The Titch Hik

Bristol

& the West Country

9th Edition

Editor

Lindsey Potter

Titch Hikers' Guide to Bristol & the West Country

9th Edition

Published by

Titch Hikers' Guide (UK) Limited
PO Box 296, Bristol BS99 7LR

Published

March 2004

ISBN

0-9534648-3-0

Cover design

Liz & Marcus Parnell, Coastal
01803 669258

Printed by

APB Colour Print Ltd
www.apbcolour.co.uk

Cover photographs courtesy of

Bristol Ferry Boat Company
Waterbabies (swimming baby)
Undercover Rock (climber)
Paul Box, Vital Health
Martin Chainey, @Bristol (girl with insect)
Bristol Zoo Gardens (runners)

Special thanks to

- Bristol Conference & Tourism for their support, advice and loan of maps
- Bristol City Council's departments for Traffic & Transport and Early Years and Children
- Bristol Community Sports
- Children's Information Service
- John Lewis Partnership
- Our advertisers
- See also the acknowledgements at the back of the book

Book orders

Email: books@titchhikers.co.uk
Tel: 0117 914 4867

First Published as Titch Hikers' Guide to Bristol by The National Childbirth Trust (Bristol Branch): First Edition 1983, revised editions 1985, 1987, 1989, 1992, 1994,
Seventh Edition published by Titch Hikers' Guide Limited, 1998, revised edition 2001.

titch hikers' guide

CONTENTS

How to navigate

The central Reference Section holds
- Symbol keys for entry facilities
- Maps of Bristol & the West
- Tables listing sporting facilities across the region

The Index lists subjects as well as entry names. The chapter contents give an overview of the topics covered.

LETTER FROM THE EDITOR

Welcome

If you want to have a fantastic time with your childen but save time and money, this book is for you. Whether you have babies in arms or children in their late teens, we provide you with endless ideas and helpful information.

It started 20 years ago as a small booklet put together by a group of local parents. Over the years, it has grown to become the "must have" book for parents in Bristol and the West. In fact, we've had praise from readers without children in tow.

Having listened to feedback on the last edition we have made this the biggest edition ever, by adding new chapters on holidays, education and the teenage years. We have added numerous new recommendations and improved the chapter structure. For the first time there are tables, colour maps, a central reference section and a detailed index, making it easier to flick through and find what you are after.

This guide is unique and envied by many UK cities. What makes it good is that the listings are only there because our Titch Hikers' readers say they should be. So please keep sending us your feedback:

info@titchhikers.co.uk or **www.titchhikers.co.uk** or **PO Box 296, Bristol BS99 7LR**

This project has been a huge task, but tremendous fun. The research team consisted of parents and grandparents working from kitchens, landings and garages! All enthusiasts about our great city and surroundings. We hope that you enjoy using this book and tell your friends about it.

Have fun in Bristol and the West Country.

Lindsey Potter
Editor

PS - What's worth doing?

I am amazed at what can be done on a low budget. Here are some places and ideas to search for within the chapters:

- Enjoy free admission to city farms, and museums in Bristol and South Wales
- Explore the many walks and cycle routes
- Visit your local library - take advantage of the storytimes, internet access, videos and books
- Enrole in a course with supporting free or low cost crèche
- Visit the parks and check out their seasonal events and holiday fun-days
- Use the inexpensive sporting facilities around the West
- Take up camping - great value holidays
- Register your pre-school child at a subsidised toddler group/nursery
- Watch the press for information on festivals and events - family days out to remember

TRANSPORT

Isabelle Whiteman

CHAPTER 1

INTRODUCTION

Getting there is often half the fun of a day out. So here are some ideas to transport you around the region, whether it's under your own steam or letting someone else ferry you about. As well as details of cycle routes and railway journeys, I've also included details of ferry and boat trips from the many seaside resorts and riverside locations in our region. I hope you'll enjoy discovering new ways to explore our wonderful cities, towns and countryside.

Travel Information
www.travelbristol.org
This new website, designed by Bristol City Council provides a range of travel and transport information. This includes a trip planner whether you are on foot, public transport or bike and 'real time' information for selected bus services as well as links to other travel information websites.

RAIL

National Rail Enquiry Line
08457 484 950 (24 hours)
www.nationalrail.co.uk

National rail telesales
08457 000125

First Great Western
0845 600 5604 Customer service
08457 413775 Mobility impaired

Virgin Trains
www.virgin.com/trains
08457 222333 Bookings and information

Bristol Parkway
This station underwent a major refurbishment in 2002 and now provides a number of new facilities including lifts to the platforms, shop and café on the 1st floor. Ticket office and toilets are at the entrance. Regular bus services.

Parking
£3.70/day

Bristol Temple Meads
Beautiful historic station. Lifts down to subway then up to platforms. Main toilets in subway, mother's room (baby changing) off the Ladies'. Refreshment outlets to be found on Platforms 3 and 10, as well as in the subway. WH Smith in main entrance. Shuttle bus operates to the airport (Bristol Flyer).

Parking
£1/hr short term parking on station forecourt (up to 20 mins free)
£8/24hr under cover longer term parking
£6/24hrs open air longer term parking

SEVERN BEACH LINE
From £2 day rtn, free U5's, pay on train
Information points available at every station
Mon-Sat, hrly Mon-Fri from 6.30am

The Bristol to Severn Beach railway line runs for 13½ miles from Temple Meads to the shores of the Severn estuary at Severn Beach. Calling at Lawrence Hill, Stapleton Rd, Montpelier, Redland, Clifton Down, Sea Mills, Shirehampton, Avonmouth, St Andrews Rd (request only).
This is an excellent local service, use it to:
- Clifton Down station: Go shopping or eat out on Whiteladies Rd
- Severn Beach or Lawrence Hill: go cycling, access to the Bristol-Bath cycle path
- Go walking: Severn Beach for the sea wall and Severn Way; Sea Mills for river Trym, Blaise Castle and Shirehampton

A summer timetable is produced from May. Special events are arranged during the summer including quizzes. Further information contact FOSBR.

Friends of Suburban Bristol Railway (FOSBR)
17 Belmont Rd, Bristol, BS6 5AW
www.bigfoot.com (enter fosbr)
A campaign group whose aim is to keep, promote and improve the services and facilities on the line.

BUS & COACH
0870 6082608 Travel line
www.traveline.org.uk

City Line and Badgerline
www.firstgroup.com
City Line operate buses within Bristol, Badgerline travel throughout the South West. Both services offer tickets for all day use:
- FirstFamily ticket: unlimited travel all day on First Bus in Bristol Mon-Fri after 9am and any time at weekends and Bank holidays. £5 Family (2+3)
- FirstExplorer: travel anywhere on FirstGroup bus services in the West of England (some restrictions apply). £5 adult, £4.25 child, £12.50 family (2+2)
- City Tour Plus: includes your fare into the city centre plus all day on the Open Top Tour buses. £7 adult, £6 child

- Bus activity tickets are also available: Zoo Safari, Bus Skate Special and @Bristol. The ticket combines your bus fare with the attraction/activity

Tickets can be purchased at the Colston Street Booking Office, Bristol Bus Station Booking Office, your local Bus Shop or via the Internet.

National Express
08705 808080 enquiries & reservations
www.nationalexpress.com

Many economy fares available, but these may need to be booked in advance. Economy tickets also exclude travel on Fridays and many Saturdays. On-line booking available. Otherwise obtain tickets from Bristol Bus Station, some Bus Shops, travel agents and Tourist Information Centres.

Bristol Bus Station
Marlborough Street, BS1 3NU
0117 921 3614

Bus and coach information is located at this terminus. Short-term parking next to station. Waiting area is noisy and not very clean. Café open Mon-Sat. Snack bar open Sun. Portaloos available but disabled and baby changing available on platform level, key available from Bus Information Shop or security guards. Major redevelopment planned for 2004.

Bristol City Sightseeing Tour
01934 830050
www.bristolvisitor.co.uk
www.city-sightseeing.com
Easter-Sep: daily 10am-5pm
£7 adult, £6 children U18, free U5's. One free child per adult passenger

Tickets available on the bus or from Bristol Tourist Information Centre.

This open top sightseeing bus takes in all the major attractions, including @Bristol, Bristol Zoo, SS Great Britain, Clifton Village and the British Empire and Commonwealth museum. Discount available on entry to a number of attractions on presentation of ticket. You can hop on or off the bus at any of 20 stops en route. Includes guided tour with headphones on every seat. Children's pack available. See advertisement in central reference section.

Bristol International Flyer
01275 474444
Daily 5.30am-10.30pm
Return fares: £6 adult, £5 child, £14 family

Non-stop bus service from Bristol Bus & Coach Station or Bristol Temple Meads direct to the airport.

PARK & RIDE
0870 6082608 Traveline

Long Ashton Park and Ride
Located: A370 towards the SW of the City
Mon-Fri, 7am-7.45pm, every 10-12 mins
Thurs last bus leaves city centre at 8.23pm
Sat 8am-6.30pm

The journey time is 10-15 mins. Operates a circular route stopping at: Harbourside, Augustine's Parade, Baldwin Street, Victoria Street and The Haymarket. Saturday service stops at: St Augstine's and St James Barton, outside House of Fraser.

Brislington Park and Ride
Located: off A4, main Bristol-Bath Road, 100 School Road
Mon-Fri 7am-7.43pm, every 10 mins
Thurs last bus leaves the city centre at 8.03pm
Sat: 8am-6.30pm

The journey time is approx. 15 mins. Operates a circular route stopping at: Temple Gate, Old Market, Temple Way, Haymarket and Broad Quay.

Tollgate (M32) Park and Ride
Located: Multi-storey car park at the bottom of M32
Frequency: Mon-Fri 7am-6.40pm, every 10 mins
Sat 8am-6.40pm. Last bus from city centre Mon-Sat 6.46pm.

The journey time is 5 mins to Broadmead and central Bristol.

Portway Park and Ride
Located: A4 Portway at Shirehampton.
Frequency: Mon-Fri 6.50am-7pm, Sat 7.30am-7pm.

The journey time to central Bristol is approximately 30 mins.

FERRY & BOAT TRIPS

Bristol Ferry Boat Company

An excellent way to get around the dockland area. See Out & About in Bristol chapter.

Waverley and Balmoral

Waverley Excursions Ltd, Waverley Terminal, Glasgow, G3 8HA
0845 1304647
www.waverleyexcursions.co.uk
Jul-Sep, from £14 adult, children half price, free U5's

Sailings from Clevedon Pier, Bristol and Weston-Super-Mare (also from Minehead, Ilfracombe, Watchet, Sharpness and Bridgwater). Cruise in "Big Ship" style aboard the Waverley, the last sea-going paddle steamer in the world and the Balmoral, traditional pleasure cruise ship. Cruises around Holm Islands and the coast of Wales. For full details and timetable contact Waverley Excursions Ltd directly or the Weston-Super-Mare Tourist Information Centre. Facilities: self-service restaurant, full licensed bar, heated observation lounges, souvenir shops.

To land on Steep Holm and Flat Holm see Severn Adventures in Out & About in the West Country chapter. To land on Lundy island see Camping in Family Holidays & Weekends Away.

Bristol Queen

01934-613828
www.bristolqueen.com
Apr to Oct from £7 adult, £3.50 child

Sailings from Knightstone Harbour, Weston-Super-Mare and occasionally from Portishead. Most popular cruises are 1hr trip from Weston along the Brean Down peninsula. Also 2hr cruises around both Holm Islands, and occasional trips to Cardiff Bay and Steep Holm. Cruises from Portishead are either into Princes Wharf, Bristol or across to Cardiff Bay. Facilities: small snack shop, high weather viewing deck, toilets, and commentary. For timetable and further information contact Bristol Queen or Weston-Super-Mare Tourist Information Centre, see Out & About in the West Country chapter.

The Bath and Dundas Canal Co.

Brass Knocker Basin, Monkton Combe, Bath
01225 722292, www.bathcanal.com
Daily 8am-dusk, some seasonal variations
Canoe hire: £14/2hrs, £21/3hrs, £31/day 2ad/2ch
Electric boats: From £41/½ day, £59/day 2ad/2ch
Take A36 south of Bath, at Monkton Combe turn left at lights onto B3108.

P V ✎ WC ⊓ CP ☂ � ✂ ⊞ ⊨ 🚌 ♿

You can hire electric boats, canoes and even narrow boats for longer periods. There are no locks on the canal between Bradford-on-Avon and Bath. Also see Cycle Hire below.

The Lock Inn

48 Frome Road, Bradford-on-Avon, BA15 1LE
01225 867187
www.thelockinn.co.uk
Daily 9am-6pm
Canoe hire: £14-£16/½ day, £26/day 2ad/2ch
Walk from back of Station car park into park. Go under bridge, along path and up steps onto tow path, turn right to Lock Inn

V WC ⊓ CP ☂ ✂ ⊞ 🚌

You can hire canoes to paddle along the canal from this pleasant spot. It's easiest to go towards Bath as there are no locks to negotiate (canoes must be carried around them) and there are plenty of pubs and tearooms along the way. Pre booking is advisable as it gets very busy in the summer. Credit/debit card necessary for deposit. Also see Cycle Hire below

For further canoe hire in the West see Outdoor Pursuits in the Teen Guide chapter.

Canal Boat Trips on MV Barbara McLellan

Wharf Cottage, 15 Frome Road, Bradford-on-Avon, BA15 1LE
01225 868683
www.katrust.org/west.htm
Apr-Oct: Sat/Sun/Wed & B/Hols
From £4 adult, £3 child, £11 family, under 5's free
Turn right out of station car park onto Frome Rd and walk 300m to cottage.

WC ♿

A relaxing way to see the canal is on this comfortable narrowboat. Three trips are offered during the summer: to Meadows Bridge, 1hr; to Avoncliff Aqueduct, 1½hrs; to Widbrook 1 hr. Times given are for return trip. Advance bookings can be made at the Cottage

Shop, except in Aug when tickets can only be bought on day of trip. Boat leaves from the cottage on Canal Wharf. See website for details of special trips.

Canal Narrow Boat Hire

If you've ever fancied taking a canal boat out yourself for a day or more, contact one of the following companies.

Sally Boats

01225 864923, www.sallyboats.ltd.uk
Operate out of Bradford-on-Avon.

Anglo-Welsh Waterway Holidays

0117 3041122, www.anglowelsh.co.uk
Have bases in Bristol, Bath and Monkton Combe.

Wessex Narrow Boats

www.wessexboats.co.uk, 01225 765243
Located 3 miles from Bradford-on-Avon, at Staverton Marina, day hire possible.

Bath Narrow Boats

Bathwick Hill, Bath
01225 447276, www.bath-narrowboats.co.uk
Mainly day hire.

AIRPORT

Bristol International Airport
0870 121 2747
www.bristolairport.co.uk
See Family Holidays & Weekends Away.

CYCLING ORGANISATIONS

Cycling around or just out of Bristol can be an excellent way to see the countryside and a pleasant escape from city life. For further information regarding cycle routes or family cycling, contact the following:

Life Cycle UK

86 Colston Street, Bristol, BS1 5BB
0117 929 0440, www.lifecycleuk.org.uk
This Bristol based charity runs several projects aimed at increasing cycle use.

Cycle Training Courses

For children, 8-11yrs, held at various locations in and around Bristol in the school holidays. Also by arrangement in schools or for private groups. Adult cycle training and other programmes available. They also offer free cycle route guides, see Cycle Routes below.

Sustrans

The National Cycle Network Centre,
2 Cathedral Square, College Green, Bristol, BS1 5DD
0845 113 0065, www.sustrans.org.uk

This sustainable transport charity works on practical projects to encourage people to walk, cycle and use public transport in order to reduce motor traffic and its adverse effects. Their main project is the National Cycle Network which currently provides more than 7,000 miles of cycling and walking routes throughout the UK. See the interactive mapping section on their website for cycle routes. Maps and free leaflets are also available.

Sustrans is also involved in a 'safe routes to school' project, encouraging children to cycle and walk to school. Free information pack available.

Bristol Cycling Campaign

Box No. 60, 82 Colston St, BS1 5BB
www.gn.apc.org/alt-transportbristol
Membership £5, concessions available

Regular Sunday rides organised, some quite short and suitable for families. BCC members also campaign to improve accessibility and safety for cyclists. For further information either obtain a leaflet (distributed in cycle shops) or visit the website.

CYCLE HIRE COMPANIES

There are many places you can hire bikes in the region, giving you an opportunity to try the recreation before investing in bikes for the family. Some of the places listed below offer guided rides, treasure hunts, look and learn orienteering, 2-3 day breaks with luggage support, call for details.

9

Bristol Bicycle Hire

Smeaton Rd, Adj to Bonded Warehouse,
Cycle Route 41, Hotwells
0117 965 5192, 0780 3651945 (mobile)
Bike hire prices from:
£10-£12 per day, £7-£9 half day, additional days half price

🚲 WC ✖ P

Hires out a variety of bikes, children's trailers and seats. Pre-booking essential. Café open on Sundays serving vegetarian food.

The Bath and Dundas Canal Co.

Brass Knocker Basin, Monkton Combe, Bath
01225 722292
www.bathcanal.com
Open daily, but between Nov-Mar ring first
Bike hire prices from:
£14 adult, £7 child per day, hourly rates available, pre-booking recommended

Offers a range of family bikes and accessories to hire. Also see Ferries & Boat Hire above.

Forest of Dean Cycle Hire

Pedalabikeaway Cycle Centre, Colliery Offices, Cannop Valley, Nr. Coleford, Glos, GL16 7EH
01594 860065
www.pedalabikeaway.com
Apr-Oct: Tue-Sun 9am-6pm
Nov-Mar: Sat-Sun 10am-5pm
Daily Jul/Aug & school holidays
Bike hire prices from:
£20/3hrs, hourly & child rates available

WC ✖ P 🔧 ♿

This friendly shop is situated on the cycleway, hiring out bikes, buggy and bike trailers. Helmets are free. Their motto is 'bikes for everyone' and are keen to assist those with special needs. Routes, maps, information, books, parts, accessories and repairs available. Try the chips at the café!

If you have got the cycling bug you may want to try other cycle hires in the region, offering hourly rates to organised cycling holidays:

Pedalaway Llangarron, Nr Ross-on-Wye
01989 770357

Pedalaway Abergavenny, Govillon, Nr Abergavenny
01873 830219

The Lock Inn

48 Frome Road, Bradford on Avon, BA15 1LE
01225 867187
www.thelockinn.co.uk
Daily 9am-6pm
Bike hire prices from:
£10 adult, £6 child per day, hourly rates available
Canoes and boats also for hire

WC ♿ ✖ 🚶

Has a wide range of cycles for both adults and children along with all the attachments. Ideally situated on the Kennet and Avon canal towpath. There is also an extensive bike shop and canal side café. Also see Ferries & Boat Hire above.

For further bike hire see Cycling & Outdoor Pursuits in the Teen Guide chapter.

CYCLE ROUTES

Some cycle routes may have bollards at their start/finish points, worth bearing in mind if you are using a buggy trailer.
Life Cycle UK, Sustrans and Bristol City Council provide cycle maps across the region.
The following cycle paths have been recommended, let us know your suggestions.

Bristol and Bath Railway Path

13 miles long: you can start either from Bristol Bridge or from St Phillips Rd, Old market. Bitton is an interesting place to stop, where there is a steam railway (or start your ride from here, as the route crosses the road) Pubs along the way include the Bird in Hand and the Jolly Sailor on the river at Saltford.

Ashton to Pill Cycle Path

Starts from the Create Centre on Cumberland Rd, or from Leigh Woods if you take the first right after the Clifton suspension bridge and follow the road for ¾ mile; it is signposted from there. Refreshments can be bought in Pill.

Ashton Court

After passing through the entrance to Ashton Court by the Suspension Bridge, take the second track on the right (after the road for the golf course). There are numerous trails through the woods but it is very hilly and quite rough.

Forest of Dean Cycle Trail

(see Cycle Hire section)
This is a beautiful area for cycling. There is a popular circular 12 mile family cycle route, with several access points (one being at Pedalabikeaway listed above.)

Kennet and Avon Canal Towpath

This travels east out of Bath, starting behind Bath Spa railway station. Three easy access points are: Bradford-on-Avon (station carpark); Hilperton Marina (car parking and toilets) and the Visitor Centre at Devizes Wharf (Pay and Display).

A cycle route with plenty to look at on the canal and several places to stop for food and drink. Besides the aqueducts at Avoncliff and Dundas, the other amazing feat of engineering is the flight of locks at Caen, west of Devizes.

Canal cycle tracks can be narrow in places, not suitable for inexperienced cyclists.

RAILWAYS FOR PLEASURE

Many children seem to have a love affair with trains; there are plenty of railways and rides to be had in the region.

Ashton Court Estate Miniature Steam Railway

Adjacent to golf area
0117 963 9174, Ashton Court Visitor Centre
Apr-mid Oct: Sun & B/H's 12pm-5.30pm
Enter through Clifton Lodge on A369, turn right, then right again
Sit astride trains on track ½ a mile long. Ramps and footbridges for pushchairs are by the ticket office. Toilets at the golf café. Santa Specials can be booked in advance.

Bristol Harbour Railway

Princes Wharf, Wapping Road, BS1
0117 925 1470
Apr-Nov selected w/e's
60p single, £1 rtn, £3.50 family ticket, free U6's
This train steams along the dockside from Bristol Industrial Museum to the SS Great Britain. Locally built engines (Henbury and Portbury) pull the wagons which once ran at Avonmouth Docks.

Avon Valley Railway

Bitton Station, Bath Road, Bitton, Bristol, BS30 6HD
0117 932 7296 Talking timetable
0117 932 5538 General enquiries
www.avonvalleyrailway.co.uk
Easter-Oct: Sun, B/H's
Tue-Thu during school holidays
£4.50 adult, £3 child, free U3's, family fares available

Fare allows unlimited travel on day of issue. This line runs along the former Mangotsfield to Bath Green Park branch of the old Midland Railway. The line has now been extended to a new platform at Avon River side with links to boat trips and the Avon Valley Country Park, see Out & About in the West Country chapter. Special events such as days with Thomas The Tank Engine and 'Santa Specials' require booking.

Dean Forest Railway

Norchard Railway Centre, Lydney, Gloucestershire
01594 843432 (information line)
01594 845840 (enquiries)
www.deanforestrailway.co.uk
Apr-Oct: Sun, B/H's & some weekdays during the summer
£5.50 adults, £3.60 child, free U5's
M4, M48 Chepstow, Norchard is on B4234 just north of Lydney, accessible by train and bus

Fare allows unlimited travel on day of issue. This line runs from Norchard to Lydney Junction, then on to Whitecroft. Special timetabled events throughout the summer and Christmas include 'Days Out with Thomas The Tank Engine', 'Teddy Bear Specials', 'Diesel Days' and 'Santa Specials'. Booking essential.

Other attractions include riverside walks, boating lake, park, Railway Museum (open daily late Mar-Jan and winter weekends), café in classic restaurant coach open on 'Steam Days'. Pushchairs can be stored in the station building or put on the train using disabled ramps provided.

Perrygrove Railway, Forest of Dean

01594 834991
www.perrygrove.co.uk
Easter-Aug: B/H weekends, July: Sun's, Aug: Sat-Sun
12.30pm-4.15pm
£3.50 adults, child £2.50, £3 U3's
½ mile south of Coleford on B4228, nearest mainline railway station Lydney

P ✏ WC 🛏 🛝 ♿ 🛍 🚻 ♿

Fare allows unlimited travel on day of issue. Narrow gauge railway runs through farm and woodland for a 1½ mile return trip. Visitors also able to walk through the woods (with pushchairs), explore the indoor village and secret passages, and take part in an optional treasure hunt (£1.80). Birthday parties welcome.

Gloucestershire Warwickshire Steam Railway Co.

The Railway Station, Toddington, Glos, GL54 5DT
01242 621405 Talking timetable
www.gwsr.plc.uk
Steam Days w/e's & B/H's & some weekdays during the summer
£9 adult, £5.50 child, free U5's, £24 family (2+3)
M5 J9, A46, B4077 junction with B4632

♿ 🛝 ♿ ✕ 🛍 P

Fare allows unlimited travel on day of issue. The railway operates a round trip of 20 miles from Toddington to Cheltenham Race Course Station with a brief stop along the way at Winchcombe. The line passes through the beautiful Cotswold Hills and you will have views over the Vale of Evesham to the Malvern Hills beyond. Special events take place throughout the season, most notably 'Days Out with Thomas' and 'Santa Specials'.

East Somerset Railway

Cranmore Railway Station, Shepton Mallet, Somerset, BA4 4QP
01749 880417
Apr-Oct: w/e's & some weekdays during the summer
Nov-Easter: Sun only
£6 adult, £4 child, free U3's, £17 family
Platform tickets, £2 adult, £1 child, free U3's
A37, A361

♿ WC ✏ ✕ 🛏 🛍 🚻

A round trip of 35 minutes. The 'static attractions' (platform ticket) includes the train shed, signal box and museum. Special events include 'Days with Thomas' and 'Santa Specials', booking essential. There is a restaurant and model shop (only open on Steam Days). The station is buggy friendly with storage space available on the train.

Severn Beach Line

See Rail above

West Somerset Railway

The Railway Station, Minehead, Somerset, TA24 5BG
01643 707650 Talking timetable
01643 704996 General enquiries
www.West-Somerset-Railway.co.uk
All year but not daily, phone for full timetable
£3-£11 dependent on journey length
M5 J25, follow tourist signs to Bishop's Lydeard

♿ 🛝 WC ✏ ✕ 🛍 P ♿

The train line runs for 20 miles between Bishop's Lydeard and Minehead along the coast and Quantock Hills. Ten restored stations along the line have a variety of signal boxes, museums, displays and steam and diesel engines to visit. Buffet facilities on all regular, timetabled trains. Special events include 'Thomas The Tank Engine', 'Mothers Day and Fathers Day Specials', and 'Santa Specials', booking essential.

OUT & ABOUT IN BRISTOL

Sarah Bruton

CHAPTER 2

INTRODUCTION

For the first time we have dedicated a whole chapter to activities, attractions and services in Bristol. For many of us busily bringing up families in the city, it is hard to keep up with the choice of exciting activities and events on offer.

Libraries, parks departments and museums put on a wide variety of events, many of them free.

See the maps in the central Reference Section and look up the annual events listings.

We hope this chapter helps you put your finger on the pulse of this great city so you and your family can get the most out of where we live.

Keep us posted of new ideas and let us know what you think about Bristol when it comes to getting out and about.

ZOO

Bristol Zoo Gardens

Clifton, Bristol, BS8 3HA
0117 973 8951
www.bristolzoo.org.uk
Daily 9am-5.30pm, 4.30pm winter
£9.50 adult , £6 child, free U3's
Annual: £39 adult, £64 2 adults, £15 child
Follow the brown tourist signs from the M5 J17 or
from Bristol city centre

One of Bristol's most famous landmarks. There are over 300 species of wildlife housed in and around the Zoo's botanical gardens. In the impressive Seal and Penguin Coasts you will come face to face with seals and penguins through transparent underwater walkways. Other favourites include Zona Brazil, Gorilla Island, Bug World, Twilight Zone, the Aquarium, the Reptile House and the children's play area. There's plenty of hands-on fun in the Activity Centre too with face painting, badge making etc. Feeding time talks around the Zoo help to make your visit educational. Membership benefits include free entry to other Zoos in the UK, Zoo magazine, entry to Zoo events and special discounts off shop purchases. Admission fee will be refunded if you take out membership during your visit.

THE DOCKSIDE

This is a fascinating and lively area of Bristol which has a lot to offer parents and children of all ages. The city has a long and distinguished history of maritime activity and attractions such as the Industrial Museum and the SS Great Britain ensure it is not lost. This largely traffic-free area makes it ideal for walking, family cycling or just boat and people watching. Parking is ample and located at the Industrial Museum, SS Great Britain and Explore@Bristol. There are cafés and restaurants on both side of the harbour so go prepared for a busy day out.

Bristol Harbour Railway

Princes Wharf, Wapping Road, BS1 4RN
0117 925 1470
Apr-Nov selected w/e's
60p single, £1 rtn, £3.50 family ticket, free U6's

This train steams along the dockside from Bristol Industrial Museum to the SS Great Britain. Locally built engines (Henbury and Portbury) pull the wagons which once ran at Avonmouth Docks.

Bristol Industrial Museum

See Museums section, below

SS Great Britain

Great Western Dock, Gas Ferry Road, BS1 6TY
0117 929 1843 Information Line
0117 926 0680 Enquiries
Apr-Oct: 10am-5.30pm, Nov-Mar: 4.30pm
£6.25 adult, £3.75 child, £16.50 family ticket

Brunel's masterpiece of ship design is housed in the original Great Western Dock where she was built in 1843. Embracing many innovative engineering ideas, the SS Great Britain was the first screw-propelled iron passenger liner and is the forerunner of all modern ships. Of more interest to school-aged children. Tickets include admission to:

Maritime Heritage Centre

This houses an exhibition on the history of shipbuilding in Bristol from the days of wood and sail, through to diesel power and plastics.

The Matthew

A replica of the ship built in the 15th century in which John Cabot sailed from Bristol across the Atlantic to discover Newfoundland in 1497. The replica successfully made the crossing in 1997. Note that disabled and buggy access to the ships is limited.

FERRIES

The Bristol Ferry Boat Company

MB Tempora, Welsh Back, Bristol, BS1 4SP
0117 927 3416
www.bristolferryboat.co.uk
Daily 10.30am-6.10pm (charters can run later)

Waterbus and historic harbour tours. This friendly company runs a waterbus service from the city centre which runs every 40 minutes, covering the middle and western end of the harbour. During Apr-Oct and in the school holidays the service covers the middle and eastern end of the harbour up to Temple Meads Station. There are many stops allowing access to tourist attractions along with cafés, restaurants and pubs with outside areas suitable for children.

Chartered trips which go beyond the harbour to the river and gorge are available Apr-Oct. There are 2 heated boats in the fleet - look out for their popular Sail with Santa on weekends in December.

The Hotwells Ferry
Apr-Sep daily, Oct-Mar Sat-Sun
Single £1 adult, 60p child,
Round trip £3 adult, £1.50 child
The Hotwells Ferry operates around the harbour between Hotwells and the city centre. The 40 minute round trip includes the SS Great Britain.

The Temple Meads Ferry
Apr-Sep Sat-Sun/daily during the school holidays
Round Trip £3.50 adult, £1.50 child, shorter fares available
Operates between Temple Meads and the City Centre. This is a 60 minute round trip that includes the SS Great Britain and Castle Park.

MUSEUMS

@Bristol
Anchor Road, Harbourside, Bristol, BS1 5DB
0845 345 1235
www.at-bristol.org.uk
Daily 10am-6pm
From £6.50 adults, £4.50 child, free U5's, £19 family ticket, various tickets combinations available

Explore @Bristol/Orange Imaginarium
An interactive science centre over two floors with experiments, games and puzzles. You can make a programme in a TV studio, experience a walk-in tornado or watch a computer-generated film on the journey of a sperm! The Orange Imaginarium, (£2) is a planetarium where you sit back and watch the universe go by.

Wildscreen@Bristol
A close-up look at evolution and the world of plants, animals, fish/birds.

Imax Theatre @ Bristol
A four storey high screen with digital surround sound. Some 3-D films.

Blaise Castle House Museum
Blaise Castle Estate, Henbury Rd, Henbury
0117 903 9818
Apr-Oct: Sat-Wed 10am-5pm
Admission free

Social history collections exhibiting domestic furnishings, costumes, textiles and toys. Of more interest to school-aged children.

Bristol City Museum and Art Gallery
Queens Road, Clifton, Bristol, BS8 1RL
0117 922 3571
www.bristol-city.gov.ukmuseums
Daily 10am-5pm
Admission free

Many interesting and varied exhibits appealing to children including stuffed animals, a bi-plane suspended from the ceiling in the entrance hall and a Romany caravan. Older children and adults can request a gallery trail. Toys are provided at some exhibitions to keep youngsters happy. Ask staff for toddler steps if required. Holiday activities and workshops. Family fun day first Sunday of every month.

Bristol Industrial Museum
Princes Wharf, Wapping Rd, Bristol, BS1 4RN
0117 925 1470
Sat-Wed 10am-5pm
Admission free

The ground floor has displays of motorised and horse-drawn vehicles and a model railway (20p to operate). First floor chronicles Bristol's aerospace and maritime history. At weekends there is sometimes the chance to try your hand at printing. Also, the steam crane may be operational: climb on it, get oily, then

15

watch it move. See also Harbour Railway, above.

On the harbour, half hour trips on various boats are sometimes available, and you might be lucky enough to see the Pyronaut fireboat's water cannon in action.

British Empire/Commonwealth Museum

Clock Tower Yard, Temple Meads, Bristol, BS1 6QH
0117 925 4980
www.empiremuseum.co.uk
Daily 10am-5pm
£5.95 adult, £3.95 child, £14 family ticket

Housed next to Temple Meads station. The museum charts the history of the British Empire and Commonwealth from Cabots's journey in 1497. Exciting children's activities during half term and school holidays.

Georgian House

7 Great George Street, Bristol, BS1 5RR
0117 921 1362
Apr-Oct: Sat-Wed 10am-5pm
Admission free

Georgian House built in 1790 furnished in period style. Of more interest to school-aged children. No buggies in the house but they can be stored.

Red Lodge

Park Row, Bristol, BS1 5LJ
0117 921 1360
Apr-Oct: Sat-Wed 10am -5pm
Admission free

Beautiful Elizabethan house with panelled rooms and a Tudor knot garden. Of more interest to school-aged children. No buggies in the house but they can be stored.

VISITOR CENTRES

Ashton Court Visitor Centre

Long Ashton, Bristol, BS41 9JN
0117 963 9174
www.bristol-city.gov.ukacm
Apr-Oct: Sat-Sun 10.30am-5.30pm, staffed some weekdays during summer
Nov-Mar: Sun 11am-4pm

Gives a history of the estate and information on how it is managed. Walking, nature trails and orienteering maps available. They also run holiday and half term events for children, 8-12yrs, such as mountain biking.

Clifton Observatory and Caves

Clifton Down, Bristol
0117 974 1242/939 3798
Mon-Fri 11.30am-5pm, Sat-Sun 10.30am-5pm
occasionally closed, phone first
£1 adults, 50p children

The Observatory houses a 'Camera Obscura' installed in 1829. In fine weather a rotating mirror in the roof reflects the panorama outside. From the Observatory a steep stepped passage through the rock leads to a viewing platform which gives splendid views of the Bridge and Gorge. Buggies can be left at the kiosk, which sells ices.

Clifton Suspension Bridge Visitor Centre

0117 974 4664
www.clifton-suspension-bridge.org.uk

New premises due to open late 2004. For further details call or visit their website. When re-opened the exhibition will graphically illustrate the story of this famous landmark. Intricate scale model of the bridge.

THEATRE

Bristol Old Vic

King Street, Bristol, BS1 4ED
0117 987 7877
www.bristol-old-vic.co.uk

Varied programme to suit all ages and tastes.
Children's productions, especially around
Christmas and Easter, often include shows
particularly suitable for a pre-school audience.
Currently reorganising children's production
schedule, ring or see website for details of
new season's events. Also see advertisement
in central Reference Section.

Colston Hall

Colston Street, BS1 5AR
0117 922 3682
www.colstonhall@bristol-city.gov.uk
Bristol's largest concert venue. See their
website or local press for details. Over half
term and Easter holidays there are often
shows featuring nursery rhymes or television
characters which are popular with children.

Other Venues

The following theatres all offer children's
productions or pantomines during the year,
often around Christmas. Contact them for a
current programme or see local press.

The Bristol Hippodrome
0870 607 7500

Redgrave Theatre
0117 315 7600

The Tobacco Factory
0117 902 0344

CINEMA

Broadmead Odeon

Union Street, Bristol, BS1 2DS
0117 929 0884 Cinema office
0870 505 0007 Bookings
www.odeon.co.uk
Family Tickets £12.60 anytime (2+2 or 3+1)
Birthday Parties now available with use of
party room. Lots of car parks nearby and bus
stop. Buggies can be stored.

Cineworld the Movies

Hengrove Leisure Park, Hengrove, Bristol, BS14 0LH
01275 831721, www.co.uk
'Kids Club' Sat 10am
£1 child, free accompanying adult
Kids Club includes half an hour of fun and
games then a choice of three films. Suitable
for under 11yrs, under 7yrs must be supervised. Phone for details of parties.

Vue Cinema (formerly Warner Village)
Aspects Leisure Park
Avon Ring Rd, Longwell Green
0870 240 6020

Vue Cinema (formerly Warner Village)
The Venue
Cribbs Causeway Leisure Complex, Merlin Rd
0870 240 6020

Opheus Cinema
7 Northumbria Drive, Henleaze
0117 962 3301

Showcase Cinema
Avon Meads, St Philips Causeway
0117 972 3434

FARMS

Hartcliffe Community Farm

Lampton Ave, Hartcliffe, Bristol, BS13 0QH
0117 978 2014
Daily 9.00am-4.30pm
Admission free (donations welcome)

The main site is 35 acres of pasture with a
collection of the usual farm animals. 'Kiddies

Corner' contains goats, rabbits and ducks. The farm now has an aviary with budgies, canaries and cockatiels.

HorseWorld

Staunton Lane, Whitchurch, Bristol, BS14 0QJ
01275 540173
www.horseworld.org.uk
Easter-Sep & school hols: daily 10am-5pm,
Oct-Easter: Tue-Sun 10am-4pm
£4.50 adult, £3 child, free U3's, £14 family ticket
A37 south of Bristol, turn left into Staunton Lane in Whitchurch

HorseWorld is an equine welfare charity. Learn about the rescue, rehabilitation and re-homing work undertaken. Great opportunity for children to meet horses, donkeys and ponies. Museum with audio-visual presentation, nature trails, pony rides and pony and pet handling make for a good family day out.

Lawrence Weston Community Farm

Saltmarsh Drive, Lawrence Weston, BS11 0ND
0117 938 1128
Tue-Sun 9.30am-6pm, winter 4pm
Admission free (donations welcome)

A city farm set in 6 acres of land with sheep, goats, pigs, chickens and rabbits. Some rare breeds. Events include Easter activities, and play schemes in the holidays for under 11's. Refreshments available Wednesday afternoons and all day Friday.

St Werburghs City Farm

Watercress Rd, St Werburghs, Bristol, BS2 9YJ
0117 942 8241
Daily 9am-5pm
Admission free (donations welcome)

This is a small community farm set among allotments. Animals include pigs, goats, rabbits, guinea pigs, ducks, geese, sheep and chickens and sometimes lambs and kids. The site includes a large wildlife pond and farm shop selling plants and organic produce. Other attractions are the adventure playground for under 8's, café (closed Mon/Tue) and children's homeopathic clinic, see Healthcare.

Windmill Hill City Farm

Philip Street, Bedminster, Bristol, BS3 4EA
0117 963 3252
www.windmillhillcityfarm.org.uk
Tue-Sun 9am-dusk
Admission free (donations welcome)

Well laid out paved farmyard with animal enclosures. Wide paths lead to paddocks, a small nature reserve, gardens and allotments. The Play Centre for 1-5's has indoor and outdoor areas. Adventure playground for 5-11's. Under 8's must be accompanied by an adult. Holiday activities and events. Educational group visits to the farm can be arranged.

LIBRARIES

Young or old, libraries are for everyone! Libraries are easy to join and free. As well as story books, there are children's non-fiction books, music and story tapes, CDs, DVDs, videos and jigsaw puzzles which may be borrowed or used in the library.

Most offer excellent pre-school storytimes, sometimes followed by a craft activity.

Libraries are also a good source of information on local groups for children and parents. All libraries have wheelchair access although some are trickier to negotiate than others. See advertisement.

Please note:

- Bristol City Libraries allow you to borrow and return books from different libraries.
- As of April 2004 opening times are changing. Many will be open for longer hours.

Library Services for Children

Bristol's Children/Young People's Librarian
Janet Randall 0117 924 7513

South Gloucestershire Children/Young People's Librarian
Wendy Nicholls 01454 868451

Avonmouth Library

Avonmouth Rd, Avonmouth, Bristol, BS11 9EN
0117 903 8580
Mon 2pm-5pm, Fri 2pm-6pm, Sat 9.30am-12.30pm

Storytime Fridays 2.15pm term time only.
Story tapes/puzzles available.

Bedminster Library

East Street, Bedminster, Bristol, BS3 4HY
0117 903 8529
Mon,Tue, Fri/Sat 9.30am-5pm,
Thu 9.30am-7pm

Storytime Fridays 10.30am term time only.
Story tapes, videos, puzzles, internet access
and computer facilities available. Please
contact library for details of children's
activities during school holidays. Car parking/
toilets in Asda nearby.

Bishopsworth Library

Bishopsworth Road, Bishopsworth, Bristol, BS13 7LN
0117 903 8566
Mon 9.30am-1pm & 2pm-7pm Tue/Thu/Fri/Sat
9.30am-1pm & 2pm-5pm

Storytime Tuesdays 2.15pm all year. Story/
music tapes, videos and puzzles available.

Bradley Stoke Library

Bradley Stoke Leisure Centre/Library, Fiddlers Wood
Lane, Bradley Stoke, BS32 9BS
01454 865723
Mon/Thu 10.30am-6pm,
Tue/Fri 10.30am-8pm, Sat 9.30am-5pm

Storytime Mondays 11am with craft activity
term time only. Story/music tapes and videos
available. Toy box.

Bristol Central Library

College Green, Bristol, BS1 5TL
0117 903 7215
Mon/Tue/Thu 9.30am-7.30pm,
Wed/Fri/Sat 9.30am-5pm, Sun 1pm-4pm

Storytime Wednesday 2pm. Story/music
tapes, videos and lots of board/picture books.
A few toys. To avoid steps at front of building,
use the disabled entrance to the right. An

excellent library for student research. PCs for
children with safe internet access.

Bristol Mobile Library

c/o Bedminster Library, East St, Bedminster, BS3 4HY
0117 903 8531
Branch Library on wheels with good adult
and children's books, tapes, CDs/videos.
Runs fortnightly service all around Bristol
(telephone for stops). Residential service for
elderly/housebound in Bristol.

Cadbury Heath Library

School Road, Cadbury Heath, Bristol, BS30 8EN
01454 865711
Mon/Thu 9.30am-1pm & 2pm-7pm, Fri/Sat 9.30am-
1pm & 2pm-5pm

Recently refurbished. Storytime Mondays
2.15pm with story-related craft activity
afterwards. Story tapes and puzzles available.

Cheltenham Road Library

Cheltenham Rd, Cotham, Bristol, BS6 5QX
0117 903 8562

Mon/Wed/Fri 10am-1pm & 2pm-5pm. Sat10am-1pm & 2pm-4pm

🏃 🏃

Storytime Fridays 2.15pm. Story tapes available. A few toys/puzzles to use in the library. Public toilets 150m away.

Chipping Sodbury Library
High Street, Chipping Sodbury, BS37 6AH
01454 865719
Tue/Fri 9.30am-5pm, Sat 9.30am-12.30pm
Closes lunchtime 12.30pm-1.30pm

🏃

Story/music tapes and videos available. No storytime.

Clifton Library
Princess Victoria Street, Clifton, Bristol, BS8 4BX
0117 903 8572
Mon/Wed/Fri 10am-1pm & 2pm-5pm, Sat 10am-1pm & 2pm-4pm

🏃

Storytime Mondays 10.30am with colouring afterwards, term time only. Tea, coffee, squash, story tapes and puzzles available. Playpen and toys.

Downend Library
Buckingham Gardens, Downend, Bristol, BS16 5TW
01454 865666
Mon/Thu 9.30am-7pm, Wed/Fri 9.30am-5pm,
Sat 9.30am-1pm & 2pm-5pm

P 🏃

Storytime Fridays 2.15pm with story-related crafts. Key available for public toilet. Tapes and videos.

Eastville Library
Muller Road, Eastville, Bristol, BS5 6XP
0117 903 8578
Mon/Wed/Fri 10am-1pm & 2pm-5pm,
Sat 10am-1pm & 2pm-4pm

🏃

Storytime Mondays 2.15pm with craft activity. Tapes and puzzles available.

Filton Library
The Shield Retail Park, Link Rd, Filton, BS34 7BR
01454 865670
Mon 9.30am-12.30pm & 1.30pm-7pm, Tue/Thu-Sat
9.30am-12.30pm & 1.30pm-5pm

P 🏃

Storytime Tuesdays 1.45pm with story- related craft activity. Tapes, videos and computer games available.

Filwood Library
Filwood Broadway, Bristol, BS4 1JN
0117 966 1671
Mon/Wed/Fri 9.30am-1pm & 2pm-5pm,
Sat 9.30am-1pm

🏃

Storytime Mondays 2.15pm with colouring activity afterwards. Story/music tapes available. Puzzles to use in library.

Fishponds Library
Fishponds Rd, Fishponds, Bristol, BS16 3UH
0117 903 8560
Mon/Tue/Fri/Sat 9.30am-5pm, Thu 9.30am-7pm

🏃

Storytime Tuesday 2pm term time only with nursery rhymes, craft activity, drink and biscuit (40p). Coffee mornings Fridays 9.30am-12pm. Story/music tapes, CD's and videos available. Car parking and public toilets in Safeway opposite the library.

Hanham Library
High Street, Hanham, Bristol, BS15 3EJ
01454 865678
Tue/Thu 9.30am-7pm, Fri 9.30am-5pm,
Sat 9.30am-1pm & 2pm-5pm

P 🏃 🏃 🔲

Storytime Thursdays 2.15pm with craft activity afterwards. Lots of story tapes and videos.

Hartcliffe Library
Peterson Square, Hartcliffe, Bristol, BS13 0EE
0117 903 8568
Mon/Wed/Fri 9.30am-1pm & 2pm-5pm,
Sat 9.30am-1pm

P 🏃

Storytime Fridays 10am-12pm, in partnership with Play Days, with simple craft activities. Story and music tapes available.

Henbury Library
Crow Lane, Henbury, Bristol, BS10 7DR
0117 903 8522
Mon/Tue/Thu/Sat 9.30am-1pm & 2pm-5pm,
Fri 9.30am-1pm & 2pm-7pm

P ✏ WC ⊙ 🏃 ♿

Storytime Tuesdays 2.30pm in children's area. Tapes and videos available. Puzzles to borrow once you have donated one!

Henleaze Library
Northumbria Drive, Henleaze, Bristol, BS9 4HP
0117 903 8541
Mon/Fri 10am-7pm, Tue/Thu 10am-5pm,
Sat 9.30am-5pm

Storytime Mondays 2.45pm with songs. Tapes, videos, games, DVDs and educational CD-Rom's. Puzzles to use in library. Toilets are available at Waitrose across the road.

Hillfields Library
Summerleaze, Hillfields, Bristol, BS16 4HL
0117 903 8576
Mon/Wed/Fri 10am-1pm & 2pm-5pm,
Sat 10am-1pm & 2pm-4pm

A few story tapes and puzzles available.

Horfield Library
Filton Avenue, Horfield, Bristol, BS7 0BD
0117 903 8538
Mon 9.30am-1pm & 2pm-7pm,
Tue/Thu-Sat 9.30am-1pm & 2pm-5pm

Storytime Tuesdays 2pm. Story tapes and videos available. Homework club Mon 4.45pm, Fri 3.45pm

Kingswood Library
High Street, Kingswood, Bristol, BS15 4AR
01454 865650
Mon/Tue 9.30am-5pm, Wed/Fri 9.30am-7pm
Sat 9.30am-1pm & 2pm-5pm

Storytime Tuesdays 2.15pm with activity, term time only. Tapes, videos and educational CD-Roms.

Knowle Library
Redcatch Road, Knowle, Bristol, BS4 2EP
0117 903 8585
Mon/Fri 10am-7pm, Tue/Thu 10am-5pm,
Sat 9.30am-5pm

Story/music tapes, videos and puzzles available. Toys.

Lawrence Weston Library
Broadlands Drive, Lawrence Weston, BS11 0QA
0117 982 2432
Mon-Fri 9.30am-5pm, Sat 9.30am-1pm

Storytime Fridays 9.30am. Story tapes, puzzles and a few toys available.

Marksbury Road Library
Marksbury Rd, Bedminster, Bristol, BS3 5LG
0117 903 8574
Mon 10am-1pm & 2pm-7pm,
Wed/Fri 10am-1pm & 2pm-5pm, Sat 10am-1pm

Storytime for pre-school children Wednesdays 10.45am. Tapes and puzzles available. After school club every other Monday.

Patchway Library
Rodway Road, Patchway, Bristol, BS34 5PE
01454 865674
Mon/Wed 9.30am-12.30pm & 1.30pm-7pm
Fri/Sat 9.30am-12.30pm & 1.30pm-5pm

Storytime Wednesdays 2pm with story-related craft activity. Story tapes, videos, music CD's, DVDs, computer games and puzzles available. Telephone for details of activities during school holidays. Public toilets next door.

Redland Library
Whiteladies Road, Redland, Bristol, BS8 2PY
0117 903 8549
Mon/Tue/Fri/Sat 9.30am-5pm, Thu 9.30am-7pm,
Sun 1pm-4pm
Storytime Mondays 2.30pm with related craft activity. Videos available. Soft toys and puzzles in library. To avoid steps, use disabled access at side. Toilets at Clifton Down Shopping Centre.

Sea Mills Library
Sylvan Way, Sea Mills, Bristol, BS9 2NA
0117 903 8555
Mon/Thu/Sat 9am-1pm & 2pm-5pm,
Tues/Wed/Fri 9am-1pm

Storytime Thursdays 11.45am. Tapes, videos and puzzles available.

Shirehampton Library
Station Rd, Shirehampton, Bristol, BS11 9TU
0117 903 8570
Mon/Wed/Fri 10am-1pm & 2pm-5pm, Sat 10am-1pm & 2pm-4pm

Story/music tapes and puzzles available. A few toys.

South Gloucester Mobile Library
c/o Yate Library, 44 West Walk, Yate, BS37 4AX
07881 813292
Wide range of adults/children's books and videos. Story tapes, CD's and internet access available. Runs fortnightly service all around South Gloucester, telephone for stops.

Southmead Library
Greystoke Ave, Southmead, Bristol, BS10 6AS
0117 903 8583
Mon/Wed/Fri 9.30am-1pm & 2pm-5pm,
Sat 9.30am-1pm

Telephone library for storytime details. Few story tapes and puzzles to use in library. Wooden train that children can sit in! Public toilets and car park at Aldi.

St George Library
Church Road, St George, Bristol, BS5 8AL
0117 903 8523
Mon 9.30am-1pm & 2pm-7pm, Tue/Wed/Sat 9.30am-1pm & 2pm-5pm.

Storytime Tuesdays 2.15pm including singing and craft activity (30p), term time only. Story tapes and videos available.

Staple Hill Library
The Square, Broad Street, Staple Hill, BS16 5LR
01454 865715
Tue/Fri 9.30am-12.30pm & 1.30pm-7pm, Thur/Sat 9.30am-12.30pm & 1.30pm-5pm.

Storytime Fridays 11am with story-related craft activity, term time only. Good selection of story tapes. Small collection of DVDs and videos available for hire. Activities for older children during school holidays. Disabled toilet available.

Stockwood Library
Stockwood Road, Bristol, BS14 8PL
0117 903 8546
Mon,Thu, Fri/Sat 9.30am-1pm & 2pm-5pm, Tue 9.30am-1pm & 2pm-7pm

Storytime Fridays 9.30am term time only. Large colourful children's area. Story/music tapes, videos and puzzles available.

Thornbury Library
St. Mary Street, Thornbury, BS35 2AA
01454 865 655
Mon/Tues 9.30am-5pm, Wed/Fri 9.30am-7pm, Sat 9.30am-12.30pm & 1.30pm-5pm

Storytime Mondays 2.15pm with rhymes, singing and craft activity. Story tapes, videos, DVDs and free internet access available. Ring for details of school holiday activities. Toilets opposite Safeways.

Trinity Road Library
Trinity Road, St Philips, Bristol, BS2 0NW
0117 903 8543
Mon/Wed/Fri 10am-1pm & 2pm-5pm,
Sat 10am-1pm & 2pm-4pm

Collection of story tapes and puzzles available. Wide range of children and adult books, many in Asian languages. Refurbished children's area with new stock of picture books and videos.

Westbury on Trym Library
Falcondale Road, Westbury on Trym, Bristol, BS9 3JZ
0117 903 8552
Mon/Tue/Wed/Sat 9.30am-1pm & 2pm-5pm,
Fri 9.30am-1pm & 2pm-7pm

Storytime Mondays 2.15pm with activity, term time only. Story tapes, videos and puzzles available.

Wick Road Library
Wick Rd, Brislington, Bristol, BS4 4HE
0117 903 8557
Mon 9.30am-1pm & 2pm-7pm, Tue/Wed/Fri/Sat 9.30am-1pm & 2pm-5pm

Storytime Fridays 9.30am with craft activity (20p) term time only. Tapes, videos and selection of puzzles.

Winterbourne Library
Flax Pits Lane, Winterbourne, South Glos, BS36 1LA
01454 865654
Tue/Fri 9.30am-1pm & 2pm-7pm, Wed/Sat 9.30am-1pm & 2pm-5pm

Storytime Wednesdays 2.15pm with crafts, term time only. Story/music tapes available. A few toys.

Yate Library
44 West Walk, Yate, BS37 4AX
01454 865661
Mon/Tue/Thu/Fri 9.30am-7pm, Sat 9.30am-5pm

Storytime Tuesdays 2.15pm with colouring and craft, term time only. Wide selection of story tapes, videos and DVDs available.

TOY LIBRARIES

For a small fee you can borrow toys from toy libraries, often with the opportunity to meet other parents and carers. These libraries often share facilities with other groups such as toddler and church groups, so opening times can be limited and may vary. Toys are generally suitable for children up to 6 years with the exceptions of Bwerani Toy Library and Barton Hill Family Playcentre, which cater for children up to 8 years.

For children with special needs there are toy libraries run by social services and voluntary organisations. Contact the National Association of Toy Libraries below for more information and venues.

National Association of Toy Libraries
68 Churchway, London, NW1 1LT
020 7255 4600
www.natll.org.uk

Barton Hill Family Playcentre
Barton Hill Settlement, 43 Ducie Road, BS5 0AX
Debbie Fitzgerald: 0117 955 6971
£1 per year

Crèche facilities, playing together, 2's group, pre-school and young mums group. For information of when the groups meet and prices, please phone.

Bwerani Multicultural Toy Library
Unit 12, 20-23 Hepburn Rd, St Pauls, BS2 8UD
Sue Lowney: 0117 915 9805
Mon/Tues 9am-12.00pm & 2pm-5pm, Wed 1.30pm-5pm, Thu 1.30pm-6.30pm, Fri 9am-2.00pm

This toy library specialises in multicultural, toys and educational resources for children aged 0-16yrs. Library membership is available to individuals and educational groups at various rates, call for details. Leaflets available in different languages, braille and audio versions.

Downend Toy Library
Mangotsfield United Reform Church, Cossham St, Mangotsfield
Cathryn Bartrum: 0117 985 9929
Fri 9.30am-11.30am

This toy library is also a weekly toddler group, and is open to anyone from Downend, Kingswood, Warmley, Staple Hill and Mangotsfield. For £1 you can borrow four items. Toys suitable for 0-6yrs including a play kitchen, ride-on toys and videos.

Freshways Toy Library
Lawrence Weston Resource Centre, Knovill Close, Lawrence Weston, BS11 0SA
Sophie Stagg: 0117 923 5353
Mon-Fri 10.30am-4pm.

The library offers a drop-in session every Tuesday between 1.30pm-3pm for coffee and play. Membership costs £1 and toy hire is then 25p per toy for a fortnight. This is a large library with a wide range of toys for under 5's as well as some games for older children and those with special needs.

Knowle Family Learning Toy Library

Knowle Day Nursery, Ruthven Road, BS4 1ST
Rachael Stenning: 0117 966 2969
Tue 1-30pm-3pm

[icons]

Toy hire 50p per item per week. There is also a selection of videos. Emphasis is on education and learning so each toy comes with an activity suggestion.

Play Days Hartcliffe Community Toy Library

Hartcliffe Methodist Church Hall, Mowcroft Road, Hartcliffe, BS13 0LT
0117 964 2353
Mon 10am-12pm & Wed 1.30pm-3.15pm.

[icon]

This is a well-established toy library which runs in conjunction with a parent and toddler group. No membership fee is charged, and toys cost 10p-20p to hire once you have been visiting the group for 6 weeks. Play sessions with simple crafts, stories and action songs. Many play activities including soft play area, play kitchen and table-top toys. Contact Hartcliffe Library, Peterson Square, Bristol, BS13 0EE for further details.

The Candle Project Toy Library

The Salvation Army Citadel, Ashley Rd,
St Pauls BS6 5NL
Christine Jones: 0117 942 4607
Mon-Fri 11.45am-12.15pm

[icons]

This toy library, up two flights of stairs, has a basic range of toys for under 5's, including puzzles and games. Toy borrowing takes place at the end of the playgroup and toddler sessions, term time only. You pay a returnable deposit of 50p and borrow one toy per week.

PARKS AND PLAY AREAS

Bristol City Council Parks, Estates and Sport

Department of Environment, Transport and Leisure, Colston House, Colston St. BS1 5AQ

0117 922 3719, www.bristol-city.gov.ukevents
Call the above number for information about your nearest park or play area.

Park Events

The parks service runs a programme of events and activities, many taking place during the school holidays. See their news and events guide produced twice a year called 'Park Life'. It can be obtained in local libraries, museums or by phoning the above number. Also take a look at the website. Examples of activities for younger children include: play days, craft days and teddy bear's picnics. For older children there are wildlife discovery events, deer feeding rambles and sports activities.

If you would like to organise your own community event in one of Bristol's parks or open spaces call the Parks Events Team: 0117 922 3808.

There are more than 200 parks in Bristol, many of which have good play facilities or are attractive parks with plenty of open space to play games. Of particular note are the two new flagship play areas at Blaise Castle Estate and at Hengrove, see below.

Blaise Castle Estate BS10

Entrance and car park on Kingsweston Rd
Events Programme: 0117 950 5899
You will find the largest play area in North Bristol at Blaise. It attracts children of all ages from all over the city. There is a play area for toddlers and one for older children. A play supervisor is on hand at most times, although parents/carers must accompany their children. There are toilets adjacent. A new visitor centre with café, upgraded toilets and an office for the play supervisor is currently under construction. Blaise also offers wonderful spacious grassed areas for picnics and ball games. There are woodlands and the castle folly to explore. Also take a look in the museum near the play area, see Museums above.

Brandon Hill BS8

Entrances on Great George St, Jacobs Wells Rd, Upper Byron Place and Queen's Parade
Climb Cabot Tower's many steps and see superb views across the city. The opening times vary depending upon the time of

year. From the tower there is a network of pathways and steps with waterfalls, ponds and trees. Toilets are on the middle terrace. Fenced-in play area with toddler swings, sprung rocker and climbing frame with slides and chute all in a huge sand pit. There are swings and a climbing structure for older children. Avon Wildlife Trust (based in The Old Police Station, Jacobs Wells Road) manage the nature park.

Canford Park BS10
Entrance on Canford Lane, Westbury-on-Trym
This is an attractive well-kept park, with a fenced play area providing a good variety of play equipment. The park itself has a large, flat lawn, excellent for ball games and picnics. There is also a sunken, ornamental rose garden with a pond. The circular path around the park perimeter is popular for learning to cycle and skate. Tennis courts for hire by the hour.

Clifton Down BS8
Off the Suspension Bridge Road
This is an unfenced play area with a good mixture of assault course style wooden climbing equipment: slides, swings and natural rock faces (great for budding mountaineers). Nearby natural rock slides attract the older child and adult! Toilets are on Bridge Road. From the play area you can walk to the Observatory and bridge.

Cotham Gardens BS6
Entrance on Redland Grove, Nr Redland Station
A small friendly park. Spacious fenced play area with large sandpit, swings and climbing apparatus. Also a grassed area for ball games and picnics. Great views of the trains passing on the railway line alongside.

The Downs BS8
Park anywhere along Ladies Mile
The Downs are made up of Clifton Down and Durdham Down. They are Bristol's most famous open space with grassland and some wooded areas. An Act of Parliament preserved it for the people of the city in 1861. It is very popular with footballers, joggers, kite flyers and dog walkers. The Circular Road

offers dramatic views of the Gorge and the Suspension Bridge. Toilets can be found near the viewpoint on the Sea Walls and at the Water Tower. New tea room, see Eating Out, below.

The Downs usually host annual events such as the Flower Show, circuses and a superb fireworks display in November.

Easton Play Park BS5
Main entrance on Chelsea Rd next to The Mission
This exciting and imaginative playground is really worth a visit. It is compact without being overcrowded, which makes it relatively easy to keep an eye on the children. There are climbing frames, slides, swings and a marvellous see-saw suitable for all ages. There is also an all-weather 5-a-side football pitch and a small area for picnics. The Bristol-Bath cycle path runs alongside.

Eastville Park BS16
Alongside Fishponds Rd and adjacent to M32 J2
A large area of grassland ideal for running about. There are two play areas, the better of the two is fenced and has a sandpit. Take a walk down to the lake, or walk through the woodland and along the river towards Oldbury Court.

Hengrove Play Park
Entrance off Hengrove Way
www.bristol-city.gov.ukhengrove
Hengrove Play Park was opened in 2002 and is next door to the leisure park on the site of the old Whitchurch airfield. The playground is one of the most exciting built in England. It features the innovative play dome, a twelve metre high domed frame enclosing chutes and walkways. There is a skateboard/BMX zone, an area for sand and water play for younger children, plus other play equipment. Within the area there is plenty of open space plus seating, a café and toilets. The play park is staffed during the day.

Monks Park

Entrances off Lyddington Road, Kenmore Crescent and Biddestone Rd

Built in 2000 for Horfield on the former Monks Park School playing fields. There are two equipped play areas catering for children of different ages, and plenty of green open space.

Oldbury Court Estate, Snuff Mills BS16

Entrances at the end of Oldbury Court Rd and via River View (cul-de-sac off Broom Hill)

Car parks at both entrances. This is a large park that extends from Snuff Mills to Frenchay, with the River Frome in its grounds. There is a large, well equipped, fenced off play area near the Oldbury Court Road entrance. Equipment includes a large wooden galleon-shaped climbing frame, several sand play areas, swings, long slides, trains, castles, a crows nest and lots more. There are pleasant walks down by the river and plenty of woodland to explore. Toilets and a small café are situated by the Broom Hill entrance. There are also toilets next to the play area.

Redcatch Park BS4

Main entrance on Redcatch Rd, behind Broadwalk Shopping Centre. Free car park

A pleasant, quiet park with an unfenced basically equipped play area. The park offers plenty of green space and also has tennis courts on-site which can be hired by the hour.

Redland Green BS6

Entrances on Redland Green Rd and Cossins Rd.

Lovely green with a fenced play area. There are swings and a whirligig for older children and a low-level climbing structure set over a large sandpit, which is particularly suited to toddlers but enjoyed by all.

Shirehampton Park BS11

Entrance off Shirehampton Rd.

Open parkland and wooded areas with walks to Penpole Wood and Kingsweston Down. Good views of both Severn Bridge crossings and of Kings Weston House. There are good connecting paths to Blaise Castle.

St Andrews Park BS6

Entrances on Effingham Rd, Leopold Rd, Maurice Rd, Somerville Rd and Melita Rd.

The play area has good play equipment and an area of grass for ball games or picnics. The park also boasts Bristol's only functioning paddling pool, seasonal. During hot weather the attraction of the pool makes the park extremely crowded. It hosts 'Music in the Park' in June, a fun family afternoon.

St George Park BS5

Entrances on Church Rd (A420), Park Crescent and Park View, with a car park off Chalks Road.

A large popular Victorian park with plenty of open space and a lake with ducks and swans. There is a fenced play area with a variety of equipment, and a 'wheels park' for skateboarding, roller-skating and BMX biking.

Southmead Adventure Playground

Doncaster Rd, Southmead, BS10 5AQ
0117 950 3607
Summer: 3.30pm-7.45pm, winter: 3.30pm-5.45pm, Tue-Sat school hols: 10am-12.45pm & 2pm-5.45pm
Free

Free adventure playground for all ages with separate outside and indoor soft play areas for under 8's. New multi games court, TV games console area and craft room. Toilets and Parking.

Victoria Park BS3

Entrances from Fraser St, Somerset Terrace, Nutgrove Avenue, Hill Ave, St. Luke's Rd and Windmill Close.

Plenty of open space with views over Bristol from the top of the hill. Small fenced playground with equipment for very small children set on a safety surface. There is a basketball backboard for older children, and a planned multi-sport facility off St Luke's Road. The water maze is fun so bring your wellies! There are toilets next to Somerset Terrace.

WALKS

Ashton Court Estate

Long Ashton, BS41 9JN
0117 963 9174
2 entrances off the A369, one at Kennel Lodge Rd and one at Clifton Lodge (opp. Bridge Road). Third entrance off A370 at Church Lodge (opp. Long Ashton)

Ashton Court Estate is a huge heritage estate with woodland, grassland and meadowland to explore. There are many tracks that are suitable for toddlers or for walking with a backpack, and some suitable for buggies. For more information visit the visitor's centre, see above. The deer herd is popular with children and the deer keeper runs regular deer feeding rambles, phone for details. Take a ride on the miniature railway, see Transport or have a game of golf on one of the two pitch-and-putt courses. A small café and toilets are available at the golf kiosk. Many large events such as the Bristol International Balloon Fiesta, International Kite Festival and Bristol Community Festival take place on the estate, see Annual Events and Festivals.

Blaise Castle Estate, Coombe Dingle

Henbury Rd, Henbury, Bristol, BS10 7QS

See Parks and Play areas section above. Park at Blaise Castle Estate car park on Kings Weston Road. Pleasant wooded walks through the grounds, leading up to the castle folly and beyond into Coombe Dingle. Can be muddy and since it is popular with dog walkers, watch your step!

Eastville Park

Opposite the Royate Hill turn-off on the A432, Fishponds Rd.

Once in the park, descend the hill to the lake, then turn right and continue along the banks of the Frome for 1½ miles to Snuff Mills. This walk is suitable for pushchairs but parts of it can be muddy.

Floating Harbour walk

This walk can be combined with a ferry trip, see The Dockside, above. It is almost possible to walk a complete circuit around the Floating Harbour (west of Prince Street Bridge), taking in the SS Great Britain, Industrial Museum, Arnolfini, Watershed, @Bristol, Lloyds TSB building and the skate boarders! This walk is flat, so great for pushchairs but watch the harbour edge with toddlers. A good place to start is from the Pay and Display car park at the SS Great Britain. The Floating Harbour also extends beyond Prince Street Bridge, along Welsh Back towards Temple Meads.

Kings Weston Wood and House

Kings Weston Lane, Shirehampton, BS11 0UR
0117 938 2299, www.kingswestonhouse.co.uk
7 mins walk to the house from the car park opposite Shirehampton Golf Course

Paths through the woods lead to the grotto and to Kings Weston House, a Palladian mansion built in 1710. Pleasant grounds for picnics with paths suitable for pushchairs. It has a vaulted tea room open Mon-Fri 9am-5.30pm, Sat-Sun & B/H's 10am-4pm.

Leigh Woods

The National Trust, Valley Road, Leigh Woods, Bristol, BS8 3PZ
0117 973 1645
From Clifton take A369 towards Portishead, through traffic lights pass a large old archway on right take right turn almost immediately after this, car park ½ km on left

Several trails to choose from. The Purple Trail which begins and ends at the car park is a fully accessible 2½ km circular route, hard surfaced, mostly level and suitable for push-chairs and wheelchairs. There are also other hard surfaced paths leading from the Purple Trail which are marked on the board in the car park and on a free leaflet available from the Reserve Office on Valley Road. However, not all are waymarked on the ground like the Purple Trail. Don't miss the bluebells in April and May.

Sea Mills walk

Walk under the railway bridge at Sea Mills station to the banks of the Avon, along which you can walk about a mile towards the centre of Bristol. Suitable for pushchairs, but can be muddy and overgrown at times.

Snuff Mills walk
Start in car park at end of River View

P 🛝

This is a delightful wooded walk of about 2 miles suitable for push chairs, following the River Frome, past a water mill and weir, ending in Oldbury Court Estate, see above.

EATING OUT IN BRISTOL
It is good to know where you can go to eat out with children, receive a warm welcome and know the food and facilities are suitable for youngsters.

Places listed below have been put into geographical areas within Bristol, so that you can link them in to where you might be spending the day; either on a walk or visiting an attraction.

CENTRAL BRISTOL

Bella Pasta
8-10 Baldwin St, Bristol, BS1 1SA
0117 929 3278
Meals from £3.95 child, £5.25 adult

P V ✏ WC ✂ ⛱ CP 👓 🛝 ♿ 🚻 ♿

Simple, bright Italian-style chain.

Boston Tea Party
75 Park St, Bristol, BS1 5PF
0117 929 8601
www.thebostonteaparty.co.uk
Tues-Sat 7am-10pm, Sun 9am-7pm, Mon 7am-6pm
Meals from £1.95

V ✏ WC ✂ ⛱ 🛝

Relaxed café, sofa lounge and heated terraced garden. Although no children's menu, smaller portions available on request.

Bristol Old Vic
King Street, Bristol, BS1 4ED
0117 987 7877

www.bristol-old-vic.co.uk
Daily 10am-7pm
All under £6 (cash only)

P V ✏ WC ✂ ⛱ CP ♿

Atmospheric place with a good menu.

Browns Restaurant & Bar
38 Queens Rd, Clifton, Bristol, BS8 1RE
0117 930 4777
www.browns-restaurant.com
Mon-Sat 11.30am-late, Sun 12-10pm
Meals from £3.50 child, £7 adult

V ✏ WC ✂ ⛱ CP 👓 🛝 ♿

Popular, lively and noisy with friendly staff and good service in large attractive licensed refectory. Extensive adult and children's menu. Buggy entrance at the side door.

Brunel's Buttery
Wapping Wharf, Bristol, BS1 6UD
0117 929 1696
Daily 8am-4pm
Meals from £1.75

P WC CP 🛝 ♿

End of old dock railway beyond the Industrial Museum. Outdoor kiosk with tables next to the harbour. Chips, tasty bacon butties and lots more. Great atmosphere and lovely views.

Chicane Café
3 Christmas Steps, Bristol, BS1
Mon-Sat 10am-6pm (4pm Sat)
Meals from £3.75

WC ✂

Oriental/mediterranean style menu. No smoking downstars. Doodle pads for kids.

Danby's Café
Queens Road, Clifton, BS8 1RL
0117 922 3571
Daily 10am-4.30pm
Meals from £3.25 child, £3.95 adult

V ✏ WC ⛱ CP 🛝 ♿ 🎨 ♿

Within Bristol City Museum and Art Gallery.

Deep Pan Pizza
Corner Unit, Silver St, New Broadmead, BS1 2DU
0117 929 8014
www.deeppanpizza.co.uk
Meals from £3.29 child, £6.50 adult

V ✏ WC ✂ ⛱ CP 🛝 ♿ 🚻

Efficient chain.

Firehouse Rotisserie

Anchor Square, Harbourside, Bristol, BS1 5DB
0117 915 7323
www.firehouserotisserie.co.uk
Daily 12pm-3pm and 5pm-9.30pm
Meals from £5.95 child, £9.50 adult

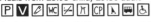

An interesting adult's restaurant that welcomes children.

Oasis Café

Southville Centre, Beauley Rd, Bristol, BS3 1QG
0117 923 1039
www.southville.org.uk
Mon 9.30am-5pm, Tue-Fri 4pm
Meals from £1.35 child, £3.50 adult

Spacious and bright community café. Wholesome inexpensive menu. Special children's tea on Mondays.

Pizza Express

31 Berkeley Square, Bristol, BS8 1HP
off Park Street
0117 926 0300
11.30am-Midnight
Meals from £4.95

Firm favourite with families. Smart, lively and comfortable. Added attraction of watching the chefs make the pizzas.

Pizza Hut

2-4 Penn St, Bristol, BS1 3AN
0117 927 2916
www.pizzahut.co.uk
Mon-Fri 11.30am-10pm, Sat 11.30am-11pm, Sun Midday-10pm
Meals from £3 child, £6.50 adult

Pizza Hut

23-25 St Augustines Parade, Bristol, BS1 4UL
0117 925 2755
Meals from £3 child, £6.50 adult

Efficient chain.

Quayside Restaurant

Jury's Bristol Hotel, Prince St, Bristol, BS1 4QF
0117 923 0333
www.jurysdoyle.com
Daily 12.30pm-2.30pm and 6.30pm-10.30pm
Meals from £4.95

Formal dockside restaurant. Pub and restaurant menus available.

Riverstation

The Grove, Bristol, BS1 4RB
0117 914 4434
Open 7 days for lunch and evening meals, ring for details
Meals from £4.50

Modern restaurant and deli café. More of an adult venue but children are welcome. Childrens menu on request.

The Galleries Food Street

Galleries, 25 Union Gallery, Broadmead, Bristol, BS1 3XD
0117 929 0569
Mon-Sat 8.30am-5.30pm, Thu 6.30pm, Sun 10.30am-4.30pm

Food court with communal eating from Fat Jackets, Burger King, Hickory Grill, Haagen Dazs, Singapore Sam Express and Zacks Deli.

The Hole in the Wall

2 The Grove, Queens Sq, Bristol, BS1 4QZ
0117 926 5967
www.beefeater.co.uk
Meals from £2.99

Beefeater chain restaurant. Upstairs, staff happy to help with buggies.

The Riverside Garden Centre Café

Clifthouse Road, Southville, Bristol, BS3 1RX
0117 966 7535
Daily 9.30am-4.30pm

Garden centre café with outside play area, Wendy House and climbing frame. Homemade meals. Childrens portions available.

Watershed Café Bar
1 Canons Rd, Harbourside, Bristol, BS1 5TX
0117 927 5101
www.watershed.co.uk
Mon 11am-11pm, Tues-Fri 9.30am-11pm, Sat 10am-11pm, Sun 10am-10.30pm
Meals from £2 child, £5.45 adult

Relaxed atmosphere but can get very busy. Children's menu available during holidays and on request.

Windmill Hill City Farm Café
Philip St, Bedminster, Bristol, BS3 4EA
0117 963 3252
Daily 9.30am-5pm
Meals from £2.50, no credit cards

Simple, healthy menu available including good breakfasts. Hot food finishes 2.30pm (2pm Sun).

CLIFTON VILLAGE

Aruba
6 Clifton Down Rd, Bristol, BS8 4AD
Top of Regents Street
0117 974 4633
Mon-Sat 8am-5pm, Sun and B/H 10am-4pm
Meals from £1.75 child, £2.30 adult

Traditional style licensed café with friendly and accommodating staff. All food homemade on the premises, small portions available, baby food heated etc. Spacious patio area for supervised play.

Avon Gorge Hotel
Sion Hill, Bristol, BS8 4LD
0117 973 8955
Daily 12pm-2pm and 7pm-10pm
Meals from £5

The main attraction is a large sun terrace with magnificent views of the Suspension Bridge. Bar food.

Emmanus House
Clifton Hill, Bristol, BS8 1BN
0117 907 9954
www.emmanus-house.co.uk
Open daily 12-2pm, recommend booking
Meals from £6.25

Fantastic views over Bristol. Terraced lawn with wheelchair access and gates at either end making it safe for youngsters, but watch the pond.

Pizza Express
2-10 Regent St, Bristol, BS8 4HG
0117 974 4259
Mon-Sat 12-11pm, Sun 12-10.30pm
Meals from £3.95 child, £4.95 adult

Dirm favourite with families. Smart, lively and comfortable. Added attraction of watching the chefs make the pizzas.

Rainbow Café
10 Waterloo St, Bristol, BS8 4BT
0117 973 8937
Mon-Sat 10am-5.30pm, Wed 10am-3pm
Meals from £2.50, no credit cards

Friendly licensed café. Small and informal, with fold up chairs and exceptionally helpful staff. Excellent homemade whole-food lunches, snacks and teas with child-friendly beakers etc. Limited parking in the street.

Splinters Coffee House
66 Clifton Down Rd, Bristol, BS8 4AD
0117 973 4193
Mon-Sat 8am-6pm, Sun & B/H's 10am-5.30pm
Prices £2-£5

Traditional style licensed café with friendly and accommodating staff. All food homemade on the premises, and small portions available, baby food heated etc. No facilities, but spacious patio area outside for supervised play.

The Lansdown

8 Clifton Rd, Bristol, BS8 1AF
0117 973 4949
Meals from £3.50 child, £5.95 adult

Children only allowed in pub garden except on Sundays when they can use the dining room. No childrens menu but children-friendly food is available.

WHITELADIES ROAD

Bannisters

3 Worrall Rd, Bristol, BS8 2UF
0117 973 6577
Mon-Fri 8am-5pm, Sat 9am-5pm, Sun 11am-3pm
Meals from £1.60, no credit cards

Small friendly café (too busy at lunchtime for buggies).

Bella Pasta

96a Whiteladies Rd, Bristol, BS8 2QX
0117 973 8887
Mon-Thu from 6pm, Fri-Sun from midday
Meals from £3.95 child, £5 adult

Relaxed, bright, Italian-style licensed chain restaurant.

Henry Africa's Hothouse

65 Whiteladies Rd, Bristol, BS8 2LY
0117 923 8300
Fri-Sun 10am-late, Mon-Thurs 3.30pm-late
Meals from £2 child, £5 adult

Relaxed and friendly licensed contemporary American restaurant. Varied food in simple surroundings. A lot of stairs to negotiate, but staff very willing to help. Balloons and crayons.

Maskrey's Restaurant

62 Whiteladies Rd, Bristol, BS8 2QA
0117 973 8401
Mon-Sat 9.30am-5pm
Meals from £2.60

Pleasant, airy second floor restaurant inside the furniture department. Reached by lift with a few steps to negotiate. Outdoor terrace.

Metro Espresso

Whiteladies Rd, Bristol, BS8 2NP
Outside Clifton Down Shopping Centre

Coffee bar, selling sandwiches, baguettes and cakes. Fruit smoothies popular with kids. No smoking at lunch time.

Planet Pizza

83 Whiteladies Rd, Bristol, BS8 2NT
0117 907 7112
Mon-Sat 11.30am-11pm, Sun 12-10.30pm
Meals from £3.95

Fast food, pizza bar. Not buggy friendly and no children's menu, but portions can be divided.

NORTH BRISTOL

Café Unlimited

209 Gloucester Road, Bishopston, BS7 8NN
Mon-Sat 9am-4.30pm
Meals from 90p child, £2.50 adult

Recently opened. Large downstairs family room (help down steps with buggies provided). Childrens tables and chairs, books and drawing material for distraction. Healthy kids food. Fairly traded produce used.

The Downs Tea Room

Durdham Down, next to the Water Tower
0117 923 8186
Daily 8.30am-6pm
Meals from £2

You couldn't get a bigger outdoor play area! On the edge of Durdham Down. Eat alfresco or inside. Good menu range.

Harry Ramsden's
Catbrain Lane, Cribbs Causeway, Bristol, BS10 7TQ
0117 950 0233, www.harryramsdens.co.uk
Mon-Thu 12-9.30pm, Fri-Sat 10pm, Sun 8pm
Meals from £4.99
Just off J17 of M5

Famous fish and chip chain restaurant; bright, welcoming and clean.

St Werburghs City Farm Café
Watercress Rd, Bristol, BS2 5YJ
0117 923 2563
Wed-Sun 10am-4pm
Meals from £1.50 child, £1.75 adult

Lively and unusual tree house café overlooking children's play area. Homemade menu and very child orientated. Notice board with 'parent space' advertising groups etc.

The Beehive
Wellington Hill West, Henleaze, Bristol, BS9 4QY
0117 962 3250, www.beehive-pub.com
Meals from £2.95 child, £1.95 adult

Friendly pub with a lounge overlooking the garden. Children's area inside, and play equipment outside. Varied inexpensive menu.

The Lamb & Flag
Cribbs Causeway, Bristol, BS10 7TL
0117 950 1490
Meals from £2 child, £6 adult

Harvester restaurant with imaginative farm-like interior and garden. Active policy to welcome family groups; 'early bird' menus.

The Mall Food Court
The Mall, Cribbs Causeway, Bristol, BS34 5QU
0117 903 0303
See Mall opening times in Shopping & Services

Food Court with communal eating surrounded by quick service outlets. Arkwrights (Fish & Chips) Bakers Oven, Burger King, KFC, Singapore Sam Express, Nandos, Druckers and Spud U Like. Starbucks, Pizza Hut & Massarella's have their own seating.

The Mill House
115 Gloucester Rd Nth, Bristol, BS34 7PY
0117 931 2706
www.millhouseinns.co.uk
Mon-Fri 12pm-3pm and 5pm-9pm, Sat-Sun 12pm-9pm
Meals from £2.95 child, £3.50 adult

Very comfortable child orientated pub, with pirate galleon ship in the outside play area.

NORTH EAST BRISTOL

The Beefeater, Emersons Green
200-202 Westerleigh Rd, Bristol, BS16 7AN
0117 956 4755
Mon-Sat 12pm-late, Sun 12-9pm
Pub meals from £3 child, £3.95 adult

Restaurant and pub meals available.

EAST BRISTOL

Café Maitreya
89 St. Marks Road, Easton, Bristol
0117 951 0100
Wed-Fri 11.30am-3.30pm, Sat-Sun 11am-4pm, Tues-Sat 7pm-9.45pm
Meals from £2.95 adult, £1.75 child

Fab vegetarian food in light airy surroundings. Menus clearly marks vegan, wheat/gluten-free and dairy free items. Kids' menu includes mini soup of the day and cheesy soldiers.

The Highwayman
Hill Street, Bristol, BS15 4EP
0117 967 1613
Daily 11am-11pm
Meals from £1.50 child, £4 adult

Traditional pub, comfortable surroundings with a separate no smoking area Mon-Fri. Paper and crayons and a room for baby changing available on request.

SOUTH EAST BRISTOL

The Brass Mill
Avon Mill Lane, Bristol, BS31 2UG
0117 986 7280
Mon-Sat 11.30am-10pm, Sun Midday-10pm
Meals from £2.99 child, £4.25 adult

Brewers Fare pub, designed for families with scenic location by the river Avon.

TGI Fridays
Avon Meads, St Philips Causeway, Bristol, BS2 0SP
0117 977 2999
www.tgifridays.co.uk
Mon-Sat 12-11.30pm, Sun 12-10.30pm
Meals from £4 child, £6 adult
Large authentic American restaurant with American service! Varied menu.

The Lock and Weir
Hanham Mills, Bristol, BS15 3NU
0117 967 3793
Mon-Sat 11am-3pm and 6pm-late, Sun 12pm-late
Meals from £3.50, no cheques/credit card
Local drinking pub with BBQs in the summer. Large garden next to the river, beware of low fence.

The Crown
126 Bath Rd, Bristol, BS15 6DE
0117 932 2846
Mon-Sat 11am-11pm, Sun 12-10.30pm
Meals from £3.99 child, £4.99 adult
Harvester restaurant, with an imaginative farm-like interior, designed for families.

SOUTH WEST BRISTOL

The Angel Inn
172 Long Ashton Rd, Bristol, BS41 9LT
01275 392 244
Mon-Fri 12-2.30pm and 6.30-9.30pm, Sat 5-9.30pm, Sun 12-2.30pm
Meals from £3.95 child, £2.50 adult

Pleasant, traditional four roomed pub with a good range of food available. Half portions and extra plates for children. Children are welcome until 8.30pm. Restaurant is non-smoking.

The Dovecote
Ashton Road, Bristol, BS41 9LX
01275 392245
Vintage Inn chain restaurant next to Ashton Court. Large garden with open views. No children's menu but smaller portions on request.

The Stables Café
Ashton Court Visitor Centre, Bristol, BS41 9JN
0117 963 3438
Daily 11am-5pm, winrter: 4pm
Café at Ashton Court Visitors Centre.

ANNUAL EVENTS & FESTIVALS

There is a huge annual programme of events across the West, many have no admission charges. Taking part can be be an excellent way for the whole family to get out and about. Event organisers are keen to appeal to all ages and tastes.

Below is a summary of the West's annual social calendar, there are however many 'one-off' events so keep an eye on the local press or visit the website:

www.visitbristol.co.uk

MAY

Bath International Music Festival
Classical, jazz, contemporary and world music. www.bathmusicfest.org.uk

JUNE

Royal Bath & West Show
Shepton mallet showground. Agricultural and animal action. Educational fun for all the family. www.bathand west.co.uk

Bristol's Biggest Bike Ride
Fun cycling on traffic-free roads, Durdham Downs

The Internatinal Westonbirt Festival of Gardens
June-Sep. www.forestry.gov.uk/westonbirt

Bristol Motor and Classic Car show

Bristol Bike Fest
Ashton Court Estate, mountain bike endurance and cross-country racing. www.bristolbikefest.com

Glastonbury Festival
Shepton Mallet, the largest greenfield music and performing arts festival in the world. www.glastonburyfestival.co.uk

JULY

St Paul's Carnival
Spectacular carnival parade, music and great food

Truckfest
Shepton Mallet showground, the ultimate trucking festival. www.truckfest.co.uk

Ashton Court Festival
Showcasing the best music, theatre and arts from the Bristol area

Bristol Children's Festival
The Bristol Downs, fun activities for under 12's. www.childrensworldcharity.org

Bristol Harbour Festival
The city's most spectacular waterside event

AUGUST

Bristol International Balloon Fiesta & Nightglow
Ashton Court Estate, 150 hot-air balloons in the sky with launches at 6am and 6pm. www.bristolfiesta.co.uk

SEPTEMBER

Bristol Internationa Kite Festival
Aston court Estate, colourful kites from around the world. www.kite-festival.org

September Bristol Half Marathon
International runners compete in the city centre

NOVEMBER

Firework Fiesta
Bristol Downs

Somerset Carnivals
Various locations. the largest illuminated procession in the world. www.somersetcarnivals.co.uk

OUT & ABOUT IN THE WEST COUNTRY

Kath Sidaway

CHAPTER 3

INTRODUCTION

Whether it's a wet weekend in winter or a special day out in the summer holidays, you're spoilt for choice around Bristol. Within roughly an hour's journey time you should find something to satisfy even the most demanding member of your family! Most attractions charge an entry fee, however there are several which are government funded and free. There are also some wonderful outings and walks which will cost only the transport to get there.

The entries in the first part of the chapter are places of interest, listed by location. They Start at Portishead, moving down the coast to Burnham, and then anticlockwise past Bath, up through Gloucestershire ending in Cardiff (my childhood home!). Refer to the maps in the central colour section. The rest of the chapter lists attractions by type e.g. castles, farms, etc.

Opening times can change, particularly over Christmas and New Year, so phone to avoid disappointment.

PORTISHEAD

Drive 20 minutes from Bristol's city centre and you will discover a peaceful escape with something for all ages. There is a new marina with working lock; the Lake Grounds are right on the coast, although you cannot swim from the beach (it's mud!) and there is a wonderful open air pool and leisure centre, see Activities 0-12 Years.

Lake Grounds

Portishead
Follow brown signs from town centre

Spacious seafront park with boating lake, playground and seasonal bouncy castle & donkey rides.

CLEVEDON

Victorian seaside town with seafront promenade and pier, ideal for walks with toddlers and pushchairs. With older children the rocky foreshore is good for fossil hunting. At the opposite end of the promenade to the pier is Salt House Fields which has play areas for toddlers and older children, seasonal bouncy castle, miniature railway, crazy golf and snack bar. See Walks to the SW of Bristol below.

Clevedon Tourist Information Centre

Clevedon Library, 37 Old Church Road, BS21 6NN
01275 873498, www.somersetcoast.com
Mon/Thu/Sat 9.30am-5pm, Tue/Fri 9.30am-7pm

Clevedon Heritage Centre

4 The Beach, Clevedon, BS21 7QU
01275 341196
Daily 10.30am-4.30pm, seasonal variations
Admission Free

Photographic history of Clevedon.

Clevedon Pier

The Toll House, Clevedon Pier, BS21 7QU
01275 878846
Mon-Wed 10am-5pm, Thu-Sun 9am-5pm
£1 adult, 50p child, free U4's

Grade 1 listed pier, a fine example of Victorian architecture. Summer sailings to islands, phone for timetable, see Transport.

Clevedon Craft Centre

Moor Lane, off Court Lane, BS21 6TD
01275 872149
Daily 10am-5pm (most workshops closed Mon)
Admission free
M5 J20, follow brown signs, Court Lane is off B3130

Craft studios demonstrating a variety of skills. Jewellery, pottery, illustrations, hand carved leather goods and stained glass. Items for sale. Feed the birds 20p/bag at the pond.

WESTON-SUPER-MARE

Seaside town, offering a vast expanse of safe flat sandy beach ideal for sandcastles and donkey rides. If you want to paddle, the tide is always in at Marine Lake at the north end of the seafront; rock pooling at Anchor Head. Seasonal seafront 'land train', bouncy castles, crazy golf, miniature railway, putting green and a horse drawn Thomas the Tank Engine. If it rains check out the pier, Weston Park Raceway slot cars, the Helicopter Museum and the model train layout in Model Masters, see index.

Weston-super-Mare Tourist Information Centre

Beach Lawns, Weston-super-Mare, BS23 1AT
01934 888800
www.somersetcoast.com
Daily exc Sundays in winter

Seaquarium

Marine Parade, Weston-super-Mare, BS23 1BE
01934 613361
www.seaquariumweston.co.uk
Daily 10am-4pm.
£4.95 adult, £3.95 child, £17 family (2+2)
Reduction of £1 on presentation of this book

Built on its own pier, the aquarium has a wide variety of marine life and an underwater walk through tunnel. New zones 'Lethal Reef' and 'Night Hunters'. Hands-on activities.

The Grand Pier

Marine Parade, Weston-super-Mare, BS23 1AL
01934 620238
www.grandpierwsm.co.uk
Feb-Easter w/ends only, Easter-Nov 10am-dusk

Covered amusement park over the sea, including dodgems, ride simulators etc. Soft play area upstairs.

North Somerset Museum

Burlington St, Weston-super-Mare, BS23 1PR
01934 621028
www.n-somerset.gov.uk/museum
Mon-Sat 10am-4.30pm
£3.50 adult, accompanied children free

Child-friendly displays and activities, Victorian dressing up clothes, interactive computers, passport trail and holiday activities.

Wacky Warehouse/The Bucket and Spade pub

Yew Tree Drive, Weston-super-Mare, BS22 8PD
01934 521235
11.30am-10pm £2/hr
Mon-Fri 9.30am-11.30am toddler sessions £2.50

Three levels of soft play, with swings, tunnels, slides and ball pools designed for under 12's (145cm). Separate play area for under 5's. Holiday activities. Bucket and Spade pub next door serves a wide range of meals.

BERROW & BREAN

Berrow has a sandy beach and sand dunes which can be reached from the nature reserve (parking free). Brean's beach car park is inexpensive. At the north end a steep climb will take you to Brean Down, a rocky National Trust headland with great views.

Animal Farm Country Park

Red Road, Berrow, Nr Burnham on Sea, TA8 2RW
01278 751628
www.animal-farm.co.uk
Daily 10am-5.30pm, closes 4.30pm in winter
£4.70 adults & children, free U3's
Annual: £14.50
50p off with presentation of this book

Large variety of animals including rare breeds, set in 25 acres of countryside. Opportunities to cuddle and bottle feed the animals. Huge indoor and outdoor play areas, with toddler zones. Treasure hunts in the holidays.

Brean Down Tropical Bird Garden

Brean Down, Brean, Somerset, TA8 2RS
01278 751209
www.burnham-on-sea.co.uk/brean_bird_garden
Mar-Oct: daily 10am-4pm
Nov-Mar: Sat-Sun 10am-4pm
Phone for school holiday openings
£1.95 adult, 95p child

Located at the foot of Brean Down. Largest selection of tropical parrots in the West.

Brean Leisure Park

Coast Road, Brean, Somerset, TA8 2QY
01278 751595
www.brean.com
April-Oct phone for details
Pool complex £3/session, free U3's

Fun park with over 40 rides and attractions including go-karts, laserquest and rollercoasters. Indoor and outdoor pools with water chutes. Attraction has more appeal to older children/teenagers.

BURNHAM-ON-SEA

Seven miles of sandy beach stretches from Burnham to Brean. Sandcastles, walking, kite flying, picnics and seasonal donkey rides. Swimming restrictions due to hazardous tides. Esplanade, pier and amusement arcade.

Burnham-on-Sea Tourist Information Centre

South Esplanade, Burnham-on-Sea, TA8 1BU
01278 787 852
www.sedgemoor.gov.uk/tourism
Mon-Sat 9.30am-4.30pm (closed 1pm-2pm)

Apex Leisure and Wildlife Park

Marine Drive, Burnham-on-Sea
Sedgemoor Parks Dept: 01278 435435

[WC] [♿] [🏛]

42 acre park, walks, ducks to feed, a skate park, BMX biking (members only) and a children's play area.

Play Centre

Pier Street, Burnham-on-Sea, TA8 1BT
01278 784693
Daily: 10am-5pm (closed Mon/Tue term time)
£2 term time, £2.35 school holidays

[P] [✏] [WC] [🎠] [CP] [♿] [🌳] [🏛] [✂] [♨]

Small indoor play area for 1-8yrs.

STREET

Clarks Village is a great day out for shopaholics with an eye for a bargain. See Shopping & Services.

The Village Pottery & Play Factory

Clarks Village, Street, Somerset, BA16 0BB
01458 443889
Daily: Mon-Sat 9.30am-6pm, Sun 5pm
Play Factory: £2.25/hr

[P] [✏] [WC] [♿] [🌳] [🏛] [♨] [♿]

In the pottery throw your own pot for £2.99 or paint a ceramic starting at £2.50. There is also an adventure play structure for 4-9yrs, separate soft play area for under 4's, table

football, videos and toy corner. Children must be supervised.

The Shoe Museum

40 High Street, Street, BA16 0YA
01458 842169
Mon-Fri 10am-4.45pm, Sat 10am-5pm, Sun 11am
Admission Free

Traces the history of shoes and shoe making from Roman times to today. Most exhibits are on the first floor - lift only on weekdays.

Greenbank Outdoor Pool

See Swimming Outdoors, Activities 0-12 years

BATH

Bath is a beautiful and fairly compact city with lots to do. It only takes 15 minutes on the train from Temple Meads to Bath Spa. If driving, there are Park & Rides at Newbridge (A4) and Lansdown (A46) or the Charlotte Street car park in the centre is convenient if coming in from the A4. You could also cycle there on the Bristol to Bath cycleway.
See also Shopping & Services.

Bath Tourist Information Centre

Abbey Chambers, Abbey Church Yard, BA1 1LY
0906 711 2000 (50p/minute)
www.visitbath.co.uk
Daily

Bath Open Top Bus Tour

Bath Bus Company Ltd, 1 Pierrepont Street, BA1 1LB
01225 330444
www.bathbuscompany.com
www.citysightseeing.co.uk, online sales
Daily 10am-5pm, reduced service in winter
£8 adult, £4 child (6-12), free U6's

Trip lasts approximately 45 minutes, tickets are valid for two days, bought on the bus, tourist office, online or from train station. Pre-recorded and live commentary tours. Tours start on High St, Grand Parade. Free kid's passport, felt tips, puzzles and games.

Roman Baths and Pump Room

Pump Room, Stall Street, BA1 1LZ
01225 477785
www.romanbaths.co.uk
Daily 9am-6pm, seasonal variations
£8.50 adult, £4.80 child, free U6's, family ticket £22
(2+4). Combined tickets to costume museum and
Roman Baths are good value and valid for 7 days

One of the best preserved Roman sites in
Northern Europe, this religious spa was built
2000 years ago and is a fine example of
ancient engineering and design. The spring
still produces over a million litres of hot water
a day. Taste it for yourself! An outing of more
interest to older children, not suitable for
pushchairs (backpacks can be borrowed).
Audio guide provided. For special needs
facilities phone 01225 477785.

Victoria Art Gallery

Pulteney Bridge, Bath, BA2 4AT
01225 477233
www.victoriagal.org.uk
Tue-Sat 10am-5.30pm, Sun 2pm-5pm, some B/H's
Admission free

An excellent audio guide and an art trolley
for children in the gallery displaying the
permanent collection. Two other galleries
have changing exhibitions of both local and
national interest.

Theatre Royal

Sawclose, Bath, BA1 1ET
01225 448844
www.theatreroyal.org.uk

One of the oldest working theatres in the
country. An impressive range of kids' shows
and workshops in half terms and holidays.
Visit their website for details.

Royal Victoria Park

Upper Bristol Rd, Bath
01225 482624
Take A4 into Bath, ¾ mile before city centre

Families tend to visit this park for its massive
well equipped playground. There are also
beautiful botanical gardens and a duck
pond. The play area caters for children of all
ages and includes a large sandpit and skate
boarding area.

Victoria Falls, Adventure Golf

Victoria Park
01225 425066
Daily 10ish-dusk
Recently opened. Fun for children and adults
who can swing a putter carefully.

Bath Boating Station

Forester Rd, Bathwick, Bath, BA2 6QE
01225 312900
Apr-Oct 10am-6pm
£5 adult for 1st hour (£2 for additional hour/s),
£2.50 child, free U5's

A couple of miles NE of the centre you'll find
this Victorian boating station with rowing
boats and punts for hire. Boat trips available
up to Bathampton taking about 1 hour, £6
adult, £2.50 child.

BATH MUSEUMS

Bath Postal Museum

8 Broad Street, Bath, BA1 5LJ
01225 460333
www.bathpostalmuseum.org
Mon-Sat 11am-5pm, winter 4.30pm.
£2.90 adult, £1.50 child, £6.90 family, free U5's

The only museum in the country telling the
story of the postal service. Children can have
fun in a reconstructed 1930's post office
weighing items, stamping forms and sorting
letters. Educational videos, discovery trails,

jigsaws, typewriters and computer games also available.

The Museum of Costume
Assembly Rooms, Bennett Street, Bath, BA1 2QH
01225 477789
www.museumofcostume.co.uk
Daily 11am-6pm, winter 5pm
£6 adult, £4 child, £16.50 family (2+4), free U5's Combined tickets to museum and Roman Baths are good value and valid for 7 days

Large collection of clothing fashions from the late 16th century to the present day. Audio guide available, activity trolley with quizzes, word games and colouring. Courtesy child carrier for babies/toddlers are available. Children's activities during school holidays

American Museum
Claverton Manor, Bath, BA2 7BD
01225 460503
www.americanmuseum.org
Museum Apr-Oct: Tue-Sun 2pm-5pm, some BH's
Gardens & exhibitions 12pm-5.30pm
3wks Dec: Tue-Sun 1pm-4pm & Wed 5.30-7.30pm
£6.50 adult, £3.50 child, all areas
£4 adult, £2.50 child, gardens & galleries
Take A36 Warminster road out of Bath, follow signs

Displays of American decorative art spanning 17th-19th Century. Authentically furnished rooms showing the American way of life from colonial times to the eve of the Civil War, of interest to school aged children. No prams in the house. Beautiful terraced gardens. Museum re-opens for 3 weeks in Nov/Dec with the rooms decorated according to the period they represent for Christmas.

MUSEUMS OF THE BATH PRESERVATION TRUST

www.bath-preservation-trust.org.uk
The Trust works to save listed buildings from demolition and to preserve the historic beauty of Bath. It runs four museums which due to restrictive planning do not allow for disabled facilities (and difficult for prams). Three of the museums have fully illustrated trails, £1.50 (aslo available on their website).

Beckford's Tower
Lansdown Road, Bath
01225 460705
Easter-Oct: Sat-Sun & B/H's 10.30am-5pm

This 120ft tower, 2 miles north of Bath, has great views of the countryside.

Building of Bath Museum
The Countess of Huntingdon's Chapel, The Vineyards, Bath, BA1 5NA
01225 333895
Mid Feb-Nov: Tues-Sun & B/Hs 10.30am-5pm.
£4 adult, £1.50 child, £10 family (2+2), free U5's
Fri 3pm, free guided tour

This museum describes how the city of Bath was designed and built. Children can join Mr Macheath, an illustrated rat, for a drawing trail and hands-on activities. Interactive play house (U5's) dressing up clothes and handling boxes. Buggies just about possible but back carriers preferable.

Number 1 Royal Crescent
1 Royal Crescent, Bath, BA1 2LR
01225 428126
Tues-Sun 10.30am-5pm, winter 4pm, Dec-Feb closed
Open B/H's & Mondays of Bath Festival
£4 adult, £3.50 child, £10 family (2+2), free U5's

First house built on the Royal Crescent in 1767. Restored as a grand town-house of the period. Join Lily the cat on an illustrated family trail to find out how people lived in the house over 200 years ago. Drawing trail, handling boxes and dressing up clothes.

William Herschel Museum
19 New King Street, Bath, BA1 2BL
01225 311342
Mid Feb-Nov: Mon-Fri 2pm-5pm, Closed Wed, Sat-Sun 11am-5pm.
£3.50 adult, £2 child, £7.50 family (2+2), free U5's

This museum may be of interest to budding astronomers. It was the home of William Herschel, who discovered the planet Uranus in 1781. An auditorium shows programmes on space travel and astronomy. Follow the family trail with Sirius the dog star or an audio guide.

BRADFORD-ON-AVON AND THE KENNET AND AVON CANAL

It only takes half an hour to get to this attractive old wool town by train from Temple Meads, but it feels a world apart from Bristol. The canal, which played such an important role 200 years ago allowing goods to be transported to and from London, has been restored and offers lots of recreational opportunities. The stretch between Bath and Devizes is one of the most attractive in the country. Colourful narrowboats, ducks and waterside pubs make cycling, walking or boating along the canal fun for everyone. See Walks below. The car park at the station is good value (£1.80/day) and well placed for seeing the sights.

Bradford-on-Avon Tourist Information Centre.
50 St. Margarets Street, Bradford-on-Avon BA15 1DE
01225 865797
www.bradfordonavontown.com
Daily 10am-5pm, winter 4pm.
This helpful office has new premises in Westbury Gardens - look for the flag pole.

Barton Farm Country Park and the Tithe Barn
The Country Park is always open.
Nearest car park is on Pound Lane, off Frome Rd, B3109 just out of town centre past station

This park, created on land belonging to the ancient Manor Farm, is set in the wooded valley of the River Avon, stretching 1.5 miles between Bradford and the hamlet of Avoncliff. See Walks below.

14th century Tithe Barn
English Heritage
Apr-Oct 10am-6pm, winter 4pm, free admission
On the edge of the park is this impressive barn, once used to store the Abbey's tithes. The granary and old cow byres have been restored as craftshops and galleries. There are also tea gardens and a children's play area.

Kennet & Avon cycling & boating
There are many options available from bike and canoe hire to relaxing narrow boat trips. See Lock Inn and Bath & Dundas Canal Co. in Transport.

Brass Knocker Basin
Brass Knocker Basin, Monkton Combe, BA2 7JD
01225 722292
www.bathcanal.com
Daily 8am-dusk with seasonal variations
Take A36 south of Bath, at Monkton Combe turn left at lights onto B3108

This is a good point from which to orientate yourself whether you're walking, cycling or boating. The visitor centre has displays and information about the canal. The Angelfish restaurant, see Eating Out, is a scenic and child-friendly option for lunch. See bike and canoe hire at Bath & Dundas Canal Co.

CHELTENHAM, GLOUCESTER AND STROUD
Very easily reached from Bristol, there's a lot to do in this area with some especially good museums. Also see Sudeley Castle below.

CHELTENHAM

Cheltenham Tourist Information Centre
77 Promenade, Cheltenham, GL50 1PP
01242 522878
www.visitcheltenham.info
Mon-Sat 9.30am-5.15pm (10am Wed)

Cheltenham Art Gallery and Museum
Clarence Street, Cheltenham, GL50 3JT
01242 237431
www.cheltenham.artgallery.museum
Mon-Sat 10am-5.20pm, Sun 2pm-4pm. Closed B/H's
Admission Free

The collections relate to the Arts and Crafts Movement with fine examples of furniture, silver, jewellery, ceramics and textiles. Other displays include oriental art, a history of Cheltenham, sparkling costume accessories, archaeology and natural history. Actively welcomes families with discovery trails and handling tables for children of all ages, with specific activities and colouring sheets for the under fives.

Sandford Parks Lido

See Swimming Outdoors, Activities 0-12 years

GLOUCESTER

Gloucester Tourist Information Centre

28 Southgate Street, Gloucester, GL1 2DP
01452 396572
www.gloucester.gov.uk/tourism
Mon-Sat: 10am-5pm, Jul/Aug: Sun 11am-3pm

There is also a tourist information point at the National Waterways Museum, see below.

National Waterways Museum

Llanthony Warehouse, Gloucester Docks, GL1 2EH
01452 318200
www.nwm.org.uk
Daily 10am-5pm
£5 adult, £4 child, £12-16 family, free U5's
M5 J12 follow brown tourist signs to Historic Docks

This award-winning museum is housed in a listed Victorian warehouse within the historic Gloucester Docks. Many exhibits ranging from touch-screen computers to interactive pulleys and water toys, all help portray the history of our canals and rivers in a hands-on and informative way. Outside the main museum building you can watch a blacksmith at work or climb aboard historic boats. From Easter to Oct (12pm-4pm), the Queen Boadicea II (a Dunkirk 'little ship') makes 45 minute trips along the canal.

Gloucester Folk Museum

99-103 Westgate Street, Gloucester, GL1 2PG
01452 396467
www.livinggloucester.co.uk
Tue-Sat 10am-5pm
£2 adult, free child
Short walk from historic docks

Child-friendly museum of social history. In the Toy Gallery there is a Wendy House, a puppet theatre and a toy cupboard. The Portal ICT Gallery has interactive quizzes for all ages. Displays include a Victorian classroom, dairy and ironmonger's. There are more toys in the garden which occasionally has farm animals.

Nature in Art

Wallsworth Hall, (Main A38 Twigworth), GL2 9PA
01452 731422
www.nature-in-art.org.uk
Tue-Sun 10am-5pm & B/H's
£3.60 adult, £3.10 child, free U8's
M5 J11A, take A417 and A40 to A38 north. Brown/green sign at entrance.

This museum is full of art inspired by nature. Sculptures, tapestries, ceramics and paintings. Feb-Nov, visiting artists can be seen demonstrating skills ranging from oil painting to chainsaw sculpting. There is an activity room for children with jigsaws and brass rubbings. Handling boxes in some of the galleries. Large range of activities during school holidays for different age groups e.g. making dream catchers, pressed leaf pictures, masks and batik. These half day sessions need to be booked in advance (U8's must be accompanied by an adult).

STROUD

Museum in the Park

Stratford Park, Stratford Road, Stroud, GL5 4AF
01453 763394
www.stroud.gov.uk
Tue-Fri 10am-5pm, Sat-Sun & B/H's 11am, some seasonal variations
Admission free
M5 J13, A419 follow signs to Stratford Park

Set in beautiful parkland, this family orientated museum has plenty to do for children of all ages with colourful interactive displays. Younger ones will enjoy finding Thomas the Tank Engine, doing a puzzle or having a story in the 'Boats and Trains' playroom. Displays include local history and a room devoted to childhood/education over the years. Quiz trails (30p), seasonal Family

Activity Packs (£1.50) and holiday workshops are fun ways of exploring the museum and park. Free parking at Stratford Park Leisure Centre (café, indoor and outdoor pools).

THE COTSWOLDS

The Cotswolds are within easy reach of Bristol and cover a large area - too much should not be attempted in one day. There are plenty of attractions, see Cheltenham Tourist Office which also has guides for family/pushchair walks in the Cotswolds.

Bourton Model Railway

Box Bush, High St, Bourton-on-the-Water, GL54 2AN
01451 820686
www.bourtonmodelrailway.co.uk
Apr-Sep: Daily 11am-5pm, Oct-Mar Sat-Sun only, Limited opening in Jan
£1.90 adult, £1.50 child

Over 500 sq ft of scenic model railway layouts. 40 British and continental trains run through realistic and detailed scenery; some are interactive. There is also a well stocked model and toy shop, with extended opening hours.

Birdland Park and Gardens

Rissington Road, Bourton-on-the-Water, GL54 2BN
01451 820480
Apr-Oct: Daily 10am-6pm, Nov-Mar: 4pm
£4.75 adult, £2.65 child, £13.50 family (2+2), free U4's, annual: £19 adult, £11 child

Over 500 birds can be seen in a natural setting of woodland and gardens. The River Windrush provides a natural habitat for flamingoes, pelicans, storks and a wide variety of waterfowl. The colony of penguins is fun to watch at feeding time (2.30pm). Over 50 aviaries contain a variety of exotic birds including parrots, hornbills and toucans. Lots of nice picnic spots and a children's play area. Café only open w/e's during winter.

Fundays Playbarn

Unit 8, Willow Court, Bourton-on-the-Water Industrial Park, GL54 2HQ
01451 822999
www.fundaysplaybarn.com
Daily 10am-6pm
Hols & W/ends: £1 adult, £4.50 child (4-11), £4.20 U4's, £1 U1's, lower prices during termtime
A429 north of Bourton, signpost on the right after Coach & Horses pub

Large indoor playbarn: ball ponds, nets, bouncy rollers and slides for 1-11yrs. Separate toddler zone. Summer outdoor area with sandpit, go-carts and giant chess. Session limited to 1½ hours during busy periods.

Bourton-on-the-Water

Has several other attractions, all accessible from its main car park.

The Dragonfly Maze
01451 822251
Use clues found on journey through maze to help you find the golden dragonfly.

The Model Village
01451 820467
www.theoldnewinn.co.uk
Detailed replica of the village built from Cotswold stone in one-ninth scale.

Cotswold Motoring and Toy Museum
See Wheels and Wings

Moreton-in-Marsh

15 mins drive north of Bourton.

The Cotswold Falconry Centre
01386 701043
Home to 70 birds of prey; flying displays throughout the day.

Butts Farm

Nr South Cerney, Cirencester, GL7 5QE
01285 862205
Easter-Oct: Wed-Sun 11am-5pm, daily sch. holidays
£3.75 adult, £2.75 child, free U3's
3 miles east of Cirencester on the old A419 towards Swindon, follow brown tourist signs

Near Cotswold Water Park. A very hands-on farm, specialising in rare breeds. A schedule of activities takes place and children earn stickers for their participation. They can milk goats, bottle-feed young animals, ride ponies, cuddle the smaller animals and go on a tractor-trailer safari. New farm shop selling local produce.

Cotswold Farm Park

Guiting Power, Nr Stow-on-the-Wold, GL54 5UG
01451 850307
www.cotswoldfarmpark.co.uk
Mar-Sep: Daily 10.30am-5pm, Sep-Oct: Sat-Sun
(daily in autumn half term) 10.30am-4pm
£4.95 adult, £3.50 chlid, £15.50 family (2+2), free
U3's, annual: £24.75 adult, £17.50 child
Follow brown signs from Bourton-on-the-Water.

P Ⓔ WC ⊓ CP Ⓛ ⓑ ⚹ 🅖 ⚒ 🍴 ⌂ ♿

Many rare British breeds, informative animal audio guide, seasonal demonstrations of lambing, shearing and milking. Children may cuddle and feed animals in the touch barn. There is a battery powered tractor driving school (3-12yrs) for first licences! (Pedal tractors for toddlers). Tractor-trailer rides, woodland walks, nature trails, adventure playground and an indoor play area. The campsite gives reduced rates to the park, see Family Holidays & Weekends Away.

Cotswold Wildlife Park

Burford, Oxfordshire, OX18 4JW
01993 823006
www.cotswoldwildlifepark.co.uk
Daily 10am-6pm, Oct-Feb: 4.30pm
£8 adult, £5.50 child, free U3's, annual: £40 adult,
£27.50 child
M4 J15, A419, A361, from Lechlade follow brown
tourist signs

P Ⓥ Ⓔ WC ✄ ⊓ CP Ⓨ Ⓛ ⚹ ✍ 🅐
⚒ 🍴 ⌂ 🚌 ♿

Spacious enclosures with rhinos, zebras, leopards, emus, wallabies, lions and more. A walled garden houses smaller creatures such as otters and meerkats. Other attractions include children's farmyard, adventure playground, miniature railway and reptile house. See advertisement in central colour section.

Prinknash Bird and Deer Park

Cranham, Gloucestershire, GL4 8EX
01452 812727
www.prinknash-bird-and-deerpark.com
Daily 10am-5pm, winter 4pm
£4 adult, £2.50 child, free U3's
M5 J11a , situated on the A46 between Cheltenham
and Stroud, follow brown tourist signs

P Ⓥ Ⓔ WC ⊓ CP Ⓨ Ⓛ ⚹ 🅐 ⚒ 🍴 ⌂

Set in the grounds of a working abbey, the bird park has aviaries housing exotic birds and a lake. Many birds including ducks, mute swans, black swans, peacocks and cranes wander freely and will feed out of your hand, as will tame deer and pygmy goats. There is a tearoom, playground by the abbey and an 80 yr old 2-storey Tudor style Wendy House to play in. See advertisement.

Cotswold Water Park

Spratsgate Lane, Shorncote, Cirencester, GL7 6DF
01285 861459
www.waterpark.org
Keynes Country Park, open daily 9am-9pm

P Ⓔ WC ✄ CP Ⓛ ⚹ ✍ 🅐 ⚒ 🍴
🚻 🚌 ♿

Britain's largest water park with over 130 lakes. Water sports, walking, nature spotting, or just relaxing on the beach - you can do it here.

Gateway Information Centre (and café)
01285 862962
At the A419 entrance to the park

For accommodation, family activities and eating out information.

Keynes Country Park

The larger of the 2 country parks. Here you will find: the Millennium Visitor Centre and a bathing beach (Jun-Sep 1pm-5pm); two large play areas; lakeside walks and cycling; a boardwalk café and picnic/barbeque areas. Boats (ranging from pedaloes to surfbikes) and bicycles can be hired here (phone 07970 419208).

Based at Keynes is the Adventure Zone, offering a range of seasonal activities for 8-16's including waterskiing, windsurfing, kayaking, sailing and horseriding. Prebooking essential: 01285 861816.

Waterland
01285 861202

An outdoor pursuit centre offering sailing, windsurfing, canoeing and kayaking, archery and raft building. It shares 'lake 32' with Keynes.

Neigh Bridge Country Park

Is the smaller of the parks. It is quieter with a picnic site, play area and lakeside walk.

Hoburne Holiday Park (Camping)
See Family Holidays & Weekends Away

THE FOREST OF DEAN & WYE RIVER

The Forest of Dean is one of the few remaining ancient oak forests. It covers 35 square miles between the Rivers Wye and Severn on the border of England and Wales. If you are looking for a peaceful day but one to exhaust your children this has to be one of the top locations. From Bristol it's less than an hour's drive, unfortunately public transport is not at its best in the area.

The forest has a huge amount to offer families of all ages e.g. cycling, walking, orienteering, bird watching, archery, canoeing and climbing. As a lot of these are weather dependent, please ring before you set off.

Coleford Tourist Information Centre
High Street, Coleford, GL16 8HG
01594 812388
www.forestofdean.gov.uk
Mon-Sat 10am-5pm, some seasonal variations

Forest of Dean Forestry Commission
Bank House, Bank Street, Coleford, GL16 8BA
01594 833057
www.forestry.gov.uk
Mon-Thu 8.30am-5pm, Fri 4pm
Many useful leaflets and information on special events such as deer and bird spotting.

Beechenhurst Lodge
Speech House Hill, Near Coleford, GL16 7EG
01594 827357
www.forestry.gov.uk
Daily 10am-6pm, winter dusk, Jan: W/E's only
B4226 between Coleford and Cinderford

This is a good base to start familiarising yourself with the forest. There's plenty of parking (£2/day) and it's the starting point for the sculpture trail as well as a good place to pick up the circular 12 mile family cycle route.

Prinknash Abbey
(off the A46 - Cheltenham/Stroud Road)

Feed and stroke our beautiful fallow deer. See one of the biggest collections of peacocks, the numerous waterfowl, the exotic pheasants and amusing pygmy goats. All are tame and feed out of your hand.

Prinknash Park, Cranham,
Gloucester, GL4 8EX
Tel: 01452 812727

Open Daily 10am to 5pm

Next to the information centre, there is a café, picnic and barbeque area and children's play equipment.

Cycling in the Forest of Dean
A great place to cycle, cycle hire available, see Transport

Forest of Dean Sculpture Trail
01594 833057
www.forestofdean-sculpture.org.uk
Daily dawn to dusk, free
This walk features sculptures inspired by the forest. It has a magical feel to it and is good fun for young children with wonderful views. The route is about 3.5 miles long, a shorter loop is possible. Pushchair accessible.

Symonds Yat Rock

Log Cabin Symonds Yat, Near Coleford
01594 834479
www.forestry.gov.uk
Log cabin, Mar-Oct: Daily 9.30am-dusk. Nov-Feb:
limited opening
Take B4432 north of Coleford.

[P] [♿] [WC] [⚑] [⚑] [✕] [⚑] [⚑] [⚑] [♿]

Fantastic viewpoint high above the River
Wye. Log cabin with snack bar, information,
souvenirs and picnic area. Waymarked walks
start from here. A pair of peregrine falcons
nest on the nearby cliffs and from mid Apr-
Aug staff from the RSPB can tell you all about
the fastest birds in the world and hopefully
help spot them with telescopes (10am-6pm).
If you're walking, there are two useful hand
ferries (seasonal) which run from The Olde
Ferrie Inne on the west bank of the Wye to
the base of the Rock, and from the Saracen's
Head Inn on the east bank to the west.

Royal Society for the Protection of Birds

The Puffins, New Road, Parkend, Lydney, GL15 4JA
01594 562852
www.rspb.org.uk

The RSPB organises a wide range of woodland
wildlife events in and around the Forest
of Dean. Last year these included badger
watching, pond-dipping, evening bat walks
and making nest boxes and bird feeders.
They'll also help you spot peregrine falcons
during the breeding season at Symonds Yat
Rock, see above. Two of their nature reserves
which you may like to visit are Nagshead and
Highnam Woods. Phone for details.

Outdoor Pursuits

The Forest is a playground for outdoor
pursuits enthusiasts.

Wyedean Canoe and Adventure Centre

Wye Pursuits

Symonds Yat Canoe Hire

See Teen Guide chapter

Kingfisher Cruises

Symonds Yat East
01600 891063

If you'd like to see the area from the water
but don't fancy paddling yourself along, take a
40 minute river trip.

Dean Heritage Centre

Soudley, Cinderford, GL14 2UB
01594 824024 / 822170
www.deanheritagemuseum.com
Daily: 10am-6pm, winter 4pm
£4 adult, £2.50 child, free U5's
B4227 between Blakeney and Cinderford

[♿] [WC] [⚑] [CP] [⚑] [⚑] [⚑] [✕] [⚑] [⚑] [♿]

History of the forest and its people in this
newly refurbished museum. Children can take
woodblock rubbings of forest scenes. In the
grounds there is a reconstructed Victorian
forester's cottage complete with Gloucester
Old Spot pig and chickens. Adventure
playground with a new hurdle maze and a
barbeque area. Some of the woodland walks
from here are accessible by pushchair and
wheelchair. A new deck at the café overlooks
the millpond with working waterwheel.

Hopewell Colliery Museum

01594 810706
www.hopewellcoalmine.co.uk
Mar-Oct: Daily 10am-4pm. Santa Special in Dec.
Underground tours £3.50 adult, £2.50 child
On B4226 Cinderford to Coleford road, a mile west
of Beechenhurst Lodge

[P] [WC] [♿] [⚑] [⚑] [✕] [⚑] [⚑] [⚑]

Local miners will take you underground to
show you the old mine workings and explain
the methods used to extract coal (45 minute
trip). The descent into the mine is steep (as
is the exit) but the route through it is level
(just over ½ mile). Not suitable for pushchairs
or back-packs; children of walking age are
welcome and will be kitted out with safety
helmets and lamps. Practical footwear and
warm clothing recommended. Above ground
there is a tea room, picnic and play area,
narrow gauge railway and a display of mining
tools and equipment.

Clearwell Caves

Near Coleford, Royal Forest of Dean, GL16 8JR
01594 832535
www.clearwellcaves.com
Mar-Oct: Daily 10am-5pm, Dec: Daily 10am-5pm
£4 adult, £2.50 child, £11.50 family (2+2), free U5's
Christmas special: £5 adult/child inc. gift for U14's
From Coleford take B4228 south for 1 mile. Turn
right at Lambsquay Hotel

These natural caves have had iron ore
mined from them for thousands of years,
(by children as young as 6yrs). 9 caverns
are open to the public. Miners' tools and
equipment are displayed to explain the history
of iron. There are no steps and single buggies
can be taken into the caves. See website for
special events.

Puzzle Wood

B4228, Near Coleford
01594 833187
Easter-Sep: Tue-Sun 11am-5.30pm Oct: 4pm
Also open B/H's & Feb ½ term
£3.90 adult, £2.60 child
B4228 ½ mile south of Coleford

Originally a pre-Roman open cast iron-ore
mine. A tangle of pathways laid out in the
early 1800's as an unusual maze has been
resurfaced to provide a mile of tracks through
deep ravines, trailing vines and moss covered
rocks. Not suitable for pushchairs. Really
weird scenery, great for hide and seek and
getting lost in! Also farm animals, an indoor
wood puzzle and tea room.

Littledean Riding Centre

Wellington Farm, Littledean, Nr Cinderford, GL14
01594 823955
www.littledean-riding.co.uk
Tue-Sun: 10.30am-4.30pm seasonal variations
£12/hr ride for beginner, £18/2 hrs
From Cinderford take the A4151 into Littledean. Turn
right by the chip shop down Grange Lane towards
Soudley. Stables are 1 mile on right

Variety of lessons and rides available
depending on age and ability. Children 4yrs+
can be led on a half hour walk into the forest.
Older children can enjoy longer rides on
traffic-free routes through the forest. Horse-
mad 10-16 year olds can have a riding holiday

here living at the farmhouse. Lessons and
rides should be pre-booked.

Mohair Countryside Centre

Little London, Longhope, GL17 OPH
01452 831137
www.royal-forest-of-dean.com/mohair
Wed-Sun 10.30am-5pm,term time, daily sch holidays
£3 adult & 10+yrs, £4.50 child, £2.50 U2's, free U1's
Bypass Gloucester on A417 and take A40 twds Ross.
In Huntley turn left onto A4136 & follow brown signs

Farm park set in secluded valley. Adventure
barn with five different soft play units, suitable
for toddlers to 10yrs. Outside a big sandpit,
play area, pets' corner, tractor rides, nature
trail and picnic area. You can see pigs and
goats in the paddocks, ride a pony or hand
milk the cow. See website for special events.

Perrygrove Steam Railway & Dean Forest Railway

See Transport

CARDIFF

45 minutes from Bristol Parkway to Cardiff Central,
short walk to centre

Cardiff has undergone a complete
transformation over the past twenty years.
New landmarks such as Cardiff Bay, the
Millennium Stadium and modern shopping
centres alongside Victorian arcades make it a
thriving and pleasant city to visit.

If you're hoping to combine a visit to the city
centre and the Bay area, there's a good bus
service linking the two which takes about
15 minutes. The Bay Xpress runs every 15
minutes between Cardiff Central station and
the Bay.

The Cardiff Festival takes place in mid July
with three weeks of theatre, music and
fairground entertainment. For the past two
years there's been an outdoor ice skating
rink outside City Hall during December and
January. Contact the visitor centre for details
of these and other special family events.

CITY CENTRE ATTRACTIONS

Cardiff Visitor Centre
16 Wood Street, Cardiff, CF10 1ES
029 2022 7281
www.visitcardiff.info
Mon-Sat 10am-6pm, Sun 4pm

Located outside Central Train Station.

Cardiff Open Top Bus Tour
01708 866000
www.citysightseeing.co.uk
Apr-Oct: Daily 10am-4pm, Nov-Dec: Sat-Sun
10.30am-3.30pm
£7 adult, £2.50 child (U15's), £16.50 family (2+2),
free U5's

Good for getting an idea of the layout of
the main attractions from the Millennium
Stadium to the new Bay area (pre-recorded
commentary). Tickets, valid for 24hrs, can be
bought from the driver, tourist info or online.
Tour starts at Cardiff Castle and lasts about
50 mins; local fares available. Kids' passport,
puzzles, games and felt tip pens.

Cardiff Castle
Castle Street, Cardiff, CF10 3RB
029 2087 8100
www.cardiffcastle.com
Mar-Oct: 9.30am-6pm, Nov-Feb: 5pm
£6 adult, £3.70 child, £17.60 family (2+3 or 1+4),
free U5's

Situated in the town centre, Cardiff Castle
spans a 2000 year history from its Roman
remains, to the Norman keep and its opulent
Victorian interior. To view the castle guided
tours (suitable for 4+yrs) start at 10am and
last 50 mins, no buggies. Large green for
picnicking; peacocks and ducks wander freely.

National Museum and Gallery
Cathays Park, Cardiff, CF10 3NP
029 2039 7951
www.nmgw.ac.uk
Tues-Sun 10am-5pm & B/H's
Admission free
Follow signs to Cardiff city centre, nr to University

Superb range of art (best collection of
Impressionists in Europe outside Paris),
natural history and science. Exhibitions on the
evolution of Wales, with life sized dinosaurs
and Ice Age creatures. The Glanely Gallery
is a new interactive area enabling children
to touch items not normally on display and
find out about things that particularly interest
them. Steps up to main entrance, access for
pushchair/disabled at a side gate. Restaurant
has some historical Welsh dishes.

Millennium Stadium
029 2082 2228
www.cardiff-stadium.co.uk
Mon-Sat 10am-5pm, Sun & B/Hols 10am-4pm.
Restaurant event days only
£5 Adult, £2.50 child, £15 family (2+3), free U5's

All budding Wilkinsons and Beckhams will
enjoy a tour of this huge stadium and even
the less sporty members of the family can't
fail to be impressed by the largest retractable
roof in Europe! Pushchair-friendly tour
includes a chance to run down the players
tunnel and sit in the Royal Box. Pre-booking
for tours advisable.

CARDIFF BAY

From Central Station: Bay Xpress bus service
Car park: Stuart St opp. Techniquest 30p/hr
Cardiff was once the busiest coal exporting
port in the world, so the decline in the coal
and steel industries had a devastating effect
on the docks. Over recent years the ambitious
regeneration of 2,700 acres of docklands
has resulted in the new Cardiff Bay with its
cultural attractions, interesting places to eat,
shops and leisure areas. Harbour Festival in
the summer.

Mermaid Quay
029 2048 0077
A shopping and leisure complex with plenty of
places to eat.

Roald Dahl Plass
A large oval space used for outdoor events
and performances. It's all pedestrianised
here and great for the kids to run around.
Following the shore line you'll see:

The Norwegian Church Arts Centre
029 2045 4899
Originally built in 1868 as a mission for
Scandinavian seamen, this has been restored

as an arts and music centre with café. The author Roald Dahl was baptised here. Beyond here is:

The Goleulong 2000 Lightship
029 2048 7609

Originally positioned off the Gower coast to warn off ships. Fun for children to explore the engine room, light tower and cabins. There is also a café.

Cardiff Bay Barrage
Harbour Authority: 029 2087 7900
Open Daily, summer closes 7pm, winter 4pm

One of the most ambitious engineering projects in Europe. The barrage, across the bay entrance is over 1km long. It provides a 500 acre freshwater lake fed by the Taff and Ely rivers. Visiting the barrage with its locks, sluice gates and fish pass (allowing fish access from the sea to the rivers to spawn) is fascinating. Penarth marina is on the other side, an easy stroll from the locks.

Access to the barrage, where there are refreshments and toilets, is by land train or boat or on foot from the Penarth end (where there is a car park).

Cardiff Bay Visitor Centre
The Tube, Harbour Drive, Cardiff Bay, CF10 4PA
029 2046 3833
www.visitcardiff.info
Mon-Fri 9.30am-5pm; Sat-Sun 10.30am-6pm, winter 5pm
10 minutes walk from Mermaid Quay

Easily recognised by its award winning tubular design. Has a vast scale model of the Bay.

Cardiff Barrage Road Train
029 2051 2729
www.cardiffroadtrain.com
April-Oct: Daily 11am-5pm from Stuart St.
Return ticket: £3 adult, £2 child.
Leaves from behind Techniquest

There's a live commentary on the land train. It takes 20 minutes to reach the barrage where there is a 10 minute stop before returning. Alternatively you could stay longer and take a later trip back, or return by boat.

Cardiff Bay Water Bus (Cardiff Cats)
029 2048 8842
www.cardiffcats.com
Easter-Oct: daily 10.30am-6pm, Nov- Easter: W/E's only, daily school holidays
Summer Return Trip: £3.50 adult, £2 child. Winter: £2 adult, £2 child, family discount available

30 minute cruises of the Bay with the opportunity to land at the barrage leave from Mermaid Quay. The water on this side of the barrage is usually calm. Tickets can be bought in advance from the quay information point. A new service running between Mermaid Quay and the Millennium Stadium in the city centre is due to start early summer 2004.

Cardiff Bay Cruises
029 2047 2004
www.cardiffbaycruises.com
Seasonal cruises, ring for times
1hr cruise: £6 adult, £3 child U16's, free U3's
½hr cruise: £3 adult, £1.50 child, free U3's

Cruise up the Taff, along the River Ely or around the Bay, with a full commentary. Boats, including the new restaurant boat, leave from in front of the Pierhead building. Pushchair access, pre-booking advisable.

Bay Island Voyages
029 2048 4110/01446 420692
www.bayisland.co.uk
Run all year dependent on weather and demand
Fast Bay Cruise: £6 adult, £3 child U14's
Bristol Channel: £18.50 adult, £10 child

Thrill seekers need look no further than a high speed trip on the 'Celtic Ranger' powered by two 225hp engines and travelling at up to 60mph! Appealing to older children although babies and toddlers can be taken. The most popular option with younger children (from about 6+yrs) is the Fast Bay Cruise, which tends to be calmer. For those with stronger sea-legs there are tours lasting between 1-2 hrs which go up the coast or around Flat Holm and Steep Holm. The boat carries 12 passengers, waterproofs and life jackets are provided. Pre-booking advisable.

Cardiff Bay Tours

029 2070 7882
www.cardiffbaytours.com
Easter-Oct: Daily 10am-4pm
£4 adult, £1.50 child

Informative 1½ hr walking tours of the Bay start at the Tube Visitors' Centre and end at St. Davids Hotel. Of interest to older children although the route is pushchair (and wheelchair) friendly. Pre-booking advisable.

Techniquest

Stuart Street, Cardiff, CF10 5BW
029 2047 5475
www.techniquest.org.
Mon-Fri 9.30am-4.30pm, W/E's & B/H's 10.30am-5pm
£6.75 adult, £4.65 child, £18.50 family (2+3), free U3's, annual family £48
Techniquest is signposted entering the Bay on A4232

On the waterfront, this large Science Discovery Centre for children has over 150 hands-on exhibits. There is an interactive Science Theatre Show and Planetarium. For younger children there are curiosity boxes in the Discovery Room.

Craft in the Bay

The Flourish, Lloyd George Avenue, CF10 4QH
029 2048 4611
www.makersguildinwales.org.uk
Daily 10.30am-5.30pm
Free admission
Five minutes walk from Mermaid Quay

Retail gallery set in old maritime warehouse displaying crafts made by members of the Makers Guild in Wales. Ceramics, jewellery, textiles, glass, furniture and paper. Café serving mainly vegetarian food.

BEYOND THE CENTRE

Roath Park Gardens & Boating Lake

Lake Rd West, Roath, Cardiff
Dawn to dusk

A 15 minute drive or bus ride from the city centre will bring you to a large park with plenty to see and do. The entire park stretches for nearly 1½ miles but the best place to head for is between Lake Roads East and West (on-street parking). Here you'll find the lake with a wide variety of hungry waterfowl. The path around the lake is about a mile long circuit and it's great for a stroll with toddlers or pushchairs. In season you can hire rowing and pedal boats; separate fenced boating area for children. On the other side of the promenade from the lighthouse is a well equipped children's play area. Further on from the play area a stream and cascade run through nicely laid out flower gardens to a huge hothouse containing tropical fish and plants. Seasonal café. Nappy changing in disabled toilet at boat stage.

Museum of Welsh Life

St Fagans, Cardiff, CF5 6XB
029 2057 3500
www.nmgw.ac.uk
Daily 10am-5pm
Admission free
M4 J33, follow brown tourist signs, bus from city centre

A village chronicling the history of Wales. A whole day is needed to see everything. Over 40 buildings have been transported here from all over Wales and rebuilt in attractive parkland. They give a fascinating insight into how people lived, worked and spent their leisure time over the past 500 years. Children will enjoy comparing a row of ironworkers' houses each furnished from a different decade, sitting in a Victorian classroom and seeing traditional crafts. Also large indoor museum.

FARMS

When visiting farms, zoos and wildlife centres it is wise to take precautions to avoid 'zoonoses' - diseases spread to humans via animal carriers. The risk is easily controlled by making sure your children wash their hands after contact with animals. If you are pregnant, or think you may be pregnant, avoid contact with pregnant ewes and newborn lambs.

Avon Valley Country Park

Pixash Lane, Bath Rd, Keynsham, BS31 1TS
0117 9864929
www.avonvalleycountrypark.co.uk
Apr-Oct: Tue-Sun & B/H's 10am-6pm, daily in school holidays
£5 adult, £4 child, free U2's
A4 towards Bath follow brown signs

Farm trail leads through several fields of farm animals and rare breeds. Other attractions include bottle feeding the lambs in the spring, a land train, a miniature ride-on railway, large adventure playground, a covered soft play area, quad bikes for any age (additional cost - U4's accompanied) and duck pond with boats for hire.

Court Farm Country Park

Wolvershill Road, Banwell, Weston-Super-Mare, BS29
01934 822 83
www.courtfarmcountrypark.co.uk
Mar-Nov: 10am-5.30pm. Nov-Mar: 10.30am-4.30pm
£4.95 adult, £3.75 child, £16 family (2+2), free U3's
ATV rides: £2 adult, £1.50 child
Season ticket: £24 adult, £18 child
M5 J21 follow brown tourist signs

A working farm with massive covered fun area and an outdoor 'Adventure Land' play area with aerial skyway and trampolines. Also: tractor and pony rides, bottle feeding lambs, handling pets and white knuckle ATV rides for the brave at heart! Maize maze from mid July to end Sept. Holiday activities include Easter egg and treasure hunts.

Greenmeadow Community Farm

Greenforge Way, Cwmbran, Gwent, NP44 5AJ
01633 862202
Daily 10am-6pm, winter 4.30pm
£3.50 adult, £2.50 child, free U2's
M4 J26, go north to Cwmbran following brown signs

Farm animals in paddocks and barns. Tractor and trailer rides, machine milking viewed from glassed-in area, adventure playground for 7+yrs and a large sandpit and tractor play area for U5's. Paddling pool with water spurting dragon in summer.

Wild, inspirational, fun

OLDOWN
COUNTRY PARK

3 days out in 1

Animal farm • Forest walks
Train rides • Adventure land
Pedal Go-karts • Tractor rides

For details of the many other exciting activities and opening times call **01454 413605** or visit **www.oldown.co.uk**
Foxholes Lane Tockington Bristol BS32 4PG

Oldown Country Park

Foxholes Lane, Tockington, BS32 4PG
01454 413605
www.oldown.co.uk
Feb-Nov: Sat-Sun 10am-5pm
Jun-Aug & all school holidays: daily 10am-5pm
£5 adult, £4.50 child, free U2's
Off A38 at Alveston nr Thornbury

Activities include a daily programme of animal feeding. You can get close to the animals, go for a tractor-trailer ride or use the miniature steam train. The park will appeal to children of all ages with a raised wooden walkway, assault course in the woods for 9+yrs and mini challenge course for 5-9yrs. Paths through the woods are generally buggy friendly. Café, education centre and parties. Seasonal fruit and veg. picking. See advertisement.

Noah's Ark Zoo Farm

Failand Rd, Wraxall, Bristol, BS48 1PG
01275 852606
www.noahsarkzoofarm.co.uk
Feb-Oct: Tue-Sat, B/H's & Mon school hols
10.30am-5pm
£7 adult, £5 child, £22 family (2+2) or £20 (1+3),
free U2's, annual: £35 adult, £30 child, £90/99 family
Bristol to Clevedon road via Failand (B3128)

This farm creatively combines religious and agricultural themes. A full day's activity with 60 different kinds of animal (offering a hands-on experience from chicks to camels and the chance to see lambs being born around Easter time), tractor-trailer rides, a huge variety of indoor and outdoor play equipment designed to meet the needs of toddlers to teenagers, a straw den with rope swings and several adventure trails. The theme of this farm (Noah's Ark and the creationist view of evolution) is explored in exhibitions, during the tractor ride and whilst feeding and handling the animals in the barn. New for 2004: an indoor maze; a lookout tower offering stunning views across the Severn Estuary to Wales and the longest hedge maze in the world planted autumn 2003.

Norwood Farm

Bath Rd, Norton St Philip, Bath, BA2 7LP
01373 834356
www.norwoodfarm.co.uk
Apr-Sep: Daily 10.30am-5.30pm
£5 adult, £3.50 child, free U3's, annual: £20 adult,
£14 child
B3110 between Bath and Frome. Hourly bus service
(No 267) from Bath

This environmentally conscious working farm, set in lovely countryside is the only Organic Rare Breeds Centre in the region. The farm opens in spring with the lambing of 12 different native breeds. A variety of goats, ponies, poultry, pigs and cattle can be stroked and fed. There are farm walks, gardens to picnic in, separate play areas for U12's and toddlers and a new organic veg and plant centre.

The Cattle Country Adventure Park

Berkeley Heath Farm, Berkeley, GL13 9EW
01453 810510
www.cattlecountry.co.uk
Easter-Early Sep: Sat-Sun 10am-5pm, daily school
holidays, some winter openings call for details
£4.90-£5.75 adult/child, free U2's, prices seasonal
M5 J14 take A38 and follow brown signs

This is a good family day out for U15's. Lots of indoor and outdoor play equipment where parents can join in too. Two dedicated play areas for the U6's. A farm trail passes a willow maze and a herd of American bison. Private party bookings available.

Other farm listings:

See The Cotswolds above for Butts Farm & Cotswold Farm Park
See Berrow & Brean above for Animal Farm Country Park

WILDLIFE

Longleat

Nr Warminster, Wiltshire, BA12 7NW
01985 844400
www.longleat.co.uk
Safari Park - Apr-Oct: Daily 10am-4pm, 5pm W/E's,
B/H's & summer hols
House openings/tours - phone for details
Passport ticket (valid for each attraction & one
season): £16 adult, £13 child, free U3's
A37 (Wells Road) south to Farrington Gurney. Left
onto A362, through Frome and follow signs.

Longleat comprises a stately home, safari park, and other attractions. Drive through the safari park (soft top cars not permitted) and see giraffes, zebras, tigers and lions in their enclosures. The monkey jungle is optional as they will clamber on your car, so not recommended for the car proud but children will love it! (Safari bus available). The other attractions include Postman Pat Village, Butterfly Garden, King Arthur's Mirror Maze, miniature steam railway, pets' corner, a large adventure playground, a safari boat trip where you can see hippos and sea lions. Not all areas are buggy friendly.

WWT Slimbridge
The Wildfowl and Wetlands Centre, Slimbridge, GL2
01453 890333
www.wwt.org.uk
Daily 9.30am-5pm, winter 4pm
£6.75 adult, £4 child, £17.50 family (2+2), free U 4's
M5 J14, follow signs

Spacious landscaped grounds offer the chance to get very close to, and feed, exotic, rare and endangered water birds. You can also view from hides and towers. Humming birds can be seen at close range in the Tropical House. The visitor centre includes the Hanson Discovery Centre, a cinema and great views over the River Severn from the Sloane Observation Tower. Also a wildlife art gallery.

Tropiquaria
Washford Cross, Watchet, West Somerset, TA23 OJX
01984 640688
www.tropiquaria.co.uk
Apr-mid Sep: 10am-6pm, mid Sep-Oct:11am-5pm
Nov-Mar: W/E's & school hols
£6.50 adult, £5.50 child, £23 family (2+2), free U3's
M5 J23, take A39 twds Minehead. It's between Williton and Washford

Housed in the old BBC transmitting station this colourful aquarium is home to frogs, snakes, lizards, birds and spiders. Outside there are lemurs, wallabies and chipmunks. Other attractions include: The Shadowstring Puppet Theatre, Wireless in the West Museum (a history of broadcasting), an adventure playground with two life-size galleon ships, a playground for the U5's and a new indoor play castle with café.

The National Birds of Prey Centre
Newent, Gloucestershire, GL18 1JJ
0870 990 1992
www.nbpc.co.uk
Feb-Oct: Daily 10.30am-5.30pm.
£6.75 adult, £4 child, £18.50 family (2+2), free U4's
M5 J11a, A40 Ross-on-Wye, B4215 to Newent, follow signs

The centre will be operating as usual until Nov 2004 when it is likely to be taken over, please ring for an update.
Impressive collection of birds including eagles, falcons and buzzards which can be seen in action three times a day.

CASTLES

Berkeley Castle and Butterfly Farm.
Berkeley, Gloucestershire, GL13 9BQ
01453 810332
www.berkeley-castle.com
Apr-Sep: Tue-Sat & B/H's 11am-4pm, Sun 2pm-5pm.
Oct: Sun 2pm-5pm
£7 adult, £4 child, £18.50 family (2+2), free U5's
Garden only (avail Tue-Fri) £4 adult, £2 child,
Annual: £20 adult, £10 child, £45 family (2+2)
On A38 between Bristol and Gloucester

24 generations of the Berkeley family have lived here since 1153 in what is England's oldest inhabited castle. It has been transformed over the years from a Norman fortress to a stately home full of paintings, tapestries and treasures. Lawns and terraced gardens surround the castle. Admission price includes an optional 1 hr guided tour plus entry to the Butterfly Farm (Apr-Sep) where you can walk amidst exotic butterflies in flight. The castle is unsuitable for pushchairs and baby back-packs are preferable outside. Tea rooms and plant centre.

Farleigh Hungerford Castle
Farleigh Hungerford, Nr. Bath, BA2 7RS
01225 754026
www.english-heritage.org.uk/farleighhungerford
Apr-Sep: daily 10am-6pm, Oct: 5pm, Nov-Mar: Wed-Sun 10am-4pm, closed 1-2pm in winter
£2.80 adult, £1.40 child, free U5's
3½ miles west of Trowbridge on A366

Ruins of a 14th century castle and chapel with museum. Audio guide and programme of events suitable for children, including exhibitions, medieval pageants. Pushchairs can be used but back-packs are preferable.

Sudeley Castle

Winchcombe, Cheltenham, GL54 5JD
01242 602308
www.sudeleycastle.co.uk
Mid Mar-Oct: daily 10.30am-5.30pm
Castle & Gardens: £6.85 adult, £3.85 child, £18.50
family (2+2), free U5's, seasonal variations on price
M5 J9 take A46, B4077, then signs to Winchcombe

P WC 🏛 ✕ 🛍 ⊞

The castle can boast many royal visitors
over the past 1,000 yrs including Anne
Boleyn, Elizabeth I and Henry VIII. Much
of the impressive collection of furniture and
paintings on display is from the Tudor period
and children doing this part of history at
school will enjoy the 'Six Wives at Sudeley'
exhibition. Attractive gardens surround the
castle, the highpoint for children being 'Fort
Sudeley', a large imaginatively designed
play area for 5+yrs. Separate small area for
toddlers. (£1.50/child, free U5's).

Caerphilly Castle

Castle Street, Caerphilly, CF83 1JD
029 2088 3143
www.cadw.wales.gov.uk
Daily 9.30am-5pm, summer 6pm, seasonal variations
£3 adult, £2.50 U16's, £8.50 family (2+3), free U5's
M4 J28 direction 'Risca' then A468 to Caerphilly.

P ✐ WC 🏃 🏃 🛍 ⊞ 🚌 ♿

This huge castle built in the 13th century is
the second biggest in Britain after Windsor.
It is a classic castle with high towers, moats,
banqueting hall, working replica siege-engines
and a leaning tower to make the people of
Pisa green with envy! Pushchair accessible
apart from the two exhibition towers.
Excellent re-enactment days through spring
and summer. Audio guide available.

Caldicot Castle and Country Park

Church Road, Caldicot, Monmouthshire, NP 26 4HU
01291 420241
www.caldicotcastle.co.uk
Mar-Oct: Daily 11am-5pm
Castle: £3 adult, £1.50 child, £8.50 family (2+3)
Annual: £24 family (2+3)
Admission to Country Park free
M4 to M48, J2 for Chepstow, A48 twd Newport then
B4245 follow signs

P ✐ WC 🏃 🏃 🏛 ✕ 🛍 ⊞ 🛏 🚌 ♿

Although founded during Norman times,
the castle was restored in the Victorian
period and inhabited until the 1960's. Some
furnished rooms remain in the towers. Adult
and children's audio guide and discovery
sheets for children to learn about its colourful
history. The surrounding country park has lots
of buggy friendly trails and a wildlife pond
with dipping platform. There is also a family-
friendly orienteering course in the grounds.
The castle hosts a wide variety of events and
re-enactments.

Castell Coch

Tongwynlais, Cardiff, CF15 7JS
029 2081 0101
www.cadw.wales.gov.uk
Apr-Oct: daily 9.30am-5pm, summer 6pm,
Nov-Mar: Mon-Sat 9.30am-4pm, Sun 11am-4pm
Closed Jan & Feb for maintenance
£3 adult, £2.50 child, £8.50 family (2+3), free U5's
M4 J32, take A470 north, follow signs.

P ✐ WC 🏃 ✕ 🛍 ⊞

Hidden in woodland, this fairytale castle
complete with conical roofed towers, working
portcullis and drawbridge, looks convincingly
medieval. It was however built in the late 19th
century for the Marquis of Bute. The inside
remains faithful to the Victorian era being
richly furnished and decorated. Worksheet
(50p) for children in shop and audio guide
(£1) available, suitable for 8+yrs. Woodland
trail around castle not suitable for buggies.
Coffee shop open Apr-Sep.

Chepstow Castle

Bridge St, Chepstow, Monmouthshire, NP16 5EY
01291 624065
www.cadw.wales.gov.uk
Apr-Oct: daily 9.30am-5pm, summer 6pm
Nov-Mar: Mon-Sat 9.30am-4pm, Sun 11am-4pm
£3 adult, £2 child, £8.50 family (2+3), free U5's
M4 J21 to M48 J2, then A466 and follow signs.

P 🛍 🚌

One of Britain's first stone-built strongholds.
Building started not long after the Battle
of Hastings in 1066 and the castle was
significantly extended over the following
centuries. Today the well preserved ruins
perch above the River Wye offering an insight
into life in a Norman castle and plenty of
scope for exploring. Steep slope from car park
(toilets) to castle entrance.

STATELY HOMES AND GARDENS

Bowood House & Gardens

Derry Hill, Calne, Wiltshire, SN11 0L2
01249 812102
www.bowood.org
Apr-Oct: 11am-6pm
Entry to House & Gardens: £6.40 adult, £4.10 U15's, £3.25 child U4's, free U2's, annual: £29 adult, £15-19 child
Off A4, Derry Hill village, midway between Calne and Chippenham

Capability Brown designed the beautiful park in which Bowood stands. The huge grounds include a lake, waterfall, cave, Doric temple and ample space for games and picnics. More formal gardens can be found in front of the stately home itself, which contains displays of furniture, art, costumes and family heirlooms. There is also a woodland garden of azaleas and rhododendrons (separate entrance off the A342) open for 6 wks during the flowering season (late April).

Bowood also has a superb outdoor adventure playground for U12's with a life-size pirate ship, high level rope-walks, giant slides, chutes, trampolines and an indoor soft play palace for younger children.

NATIONAL TRUST PROPERTIES

National Trust properties are becoming increasingly child-friendly, with many making provision for baby changing, feeding and transportation requirements. Often, trails, quiz sheets and other activities are on offer for older children. Around Bristol we're spoilt for choice, the latest Trust acquisition being Tyntesfield which can be seen on pre-booked guided tours, but hopefully will open fully during 2004. The 4 listed below are over an hours drive from Bristol, but still well worth a day trip.

Stourhead, Wiltshire (01747 841152) Superb landscaped garden and house, with temples and mature woodland set around large lake.

Avebury, Wiltshire (01672 539250) A huge megalithic stone circle encompassing part of the village of Avebury.

Dunster Castle, Somerset (01643 821314) Impressive castle atop a wooded hill set in attractive gardens.

Hidcote Manor Garden, Gloucestershire (01386 438333) A gorgeous garden designed as a series of outdoor rooms.

The National Trust

PO Box 39, Bromley, Kent, BR1 3XL
0870 458 4000
01985 843600 (Wessex branch)
www.nationaltrust.org.uk

Details of all the Trust's properties can be found on their website. Becoming a member of the National Trust may well prove cost effective if you plan to visit several properties during the year.

Clevedon Court

Tickenham Rd, Clevedon, N. Somerset, BS21 6QU
01275 872257
www.nationaltrust.org.uk
Apr-Sep: Wed/Thu/Sun & BH's 2pm-5pm
£5 adult, £2.50 child, free U5's
B3130 1½ mile east of Clevedon

This 14th-century manor house has been home to the Elton family since 1709. Eltonware pots and vases and a collection of Nailsea glass are on display. Attractive terraced garden - not suitable for buggies but some lovely slopes for rolling down. Children's guidebook and nursery rhyme trail available.

Dyrham Park

Dyrham, nr. Chippenham, Gloucestershire, SN14 8ER
0117 937 2501
www.nationaltrust.org.uk
Park, daily 11am-5.30pm
House and Garden, Apr-Oct: Fri-Tue 12pm-5pm
Phone for winter opening hours
Garden and house: £8.30 adult, £4.10 child, £20.50 family (2+3)
Garden and Park: £3.20 adult, £1.60 child, £7.50 family (2+3), free U5's
M4 J18, take A46 towards Bath for 2 miles.

House and gardens built at the turn of the 18th century, with most of the original furnishings. Family activity pack and children's guidebook available. No prams in house, baby slings and hip-carrying infant seats for loan. Spacious grounds and deer park to run around.

Lacock Abbey, Fox Talbot Museum & Village

Lacock, Nr Chippenham, Wiltshire, SN15 2LG
01249 730227
www.nationaltrust.org.uk/lacock
Museum, cloisters and garden, Mar-Oct: Daily 11am-5.30pm
Abbey, Apr-Oct: Wed-Mon 1pm-5.30pm
Museum (only) open winter W/E's
£7 adult, £3.50 child, £17.90 family (2+3), free U5's
Ticket variations available
M4 J17, take A350, 3 miles south of Chippenham

P [symbols] WC [symbols]

The Abbey was founded in 1232 as a nunnery and transformed into a family home in the 16th century. Children's quiz in house and spacious grounds to explore. Front carrying baby slings for loan. The Museum of Photography commemorates the life of William Henry Fox Talbot who made the earliest known photographic negative. The upper gallery has changing photographic exhibitions. The medieval village with its many lime washed half-timbered houses has been used as a location for several period dramas such as 'Pride and Prejudice'. The Abbey was also used to film parts of the recent Harry Potter films. There is a small children's play area and plenty of places to eat in the village.

Other National Trust listings:

See also Chedworth Roman Villa below

SEVERN ADVENTURES

The Severn Estuary has the second highest tidal range in the world - it can be as much as 50 feet. This contributes to the great natural spectacle of the Severn Bore, details below.

The estuary itself can be explored by steamships Waverley and Balmoral, see Transport chapter. See also Bay Island Voyages, Cardiff Bay.

Flat Holm and Steep Holm, the two islands between Cardiff and Weston-Super-Mare are wildlife havens with fascinating histories and well worth visiting. Although there's no pedestrian access to the new Severn Crossing you can still walk or cycle across the old bridge away from the traffic (park at Aust Services off J1 M48).

The Severn Bore

www.severn-bore.co.uk

The Severn Bore is a large surge wave in the estuary of the River Severn which makes a truly spectacular sight at its best. It occurs because of the shape of the estuary - it narrows from about 5 miles wide at Avonmouth, to less than 100 yards wide by Minsterworth. As the water is funnelled into an increasingly narrow channel, a large wave is formed as the tide rises. This occurs at least once during most months of the year, but the Bore is largest around equinoxes. Surfing the Bore has become a competitive sport. See website for timetable and viewing points. Get there early as the Bore can arrive up to half an hour either side of the scheduled time.

Flat Holm Project

The Pier Head, Barry Docks, Barry, CF62 5QS
01446 747661
www.cardiff-info.com/flatholm
Trips run from Mar-Oct, tide & weather dependent
£13 adult, £6.50 U17's, £35 family (2+2), no U4's due to life jacket restrictions

WC [symbols]

This tiny island in the Bristol Channel can be visited on a short day trip, giving you 3 hrs on the island. The crossing takes 30 minutes. Since the Dark Age the island has been used as a retreat for monks, then as a sanctuary for Vikings, Anglo Saxons, smugglers and cholera victims. Fortified in Victorian times and WW2 it is now a haven for wildlife, home to a large colony of gulls, shelducks, slow worms, goats and sheep to keep the grass mown and plenty of tame rabbits. The Flat Holm Project was set up to encourage visitor access and manages the island as a local nature reserve. Trip includes a guided walk. Best to take a picnic as shop only sells snacks.

Steep Holm

Knightstone Causeway, Marine Lake
01934 632307
www.steepholm.freeserve.co.uk
Trips run Apr-Sep, tide & weather dependent
£16 adult, £8 child accompanied (5-16). No U5's due
to life jacket restrictions
M5 J21, take A370 to seafront then head north up to
Knightstone

Visiting Steep Holm on a ferry from Weston-Super-Mare is also possible. There are great views of the Severn Bridges and as far down the coast as North Devon. There is a variety of wildlife including muntjac deer, cormorants and gulls. In Jul/Aug you may see grey seals fishing. Fortifications include Victorian cannons. Visitors need to be reasonably fit as there is no landing stage on the island and the paths are steep in places. The visitor centre has toilets and offers light refreshments and souvenirs. You should have around 6 hours on the island depending on the tides and there's a trail guide (£1.70) to help you navigate the sights. Take a torch to explore underground ammunition stores, binoculars, non-slip shoes and a picnic.

Oldbury Power Station Visitor Centre

Oldbury-on-Severn, South Gloucestershire, BS35
01454 893500
Mar-Oct: Daily 10am-4pm, pre booked winter visits
Admission free
A38 north, take B4061 through Thornbury, then left
to Oldbury-on-Severn and follow signs

Find out how a nuclear power station works with interactive displays and videos. Outdoor play area & nature trail.

Severn Bridges Visitor Centre

Shaft Rd, Off Green Lane, Severn Beach, BS35 4HW
01454 633511
www.onbridges.com
Easter-October: Sat/Sun & B/H's 11am-4pm, pre-booked visits in winter
£1.50 adults, 70p child
M5 J17 take B4055 through Pilning. Continue straight on. At mini-r'about follow Green Lane over M49. Right at lights into Shaft Rd

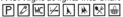

Educational exhibition showing history of the River Severn crossing and the construction of the two road bridges. There is a video which is quite technical for children but staff offer child-friendly information.

ROMAN BRITAIN

As well as the Roman Baths, see Bath, there are several other Roman sites near Bristol worth a visit. Always useful for bringing that school project to life!

Chedworth Roman Villa

Yanworth, Near Cheltenham, GL54 3LJ
01242 890256
www.nationaltrust.org.uk
Mar-Nov: Tue-Sun & B/H's 11am-4pm,
summer 10am-5pm
£3.90 adult, £2 child, £9.80 family (2+3), free U5's
M5 J11A take A417 east, A436 then right via
Withington, follow signs

Owned by the National Trust, this is one of the best examples of a Roman villa in England. The remains of this substantial dwelling indicate that it would have been inhabited by a very wealthy family. There are 2 well preserved bathhouses, hypocausts (demonstrating how the Roman invention of under-floor heating worked), beautiful mosaics, a latrine, and a museum housing objects from the villa. Entertaining audio guide for children, 6+yrs. If you can, coincide your visit with one of the Living History Days where you can join in with demonstrations of day to day Roman life. Children's activities during the holidays. Pushchairs can be used but there are quite a few steps to negotiate. There are good walks in Chedworth Woods which surround the villa and along the disused railway track.

Roman Legionary Museum Caerleon

High Street, Caerleon, Gwent, NP18 1AE
01633 423134
www.nmgw.ac.uk
Museum: Mon-Sat 10am-5pm, Sun 2pm-5pm
Fortress Baths: Mon-Sat 9.30am-5pm, Sun 11am-5pm, winter 1pm-5pm
Museum, Barracks and Amphitheatre: free
Fortress Baths: £2.50 adult, £2 child, £7 family (2+3)

M4 J24 follow signs to Caerleon and Museum

🖉 ⛨ 🔲 ♿ 🔳

Nearly 2000 years ago the Romans established a fortress at Caerleon. In the museum you can discover how the Roman soldiers lived, fought and worshipped. At weekends and during the holidays a barrack room can be visited where you can try on replica suits of armour and take part in the daily activities of a soldier. Also see the remains of the fortress baths, with video, sound and light displays. A short walk from the museum is Britain's best example of a Roman amphitheatre where gladiators battled to the death. Impressive re-enactments are held here every June (ring 01633 430041 for details).

Caerwent
10 miles from Caerleon on A48 or from Bristol M4 then M48 J2.

Having visited the museum at Caerleon you could stop off at the wonderfully preserved town of Caerwent where the remains of shops, a courtyard house, temple and forum can be seen. In the 4th century A.D. when the Romans were struggling to retain power, a high wall was built around the town, most of which still stands today.

WHEELS & WINGS

Many children go through a stage of being fascinated with transport, be it wheeled or winged. The places listed below all display the life sized article. If you fancy something smaller there's Bourton Model Railway, see Cotswolds and for the hands-on approach try Diggerland, see Fun Stuff.

Cotswold Motoring Museum and Toy Collection
The Old Mill, Bourton-on-the-Water, GL54 2BY
01451 821255
www.cotswold-motor-museum.com
Feb-Oct: Daily 10am-6pm
£2.95 adult, £1.95 child, £8.95 family, free U4's
Park in main village car park

🖉 ⛨ 🔲 ♿ 🎪 🎡 🔳

As well as a car collection dating back to the 1920's the museum has lots of other transport

memorabilia including over 800 enamel signs. As well as a big toy collection (including children's pedal cars and dinky toys), a workshop based on a 1920's village garage, and a blacksmith's, this is also where Brum the little car lives. Children's quizzes, puzzles and jigsaws.

Haynes Motor Museum
Sparkford, Nr Yeovil, Somerset, BA22 7LH
01963 440804
www.haynesmotormuseum.co.uk
Daily 9.30am-5.30pm, some seasonal variations
£6.50 adult, £3.50 child, £8.50-£19 family, free U5's
M5 J25 then A358 & A303 to Sparkford. Or A37 south to A303

🅿 🆅 🖉 ⛨ 🔒 🔲 CP 🔳 🔳 🔳 🔳
🔳 ♿ 🎡 🔳

If you've got car fanatics in your household, Britain's most extensive car collection on permanent display should keep them happy. Hundreds of cars ranging from the Chevrolet Corvette to the Sinclair C5. There is also a Hall of Motor Sport, motorbike display, a bus full of soft play equipment (open summer hols), an indoor children's activity centre and a themed outdoor play area.

STEAM - Museum of the Great Western Railway
Kemble Drive, Swindon, SN2 2TA
01793 466646
www.steam-museum.org.uk
Mon-Sat 10am-5.30pm, Sun 11am-5.30pm, earlier closing in winter
£5.95 adult, £3.80 child, £14.70 (2+2), free U5's
M4 J16, follow signs to 'Outlet Centre'

🅿 🖉 ⛨ 🔲 🔳 🔳 ♿

Here you can get an idea of what it was like to work on and use the GWR with lots of hands-on exhibits. Reconstructed platforms, a cab simulator, and family activities during the school holidays. Special appearances by Thomas the Tank Engine and engines 'in steam', help bring railway history to life.

The Helicopter Museum
The Heliport, Locking Moor Road, Weston-s-Mare
01934 635227
www.helicoptermuseum.co.uk
Wed-Sun & B/H's 10am-5.30pm, earlier closing in winter, open daily at Easter and in summer hols
£4.95 adult, £2.95 child, £13 family(2+2)
M5 J21. Situated on the A368/A371, follow signs

The world's largest dedicated helicopter museum housing the oldest, fastest and ugliest helicopters! Themed play area. Special events include 'Helicopter Experience Flights' (£29 adult, £24 child) and the annual 'Heliday' (usually the last weekend in July), a static helicopter display on Beach Lawns, the seafront. This features civil and military helicopters from all over the world and pleasure flights from the beach.

Fleet Air Arm Museum

RNAS Yeovilton, Ilchester, Somerset, BA22 8HT
01935 840565
www.fleetairarm.com
Daily 10am-5.30pm, winter 4.30pm
£8.50 adult, £5.75 child, £27 family (2+3), free U5's
Take the A37 south of Bristol (50mins)

Displaying the largest collection of Naval aircraft in Europe, this museum will appeal to children of 6+yrs along with aircraft enthusiastic toddlers. Follow the development of British aircraft from wooden bi-planes through to Concorde. You can sit in the cockpit of a jet fighter, or even experience life aboard an aircraft carrier, arriving on the flight deck via a simulated helicopter ride. Being next to the air base, there's a good chance of seeing Sea Harriers and helicopters going through their manoeuvres outside.

RNAS Yeovilton Airday

www.yeoviltonairday.co.uk
Entertainment on the ground as well as flying displays at this annual event. See website for details.

Royal International Air Tattoo

RAF Fairford, Gloucestershire, GL7 4NA
0870 758 1918
www.airtattoo.com
M4 J15, follow signs.

This weekend event takes place annually in mid July at RAF Fairford. It is the biggest display held in the UK. See website for details.

GOING UNDERGROUND

Going down into a mine or through caves can have a lasting impression on a child, entering a fantasy world in the semi-darkness.

Cheddar Caves & Gorge

Cheddar, Somerset, BS27 3QF
01934 742343
www.cheddarcaves.co.uk
Daily 10am-5pm, minor seasonal variations
£9.50 adult, £6.50 child, £26 family (2+2), free U5's
SW of Bristol on the A371, between A38 & A37

Impressive caves located in a spectacular gorge. The 2 main caves to explore are Gough's with its cathedral-like caverns and Cox's with its stunning formations and colours. Excellent new explorer audio guide of Gough's cave (suitable 5+yrs). Buggies can be taken into the caves, although they will have to be left in certain places and picked up later. Baby back-packs are fine, watch the head room. Also: The Cheddar Man Museum, home to the oldest complete skeleton in the UK; The Crystal Quest - discover dimly lit caves inhabited by wizards, goblins, fairy princesses and dragons; an open top bus tour of the Gorge during summer; Jacobs Ladder - a 274 step climb to the top of the gorge with fantastic views of the Mendips from the lookout tower. From here there is a 3 mile waymarked circular walk around the gorge. The caves also offer caving, climbing and abseiling - see Teen Guide chapter. Further down the gorge you can watch the famous cheese being made.

Wookey Hole

Wookey Hole, Wells, Somerset, BA5 1BB
01749 672243
www.wookey.co.uk
Daily 10am-5pm, winter variations
£8.80 adult, £5.50 child, free U4's
2 miles north west of Wells, follow brown signs

A guided tour (approx 40 mins) takes you through this impressive series of caves carved out by the River Axe. The route is not suitable for pushchairs; there is enough headroom for child back-packs. Other attractions include a museum, an interactive Victorian paper mill, a mirror maze and a collection of playable Edwardian penny arcade machines.

Big Pit National Mining Museum

Blaenafon, Torfaen, Nr. Newport, NP4 9XP
01495 790311
www.nmgw.ac.uk/bigpit
Mid Feb-Nov: daily 9.30am-5pm, underground tours from 10am-3.30pm
Admission free
M4 J25a follow brown signs, 80 mins Bristol

Blaenafon has recently been given World Heritage status. Walk around this coal mine and find out how men, women and children worked here for over 200 years. Children over 1 metre tall can go underground, and wear hard hats. New museum exhibitions in the original pithead baths and multi-media displays of modern mining will help to answer all their questions. Allow 4 hours for visit.

Hopewell Colliery Museum & Clearwell Caves

See Forest of Dean above

FUN STUFF

You'll find other similar ideas listed under the place/town in which they're located. These two were simply geographically isolated.

Boomerang

Bowerhill, Melksham, Wiltshire, SN12 6TJ
01225 702000
Mon-Thu 9am-6pm, Fri 9pm, Sat-Sun 7pm
Closed Aug B/H
Peak time 1½ hours: £3.50 child U11's, £2.45 U2's, free U1's
M4 J17, A350 to Melksham then follow signs for Bowerhill & Sports Centre

Huge area of softplay equipment for U11's or 1.5m offering unlimited playtime when not full. Separate room for U1's with activity centres, play mats, bottle warmers etc. Fri night disco for 5-11yrs and Club Boom for

11-15yrs on Wed nights. Also a selection of parties on offer and bouncy castle hire.

Diggerland

Verbeer Manor, Cullompton, Devon, EX15 2PE
08700 344437
www.diggerland.com
Feb-Nov: W/E's, B/H's and daily during school hols, 10am-5pm
Entrance £2.50 pp, free U2's. Buy 'credits' for riding/driving motorised diggers
M5 J27 take A38 east and follow signs for 3 miles

This adventure park revolves around the fascination children have with mechanical diggers. Children and adults can ride in, and drive different types of construction machinery including dumper trucks and diggers under strict supervision. Age limits apply. Other attractions include pedal power diggers, a digger sandpit, bouncy castle and computer digger games.

WALKS AND DAYS OUTSIDE

Thanks to Peter Stonham for his research and editing of this section.
When the weather is OK it's nice to get outside for a few hours and most children enjoy it even if the idea isn't initially met with boundless enthusiasm! You don't have to travel very far out of Bristol to find a variety of places to stretch your legs, whether it's a gentle potter with toddlers or a proper hike you're after. Below you'll find a few ideas, some requiring basic map reading skills, others just being nice places to wander around. Where possible we've tried to give an indication of age/pushchair suitability.

Other Walks

Bristol City Coucil have just produced a set of free laminated walks accessed by public transport, phone 0117 903 6701 for details. Roger Noyce has written a book 'Pub Strolls Around Bristol & Bath' which is popular with families, published by Countryside Books.

WALKS TO THE SW OF BRISTOL

Ashton Hill, Failand
OS Map 172 Bristol and Bath
Access: The car-park is on the B3129 at the southern tip of Failand village.

A beautiful walk through woodland areas, don't miss it in the autumn. There are several walks of up to a couple of miles, through mature woodland. The terrain is rough and can get muddy, unsuitable for pushchairs.

Clevedon Poet's Walk
Access: Pay & Display at Salt House Fields or street parking

A wonderful, easy-going, short walk (about 1½ miles) around the headland with good views across the Severn. Suitable for pushchairs (two flights of steps) with a nice clean public toilet.

Start at the Salt House Fields car park, walk along the front towards the headland, up the first flight of steps, and along the path. Continue along the undulating, fenced tarmac path on the top of the cliff to St Andrews Church. On the right hand side of the church you should see a sign for the walk, follow the path back towards your starting point.

Brockley Wood, Cleeve
OS Map 172 Bristol and Bath.
Access: Take A370 towards Congresbury, turning left in Cleeve immediately before the Lord Nelson pub, down Cleeve Hill Road. Continue for approximately 600 yards and turn left into Goblin Coombe car park.

Many pretty walks of up to 4 miles through the woods, beautiful in autumn. No toilets but the Lord Nelson pub on the A370 is close by.

Blagdon Lake
Blagdon Visitor Centre, Blagdon Lake
Visitor Centre, May-Aug: Sun 2pm-5pm

Peaceful and pretty woodland walk along the banks of the lake - but beware fishermen casting. Good walking for toddlers. Park on bridge abutting lake.

Burrington Coombe, near Churchill
OS Map 172 Bristol and Bath.

Access: From A 368 (Churchill to Blagdon) take the B3134. Drive up the valley for nearly 2 miles to the plateau and there is a car park on the left

A great starting point on the Mendips for young children. Fantastic views, wonderful heathland vegetation (wild grassy meadows, heather, bracken, gorse, silver birch etc.) and wildlife. Suitable for a quiet picnic, gentle stroll or a few miles with the back-pack. For picnics and short walks take the path at the back of the car park (north, towards Bristol), up 10 yards of rocky path and onto grassy meadow. For longer walks, walk up the road 30 yards and take the track on the right (going south) onto Beacon Batch and head right towards the peak. Continue west through Black Down, into Rowberrow Warren, Dolebury Warren to the Ancient Hill Fort above Churchill then back along the ridge in the direction of the car park. This is about a 7 mile circuit but can be shortened and there are other access points from Churchill and Shipham areas.

Chew Valley Lake
Chew Valley Lake Information Centre, Chew Stoke
01275 333345
www.bristolwater.co.uk
Daily 10.30am-5.30pm, 4.30pm winter
Parking £1

P V [icons] WC [icons] CP [icons]

Beautiful lake with wonderful views and the chance to see birds, insects and animals. Ideal for toddlers. Park at information centre where there are walk details.

Glastonbury Tor
Tor is open 365 days/year.
Access: 15 minute walk from village to bottom of Tor. Easter-Sep a tour bus costing approx £1 runs every half hour from the car park by the Abbey and you can just hop off at the Tor

This steep hill is a striking feature of the local landscape offering stunning views over Somerset, Dorset and Wiltshire. Renovated in 2003, the 15th century tower on top of the Tor is all that remains of a mediaeval church. Up there you get a sense of why this place is a focus for legend and superstition. The Tor is 158m high and a steep climb, but well worth the effort. Unsuitable for pushchairs but determined toddlers will make it to the top!

WALKS TO THE SE OF BRISTOL

Willsbridge Mill
Avon Wildlife Trust, Willsbridge Hill, BS30 6EX
0117 932 6885
www.avonwildlifetrust.org.uk
Nature Reserve open all year, mill seasonal
Admission free
A431 Bristol to Bath road, turn into Long Beach
Road. Car park on left.

This converted mill housing hands-on wildlife
& conservation displays is currently only open
when schools are visiting, but there is plenty
to do outside. The Valley Nature Reserve
which includes a Heritage Sculpture Trail,
a Wild Waste Garden and plenty of lovely
sculptural seating areas for picnics is open all
year. Pond-dipping equipment available for
hire. All paths pushchair friendly.

Dundas Aqueduct to Avoncliff
Access: Take A36 from Bath to Monkton Combe, turn
left on B3108 and park at Canal Visitor Centre.
This walk starts at Brass Knocker Basin, see
Bradford-on-Avon. It passes through pretty
cuttings and embankments. Take towpath
and follow the signs to Avoncliff. Lots of wild
flowers, ducks and cyclists. Fordside Tea
Gardens is about ¾ mile from the start of
the walk, open daily. The walk to Avoncliff
Aqueduct is about 4 miles. There are many
other walks that are possible along the Kennet
and Avon canal and it's easy for family cycling
(novice cyclists watch the edge). In the other
direction it is about 4 miles to Bathampton
where The George is a child-friendly pub for
lunch.

Bradford-on-Avon to Avoncliff
Access: Bradford-upon-Avon station car park
A canal side walk between two villages.
Take the path at the end of Bradford-on-
Avon station car park that leads into Barton
Country Park. Follow the river until it joins
the towpath. Walk along this for a mile or so
past narrow boats, until you come to Avoncliff.
Here you will find The Madhatter café, see
Eating Out and The Cross Guns pub (lots
of steps but a nice garden, often busy over
lunch).

Brokerswood Country Park
Brokerswood, Nr. Westbury, Wiltshire, BA13 4EH
01373 822 238
www.brokerswood.co.uk
Daily from 10am, closing times seasonal
£3 adult, £1.50 child, free U5's, train 75p
A36 12 miles south Bath, follow brown tourist signs

Attractive woodland country park, with a
lake (fishing possible) and miles of paths to
explore, many pushchair accessible. Narrow
gauge railway operates Easter-Oct, w/e and
school holidays (Santa Special in Dec). There
are 2 outdoor adventure playgrounds for
2+yrs and an undercover play area for U7's.
Caravan/camping available in park.

WALKS TO THE NE OF BRISTOL

Splatts Wood, Cotswolds.
OS Map 172 Bristol & Bath.
Access: 2 miles North of Hawkesbury Upton. Parking
on verge between Hawkesbury Upton and Hillesley
at 772880. Alternatively, park in Hawkesbury Upton
and adjust the route accordingly
A gentle 2-3 mile walk through peaceful,
lush meadows beneath wooded ridges and
woodland, including a stretch of the Cotswold
Way. Suitable for babies in backpacks and
children.
Take the right hand of the two tracks going
north, which bears right as it goes into the
woods. Follow it round to north east, into
the meadows below Splatts Wood. Continue
for 1.5km to the lane at the bottom and turn
right. Turn right after 100m up the track on
the right and continue back to the car through
woods and fields. Alternatively, continue
South East along the lane, fork right and
take the footpath on the right 300m after the
fork. Walk up the valley taking a choice of
footpaths towards Hawkesbury Upton. At the
lane either turn right 1.5km back to the car,
past the monument or wander through the
village to the pub on the crossroads then back
to the car.

The National Arboretum Westonbirt

Nr Tetbury, Gloucestershire, GL8 8QS
01666 880220
www.forestry.gov.uk/england
Daily 10am-5pm (or dusk if earlier)
£7.50 adult (£6 in winter), £1 child, free U5's
Annual family: £42
M4 J18, take A46 towards Tetbury, follow signs

P ⊘ WC ⛺ ⛏ ♿ ♨ ✗ ⛺ ⊞ ⊞ ♿

The Arboretum consists of miles of beautiful, well-marked tree-lined paths, most of them suitable for pushchairs. The Old Arboretum is dog free. The area is especially beautiful in the autumn and hence busier. Ring for details of seasonal events such as Christmas lights. Shop with information & plants for sale.

Lasborough Park, Cotswolds.

OS Map 162 Gloucester & Forest of Dean
Access: 5 miles east of Wotton-under-Edge, parking on wide grass verge by Chapel in Newington Bagpath at 815948

A 4 mile circular walk through delightful Cotswold valleys. A walk for all seasons, enjoy it during crisp frost in winter, lambing in spring, warm afternoons in summer or grouse, blackberries and colourful leaves in autumn. Stout footwear required, boots if recent rain. Not suitable for buggies or pre-school children. Ideal if babies in back-packs and for school age children.

Behind the chapel pick up footpath west to Bagpath. At the lane turn left going south for 300m and take footpath on right after last building. Cross the fields and down into the woods, to the stream at the bottom. Turn left (south) and follow the stream for 1km across several fields. Cross to the west bank when convenient as you approach the derelict stone bridge in the trees. Follow the track as it swings right then take a left along the track alongside the woods below Ozleworth Park. Continue into the woods then after 200m take the track on the left, going due east along the stream. After 1km take the path into the left valley going north east. There are fishing lakes in this area so keep an eye on young children. After the large lake take the gate into Lasborough Park, walking below the house and continuing through the park to the gate at the top corner, and the path rises towards the chapel where you started.

Brackenbury Ditches, Cotswolds.

OS Map 162 Gloucester & Forest of Dean
Access: Parking on roadside 1 mile north of Wotton-under-Edge at 757943 or at 754941

A fairly level walk of 2-4 miles through mixed woodland, some mature beech areas, plus some great views. Suitable for all-terrain buggies and children, but toddlers might struggle. Trainers OK as long as no recent rain. Mind you don't lose your bearings in the woods. Take the track going north west, or the footpath across the fields depending on where you parked. Take your pick of the tracks through the woods, but aim for the fort and Nibley Knoll in a north westerly direction for the better woodland and views.

EATING OUT

It is good to know where you can go to eat out with children, receive a warm welcome and know the food and facilities are suitable for youngsters.

Places listed below have been put into geographical areas in relation to Bristol, so that you can link them in to where you might be spending the day; either on a walk or visiting an attraction.

NORTH OF BRISTOL

Bowl Inn

Church Road, Lower Almondsbury, BS32 4DT
01454 612757
www.theoldbowlinn.co.uk
From £3.95

P V WC ⛺ CP ♀ ♿ ♿ ⊞

Traditional village pub with à la carte restaurant and bar menu. Tables outside.

The Golden Heart

Down Rd, Winterbourne Down, BS36 1AU
01454 773152
From £3.50

P V ⊘ WC ⊞ ⛺ CP ♨ ♀ ♿ ♿ ▯

A friendly family pub with good quality food.

The Mason's Arms
94 Gloucester Rd, Rudgeway, BS35 3QJ
01454 412370
From £6.25 adult, £2.40 child
On the A38

⬚ P ⬚ V ⬚ ✎ ⬚ WC ⬚ 🔒 ⬚ 🪑 ⬚ CP ⬚ 🕐 ⬚ 🍽 ⬚ 👤 ⬚ 👣 ⬚ ♿

A popular no smoking family orientated pub
and restaurant where children are definitely
welcome.

The Star Inn
Stone Edge Batch, Clevedon Rd, Tickenham, BS21
01275 858836
From £7.95 adult main meal, £3.95 child

⬚ P ⬚ V ⬚ ✎ ⬚ WC ⬚ 🔒 ⬚ 🪑 ⬚ CP ⬚ 🕐 ⬚ 🍽 ⬚ 👤 ⬚ 👣 ⬚ ⬚ ♿

Large pub under new ownership, serving
traditional food with an activity room and a
large garden. Theme night held once a month
in aid of local children's hospice.

The Swan
Tockington Green, Tockington, BS32 4NJ
01454 614800
From £3 adult, £2.45 child

⬚ P ⬚ V ⬚ ✎ ⬚ WC ⬚ 🔒 ⬚ 🪑 ⬚ CP ⬚ 🍽 ⬚ 👤 ⬚ 👣 ⬚ ♿

Atmospheric village pub, with child-friendly
area and large garden.

The White Hart
Littleton-on-Severn, Nr Thornbury, BS35 1NR
01454 412275
From £7 adult, £3.95 child

⬚ P ⬚ WC ⬚ 🔒 ⬚ 🪑 ⬚ CP ⬚ 🍽 ⬚ 👤 ⬚ 👣

A lovely old country pub with good beer and
food. Large attractive family room & garden.

NORTH EAST OF BRISTOL

Lamb Inn
Wotton Road, Iron Acton, BS37 9UZ
01454 228265
Mon-Sat 12pm-11pm
From £3.95 adult, £2.95 child

⬚ P ⬚ V ⬚ ✎ ⬚ WC ⬚ 🔒 ⬚ CP ⬚ 🍽 ⬚ 👤 ⬚ ⬚

Quiet, cosy historic village pub with small
family dining area. Attractive shaded grassy
garden and covered patio. Large function
room available for hire.

Snuff Mill Harvester
207 Frenchay Park Rd, Frenchay, BS16 1LF
0117 956 6560
Mon-Sat 12pm-10pm
From £8.45 adult, £3.99 child. 1/3 off before 6.30pm

⬚ P ⬚ V ⬚ ✎ ⬚ WC ⬚ 🔒 ⬚ 🪑 ⬚ CP ⬚ 🕐 ⬚ 👤 ⬚ 👣 ⬚ ♿

Imaginative farm-like interior including a
central indoor pond stocked with fish.

The Cottage Tea Rooms
16B Horse St, Chipping Sodbury, BS17
01454 321121
Mon-Sat 9.30am-5pm

⬚ P ⬚ V ⬚ WC ⬚ 🔒 ⬚ 🪑 ⬚ CP ⬚ 👤 ⬚ 👣

A comfortable coffee shop with inexpensive
meals and smaller children's portions.

The Dog Inn
Badminton Rd, Chipping Sodbury, BS37 6LZ
01454 312006
From £4.95 adult, £2.95 child

⬚ P ⬚ V ⬚ ✎ ⬚ WC ⬚ 🔒 ⬚ CP ⬚ 🍽 ⬚ 👤 ⬚ 👣 ⬚ ⬚ ♿

A busy pub with a large garden. They have an
adventurous selection including a fun menu of
good food for children.

The Golden Lion
Beesmoor Rd, Frampton Cotterell, BS36 2JN
01454 773348
From £3.50 adult, £2 child

⬚ P ⬚ V ⬚ WC ⬚ 🔒 ⬚ 🪑 ⬚ CP ⬚ 🚼 ⬚ ♿

Traditional spacious family pub offering an
extensive menu.

EAST OF BRISTOL

Codrington Arms
Wapley Rd, Codrington, BS17 6RY
01454 313145
From £6.50

⬚ P ⬚ V ⬚ WC ⬚ 🔒 ⬚ 🪑 ⬚ CP ⬚ 🍽 ⬚ 👤 ⬚ 👣

A comfortable, unspoilt family country pub
with a large attractive garden. Friendly staff
and an extensive menu. Food outside until
8pm. Book for indoor tables at the weekends.

The Compass Inn
Nr Badminton, Tormarton, GL9 1JB
01454 218242
www.compass-inn.co.uk
Mon-Sat 7am-11pm, Sun 8am-10.30pm
From £4 adult, £3.50 child

A family run pub with a large, pleasant family conservatory and à la carte restaurant. Pub is on a busy road. Half portions available.

SOUTH EAST OF BRISTOL

Compton Inn
Court Hill, Compton Dando, BS39 4JZ
01761 490321
Open all day at weekends
From £4

A small, unspoilt traditional pub with a large grassy garden. Suited to older children.

Dundry Inn
Church Rd, Dundry, BS41 8LH
0117 964 1722
Mon-Thu 12pm-3pm, Fri-Sun all day
From £2.50 child

Quiet local pub with garden. Friendly staff (paper and crayons on request) and an excellent menu. Open all day in the summer.

The Crown
500 Bath Rd, Saltford, BS31 3HJ
01225 872117
From £4.25 adult

Large garden. Families particularly welcome.

The Riverside Inn
The Shallows, Saltford, BS31 3EZ
01225 873862
Open for food all day throughout summer.
From £4 child

Adjacent to Saltford river and lock. The upstairs pub and restaurant is smart and there

is a conservatory for families and garden overlooking the weir. Very comfortable with an extensive menu.

SOUTH OF BRISTOL

Blue Note Café
2-4 High St, Glastonbury, BA6 9DU
01458 832907
Mon-Sun 9.30am-5pm

An extremely busy, quick, casual and alternative licensed café serving wholesome vegetarian dishes. Parking 5 mins away.

Chew Valley Lake Tea Shop
Chew Valley Lake Picnic Area, Chew Stoke, BS40 8TF
01275 333345
www.bristolwater.co.uk
Daily 10.30am-4.30pm
From £2

Landscaped picnic area bordering the Chew Valley Lake. Information and gift shop.

Cloister Restaurant
West Cloister, Wells Cathedral, BA5 2PA
01749 676543
Mon-Sat 10am-5pm, Sun 12.30pm-5pm
From £2.50

A relaxed licensed restaurant in beautiful surroundings with imaginative range of homemade dishes/cakes. Parking 10 mins away.

The Blue Bowl
Bristol Rd, West Harptree, BS40 6HJ
01761 221269
Food served: Mon-Sat 12pm-2pm & 6.30pm-9.30pm, Sun 12pm-9pm
From £4 adult, £3 child

Comfortable country pub that accommodates children.

The Crown at Wells and Antons Bistro

Market Place, Wells, BA5 2RP
01749 673457
www.crownatwells.co.uk
Daily 12pm-2.30pm and 6pm-9.30pm
From £7.95 adult, £3.95 child

[symbols]

A medieval inn serving good food and fine wine. Has an outdoor café serving food all day (summer only). Parking 10 mins away.

The Good Earth Restaurant

4 Priory Rd, Wells, BA5 1SY
01749 678600
Mon-Sat 9am-5pm
From £4.25 adult

[symbols]

Simple, quality whole-food restaurant and gift shop, with a wide range of vegetarian and vegan dishes. No children's menu, but happy to adapt to your requirements.

The Hunters' Rest Inn

King Lane, Clutton Hill, BS39 5QL
01761 452303
www.huntersrest.co.uk
From £2.25 child and £6 adult
Take the A37 through Pensforde village, left at r'about to Bath and after 150m, turn right into country lane, up hill 1.5 miles

[symbols]

A popular pub with family room, large garden with a miniature passenger railway. Remote but worth the effort.

Warwick Arms

Upper Bristol Rd, Clutton, BS39 5TA
01761 452256
All day, every day
From £6.70

[symbols]

Busy pub offering good playground and garden area.

SOUTH WEST OF BRISTOL

Bridge Inn

North End Rd, Yatton, BS49 4AU
01934 839100
www.inlodge.com
From £2.95 adult, £1.95 child

[symbols]

A traditional family inn that has been extended and modernised to cater for family needs. A ball pit and an outdoor playground. A wide selection of food.

Bucket and Spade Pub

Somerset Avenue, West Wick Island, Weston-s-Mare
01934 521235
Every Day 11am-11pm
From £4.95 adult, £2.25 child

[symbols]

Attached to Wacky Warehouse (soft play). See Weston-super-Mare, above.

Full Quart

Hewish, Yatton, BS24 6RT
01934 833077
Food served: 12pm-3pm & 6pm-9.30pm every day.
From £5.45 adults, £3.50 child
About 3 miles outside WsM on A370

[symbols]

Pub with a family room, dining room and bar area. Outside there is a large garden with seating and excellent play area (assault course).

Hobbs Boat

Bridgwater Road, Lympsham, Weston-s-Mare, BS24
01934 812782
Mon-Sat 12pm-11pm, Sun 12pm-10.30pm
From £4.25 adult, £2.99 child

[symbols]

Part of the Brewers Fayre chain of pubs. It has a small play area and children's menu.

Langford Inn

Lower Langford, Nr Churchill, BS40 5BL
01934 863059
Every day 12pm-11pm
From £3.95 adult, £2.75 child

[symbols]

An old restored coaching inn with a family room, patio area, walled garden and restaurant. Varied children's menu or small portions from adults' menu. A room available for baby changing on request. Situated off the A38.

Ring O'Bells
Main St, Compton Martin, BS40 6JE
01761 221284
Food served: 11.30am-2.30pm & 6.30pm-9.30pm
From £3.25 adult, £1.85 child
[P] [✎] [WC] [✂] [☂] [♀] [⚁] [↑] [✗] [◢] [CP]

A cosy country pub with a comfortable no smoking family room. Excellent facilities. Adjacent to a large orchard garden.

The Airport Tavern
Bridgewater Rd, Lulsgate, BS40 9XA
01275 472217
Mon-Sat 12pm-3pm, Sun 12pm-6pm
From £4.95 adult, £3.50 child
Next to airport
[P] [V] [WC] [✂] [☂] [CP] [♀] [↑] [✗] [◢] [🖽] [🛏]

A pleasant family orientated pub. Nice patio and garden with play equipment and the added attraction of low flying aircraft.

The Bell Inn
2 Kent Rd, Congresbury, BS49 5BE
01934 833110
Mon-Fri 12pm-3pm, Fri-Sun All Day
From £2.95 child
[P] [V] [WC] [✂] [☂] [CP] [⚁] [♀] [↑] [✗] [◢] [♿]

Comfortable pub.

The Crown
Skinners Lane, The Batch, BS25 5PP
01225 314864
From £2.20, snack, £3.95 main course

Small old country pub. With homemade food. Children allowed only in side rooms. Lovely garden. Adult menu can be adapted for kids.

The Goat House Restaurant
Bristol Road, Brent Knoll, Burnham-on-Sea, TA9 4HJ
01278 760995
Tues-Sun 12pm-2.30pm and Wed-Sat 7pm-9pm
From £5
[P] [✎] [WC] [✂] [☂] [CP]

Lunches and evening meals available, prepared using fresh local produce, fully licensed.

The Lock Inn Café
48 Frome Road, Bradford-on-Avon, BA15 1LE
01225 868068
www.thelockinn.co.uk
Sun-Wed: 8.45am-6pm, 9.30pm school hols,
Thu-Sat: 8.45am-9.30pm
[V] [WC] [☂] [CP] [♀] [↑] [✗] [✗] [🖽] [🛏]

A pretty canal-side spot for a meal or snack. Try the famous 'Boatman's Breakfast'. Several seating areas in and out. Licensed.

The Lord Nelson
58 Main Rd, Cleeve, BS49 4NR
01934 832170
From £2.49
[P] [V] [✎] [WC] [✂] [☂] [CP] [⚁] [♀] [↑] [✗] [◢] [🄰]

Family pub. Play areas inside and out.

The Terrace Café
Cadbury Garden Centre, Smallway, BS49 5AA
01934 875767
Mon-Sat 9.30am-5.30pm, Sun 10am-4.30pm
From £4.75 adult, £2.25 child
[P] [V] [✎] [WC] [✂] [☂] [CP] [↑] [✗]

Bright and airy licensed restaurant at this popular garden centre.

WEST OF BRISTOL

Rudgeleigh Inn
Martcombe Rd, Easton in Gordano, BS20 0QD
01275 372363
Mon-Sat 12pm-11pm, Sun 12pm-10.30pm
From £5 adult
[P] [V] [WC] [✂] [☂] [CP] [⚁] [♀] [↑] [✗] [◢] [🄰] [🛏]

Friendly pub, older children are particularly well catered for, good outdoor play area.

The Little Harp Inn
Elton Rd, Clevedon, BS21
01275 343739
From £5.95
[P] [V] [WC] [✂] [☂] [CP] [♀] [↑] [✗]

Restaurant style pub on the seafront by the pier with a family section and beer garden.

The Moon and Sixpence
15 The Beach, Clevedon, BS21 7QU
01275 872443
Open all day
From £3.50

Ⓟ Ⓥ ⓌⒸ ✍ ⛫ CP 🏃 🖼

Pleasant pub, overlooking the pier and car park! A family area provides restaurant meals.

The Old Farm House
Chelvey Rise, Trendlewood Way, Nailsea, BS48 2PF
01275 851889
Mon-Fri 11.30am-3pm, Sat-Sun 12pm-11pm
From £5 adult

Ⓟ Ⓥ ✎ ⓌⒸ ✍ ⛫ CP 🍷 🏃 🖼 🛏 ♿

Farm buildings have been converted into a traditional pub. Fresh produce.

The Old Inn
Walton Rd, Clevedon, BS21
01275 790052
Open daily
From £3.25

Ⓟ Ⓥ ⓌⒸ ✍ ⛫ CP 🍷 🏃 🖼 🛏

A very busy traditional pub offering a simple menu. It has a big fenced garden full of play equipment.

WEST OF BRISTOL

Gordano Gate
Whyndham Way, Portishead, BS20 7GA
01275 846526
www.whitbread.co.uk
Mon-Sat 11.30am-10pm, Sun 12pm-10pm
From £6 adult, £3 child

Ⓟ Ⓥ ✎ ⓌⒸ ✍ ⛫ CP ⏱ 🍷 🏃 🖼 🖾 ♿

A Whitbread "Brewsters" pub, completely family orientated. See Activities 0-12 years.

Marine Lake Café
Lake Grounds, Portishead, BS20
01275 842248

ⓌⒸ 🏃 🖼

A parents' refuge while the children play. Basic but clean. Snacks and fast food served. Open during the summer months, staff dependent.

The Anchor
Ham Green, Pill, BS20 0HB
01275 372253
Mon-Sat 11am-11.30pm, Sun 11am-11pm
From £4.25 adult, £2.25 child

Ⓟ Ⓥ ⓌⒸ ✍ ⛫ CP 🍷 🏃 🖼 🖾 🚌 Ⓟp

A village pub with a separate family room. There is a garden and play area. Snacks available as well as main meals.

ACTIVITIES 0-12 YEARS

Astrid Pestell

CHAPTER 4

INTRODUCTION

Hobbies and interests for youngters seem more accessible than ever and need not break the family purse strings.

There really is something for everyone in this chapter. It covers physical and artistic activities for the very young, along with a wide variety of sports, hobbies and clubs for primary-aged children. Understandably there has been some overlap with the Teen Guide, so we have cross referenced where necessary. Some of the listings require no booking, well worth remembering on a wet day when cabin fever has set in! However, it is still advisable to call beforehand to check on opening times. Don't forget to check out our popular Parties subchapter. It has loads of ideas to help you and your family celebrate life's milestones.

SPORTS DIRECTORY

There are some great sporting facilities in and around Bristol, see the central Reference section. All of them have excellent websites.

BOWLING

Bowlplex
Unit 4, Aspect Leisure Park, Longwell Green
0117 961 0000, www.bowlplexuk.com
Open daily
Mon-Fri £2.70 before 6pm, Sat-Sun £3.70, varying rates in the evenings, free U4's before 7pm

Hollywood Bowl
Avonmeads Retail Park, St Philips Marsh, BS2 0SP, 0117 977 1777, www.hollywoodbowl.co.uk
Open daily
£1.50 child after school, Sat-Sun 10am-12pm
Children go free with paying adult, call for other prices

'Munchbox Meal offers'. U4's bowl free with a paying adult anytime.

Megabowl
Brunel Way, Ashton Gate, Bristol, BS3 2YX
0117 953 8538, www.megabowl.co.uk
£9.99 Mon-Fri 12pm-6pm, Sat-Sun 10am-12pm family hr (6 people, one must be under 16yrs)
£1.50 Mon-Fri 12pm-6pm Time Out Club
Prices listed do not include school or B/H's

Time Out Club includes bowling or adventure golf. Available for youth clubs, community groups, disabled groups and others, call for details.

CRICKET

Cricket may not be a promoted activity at your child's school but there is a thriving league in and around Bristol.

Bristol Youth Cricket League
Sally Donaldson: 0117 330 6502
bycl@ukonline.co.uk

There are around 40 youth cricket teams in and around Bristol catering from U11's through to U17's. Many teams have facilities for indoor nets (Feb-Apr), the season starts in April through to July. Whether you live in Bristol or outside call to find your nearest team.

The Bristol YMCA CC
Golden Hill, Henleaze
Gerry Mulholland: 0117 942 2957
www.ymcacricket.pwp.blueyonder.co.uk
This is one of Bristol's oldest surving cricket clubs founded in 1878. It has an excellent youth set up which attracts junior cricketers from across the district. During the winter it provides winter indoor net sessions and competes in the Bristol Indoor Cricket League. It hosts numerous social events, with a cricket theme, for all the family.

FOOTBALL

Many leisure centres run indoor football training sessions from primary age upwards. See the leisure centres tables (central reference section). There are also many football teams coached by parents at your child's school. If you are looking for more and there is lots more, check out our Teen Guide chapter.

Avon Sports Academy - Soccer Camps
0117 904 6686, www.avonsportsacademy.co.uk
Sessions offer a balance between coaching skills and small-sided team games, for children 5-11yrs. Venues: Stoke Lodge Playing Fields and Combe Dingle Sports Complex in Stoke Bishop.

Bristol Rovers Girls Foootball (Community Dept)
Debbie Arrowsmith: 0117 924 4040
Training sessions open to all girls 8-12yrs at The Grange School in Warmley and Golden Hill Training Centre in Horfield.

Gloucestershire Football Association

Youth Committee has 12 affiliated leagues some of which cater for U9's - U12's. For contact details see Teen Guide chapter.

GYMNASTICS

Bristol Hawks Gymnastic Club

Gymnastics World, Roman Rd, Lower Easton, BS5
0117 973 7481/935 5363

Parent & Toddler (18mths-3yrs)
Tue/Wed/Thu am, £3.20 per session, £16.20/6 wks

Pre-School Gym Class (2-5yrs)
Tue/Wed/Thu am, prices as above

Young Beginners (4-6yrs)
Wed pm, £3.20, £16.20 for 6 weeks

Play Gym (U5's) Sat am
£2.00 per session

Open Gym (4-6yrs) Sat am
£2.80 per session

Sessions for primary aged children after school & Saturdays phone for details. Fun, challenging, stimulating and safe. All coaches qualified. BGA grades followed. Drinks & snacks available. Buggies left in changing rooms. Holiday schemes.

Bristol School of Gymnastics

Old Bishopston Methodist Church, 245 Gloucester Rd
0117 942 9620

General gymnastics with apparatus, taught by qualified coaches.

Under 3's
£24/8wks

Play based, including songs finishing with juice/biscuit, parent stays.

Over 3's
£26.40/8 weeks, parents encouraged to leave

Open Sessions 4-10yrs
Sat am, £3 per session

Other sessions available for pre-school, U7's and 7+yrs.

Kingswood Gymnastic & Trampoline Centre

The Wesley Studios, Kingswood Foundation Estate, Britannia Road, BS15 8DB
0117 947 6449
Tue/Wed 18+mths
Mon-Fri after school, 4-11yrs

A social, physical and educational activity programme is offered leading up to the junior gymnastics programme. Fun sessions by qualified & experienced staff.

BAGA award scheme. Offering a variety of other activities including: bar, beam, rythmic gymnastics, trampolining, team games, group activities, parachute and ball games. Holiday fun sessions. Also see Parties section, below.

HOCKEY

Redlands Ladies Hockey Club
Sun 10am-12pm
£30 per season

U11's mixed hockey team playing in a Bath league. See Teen Guide chapter.

HORSE RIDING

Kingsweston Stables

Lime Kiln Cottage, Kingsweston Road, Lawrence Weston, Bristol, BS11 0UX
0117 982 8929
Wed-Sun
£10 for ½hr non-riders , £13/hr riders

Riding lessons and hacking for over 3's. Pre-booking required. Also see Little Dean Riding Centre.

ICE SKATING & SKIING

Bristol Ice Rink

Frogmore Street, BS1 5NA
0117 929 2148, www.nikegroup.co.uk
Session times vary, call for details
From £5 including skate hire

General, family and disco sessions available for all abilities. Boots from child size 5.

Long sleeves, trousers and gloves are recommended. Tuition available for all ages and abilities and courses run to the NISA fun skate program. Junior Ice Hockey (U19's) on Tuesdays, booking is advisable. Sledges available for disabled. Disabled access to building is difficult but staff are happy to assist.

Also see Parties section, below and Teen Guide chapter.

Gloucester Ski & Snowboard Centre

Robinswood Hill, Matson Lane, Gloucester, GL4 6EA
08702 400375, www.gloucesterski.com
Daily 10am-10pm, except Thu/Sat/Sun 6pm
£11/hr child, £15/2hrs, £18 all day in winter. From £6/hr in summer

P WC ↟ ✗ ♿

Crazy Kids Club (must be competent on skis). Private & group lessons available from 6yrs, snowboarding from 12yrs. Adapted equipment available for disabled customers.

High Action Avon Ski Centre

Lyncombe Drive, Churchill, N Somerset, BS25 5PQ
01934 852335, www.highaction.co.uk
9.30am-10pm, costs vary according to activity (from £4.50 for toboganning)

P V ✐ WC ⛷ ♞ CP △ ▣ ✗ ♨ ⊢ ▦

Floodlit dry ski slope open all year. Any age permitted providing they can snowplough, stop, turn & use button drag lift, booking not necessary. Lessons available for all abilities from 6yrs. Snow Blading for skiers 6+yrs. Tobogganing for 5-13yrs under parental supervision and snowboarding for 14+yrs. Activity days run by a qualified instructor, teaching skiing, horse riding, archery and rifle shooting. Booking essential for all activities except recreational ski-ing. Also see Parties section, below.

KARTING

Castle Combe Kart Track

Castle Combe Circuit, Wiltshire, SN14 7EQ
01249 783010
Junior kart racing for 10-15yrs (with a min. height of 4'8") on 1st & 3rd Sunday of every month. Pre-booking essential. 'Phone for possible summer school sessions.

West Country Karting

The Lake, Trench Lane, Winterbourne, BS36 1RJ
01454 202 666, www.westcountrykarting.com

P WC ✗

350 metre outdoor karting circuit. Must be at least 4'10" (min age 10yrs).

MARTIAL ARTS

ShotoRyu Karate

Nick Moller: 0117 969 5697,
www.shotoryukarate.co.uk
Sesssions are held throughout the week at Horfield, Easton & Robin Cousins Sports Centres, see Leisure Tables; also at Greenway Centre and Kingswood Community Centre, ring for details.

Taekwon-Do

Ray Gayle: 07968 1903060
www.bristolmartialarts.com
Taekwon-Do is the Korean martial art of punching and kicking, offering improvements in strength, endurance, flexibility, stamina, self-control, confidence and relaxation. Sessions held at Newman Hall, Grange Court Rd, Henleaze; Claremont School, Henleaze and Christ Church Primary School, Clifton for Little Pumas (4-6yrs).

OUTDOOR PURSUITS

There are many outdoor pursuits that children of primary age may like to try. Mountain Biking, canoeing, climbing etc. See Teen Guide chapter.

RUGBY

There is an active rugby scene in the region. Also see Teen Guide chapter for details.

Clifton Rugby Club

Cribbs Causeway
0117 950 0445, www.cliftonrugby.com
Sun 10am-12pm
£40 per season, £30 2nd child

Mini and junior rugby for all age groups from U7's upwards. Touch rugby for those U8yrs.

Saracens Rugby Club

Sun 10.30am
Training for U8's and U10's. Each group has a coach dedicated to them.

Shoguns - Bristol Rugby Club's Community Programme

Nicola Goodrick-Turner: 0117 311 1474
www.bristolrugby.co.uk
Coaching in primary schools across the region. Half term rugby camps available for 7-12yrs.

SOFT PLAY & PRE-SCHOOL GYM

Gordano Gate

Whyndham Way, Portishead, BS20 7GA
01275 846 526, www.whitbread.co.uk
Mon-Sat 11.30am-10pm, Sun 12pm-10pm
From £6 adult, £3 child

A Whitbread Brewsters pub, completely family orientated. "Fun Factory" supervised soft play for older children with face painting, juggling, TV etc. Ball Swamp soft play for U3's inside, and play equipment outside. Child tagging and CCTV for parental peace of mind.

Parent and Toddler sessions

Mon/Wed & Fri 10am-12pm

Castaways Children's Indoor Playland

Waters Road, Kingswood, Bristol, BS15 8BE
0117 961 5115
Tue-Sat 9am-6.30pm
General play: free 0-6mths, £1.25 7-17mths, £2.60 18+mths

Two tiers of fun for U11's which includes small inflatable bouncy climbing equipment, 2 ball pools, slides, softplay area, separate toddler/baby area based on under water theme. See Parties section, below.

Treasure Tots (preschool)

Tue/Thu 10am-12pm term time, £3.20
Includes activities, toys, drink, fruit & biscuits. Very popular with limited spaces.

Elmgrove Centre Rumpus Room

Redland Road, Cotham, Bristol, BS6 6AG
0117 924 3377, www.elmgrovecentre.org.uk
Mon-Fri 9.30am-1.30pm, 50p per child
Drop-in Soft Play U7's, occasionally pre-booked for a party.

Fromeside Gymnastics Club

Watleys End Road, Winterbourne, Bristol, BS36 1QG
01454 776 873
All classes taken by British gymnastics qualified coaches. Children participate in the Persil Funfit Reward Scheme.

Jellies (walking U2's with parent)

£2.50, no pre-booking

Parent & Toddlers (2-3yrs with parents) & Gym Tots (3-4yrs without parents)

£15 Registration fee, £3.50 weekly charge, pre-booking required
Free trial session available. See Parties section, below.

Jack in a Box

Waterford Hall, Waterford Road, Henleaze, BS9 4BT
Kate Wright: 0117 962 3758
katewrightjackbox@hotmail.com

Soft play for tinies (under 20mths)

Tue/Wed & Fri 9.25am-10.15am, £3
Wide variety of equipment with free play and music. No pre-booking necessary.

Mini-gym (20ths-3 yrs)

Tue/Wed & Fri 10.45am-11.35pm
£3.30 per sessionn, payable half-termly
Working with carer round circuits of apparatus. Pre-booking necessary.

Pre-school gym (3-5yrs)

Tue/Wed & Fri pm
£3.30 per session, payable half-termly
Working independently in small groups and following B.G.A badge schemes.
All classes supervised by qualified staff. Popular and friendly group.

Parent Play & Stay/Time Zone Kidz

Time Zone Kidz, The Mall at Cribbs Causeway, Bristol, BS34 5UR
0117 9155 802, www.cribbs-causeway.co.uk

Parent Stay and Play
Mon-Fri 10am-3.30pm, term time only
Up to 9yrs, £2.25/2hrs
Soft play with ball pit, trikes, construction toys, dolls, books etc and adventure play room. Tea and coffee available for parents. Buggy store available in reception.
Crèche: £1.80/½hr, max stay 2/hrs

Planet Kids
Mega Bowl, Brunel Way, Ashton Gate, BS3 2YX
0117 953 8538, www.megabowl.co.uk

P WC CP ♿ ♿ ✕ ♿

Adventure Play Centre (under 12's)
Fri 4pm-8pm
Sat-Sun & school hols 10am-8pm
£3 (or £10 for 4 children)

Adventure Golf Centre
Daily, school hols 10am-12pm, 4+yrs, £1.50

Riverside Leisure Club
Station Road, Little Stoke, Bristol, BS34 6HW
01454 888 666
Daily 10am-6pm
1½hr sessions, £2.50 U5's, £2.95 5+yrs

P V ✎ WC ✂ ⛴ CP ☺ ♿ ♿ ✎
✕ ⛪ ♿ ♿ ♿ Pp

Mayhem Soft Play
3mths-10yrs, under 4'11" only
Separate areas for toddlers and older children. Usually busy in holidays and weekends.

The Alphabet Zoo Children's Playcentre
Old Bingo Hall, Winterstoke Road, Bedminster, BS3
0117 966 3366
Daily 10-7pm, last admission 5pm
w/e's, school & B/H's £3.49 for 1½ hr

P ✎ WC ✂ ⛴ ♿ ♿ ♿ ☒ ✕ ♿ ♿

Play centre for 1-12yrs. Large area filled with huge variety of interesting, colourful and challenging equipment. Good separate toddller area including junior bouncy castle and ball pool. Equipment for over 5's available to toddlers when quiet during school hours if supervised by parent/adult. Some steps although wheelchair access if requested.

Tumble Tots
Pauline Fortune: 0117 377 9604

Physical pre-school play programme with structured, fun activities designed to help children with agility, balance, co-ordination and communication skills. Uses bright and stimulating equipment and helped by trained staff. Gym Babes, 6+mths through to Tumble Tots, 5yrs.

Classes held at Downend, Hanham, Saltford, Westbury-on-Trym, Stoke Gifford, Headley Park and Long Ashton with new areas opening soon. See advertisement.

SWIMMING
Safety and confidence in the water is considered an important skill for everyone. There are a wide variety of lessons available. Most pools have 'Leisure Sessions' where any age can go along, but as times frequently change it's best to ring first. Babies should have their first triple vaccine before going swimming and most pools require babies to have a swim nappy. An adult must accompany every child under 8yrs. Each pool has different adult to child ratios, some 1:2 and others 1:1 for young children, so check first.

For a list of pools in your area see the Reference Section.

SWIMMING CLASSES
Also see the Teen Guide chapter for further listings.

Bristol Henleaze Swimming Club
0117 924 5057, www.bristolhenleazesc.org.uk
Takes children from 5yrs who can swim 1 width unaided. They progress to the Development Squad at about 8/9yrs. See Teen Guide chapter.

Clifton Swim School
Pat Holmyard: 0117 973 7245
From £5 per lesson
Long established (1972) Easter and summer swim school. Courses for children from 5yrs. Beginners to ASA challenge awards, snorkelling and diving. Blocks of 10 lessons every morning over 2 weeks. Friendly tuition

in small groups held in warm pool in Clifton. Call for reservations and further information.

Splash Happy Swim School

0117 979 8266
30 min sessions (8 max per group)
Swimming lessons with qualified teachers at Henbury School pool (Wed & Fri eve) and Badminton Girls' School pool (Sun all day) for children up to 16yrs of all abilities including special needs.

Waterbabies

3, Richmond Park Rd, Clifton, Bristol, BS8 3 AS
0117 904 9090, www.waterbabies.co.uk
£8/½hr session (blocks of 10) max 10
Swimming lessons designed to introduce babies to water. Word association, repetition, games and songs are used to encourage the development of natural swimming skills including the ability to swim underwater. There are also courses for over 1's. All are taught without the use of armbands. Lessons take place at: Bristol Royal Infirmary pool, the Freeways pool at Leigh Court, Esporta in Stoke Gifford and the Cadbury House Club nr. Congresbury.

SWIMMING OUTSIDE

Swimming outside when the weather is fine can make a great day out.

Greenbank Outdoor Swimming Pool

Wilfrid Road, Street, Somerset, BA16 0EU
01458 442468, www.greenbankpool.co.uk
May-Sep: Mon-Fri 12am-6.45pm, w/e's & school hols longer openings
£3.80 adult, £2.80 child, free U2's
[P] [WC] [symbols]

This pleasant heated outdoor pool surrounded by grass is less than 5 minutes walk from Clark's Village. There's a separate children's area, a new 'Wet Play Area' and refreshments. Small car park. Picnics welcomed!

Portishead Open Air Pool

Esplanade Rd, Portishead, BS20 9HD
01275 843454
May-Sep

Help your child develop the vital physical skills and confidence needed for life with Tumble Tots, Britain's leading activity play programme. Each session includes fun action songs and rhymes, and stations focused on climbing, co-ordination, agility and balance.

It's just so much fun!

Spaces available for children aged 6mths-7yrs at: Saltford, Downend, Hanham, Westbury on Trym,

Telephone 0117 3779604

Heated open air swimming pool with separate toddler pool ideal for families. Poolside and promenade verandas, indoor changing rooms and showers and sunbathing terraces. 1:1 ratio for U5's.

Sandford Parks Lido

Keynsham Road, Cheltenham, GL53 7PU
01242 524430, www.sandfordparkslido.org.uk
Apr-Sep: daily 11am-7.30pm
£3 adult, from £4.20 family (1+1), free U5's, various season tickets available
M5 J11, A40 to Cheltenham then follow signs. Next door to Gen. Hospital
[P] [V] [symbols]

Large heated outdoor pool set in landscaped gardens with spacious terraces for sunbathing and a café. Separate children's pool for U8's, paddling pool and slides for toddlers. Two children's play areas along with table tennis and basketball. Lockers in the heated changing rooms. Pay and display carpark next door. Ring for details of early morning adult swims.

WEST COUNTRY THEMED SWIMMING POOLS

Bradford-on-Avon Swimming Pool
St. Margaret street, Bradford-on-Avon, BA15 1DF
01225 862 970
www.kinetika.org/sites/bradfordonavon/swimming
Daily please call for details

P WC 🔒 ⚡ ♿

Parent & Toddler, U5's, swimming sessions are run 4 days a week in the warm smaller pool, cost £2.55. Adult to child ratio of 1:2. Two elephant slides, rings, floats, toys and balls and playpen available. Sat 10.45-12pm, fun swim for over 8's (and U8's accompanied) with floats and inflatables. Lessons from 1yr. Sloped entrance at rear.

Newport Centre
Kingsway, Newport, South Wales
01633 662 662
Daily

P ✎ WC 🔒 ⚡ ✂

Warm leisure pool with splash area, wave machine, slide and various play equipment. Spacious changing rooms and car park nearby. U5's 1:1 adult to child ratio, 5-7yrs 1:2. Swimming lessons and soft play also available.

Sedgemoor Splash
Mount Street, Bridgwater, Somerset, TA6 6HZ
01278 425 636
Daily please call for details
£3.50 adult, £2.50 child, free U4's, £9.50 family

P ✎ WC 🔒 ⚡ ✂

Excellent warm fun pool with 2 water flumes, river run, bubbles, water jets & wave machine. Gently sloping splash area and separate children's pool with bubbles. Adult to child ratios U4's 1:1, 5-7yrs 1:2.

TENNIS
Also see Teen Guide chapter

Kings' Tennis Club
Sat 9.30am-10.30am, 3-9yrs
Sat 10.30am-11.30am, intermediates
£1.50/hr

Both these sessions focus on technique and are less competitive than the final session, 11.30am-1pm which is for teenagers and good intermediates.

Mini Tennis
Coombe Dingle Sports Complex, Combe Lane, Bristol, BS9 2BJ
David Hudgell: 0117 962 6723

Mini Tennis, 5-10yrs is available at various venues across the city, sessions cost £1. For further club information, see above.

Eastville Park Tennis Club	Sat 9am-10am
St George's Park Tennis Club	Sun 1.30pm-2.30pm
St Paul's Tenniss Club	Wed 4pm-5pm
Knowle West Tennis Club	Sun 12pm-1pm
Withywood Tennis Club	Wed 5pm-6pm

ARTS & ENTERTAINMENT

ARTS & CRAFT

Ticky Tacky
Church of the Good Shepherd Hall, Bishop Road, Bishopston, BS7 8NA
0117 951 6206
Fri 10-11.15am, 2-4yrs 75p pp, term time

Painting, sticking, drawing, singing and baking activities on a Biblical theme. Friendly and involved leaders. There is a waiting list so regular attendance is appreciated.

Make Your Mark
97 Whiteladies Rd, Clifton, BS8 2NT
0117 974 4257
www.makeyourmarkbristol.co.uk
Mon/Fri 11am-6pm, Tue-Thu 11am-10pm, Sun 11am-5pm
Studio fees: £5 adults, £4 U16's & students, group discounts available, pre-booking recommended

✎ WC 🔒 ⚡ ♿

Hands-on art café. Choose from a wide selection of ceramics, plaster models and t-shirts to decorate. Parking available in Clifton Down Shopping Centre. See advertisement.

CIRCUS SKILLS

Circus Bugz & Circus Maniacs
Office 8A, The Kingswood Foundation, Britannia Road, Kingswood, BS15 8DB
0117 947 7042, www.circusmaniacs.com
Saturday sessions, term time only
11 weeks course, £30 3-5yrs (45mins), £50 5-7yrs (1½hrs), 7+yrs £70 (2½hrs)

P WC ♿

Circus unites aspects of both sport & arts providing the creative freedom to be original and unique.
Circus Bugz is suitable for 3-7yrs. A range of activities designed to enhance hand/eye co-ordination, posture, balance, movement and creativity. "Caterpillar Awards" for 3-5yrs and "Butterfly Awards" for 5-7yrs. Parents and carers are welcome to participate.
Circus Maniacs suitable for over 7's.
Opportunity to get physical by learning skills inc. trapeze, tight-wire, acrobatics, juggling, unicycling & stilt-walking. Taster sessions available.

MakE YOUR MaRK
Hands-On Art Café
97 Whiteladies Road
Clifton, Bristol BS8 2NT
0117 9744257

Birthday parties!
A great day out!
Baby's footprints!
Make great presents!

www.makeyourmarkbristol.co.uk

DANCE & DRAMA

344 Dance Centre
Alexandra Pk, Fishponds, Bristol, BS16 2BG
0117 965 5660, www.344dance.freeserve.co.uk

P WC ♿ ☕

Ballet, modern jazz, tap, drama, singing, Irish dancing & shows children of 2+yrs. Sessions weekdays and Sat. Dancewear and tuck shop. Branches also at: Fishponds, Bradley Stoke & Bedminster and Wick. Holiday workshops.

Bristol Old Vic
King Street, Bristol, BS1 4ED
0117 987 7877, www.bristol-old-vic.co.uk
Friday 11am-11.45am, U5's, £1 pp

P ✏ WC ✂ ♿ ♿ ✖ ☕

Fun sessions for pre-school children with songs, stories, performing and a chance to meet some of the people who work at the theatre. No need to book but phone to check times and dates. Holiday workshops. See advertisement in Reference Section.

Bristol School of Dancing
Lansdown Road, Clifton, Bristol, BS8 3AB
Ms Redgrave: 01278 434 081
From £35 per term, dependent on age
Classes, for 2-11yrs, in dance and movement. 1hr sessions held daily.

Bristol School of Performing Arts
Elmgrove Centre, Redland Road, Cotham, BS6 6AG
Ms Redgrave: 01278 434 081
Sat, term time, £75, 10 wks
Drama classes for 6-16yrs. Sessions last 2hrs. Holiday workshops available.

Danceblast@the tobacco Factory
Tobacco Factory, Raleigh Road, Southville
Anne Taylor: 0117 964 6195
Sat 3-13yrs, £4 per session

P WC ♿ ✖

All types of dancing: ballet, jazz, lyrical and hip hop as well as some singing and acting included. All working towards an annual show. Sessions one hour, 3-5yrs encouraged to bring favourite teddy/doll.

Dauphine's of Bristol

32/34 Cloud Hill Rd, St George, Bristol, BS5 6JF
0117 955 1700

Theatrical activities for children, including stage craft and face painting for ages 6-18yrs. Sessions take place most Saturdays. These can also be tailor made for youth clubs, school classes and parties. Holiday workshops.

Helen O'Grady Children's Drama Academy

Alison Mazanec (Principal): 0117 924 4944
www.helenogrady.co.uk
Classes for:
Lower Primary (5-8yrs)
Upper Primary (9-12yrs)
Youth Theatre (13-17yrs)

The programme offered at the academy aims to provide ongoing confidence and skills in verbal communication through drama. Venues: Frampton Cotterell, Keynsham, Bishopston, Portishead, Westbury-on-Trym, Almondsbury, Redland and Kingswood.

Henleaze School of Dancing

St Peters' Church Hall, Henleaze & Stoke Bishop
Village Hal, Stoke Bishop
Joyce Harper: 0117 962 3224
Mon-Fri

Pre-school dance classes. Ballet & tap classes for ages 5-11yrs.

Ivy Arts Theatre School

Torwood House, Durdham Park, Redland, BS6 6XE
Miss K. Allen: 07748 983 436
Sat am & pm session
From £10 per session

Qualified teachers offer a broad range of theatre crafts. Classes include: performing, singing, movement & dance for ages 4-14yrs. Pre-booking essential. Children split into age related groups, but also spend some time integrated together. Holiday workshops.

Kick Off Youth Theatre

The Hope Chapel, Hope Chapel Hill, Hotwells
0117 929 1883
Mon 5pm-6.30pm
£3 per session, £2 concessions, payable half termly

An opportunity for children, 8-11yrs, to learn skills such as acting, voice, mime, masks and perform shows. Members must be prepared to have 'a great time and show commitment

to attendance and rehearsal'. Qualified drama teacher.

Music Box

The Tobacco Factory, Raleigh Road, Southville, BS3
Kate Hargreaves: 0117 924 5601

An opera group specialising in high quality serious music theatre for children 8-13yrs. Participants required 'to have the enthusiasm and commitment to work'. Musical boys particularly welcome. Meets once a week in term time.

QEH Youth Theatre

QEH Theatre, Jacobs Wells Rd, Bristol, BS8 1JX
Tracy Cavalier: 0117 914 5805
www.qehtheatre.co.uk
Mon 4.15pm-5.45pm
£5 per session (max 10 children) payable half-termly

Youth theatre for 7-10yrs. Classes include: movement, sound, art and craft, games, storymaking and telling, improvisation, role-play, mime and plays.

Southville Centre

Beauley Road, Southville, Bristol, BS3 1QG
0117 923 1039

P ✎ ✄ 🏠 ✕ ♿ .

Bristol School of Dancing & Ballet Classes (3+yrs)

Mon 4pm-7.30pm, 45 min sessions
Run by Royal Academy of Dancing teachers.

Toddler Creative Dance (2-4yrs)

Emma: 07879 483106
Thurs 10.30am-11.30am
£2.50 pp, £4 for two

Informal drop-in. Interactive session aims to develop mobility and co-ordination skills. For children, 2-4yrs, with accompanying adult. Also runs a session at:

St Bartholomews Parish Hall

Sommerville Rd, St Andrews
Thu 2pm-2.45pm

Stage Coach

www.stagecoachbristol.co.uk

Ashton/Bedminster	0117 986 2500
Totterdown/Keynsham	0117 330 5953
Cotham/Portishead & Winterbourne	0117 959 3995

Offer part-time training in drama, singing and dance for ages 4-16yrs, of all abilities. There are no auditions. Their ethos concentrates on 'confidence and self-esteem'. See advertisement.

Stapleton School of Dancing
Miranda Beard: 01453 844 430
From £23 per term
Ballet, modern & tap for children over 2yrs. Venues: Begbrook Primary School, Stapleton; Christ Church Hall, Quaker Road, Downend and The Ridgewood Community Centre, Yate. Summer School available for over 5's during the last week of July.

Twinkle Toes
Mrs Terry Cross: 0117 962 8964
Baptist Church, Westbury-on-Trym
Tue 10.15am-10.45am
St. Mary Magdalene Church Hall, Stoke Bishop
Fri 2pm-2.30pm
£30 per term

Dance/movement class for boys and girls 3-4yrs (those over 2½yrs may be considered). Parents observe.

Westbury Park Dance Centre
St Alban's Church Hall, Westbury Park, BS6
Pauline Reynolds: 0117 968 3682
After school & Sat

Classes following RAD Ballet and ISTD Jazz/Modern/Tap syllabuses. Children, 3+yrs, will work towards occasional shows.

Wingfield School of Ballet
The Pembles, Fishpool Hill, Brentry. BS10 6SW
Pamela Wingfield: 0117 950 3916

Ballet classes for 3+yrs. Tap & modern dance for those over 4½+yrs. Prepares children for RAD & ISTD examinations, shows & Eisteddfod. Classes are held after school in: Patchway, Little Stoke, Thornbury, Almondsbury & Brislington and Sat am at Bradley Stoke Leisure Centre.

MUSIC & MOVEMENT

Child's Play at the Crotchet Factory
1 Edward Street, Eastville, Bristol, BS5 6LW
0117 951 8015 24 hrs

Music workshops providing a fun, hands-on introduction to a mixture of music. Holiday and private sessions available.

Baby class
Tue/Fri 9.45am-10.15am, £3.60 per session

2-3yrs
Mon 1.15pm-1.45pm, Tue/Fri 10.30am-11.00am, £3.60 per session

Over 3's (10 children max)
Mon 2pm-2.45pm, Tue/Fri 11.15am-12pm, Sat 10.45am-11.30am, £4.20 per session

Workshops 4-7yrs (12 children max)
£4.90 for 45min., £5.90 for 1hr
Percussion, recorder, keyboard and guitar

Christchurch Choir & Music Group
Christchurch, Clifton Down Road, Clifton
Ross Cobb: 0117 973 2011
Free, call for details.
A weekly choir and music group for children aged 5-16yrs.

Hum and Drum
28 Dublin Crescent, Henleaze, Bristol, BS9 4NA
Penny Rawlings: 0117 962 1328/924 3159
Mon-Fri am & pm, Sat am
£45 per term, weekly 45min. session

Introduction to basic musical concepts through playing a wide variety of instruments. Classes for 6mths-11yrs. Carers of younger children stay, but are encouraged to leave over 3's. Sat 4-11yrs music workshop. Piano, violin & recorder lessons after school, up to 18yrs. Holiday workshops.

Jo Jingles
Pamela MacLeod: 01454 610553
www.jojingles.co.uk
Weekly classes at various venues for pre-school children. Introduction to music, singing and movement including percussion instruments, action songs, sound games and nursery rhymes. Occasional children's parties.

Jolly Babies
Julie Thompson: 01454 619 773
From £2.50 per ½hr session, payable half termly

Groups held at various venues:

Julie Thompson, Bradley Stoke	01454 619 773
Deb Denny, Downend	0117 957 4443
Anne-Marie, Frampton Cottrel	01454 773 267
Marie Vise, Henleaze/Redland	0117 940 5803
Ruth Wong, Thornbury	01454 413 905
Diane Dickerson, Totterdown	0117 904 0863

Share your baby's first musical experiences. Classes designed for babies 0-14mths.

Music with Mummy
From £2.50 per session payable half termly

Classes for U4's with carers. Fun with music through movement, games and using simple instruments. Some sessions during school holidays. Contacts as above.

Lucy Time
Cotham Parish Church, Cotham Road, Cotham, BS6
Lucy Livingstone: 0117 924 9455
Tue-Thu
£4 per 45 min session payable half termly

Uses themes from nature to sing, dance, and celebrate the festivals. Children, 18mths-4yrs, are grouped according to age. Carers of younger children join in sessions but can leave over 3's. Also sessions for parents with young babies.

Music Makers
33 Cornwall Rd, Bishopston, Bristol, BS7 8LJ
Vicki Meadows: 0117 924 1124
Tue am & pm

From £2 per session, term time

Introduction to music & movement for under 5's using accordion, percussion and additional props. Children 18mths-4yrs, attend sessions, grouped according to age, lasting 30 or 45 mins. Carers settle children into groups and have a tea and coffee in the kitchen. Occasional children's parties. Pre-booking required.

Opus Music Workshops
1 Bridge Road, Bath, BA2 1AA
01225 460 209 24 hr
£3.65 per 45 min session payable termly

Developing interest, enjoyment and early skills in music through the use of instruments and constructive play in a friendly environment. Groups for: Minors (under 2's), Crotchets (2-3yrs) and Minims (3-4yrs). Two sampler sessions available for £5 before committing to full term. Sessions are run at various venues in Bath.

Rhymetime
Ebenezer Methodist Church, British Road, Bedminster
Esther Mclean: 0117 9667028
Thu 10.45am-11.15am, 0-18mths, 11.30am-12pm, toddlers 18mths-2½yrs
£2 per family, payable on the day

A lively music and action group. Sit in a friendly circle on the floor and sing along with the guitar to many favourite nursery rhymes and songs. Children join in with the actions using the musical instruments provided. Just turn up to take part.

Sing and Sign
Helen Hill: 0117 950 0017
£40 per 45 min session, 11 weeks

Sing and Sign is a programme of songs and rhymes for babies from 7-22mths. It teaches simple gestures (derived from sign language) which parents can use to enhance communication with their babies. Venues: Westbury-on-Trym, Stockwood, Portishead, and Westbury Park.

Toddler Tunes
Helen McGarry: 0117 962 2336
Newman Hall, Grange Court Rd, Westbury-on-Trym
Mon/Thu 10am & 11am
Horfield Baptist Church, Gloucester Rd
Tue 10am & 11am
£2.40 per 40 min session
WC A A Pp

Singing classes with action songs and rhymes, instruments and puppets. Informal and fun atmosphere, parents/carers expected to participate. No pre-booking required. Suitable for pre-school children.

GROUPS

ACTION GROUP

The Boys' Brigade & The Girls' Brigade
Brigade Centre, Garnet Street, Bedminster, BS3 3JS
0117 966 0650, www.avon.boys-brigade.org.uk
Christian organisations based on fun, friendship and training for life. For those aged between 5 & 19yrs.

SCOUTING MOVEMENT
Also see Social and Action Clubs in the Teen Guide chapter.

Beavers and Cubs
The Scouting Association runs Beavers for boys and girls aged 6-8yrs and Cubs for those aged 8-11yrs. Packs meet weekly during the term time. Activities include: sports, games, trips, camps and pioneering skills. To find out more about a pack in your area contact the numbers below.

Rainbows & Brownies
The Guiding Association includes Rainbows for girls aged 5-7yrs and Brownies for those aged 7-10yrs. Packs meet weekly during the term time. Activities include: art and crafts, games, sports, trips and basic pioneering skills. To

find out more about a pack in your area contact the numbers below.

Avon County Office, Scout Association
01454 613 006
www.avonscouts.org.uk

Girlguiding UK
0207 834 6242
www.girlguiding.org.uk

Guide Association, Bristol & South Gloucestershire
HQ, Westmoreland Rd, Redland, BS6
0117 973 4776

Scouts Information Officer, Bath
Beavers, Cubs or Special Needs enquiries:
Bill Oatley: 01225 314457
Scouts enquiries:
John Allison: 01225 442450
Dave Newman: 01761 233644

The Scout Association UK
08245 3001818
www.scoutbase.org.uk

FAITH & CULTURAL BASED GROUPS

Introduction
Many faiths based groups provide activities for young and older children on their day of worship. Alongside these, there may be holiday clubs and youth groups with a spiritual/cultural theme. To find out more either visit your local place of worship or see the contacts below. Also see Minority Groups in Advice and Support chapter.

USEFUL CONTACTS

Bangladeshi Association
0117 951 1491

Bristol Jamia Mosque
0117 977 0944

Catholic Youth Service
Ronnie Mitchinson: 0117 902 5594

Church of England
Diocesan Children and Youth Officer
0117 906 0100

Horfield Baptist Church
0117 924 3608

Lam Rim Buddist Centre
0117 923 1138

Methodist Training & Development Office
0117 908 2348

Sikh Resource Centre
0117 952 5023

AFTER SCHOOL CARE & HOLIDAY CLUBS

Run outside school hours by playworkers who help children learn, play and relax with their friends. There are different types of out of school services: breakfast clubs, after school clubs and holiday play schemes.

There are also some excellent childminders and nurseries who provide after school care. To find out more about after school services contact:

BAND (British Association For Neighbourhood Day Care Ltd)
81 St Nicholas Rd, St Pauls BS2 9JJ
0117 954 2128, www.bandltd.org.uk
Provides lists of afterschool clubs, playschemes, holiday schemes and other daycare facilities. BAND can help groups apply for funding to set up childcare facilities locally.

Children's Information Service (Bristol)
0845 129 7217, www.childcarelink.gov.uk

Bristol Early Years and Childcare Partnership
www.bristoleycp.org.uk

South Gloucestershire Children's Information Service
01454 868666, www.southglos.gov.uk/ed/cis

North Somerset Childcare Service
01275 888778

Bath and North East Somerset Family Information Service
01225 395 343

Childcare Emploment Agencies
See Childcare chapter for a list of agencies which may be able to provide you with temporary childcare in the holidays.

HOLIDAY CLUBS

Many of the entries in this chapter run holiday clubs and play schemes which are good for one off sessions or a weekly course.

Below are some additional listings that fit this category and some that provide regular after school care.

Clevedon Montessori School
34 Albert Road, Clevedon, BS21 7RR
01275 877743
Mon-Fri 3-5pm
£3.60/hr pp, £7.20/2hrs pp, tea included
P 👶 🚶 🏠 🏫 🚌 📋
Term time after school club run for 3-8yrs.

Southmead Adventure Playground
Doncaster Rd, Southmead, BS10 5AQ
0117 950 3607
Tue-Fri 3.30pm-7pm
Sat & school holidays 10am-1pm & 2pm-6pm
Free
A variety of activities for under 16's including sport and craft. Facilities include an all weather pitch, play area for U8's and a climbing area. U6's must be accompanied by an adult.

Clifton College Holiday Activities
Clifton College Services Ltd, 2 Percival Road, BS8 3LE
0117 315 7666
www.cliftoncollegeuk.com
From £21/day, £12 ½ day
Run a range of holiday activities suitable for 4-13yrs which include a mix of football, tennis, arts and craft, fun water sports and games. They also run a programme for 13-15yrs. Weekly courses covering tennis coaching, horseriding, sailing and pottery. The courses have become very popular, so all booking must be made in advance.

Ecole Française de Bristol
c/o St Ursulas High School, Brecon Road, Westbury-on-Trym, BS9 4DT
0117 962 4154

After school classes and holiday activity weeks and workshops for 5-12yrs. Also provides GCSE classes, adult classes and preschool activities. See also Playgroups & Early Education 0-4 Years chapter.

King's Camp, Bristol

King's Camp, Badminton School, Westbury-on-Trym
0870 345 0781, www.kingscamp.org
From £75 (4 days)

Activity day camps in the Easter and Summer holidays for 5-17yrs. Activities have a sports emphasis but there are also art and crafts, games and team building excercises. Camps are registered with Ofsted.

Sport & Leisure Centres

Many offer additional sessions in the holidays along with courses and fun filled days for older children. See listings in the central Reference Section.

The Art Raft

Lower Ground Rooms, Victoria Methodist Church,
1a Whiteladies Road, Bristol, BS8 1NU
0117 983 5234, www.artraft.com
8am-5.30pm
£16/day, £8/½ day

Holiday schemes, for 4-12yrs. Giving children the opportunity to access a whole range of artistic materials and practices.

Torwood House

Durdham Park, Redland, BS6 6XE
0117 973 5620
Mon-Fri 8am-6pm
£31/day £19/½ day preschool
£23/day £15/½ day 5+yrs

Offer holiday care for 3-11yrs. Activities include PE, games, drama, music, cookery, arts and crafts, trips and outings.

CHURCH SCHEMES

Chat-a-Box

Redland Parish Church, Redland Green, Redland, BS6
0117 973 7423, www.redland.org.uk
From £15/week

Activity week for 100 children, 6-11yrs. Runs in the first full week of the summer holidays.

Themed programme with various fun groups and lively Christian teaching.

Easton Christian Family Centre

Beaufort Street, Easton, BS5 0SQ
0117 955 4255
Mon-Fri 8.30am-5.30pm, all school holidays
From £12/day.
Mon-Fri after school until 6pm , £5/day

Activities aim to be fun, stimulating, educating and challenging. A homework room is available. Suitable for 4-11yrs.

Fun Factory

Bristol Community Church, Bourne Chapel,
Waters Rd, Kingswood, BS15 8BE
0117 947 8441
6.30pm-8pm

Fun filled club for children 7-10yrs, activities include outings, theme nights, crafts, games & cooking.

PARTIES

The build up to birthday parties is very exciting, particularly for children. However this is not always the case for their parents. When the novelty of pass the parcel and all those other games has gone you may need some inspiration. Here are some ideas.

CHILDREN'S ENTERTAINERS

Arty Party Ceramics

Charlie Stockford: 01275 333740
www.artypartyceramics.co.uk
From £9.50 pp (min 8), £2.50 pp fairs and fundraisers

Paint your Own Pottery at a venue of your choice, within a 15 mile radius of south Bristol. Parties, fairs, mum and baby/toddler sessions. Age range 0-99yrs!

Avon Sports Academy - Football Parties

0117 904 6686, www.avonsportsacademy
£40

One hour of qualified football instruction at a venue of your choice, 20 children max. Includes, bibs, cones and goals.

Cassandra, Storyteller

0117 966 3864

A professional performer since 1991, she fell into storytelling by accident via the flying trapeze! Trained in circus, theatre and dance; she involves her audience in every twist and turn of the story. "Children's and adults' imaginations are totally engaged by her unique and participative style of performance." See advertisement.

Cats Whiskers

15 The Ridge, Coalpit Heath, Bristol, BS36 2PR
Helen Eyre: 01454 853454
www.catswhiskers.biz
From £50

Face painting, body art and temporary tattoos for parties, events and promotions. Strict code of practice regarding hygiene and use of safe professional paints, for sensitive skin. A maximum of 24 children for a 2 hour party session.

Jack Stephens Magician

01380 850453, www.jackstephens.co.uk
£90

Jack's fun shows feature magic, puppets, singing with a guitar, games, balloon modelling and lots of audience participation. Performances geared to venues and occasions.

Mad Platter

Nicky Houghton & Louise Mosely: 07801 232 886
www.themadplatter.co.uk

Run ceramic painting parties in your home. All you need is a table big enough to seat your guests. Nicky and Louise bring a choice of ceramics to paint ranging from Christmas decorations to plates. Ceramics are taken away for firing and returned. Suitable from 4yrs, 8 children min. See website for baby hand/foot print ceramics.

Magical Mandy

Amanda Farrell: 01225 429876
www.magicalmandy.co.uk & www.rentawizard.com
From £95

Now among the "wonderful" magic shows on offer is one with a wizardly theme. The wizard (Mandy!) will organise games, prizes, balloon modelling and of course magic. Fancy dress competition optional. Mandy is a member of the Magic Circle.

Mr Brown's Pig - Puppet Shows and Pirate Pantomine

Chris Brown: 0117 963 4929
www.puppetsonline.co.uk
From £80

These "excellent" puppet shows are performed, for children aged 3+yrs from an elaborate puppet booth with lights and music. Lots of audience participation and humour. The Pirate Pantomine features puppet comedy, music, magic and mayhem. Face painting and children's songs can also be included. See advertisement.

Pizzazz

Top Floor Flat, 6 Charlotte Street, Bath, BA1 2NE
01225 333093
From: £75

Circus skills parties/workshops with balloon modelling, face painting, caricatures, giant bubbles and parachute games. "Steve manages to include all children (and adults) with patience and humour!" Also parties with giant games and circus skills for 15+yrs.

Punch & Judy

John & Trevor Harvey: 0117 965 7761

Traditional English Punch and Judy for 3+yrs. Entertainment can also include magic and/or balloons depending upon the individuals requirements. Shows last up to 1 hour.

Tallulah Swirls
0117 377 4543, www.tallulahswirls.co.uk
Amy's "beautifully" hand crafted puppets perform to all ages. Lots of audience participation, singing and laughing followed by a chance for everyone to see how the show operates. Face painting and workshops also offered. See advertisement, below.

The Pink Strawberry Puppet Co.
The Arcarde, Boyces Avenue, Clifton, BS8 4AA
Anthony Churchill: 0117 923 9242
www.strawberrygallery.com
From £75-£150
Anthony Churchill is a puppeteer who both teaches and performs. Performances can be geared to audience age and size. Workshops and puppet clubs teach puppet making, performing and its history.

Wastenot Workshops
Nicola Gilla: 0117 941 4447
From £65 within Bristol area
Children can create their own masterpieces from recycled materials - anything from puppets to costumes and masks. Themes include mermaids, pirates, dragons and princesses. Face painting can also be included.

Wizzo the Wizard
Louis Taylor: 0117 950 8312
www.wizzothewizard.com
Magic for children of all ages; there are puppets, balloon modelling and prizes for all. Wizzo also does Educational Road Safety Shows.

BOUNCY CASTLE HIRE

Bristol Bouncy Castles
Paul Tree: 07796 775522
From £45
Hires out assorted bouncy castles, slides, ball ponds and gladiators (!) for indoor and outdoor parties and events. Delivery, within 25 miles of Bristol, and setup are free.

Time to Bounce
Lesley Grant: 0117 937 4424
www.timetobounce.co.uk
From £35
Friendly family run service. Delivery and set up in Bristol area free.

PARTY GOODS

A Swell Party
37a Princess Victoria Street, Clifton Village, BS8 4BX
0117 923 7644
Mon-Sat 10am-5pm
All types of party goods and complete balloon decoration service.

Cakes by Alison
Alison Chomette: 01454 315742
www.cakesbyalison.co.uk
From £20
Cakes for all occasion; birthdays, Christenings, weddings etc. Personalised to your requirements, will deliver free within 20 miles of Bristol.

Party Pieces

01635 201844, www.partypieces.co.uk
Mon-Fri 8.30am-6pm, Sat 9pm-5pm

Mail order service for unusual plates, invitations, prizes etc.

PARTY VENUES

Bristol Ice Rink

Frogmore Street, Bristol, BS1 5NA
0117 929 2148
www.nikegroup.co.uk
Available on all sessions
£9.50 pp, min 8 children

Ice skating birthday party for 5+yrs (min 8). Price includes ½hr private tuition, skating on public session, skate hire, 2 adult spectators, meal in party area, party bags and gift for birthday child.

Bristol Old Vic

King Street, Bristol, BS1 4ED
0117 949 3993, www.bristol-old-vic.co.uk
From: £2.50 (not inclusive of ticket price)

Any performance can be combined with a party, in your own private area, before or after the show (max 30). You can bring your own cake. See advertisement central colour pages.

Bristol Zoo Gardens

Clifton, Bristol, BS8 3HA
0117 974 7300, www.bristolzoo.org.uk
£4 pp (min 8) plus Zoo admission

Jungle Tea parties are held in the Pelican Restaurant at the Zoo. The package includes invitations, gift for each child, jungle mask, activity mat, party tea and free admission for the birthday child. Tea time at 3pm or 3.30pm. Also see Out & About in Bristol chapter and advertisement inside the front cover.

High Action Avon Ski Centre

Lyncombe Drive, Churchill, N. Somerset, BS25 5PQ
01934 852 335
www.highaction.co.uk
From £4.50 for tobogganning
Hot Food can be provided, kid's menu £3.50 pp, teenager's menu £4.95 pp

Parties available all year round for children 6+yrs. Choose one from the many activities on offer: quad bike, tobogganing, snowblading, skiing, snowboarding, archery and rifle shooting (age restrictions may apply depending on activity). Party food is available in a dedicated room.

HorseWorld

Staunton Lane, Whitchurch, BS14 0QJ
Mr Chris Kemp: 01275 540173
www.horseworld.org.uk
£4.50 pp, min 10

If your child is mad about horses this is the place to party. Price includes entry, sandwiches and goodie bag. For £10 extra you get an hour long ranger guided tour. Also see Bristol Out and About chapter.

Make Your Mark

97 Whiteladies Rd, Clifton, BS8 2NT
0117 974 4257
www.makeyourmarkbristol.co.uk

Creative ceramic decoration parties for all ages, also plaster model and t-shirt painting parties.

Oldown Country Park

Foxholes Lane, Tockington, BS32 4PG
01454 413605, www.oldown.co.uk
£7 pp, mid range party price

A party venue with activities to suit most childrens tastes. Price includes half an hour with an Oldown ranger (tractor-trailer rides, feeding the animal etc), party bags and hire of party room. See full entry in Bristol Out and About chapter.

Windmill Hill City Farm

Philip Street, Bedminster, BS3 4EA
0117 963 6252, www.windmillhillcityfarm.org.uk
Times, availability and cost varies

Party room hire includes: tables, chairs and kitchen. There is a café or bring your own food. Free access to the farm park.

SPORTING AND SOFT PLAY PARTY VENUES

Sport & Leisure Centres
Many offer excellent facilities for children's parties, see central Reference Section. Prices start from £5 pp. This usually includes 1 hour of activity followed by the use of a dedicated party room where you can serve your own party food. Some will provide party tableware, invitations and 'going-home' presents. The activities on offer are varied: soft play, bouncy castles, football, roller skating, basketball, trampolining, unihockey and swimming. At Yate and Bradley Stoke you will even find electric cars for would-be Formula 1 drivers! You will need to book early as weekends are very popular.

Bristol Hawks Gymnastic Club
Gymnastics World, Roman Road, Lower Easton, BS5
0117 973 7481/935 5363
£60 for 15 children, £4 per additional child

Gym parties, 1-12yrs, available Fri & Sat between 1pm & 6pm. 1hr in gym & 1hr in tea room, bring your own food.

Bristol School of Gymnastics
Old Bishopston Methodist Church, 245 Gloucester Rd
0117 942 9620
Parties available Sat & Sun pm
From £50 for 1½hrs for up to 20 children

Coach supervised gym parties with trampoline, for girls 0-9yrs, boys 0-7yrs. Bring your own food.

Castaways Children's Indoor Playland
Waters Road, Kingswood, Bristol, BS15 8BE
0117 961 5115
£6.75 pp, min 12 children

Two hour parties can be booked at this indoor adventure play area. 1hr playing and 1hr in the party room for the birthday meal. Invitation, party bags, gift and a photo for the birthday child. The play area is not for the sole use of the party. Suitable for 0-10yrs.

TALLULAH SWIRLS PUPPET THEATRE
Create a Delightful Event
Magical & Original Characters
Laughs & Surprises for all ages!
Face Painting

Tel: 0117 377 4543
Mobile: 07785 564429
22 Cleave St, Bristol BS2 9UD
www.tallulahswirls.co.uk

Elmgrove Centre Rumpus Room
Redland Road, Cotham, Bristol, BS6 6AG
0117 924 3377

The Rumpus Room provides soft play suitable for under 7's. Adjoining room available for hire, £20/2hrs. Large hall parties for over 6's, £40/2hrs. The large hall can accommodate bouncy castles which must be hired independently by the party organiser.

Fromeside Gymnastics Club
Watleys End Road, Winterbourne, Bristol, BS36 1QG
01454 776873
Saturday pm
£55-£60 15-20 children

Qualified coaches supervise 1hr in gym followed by 30mins in coffee bar, where you provide the food. Pre-school parties can be arranged.

Kingswood Gymnastic & Trampoline Centre
The Wesley Studios, Kingswood Foundation Estate, Britannia Road, BS15 8DB
0117 947 6449
From £55, 20 children, 1hr

Supervised gym and disco parties for 5-12yrs. Activities include: trampolining, football, parachute & softplay games

Planet Kids
Bristol Mega Bowl, Bristol, BS3 2YX
0117 953 8538, www.megabowl.com
£7.99 pp, min 6 children

Party package includes 1hr in the play area and 1hr in private party room. A 'Party Captain' is there to help, but parents must stay. Suitable for 0-11yrs. Includes: invites, food, balloons, gift for every child and special gift for birthday child.

Riverside Leisure Club
Station Road, Little Stoke, BS34 6HW
01454 888 666, www.riversideleisure.com
From £40-£52 for 15-20 children

Mayhem, soft play, parties. Party room available, food provided from £2.50 pp or BYO. Suitable for 0-10yrs, height restriction 4'11".

The Alphabet Zoo Children's Playcentre
Old Bingo Hall, Winterstoke Road, Bedminster, BS3
0117 966 3366
Daily between 11am and 5pm, min 9 children
From £4.99 pp

Parties booked for 2hrs, 1½hrs play in centre and ½hr eating. Separate party gallery for food. Suitable for 0-11yrs.

Time Zone Kidz
"Parent Play and Stay", The Mall, Cribbs Causeway, 0117 915 5802
Mon-Thu £50, Fri-Sun £55 for 1½ hrs, £60 2hrs

Soft play area available, 24 children max up to 9yrs. Small kitchen and separate seating area for children to eat, either BYO or use nearby fast food outlets. Parents must stay with party.

PARTY VENUES OUTSIDE BRISTOL

Boomerang
Melksham, Wiltshire, 01225 702096
Huge indoor soft play centre. See Out and About the West Country chapter.

Faerie Parties
The Faerie Shop, 6 Lower Borough Walls, Bath
01225 427 773, www.fairyshop.co.uk
Sat 11.45am, 1.30pm, 3.15pm
£80 max 15 children

Children, 4+yrs, can escape into a faerie wonderland. On arrival there are cakes and lemonade, then a meeting with the Faerie Queen for stories and games. There is time to eat your own picnic. Balloons and optional party bags are given on departure.

Perrygrove Birthday Parties
Perrygrove Railway, Coleford, GL16 8QB
01594 834991, www.perrygrove.co.uk
A party with a difference. Time on the steam train, then picnic in their Stable Room or party food boxes can be supplied. For further details see Transport chapter.

Play Centre
Burnham-on-Sea, 01278 784693
Small indoor play area near the beach. See Out and About the West Country chapter.

The Village Pottery & Play Centre
Street, 01458 443889
See Out and About the West Country chapter.

Togas & Tunnels
The Pump Room, Stall Street, Bath, BA1 1LZ
01225 477785, www.romanbaths.co.uk
w/e's & school holidays
£5.75 pp, min 10 children
The Roman Baths in Bath, provide an unusal party venue for children aged 6-11yrs. Over the course of an hour children can explore secret tunnels, act as archaeologists, dress as real Romans and process around the Roman Baths. Party bags and invitations are included in the price. 2 adults required to accompany the party.
See Out and About the West Country Chapter

Weston Park Raceway
25 Meadow Street, Weston-super-Mare, BS23 1QQ
01934 429812, www.westonparkraceway.co.uk
Two hours of racing fun. Upstairs 180ft 4 lane slot car racing track, suitable for 8+yrs, £6 pp. Downstairs 37ft 4 lane track, suitable 5-7yrs, £5 pp, with wheel chair access.

TEEN GUIDE

by Joanna Thirlwall

CHAPTER 5

INTRODUCTION

I've written this chapter primarily for teenagers but I hope that older generations will use it too.

A lot of what goes on happens by word of mouth so I asked teenagers, including the pupils of St Bede's School, to complete a detailed questionnaire about how they spend their time. Their answers pointed me to a huge variety of activities, clubs and hobbies which are included here, although it is by no means an exhaustive list. Please feedback anything I've missed - who knows, there may be a separate Teen Guide one day!

Although the listings may lack the more detailed contact information contained in the rest of the book, I have worked on the basis that if you are particularly interested in taking things further you will use the phone or Internet like all 21st century teenagers.

BEFORE YOU START

There are other other chapters well worth looking at:

Out & About in Bristol and
Out & About in the West Country

These two chapters have plenty of teen appeal.

Schools & Educational Support

If you need help with homework, extra tuition for exams or advice on life beyond school.

Advice & Support chapter

If you are in need of help there are many support groups and charities out there to help you and your family.

SPORTS DIRECTORY

We have included a whole collection of sporting activities here, from outward bound type experiences to main stream sport. There are ideas for regular exercise or one off experiences. There is some overlap with the Activities 0-12 chapter, as indicated. The listing is alphabetical.

Useful sports websites:

Bristol Community Sport
www.bcsport.co.uk

UK Sports Directory
www.sportslinks.info

South Gloucester Sport
www.southglos.gov.uk/sportsdevelopment/clubs

ATHLETICS & RUNNING

Bristol Athletics Club

Whitchurch Stadium
01275 833911, www.bristol-ac.uk
All track and field events including road and cross country running.

Bristol BUPA Half Marathon

01538 703 111
www.bristol-city.gov.uk/halfmarathon
For those runners looking for an endurance challenge, a popular autumn event.

Cancer Research Race For Life

0870 513 4314, www.raceforlife.org
5km Bristol race, in May (women only).

Triathlon

www.sped-web.pwp.blueyonder.co.uk
If swimming, cycling and running are your thing and you fancy a challenging sport involving all three, then the triathlon is for you!

Kingswood Triathlon Club

0117 909 1435, www.kingswoodtri.co.uk
Contact: Eric Dawney

Yate Tristars

www.yatetristars.org.uk
Junior triathlon club 8–18yrs

UK Athletics

0121 456 5098, www.ukathletics.net
For information on athletics facilities near you.

Westbury Harrier and Cross Country Running Club

University of Bristol Sports Complex, Coombe Dingle
www.westburyharriers.co.uk
Rod Jones: 0117 908 9003
Mon/Thu 7pm-8.30pm, Combe Dingle
Tue/Thu 7pm-8.30pm, Sun 11am-12pm, Yate ACT
50p per session
The club offers qualified coaching for all levels from beginners to elite runners, 10+yrs. Also meet at Yate Athletics Club Track.

CRICKET

See Activities 0-12 Years chapter

CYCLING

For further information on cycle paths and cycle hire see Transport chapter.

Black Mountain Activities

Three Cocks, Brecon, Powys, LD3 0SD
www.blackmountain.co.uk
01497 847897
Bike hire: £20 for full day, £12 half a day
Offers mountain biking along with many other outdoor adventures. See Outdoor Pursuits, below.

The Burnham Tigers

www.burnhambmx.co.uk
Tue &Thu 6pm-9pm

Their track at Apex Leisure and Wildlife Park is considered by the British Cycling Federation to be one of the UK's best venues.

High Action Avon Ski Centre
www.highaction.co.uk
Offers mountain biking. See Skiing, below.

Life Cycle UK
www.lifecycleuk.org.uk, 0117 929 0440
Offers a selection of free maps showing the cycle paths.

Mountain Bikers
www.mtbr.com
A website which reviews trails, giving directions, length, level and type.

Skate & Ride
74 Avon Street, St Philips, Bristol, BS2 0PS
0117 907 9995
An indoor skate park with wooden ramps for BMX bikes. See Skateboard & Skating, below.

DIVING
Although public diving pools are few and far between, those swimming pools with diving facilities have active diving clubs offering weekly training sessions and competitive diving from club to national levels.

Soundwell Swimming and Diving Club
Kingswood Leisure Centre
www.soundwellswim.org.uk
Steve Webb: 0117 985 3282
Membership: £10 annual, £21 monthly subs
Wed 6pm–7pm
Teenage swimmers of a reasonable standard, are welcome to come along and try out a training session for free. No previous diving experience necessary.

Badminton School Pool
Judy Atkinson: 0117 962 7972
Occasional diving courses are run, taught by Mary and Steve Webb

Thornbury Swimming Club
01454 865778
Sun 6.30pm
Term time and half term diving courses.

Henleaze Lake
Henleaze Swimming Club
Al fresco diving. See Swimming, below.

DIVING - SCUBA DIVING
See Scuba Diving, below

DRIVING

The Under 17 Driving Club
www.under17-carclub.co.uk
£150 per person, £225 for 2 or more, £50 joining fee per family
Venues vary, Sat or Sun, Mar-Nov
12-17yrs
An opportunity for under 17's to practice and improve their driving skills legally and safely in a variety of different vehicles. Supervisors encourage an active interest in cars and motor sports. Members are taught to drive by their parents in their parents' cars, with the help of club instructors. Members must have an Associate Member (who is preferably, though not necessarily, a parent) responsible for him/her.

Additional one-off events are held giving members the chance to drive rally cars, go off road in 4x4 vehicles, and drive trucks and single seater racing cars. The club is a non profit making organisation.

FISHING

Henleaze Lake
For contact informations see Henleaze Swimming Club, below.

The Royal Forest of Dean Angling Club
07769 684458, www.fweb.org.uk/dean
Offers mixed fishing at its numerous pools and lakes. You need a permit and must hold a current fishing licence.

Big Well Fly Fishing
Tinmans Green, Redbrook, Monmouth, NP25 3LX
01600 772904 or 07748 227347
Open daily, dawn to dusk
This trout fishery in the Wye Valley has three lakes and a novice pond, which provides anglers with the opportunity to practice and improve technique. Free tuition, with a range of refreshments and rod hire. Inexperienced anglers are initially encouraged to attend with an adult.

Chew Valley Lake Activities
01275 332 339

FOOTBALL

Football is played all over the city and whatever your aspirations, prowess or gender there's bound to be something for you. There are regular training sessions, half term coaching days, holiday courses, league matches – even the chance of a professional football career!

The Football Foundation
www.reff.org.uk

By using your town or postcode on this website you will find all the pitches in your area. It tells you the size and kind of pitch, amenities (e.g. floodlights, changing facilities etc) and contact information. Within this website viewers are signposted to, www.football-devt.co.uk

This site allows clubs using the pitches to register their details, although none are yet listed for this area. So if your club is looking for new players, get registering.

Girls' Football Teams
Amateur Football Alliance
0845 310 8555.

Their free action pack includes information about girls' clubs and leagues in your area.

The Avon Youth League
www.avonyl.co.uk

This is a club news link, which includes a section where clubs wanting players, or players wanting a club, can advertise their vacancies and skills.

Avon Sports Academy
0117 904 6686
www.avonsportsacademy.co.uk

Run soccer courses across the region for under 14's at after school clubs.

Soccer camps at Redland Sports Ground on Saturdays 10.30am–12pm. Offering skills coaching and small-sided games. No need to book.

Soccer weeks held during the holidays at various locations, 10am-3pm. Talented players may be invited to play at their development centre.

Gloucester Football Association
01594 543186
Youth Football Liaison Officer: Denis Broughton

The GFA covers the Bristol area. It has a Youth Committee with 8 boys' and 2 girls' affiliated leagues for under 18's.

Bristol City Football Club
Football in the Community Office
0117 963 0630, www.bcfc.co.uk

BCFC has a 'Football in the Community' programme which offers 2-day soccer schools at half terms and holidays. They are open to boys and girls and take place at various locations:

- City's ground, 8-14yrs
- Hartcliffe and Withywood comprehensive schools, 12-14yrs

Prices vary depending on the venue. Soccer schools are planned for Henbury and Southmead. The club also runs residential camps for 8-14yrs, accessed through the soccer schools. Talented players will be chosen to play for City's Academy, training with professional coaches twice a week for weekend matches.

Bristol Rovers
0117 907 6555, www.bristolrovers.co.uk
Contact: Peter Atkins

Run an active 'Football in the Community' programme for boys and girls.

Boys - Holiday Soccer Fun Days
Locations: Memorial Ground, Thornbury, Yate and Gordano
3-4 days, 10am-3pm, 8-16yrs
£10 per day (includes free match day ticket)

Run at half terms and holidays, popular with boys 13-14yrs.

Advanced Community Training Programme

Keen players aged 9-16yrs may take part in this programme held at venues all over the West Country. Talented players from here will be selected for Rovers' School Of Excellence and earn the opportunity to play other regional clubs.

Girls
0117 924 4040
Contact: Debbie Arrowsmith

Rovers' Girls Football Development s Scheme operates in many of the city's comprehensive schools, running 6-8 weekly training sessions and after school clubs. There are also training sessions open to all girls 8-12yrs held at The

Grange comprehensive school, Warmley, and for girls 8-15yrs at Golden Hill Training Centre, Horfield. Players showing talent will be selected for the Girls' School of Excellence training at Golden Hill.

HOCKEY

Bristol Firebrands Juniors
Firebrand Ground, Longwood, Failand, Bristol, BS8
David Atkinson: 0117 940 0927
Tue 6.10pm-7.30pm, boys 8-14yrs
Tue 7.30pm-9.30pm, boys advanced
Wed 6.30pm-8pm, girls
£1 per session

Redland Ladies' Hockey Club
Clifton College Sports ground, Abbots Leigh
Catherine Combes: 01454 898384
Sun 10am-12pm
Annual fee £30

A mixed session. They have an under 11 side who play in a Bath league, and single sex under 13 teams who play in a league orgainsed by Sports West. Boys feed into Robinson's Mens' Hockey Club and girls into Redland Ladies.

Useful hockey website
www.n-somerset.gov.uk
Click on Enjoying/Sport/Hockey Development. This gives details of hockey clubs in north Somerset and Bristol, details of age groups and training times.

HORSE RIDING
See Activities 0-12 Years chapter

ICE HOCKEY

Bristol Ice Hockey Club
Bristol Ice Rink, Frogmore Street, Bristol
0117 929 2148
Tue 5pm
Competitive league team training for U12's through to U19's.

ICE SKATING

Bristol Ice Rink
Frogmore Street, Bristol, BS1 5NA
0117 929 2148, www.jnll.co.uk

The rink holds several sessions that have particular teen appeal. Prices do not include £1 skate hire. See Activities 0-12 Years chapter.

Pop On The Rocks	Sat 4.30pm–6pm, £4
Ibiza Ice*	Wed 8.30pm–10.30pm, £4.10
Pop On The Rocks*	Fri 8.30pm–10.30pm, £4.30
Saturday Freezer*	8.30pm–10.30pm, £4.30

*For older teens, with a speed skating session for competent skaters only

KARTING

Castle Combe Kart Track
Castle Combe Circuit, Wiltshire, SN14 7EQ
01249 783010, www.combe-events.co.uk
1st & 3rd Sunday each month (booking essential)
Sign posted from M4 J17

This kart track holds junior kart racing for 10–15 yrs (height restrictions). Summer school session also available.

West Country Karting
The Lake, Trench Lane, Winterbourne, BS36 1RJ
01454 202666, www.westcountrykarting.com

Karting for 10+yrs (height restrictions) on its 350m outdoor karting circuit.

OUTDOOR PURSUITS

These include outward bound type activities such as canoeing, rock climbing and abseiling along with more obscure ideas for fun.

Black Mountain Activities
Three Cocks, Brecon, Powys, LD3 0SD
01497 847897
www.blackmountain.co.uk
Offers rock climbing, abseiling, caving, mountain biking, canoeing, raft building and white water rafting. Also see Cycling, above.

The British Mountaineering Council
0870 0104878, www.thebmc.co.uk
Give information on where to climb walls, hills and mountains in your area

Bristol Climbing Centre
St Werburgh's Church, Mina Road, St Werburgh's, Bristol, BS2 9YH
0117 941 3489, www.undercover-rock.com
This dedicated indoor climbing centre features over 200 climbs up to 12 metres high, catering for all abilities from complete beginners to national champions.

Cotswold Water Park
See Out & About in the West Country chapter

Cheddar Caves and Gorge
Cheddar, Somerset, BS27 3QF
01934 742343, www.cheddarcaves.co.uk
11–17yrs (height restrictions apply)
This centre offers caving every day lasting up to 1½ hrs. There is also climbing and abseiling on their 50' abseil pitch in the Gorge.

Chepstow Outdoor Activity Centre
01291 629901
www.chepstowoutdooractivities.co.uk
www.spheremania.com
Offer paintballing, quad biking, archery and 'Spheremania'. The sphere is a 4 metre high transparent inflatable ball. Two riders are harnessed/suspended within in the 2 metre sized capsule and then rolled downhill!

Motiva
The Firs, Hangerberry, Lydbrook, Gloucestershire, GL17 9QG
01594 861762, www.motiva.co.uk
Offers rope courses and youth adventure.

Symonds Yat Canoe Hire
Symonds Yat West, Herefordshire, HR9 6BY
Geoff Simons: 01600 891069
www.canoehire.com
Mar-Oct: 9am-6pm
Found on the opposite bank of the River Wye from Symonds Yat Rock. Different sized canoes and kayaks can be rented from 1 hour to a week. They can also transport boats up river, so you just paddle down. Camping available.

Wyedean Canoe and Adventure Centre
Holly Barn, Symonds Yat Rock, Coleford, GL16 7NZ
01594 833238, www.wyedean.co.uk
Easter-Oct: daily 8.30am-5pm, winter by appt.
As well as offering canoe and kayak hire, this outdoor centre offers a vast range of activities for adults and children 8+yrs. On offer: canoeing, kayaking, raft building, abseiling, climbing, high and low ropes courses, team building, caving and archery. They cater for individuals and groups (schools, youth groups, guides and scouts). It is essential to book in advance.

Wye Pursuits
Riverside House, Kerne Bridge, Nr Ross, HR9 5QX
01600 891199
www.wye-pursuits.co.uk
Mar-Nov: daily, weather dependent
Large range of outdoor activities on offer as well as canoe and kayak hire. Activities for groups of 8, families welcome. On offer: climbing, abseiling, caving and white water rafting. For all water activities you must be able to swim 50 metres.

PAINTBALLING

www.paintball.com
For general information

Bristol Outdoor Pursuits Centre
Hamburger Hill, Common Wood, Hunstrete, Nr Pensford, Bristol, BS39 4NT
0800 9803980
www.bristoloutdoor.co.uk

1st Twilight Zone
Coast Road, Portishead
0800 915 4289
www.tzpaintball.co.uk
Offer junior days for 12yrs+ in woodland based paintball site.

MARTIAL ARTS

Karate
Clifton College Sports Centre
32 College Rd, BS8
Tim:07980 863061
Fri 7pm-8pm

Kick Boxing
Clifton College Sports Centre
Jay: 07970 236945
Thu 7pm-9pm

Ningisu
Clifton College Sports Centre
Michelle: 07776 202011
Mon & Wed 8pm-9pm

Matt Fiddes Academies
Call for venue
08707 422118
Black belt academy

RUGBY

There is a great tradition of rugby in the south west and this is reflected in the number of clubs offering junior coaching and match play.

Bath R F Club
01225 323 200, www.bathrugby.com
Contact: Jimmy Dean, Community Dev. Manager
Has a thriving community programme with development for talented players.

Bristol Shoguns R F Club
0117 331 1474, www.bristolshoguns.co.uk
Contact: Nichola Goodrick-Turner
The Shoguns have an active community programme in local schools & sports clubs, as well as holiday rugby camps for 12-14 yrs.

Clifton Rugby Club
Station Road, Cribbs Causeway, Bristol
www.cliftonrugby.com
Sue Ingram: 0117 962 9720
Sun 10am-12pm
£40 per season (£30 for sibling)
Training for U12's to U19's

Bristol Saracens R F Club
Bakewell Memorial Ground, Station Road, Cribbs Causeway, Bristol
0117 950 0037, www.bristolsaracensrfc.co.uk
Wed 6.30pm
Offers training and competitive match play for U12's through to U17's.

SKATEBOARDING AND SKATING

Bristol has an active and competitive skateboarding scene. Although there is no outdoor skate park in Bristol, there is enthusiasm and expertise in abundance. The area around the Lloyds TSB building is world famous for its skaters, featured in magazines and attracting professional skaters from the UK and overseas. Hone your skills here and you just might be invited to join the 50:50 skate team.

50:50
16 Park Row, Clifton, Bristol
0117 914 7783
www.fiftyfiftyskateboardsupplies.co.uk
One of Bristol's best skate shops has its own team, which has won the UK Shop Team Challenge two years running.
Membership strictly by word of mouth and invitation.

Apex Leisure and Wildlife Park
Marine Drive, Burnham-on-Sea
www.sedgemoor.gov.uk
Their skate park is in the south east of The Apex. It is a floodlit, open access facility with half and quarter pipes, and box ramp with grind and curb rails.

The Old Bus Depot
Alcester Road, Moseley
0121 442 2425
www.epicskateparks.com
Birmingham's epic skate park is recommended by 50:50. Keen female beginners might like to check out their Powderpuff Girls' Skate Academy, offering free skate classes, boards, helmets and pads.

Cardiff Skate Park,
Rhymney Riverbridge Road, Cardiff
www.cardiffskatepark.com

Dreamfields
Hamilton Road, Taunton, Somerset
www.dreamfields.org.uk
This site exists with the support of the local church and its members, so a certain level of behaviour is expected. Helmet, knee pads and wrist guards must be worn.

Skate & Ride
74 Avon Street, St Philips, Bristol, BS2 0PS
0117 907 9995
Mon-Fri 9am–11pm, Sat 9am–12 midnight, Sun 10am–10pm

Chapter 5

This indoor skate park has wooden ramps for BMX bikes, roller blades and skateboards. Skates, padding and helmets are all available for hire.

Useful website
www.skatepark.co.uk
Lists events and parks. Always on the lookout for photos for their gallery, contact@skatepark.co.uk

Horfield Sports Centre & Lawrence Weston Sports Centre
Roller Discos & roller skating sessions
See central Reference Section

SKIING, TOBOGGANING, SNOWBOARDING & SURFING

Gloucester Ski and Snowboarding Centre
Robinswood Hill, Madson Lane, Gloucester, GL4 6EA
08702 400375 (24hr)
www.gloucesterski.com
Ski schools for up to 16yrs, private and group skiing lessons, and snowboarding for the over 12's.

High Action Avon Ski Centre
Lyncombe Drive, Churchill, N. Somerset. BS25 5PQ
01934 842 335, www.highaction.co.uk
Ski schools and holiday classes available.

Simon Tucker's Surfing Academy
Porthcawl, Mid Glamorgan
07815 289761
£25/2hr session
Former British Champion, Simon Tucker coaches the Welsh U16's team and his academy teaches beginners who can swim 100 metres. Many pupils come from the Bristol area.

SWIMMING

For information on swimming pools in your area see central Reference Section.
For those keen, competent, aspiring Olympians among you who are after serious training and competition, there is a thriving competitive swim scene in the region.

Backwell Swimming Club
www.backwellswimmingclub.me.uk
Training and competitive swimming in friendly galas and larger sponsored tournaments. The club encourages interested swimmers to come along to the club, view the facilities and talk with the coaching staff.

Bristol Henleaze Swimming Club
0117 924 5057
www.bristolhenleazesc.org.uk
Contact: Judith Bush
A competitive club for boys and girls. Many will have swum their way through the Development squads reaching the Senior squad at about the age of 12. Club training sessions at various locations.

Soundwell Swimming and Diving Club
Kingswood Leisure Centre
www.soundwellswim.org.uk
The swimming and diving sections of the club are separate. See website for training sessions for the competitive swim team. For Diving, see above.

Thornbury Swimming Club
www.southglos.gov.uk/sportsdevelopment/clubs/swimming

Henleaze Swimming Club,
Henleaze Lake, Lake Road, Henleaze
PO Box 140, Westbury on Trym, Bristol, BS10 6YD
(send SAE)
For those who prefer natural surroundings, this former quarry with its rolling lawns, leafy outlook and diving boards is hard to beat. It is a members only club. Applications by post.

Useful Websites
Amateur Swimming Association
www.britishswimming.org/clubs

UK Sports Directory
www.sportslinks.info

LIFEGUARDING COURSES

Rookie Lifeguard Qualification
Bristol North Swimming Pool
0117 951 5868, www.bristolnorthsc.co.uk
Training includes lifeguard rescue, throw and tow, first aid and resuscitation. The course is open to swimmers, 10–15yrs who can swim at least 400 metres

National Pool Lifeguard Qualification
Winterbourne School & David Lloyd Centre (open to non-members)
07714 961508
Contact: Mandy Osborne

This 33-hour training programme over 8–12 weeks is open to competent swimmers 16+ yrs and leads to a professional qualification. Cost is dependent on the venue.

TENNIS

Tennis is played in tennis clubs, private members' sports clubs and public parks all over the region. For listings of private sports clubs see Time Out for Adults chapter.

City Tennis Programme
Bristol Tennis Development Officer
0117 962 6723
Contact: David Hudgell
Bristol has a LTA accredited City Tennis Programme spanning the city from Lawrence Weston in the north to Withywood in the south. Some 21 schools benefit from coaching initiatives in term time. There are also new clubs set up as part of this initiative, intended to make tennis more affordable to many new players. Check out the coaching and play sessions at:

St George's Park Coaching
Sun 2.30pm–3.30pm, 10–16yrs, £2

Eastville Park Tennis Club
Sat 10am–11am, 10–16yrs £2

St Paul's Tennis Club
St Paul's Sports Academy, Newfoundland Rd, BS5
Wed 5pm–6pm, 10–16yrs, £1.50

Further clubs are planned for Horfield Park and Canford Park.

Municipal tennis courts

Bristol City Councils Tennis Courts
0117 922 2789 hireline

Tennis clubs

Most tennis clubs have junior coaching programmes, which are open to non-members.

Bristol Lawn Tennis and Squash Club
Redland Green, Redland, Bristol
0117 973 1139
Contact: John Carver

Bristol Central TC
Derby Road, St Andrew's Park, Bristol
0117 967 8094

Clifton TC
Beaufort Road, Clifton, Bristol
0117 968 2653

Coombe Dingle Tennis Centre
Coombe Dingle Sports Complex, Coombe Lane, Stoke Bishop, Bristol
0117 962 6718
Peter Bendall: 07973 641132
Mon 6.30pm–7.30pm, 9-13yrs
Sat 11.30am-12.30pm, boys 11-14yrs
Sat 12.30pm-1.30pm, girls 11-14yrs
Sun 11.30am–12.30pm, mixed teens
£73 for 10 week course (£65 for members)
Times and prices may vary, call for details.

Cotham Park TC
71 Redland Road, Cotham, Bristol
0117 923 7500
Contact: Peter Coniglio

Henleaze TC
Tennessee Grove, off Springfield Grove, Henleaze
01275 543449
Contact: Ondrej Toman

Kings TC
Maplemeade, Kings Drive, Bishopston, Bristol
0117 942 7667, www.kings-tennis.net
Contact: Scott Dobson
Invitation squads held after school, Mon–Fri & Sun
Sat 10am–11.30am, drop-in, intermediates
Sat 11.30am–1pm, drop-in, teenage players
£1.50/hr
The word on the street is that this is a vibrant place to be for aspiring Wimbledon champions. Abilities span from absolute beginners to national level competitors. You don't have to be a member to benefit from any of these coaching sessions. The intermediate session is for those who have not played much tennis.

Knowle TC
Wells Road, Knowle, Bristol
01761 462779
Contact: Richard Douglas

Westbury Park TC
Russell Grove, Westbury Park, Bristol
0117 962 1964
Contact: Bryan Smith

Useful tennis info

Tennis in the Parks
www.bristol-city.gov.uk/
View this website if you are over 16 and wish to try one of the coaching programmes held at Horfield Tennis Club, Canford Park, Redcatch Park and St George's Park.

Bristol Box League
0117 923 8896
Contact: Julie McCarthy
Why not enter this league, which operates all year in 6–8 week periods during which players organise their own matches against others in their box. This league is not club based and is for players of all abilites up to 16yrs who want to play friendly competitive tennis.

SAILING & CANOEING

Bristol Avon Sailing Club
01225 873472
www.bristol-avon-sailing.org.uk
This family-friendly dinghy sailing club is based on the Avon between Bath and Bristol. The club runs a RYA approved 6 week sailing course (boats provided) around Easter.

Baltic Wharf Sailing School
c/o 56 Bath Road, Longwell Green
0117 907 3019,
www.balticwharf.com
Offers junior sailing at Bristol Harbour.

Bristol Canoe Club
Baltic Wharf, Bristol Docks
0117 965 3724
www.bristolcanoeclub.org.uk
Apr–Dec: Thu 6pm
Bristol South Pool, Bedminster
Pool sessions and polo training
Dec-Mar: Wed 8pm

This club, which has a youth section for keen paddlers, is active in white water trips, slalom, polo and surfing. They offer occasional formal beginners courses.

Chew Valley Lake Sailing Club
01225 783246,
www.chewvalleysailing.org.uk
Contact: Kevin Podger, Youth Co-ordinator

Portishead Yacht and Sailing Club
The Club House, Sugar Loaf Beach, Belton Road, Portishead
01275 847049

Thornbury Sailing Club
Church Rd, Oldbury-on-Severn
www.thornburysc.org.uk
01454 281947

Weston Bay Yacht Club
Uphill Beach, Links Road, Weston-super-Mare
01934 413366
Also see Outdoor Pursuits, above

SCUBA DIVING
There are a number of sub aqua clubs that meet in the south west but some words of warning before you go and order your wet suit. It can be very expensive to kit yourself out. Many clubs will not train minors (due to child protection issues) unless their parents are also members of the club and involved in the training process. Some clubs are open only to over 18s, and those under 14 may struggle with the theory involved. That said, kit can be bought second hand, if you know where to look, and there are diving schools where you can learn. And it seems that once you get the scuba diving bug, you're hooked.

Bristol Channel Divers at Happy Landings
Wells Road, Knowle
01934 844909
Contact: Mr J Prince
Mon 9pm

Severnside Sub Aqua Club
Henbury Pool
01823 490046
Contact: Andy Moll
Mon 8pm

Underwater Future Dive School
1 Pontispool Cottages, Pontispool, Norton Fitzwarren, Taunton, Somerset, TA4 1BG
01823 461 759
This diving school, run by Ron and Vicky Moore, welcomes aspiring teenage divers.

Yate Sub Aqua Club
01454 544687, www.yatebsac.co.uk
Contact: Andy Wallis

British Sub Aqua Club
0151 350 6200, www.bsac.com
www.southglos.gov.uk/sportsdevelopment/clubs
To find a subaqua club near you that welcomes under 18's.

ARTS & ENTERTAINMENT

ARTS & CRAFTS

Creative

B'delicious
2 Triangle South, Clifton, Bristol
0117 927 2567
This little gem, tucked away in the far corner of the Triangle, offers you the opportunity to be creative with beads – make yourself some jewellery or a decorative frame, hairband, belt, or if you're having a princess moment, a tiara. Be as imaginative and as individual as you like with, or, if you prefer, without the expert help and advice of staff.

Make your Mark
97 Whiteladies Road, Clifton, Bristol
0117 974 4257, www.makeyourmarkbristol.co.uk
Chose from the huge selection of pottery and make your mark upon it! Chat, paint, munch and drink – in this art café. See advertisement in Activities 0-12 Years chapter.

Bristol City Museum
Queens Road, Clifton, Bristol
0117 922 3571
www.bristol-city.gov.uk
Holds holiday workshops.

COOKERY

Quartier Vert
85 Whiteladies Road, Bristol
0117 904 6679
This creative cookery school offers workshops and courses.

D J COURSE

The Mark Davis DJ Academy
07770 940 930
Mark Davis runs DJ courses at over 40 venues across the south west. Most are held in schools, but evening classes are planned for 2004.

ENTERTAINMENT CENTRES

Laserquest Bristol
The Old Fire Station, Silver Street, Bristol, BS1 2PY
0117 949668,
www.laserquest.info
Daily 10am–10pm
This is an interactive laser game suitable for teenagers. See also Brean Leisure Park in Out & About in the West Country chapter.

Harry's Quasar
Harry's Amusements, All Saints St, Bristol, BS1 2LZ
0117 927 7671
www.laserarena.co.uk
Daily 10am–10pm
£2.50 per game, £6 for 3 games

ENTERTAINMENT/INTERACTIVE
There are many cinemas, film clubs and internet cafés across the region – here are a few of them that have proven teenage appeal.

CINEMAS

The Orpheus
7 Northumbria Drive, Henleaze, Bristol
0117 962 3301 (general enquiries)
0117 962 1644 (programme details)
Deserves a mention as one of a rare breed of independent cinemas that has survived the multiplex competition. You can even hire it for a private screening of your favourite film!

Cinephiles at the Watershed
1 Canon's Road, Harbourside, Bristol
0117 927 5100
Meet once a month on a Monday evening to discuss three films from Watershed's recent programme. Some of the films chosen may be 15's or 18's, check your eligibility with the box office.

FILM

Keeping It Reel
Watershed, 1 Canon's Road, Harbourside, Bristol
0117 927 5100
£3, 12-15yrs
Hands-on workshops in film-making skills such as animation, scriptwriting and editing.

Held every couple of months on Saturday afternoons.

Bath Film Festival
01225 401149, www.bathfilmfestival.org
Takes place in the autumn. Check the website for film making workshops for 14-18yrs.

INTERNET CAFES

Internet Exchange
23-25 Queens Road, Clifton, Bristol
0117 929 8026
Mon–Fri 8.30am–8pm, Sat 9am–7pm, Sun 11am–6pm
Training for novices. Snacks and drinks. Clean reasonable and comfortable.

onCoffee.net
11 Christmas Steps
0117 925 1100
Mon-Fri 8am–8pm, Sat 10am–6pm
Internet access and great coffee on offer here.

Public libraries
Don't forget these excellent sources of internet access. See Out & About in Bristol chapter.

VOLUNTARY & SPECIFIC INTEREST GROUPS

VOLUNTARY GROUPS

The closer you look, the more there is for you to do with your time. There are plenty of organisations just waiting for your help, either on a regular basis or during the holidays. Not only will you be doing something useful and fun, you will also be developing your CV.

BTVC-Avon
0117 929 1624, www.btvc.org
A local group, looking for young volunteers to help them improve the environment by undertaking practical conservation work.

Bristol Zoo Volunteers
Volunteer Services, Bristol Zoo Gardens, Clifton, Bristol, BS8 3HA
0117 974 7300

Volunteers over 18 can become involved in fund raising, animal encounters, enclosure talks and outreach events. You will need to commit a minimum of 6 hrs every fortnight for a year.

Charity shops
Most local charities and charity shops are grateful for volunteers.

Millennium Volunteers
01225 318879, www.mvonline.gov.uk
Contact: Harri Harrison
This national scheme, promotes sustained volunteering, for those aged between 16–24yrs. "It's about building on what you're into and making a difference, to yourself and the community." There are a variety of projects accessed in Bristol by Young Bristol Action.

Young Bristol Action
32 Bond Street, Broadmead, Bristol
0117 907 1010, www.youngbristol.com
This group, with its city centre drop-in, offers young people aged 13–19 the chance to volunteer (via Millennium Volunteers) through placements and youth-led projects. You may find yourself involved in the city's social and celebration events.

St John Ambulance Brigade
The Harry Crook Centre, Raleigh Road, Bedminster, Bristol, BS3 1AP
0117 953 3880, www.avonsja.org.uk
The UK's leading first aid, transport and care charity. See also Action Clubs, below.

HOLIDAY VOLUNTARY WORK SCHEMES

The schemes below offer a variety of unique work experience. The courses are residential (suitable for Duke of Edinburgh's Gold Award) and the prices quoted are per week, including food and basic accommodation.

British Trust For Conservation Volunteers
01491 821600, www.btcv.org.uk
16+yrs, £30-60pw

Canal Camps
01923 711114, www.wrg.org.uk
17+yrs, £35pw

Cathedral Camps
01525 716237

www.cathedralcamps.org.uk
16–30yrs, £65pw

National Trust Acorn Holidays
0870 429 2429, www.nationaltrust.org.uk/volunteers
17-28yrs, £55pw

VSO Undergraduate Scheme
www.vso.org.uk
See 18 and Beyond, below.

World Challenge Expeditions
020 8728 7200, www.world-challenge.co.uk
16-24yrs
Specialise in the provision of leadership, teamwork and personal development training. If you are up for a challenge in your school/college holiday, choose from a variety of voluntary and paid placements in 12 different countries. A fundamental part of every WCE programme is to raise a proportion of the cost of the expedition yourself.

SPECIFIC INTEREST GROUPS

ARCHAEOLOGY

Young Archaeologists Club
www.britarch.ac.uk/yac
8-16yrs
Branches all over the UK. See their website for activities and details of your nearest branch.

Bath & Bristol Young Archaeologists Club
joannamellors@blueyonder.co.uk
Membership £3 pp, £5 family (occasional additional charge for hall hire etc)
Meet once a month at venues across the West. Meetings include dig visits, survey work, studying original documents and aerial photographs. Events include a mediaeval Bristol trail, reconstruction drawing, gladiator school workshop, and a roman picnic. Some events are for members, others have more of a family flavour.

Bristol and Avon Archaeological Society
www.digitalbristol.org/members/baas/
The winter lecture series, summer walks and visits and occasional fieldwork will appeal to older enthusiasts.

Bristol City Museum
Queen's Road, Clifton
0117 922 3571, www.bristol-city.gov.uk/museums

Holds a number of events during the year with an archaeological theme.

Chedworth Roman Villa
Yarnworth, Cheltenham, Glos, GL54 3LJ
01242 890256
Holds archaeology activity weekends, national archaeology days, summer lectures and training excavations. See Out & About in the West Country chapter.

Useful websites
www.britarch.ac.uk/archabroad
A searchable directory of organisations involved in British archaeology.
www.archaeovolunteers.org
For those who are looking to volunteer their services.

ARCHITECTURE

The Architecture Centre, Narrow Quay, Bristol
0117 922 1540, www.arch-centre.demon.uk
Membership is open to anyone with an interest in architecture. Events include lectures, trips and exhibitions.

GEOGRAPHY

Young Geographers
Royal Geographical Society, 1 Kensington Gore, London, SW7 2AR
0207 591 3086, www.rgs.org
14-24yrs or in full time education
You will need a Fellow of the RGS or a head of department to sign your application form for this society. Alternatively see if your school or college has Educational Membership.

ACTION & SOCIAL CLUBS

ACTION CLUBS
There are numerous groups across the region where young people can meet, socialise and get involved in a whole range of activities with other like minded people. Apart from being very sociable, these clubs also provide young

people with the opportunity to acquire and develop a diverse and exciting range of skills.

Air Training Corps (ATC)
The Tower, Westbury College, College Road,
Westbury on Trym, Bristol
0117 959 3269/904 8338
Tue/Thu/Fri 7pm-9.30pm
Contact: Flt Lt Philip Lowndes
13-19yrs

An exciting variety of activities on offer to both male and female cadets: night exercises, ambush, camouflage, gliding, shooting, flying, hiking, Duke of Edinburgh Award scheme and sports. There are 28 active ATC squadrons in the Bristol/Gloucester area, for one in your area see contact details above. Also view one of the squadron's websites:
www.2442squadron.fsnet.co.uk

Manor Farm Boys' Club
Wellington Hill, Horfield, Bristol, BS7 8ST
0117 924 0560
Mon-Fri 6pm
8-18yrs

Affiliated to the National Association of Clubs for Young People. It draws its membership from many different districts across the city.

Sea Cadets
South West Area Sea Cadets
HMS Flying Fox, Winterstoke Road, Bristol, BS3 2NS
0117 953 1991/953 2009
www.sea-cadets.org
13-18yrs, £2 pw

A nautical youth charity which offers serious fun. Activities range from sailing/boating, camps, engineering, music and sporting events.

St John Ambulance
The Harry Crook Centre, Raleigh Road, Bedminster,
Bristol, BS3 1AP
0117 953 3880, www.avon.sja.org.uk
10-18yrs, membership free

As a cadet in their youth division you will learn first aid, communication skills, sports and administration skills. You will also have public duties, providing essential first aid cover at events around the country.

Girlguiding & Scouting
See Activities 0-12 Years chapter.

YOUTH AND SOCIAL CLUBS

These clubs are provided mainly by either your local authority or by church and faith based groups.

Local Authority youth groups
0117 927 6301
customerservicesetl@bristol-city.gov.uk

Bristol City Council runs a countywide programme of projects, activities and events accessed mostly through the 16 youth projects it has in the city.

Youth club members may get involved with the City of Bristol Young People's Forum, whose aim is to get young people involved in decision making in the city. (Young People's Forum, 32 Bond Street, Broadmead Tel: 0117 903 1330.) Projects also involve Bristol's twin cities and International Youth Work, giving members experience in another country.

For details of youth centres outside Bristol:

Bath and NE Somerset
Youth and Community team
01225 396980

North Somerset
Youth in the Community Service
01934 644075

South Gloucestershire
01454 868537

Holiday schemes
Generally based at the youth clubs. They are open to anyone, and offer activities like ice-skating and days out to Alton Towers at subsidised rates.

Faith based youth groups
Most faiths have active youth groups, some of which promote a particular culture or language. For further information see Activities 0-12 Years.

DANCE & THEATRE SKILLS

Bristol has a great theatrical tradition. Not surprisingly there is no shortage of dance and drama groups in the city and its surrounding area.

DANCE

Bristol Community Dance Centre
Jacobswell Road, Hotwells, Bristol, BS8 1DX.
0117 929 2118, www.bristoldancecentre.org.uk
£2.80 per class, no booking required

A popular dance centre which celebrated its 25th birthday in 2002. A wide and varied programme.

Youth Dance Company
Directed by Julia Thorneycroft
Tue 5pm–6.20pm (11-15yrs)

Learn contemporary techniques and creative skills which build towards an end of term performance. "Enthusiasm, commitment and a sense of adventure is vital!"

The Fandango Community Dance Show takes place at the end of term and showcases all the work undertaken at the centre.

The Centre also has a vast array of adult classes which appeal to those aged 14+yrs e.g. Hip hop, Thur 6.15pm–7.15pm.

Bristol School of Dancing
The Studio, Lansdown Road, Clifton, BS8 3AB
01278 434081

All aspects of dance are catered for. Teenagers with or without previous dance experience are welcome to attend, provided that they are enthusiastic and committed. Classes are held in Bristol, Bath, Backwell, Clevedon, Nailsea and Portishead. This school has close links with the Bristol School of Performing Arts, listed below.

344 Dance Centre
Alexandra Park, Fishponds, Bristol
0117 965 5660
www.344dance.freeserve.co.uk
Branches at Bedminster, Bradley Stoke and Wick.

Classes for all ages include ballet, tap, modern, drama, pilates, Irish, hip-hop and flamenco. Some classes need to be pre-booked, some suitable for 14+yrs, check prior

to attending. Full time courses are available for 16+yrs leading to careers in dance.

Danceblast at the Tobacco Factory
See Theatre Skills, below

THEATRE SKILLS

These groups incorporate a combination of some or all of the following: dance, acting, singing and behind the scenes production skills.

Bristol Arts and Music Service of Bristol City Council
Drama
Horfield Methodist Church
Sat 9.30am–11.30am, 8–16yrs
£40 per term

Covers all aspects of theatre skills, dance and singing.

Dance
0117 903 1297
Contact: Arts Co-ordinator

The 'Stages' dance performances takes place in January at Bristol Old Vic Theatre and The Victoria Rooms and in the spring at the Hippodrome. All are co-ordinated by the Arts Section of the BAMS. Talented dancers are referred to the Kenesis dance group.

Bristol Amateur Operatic Society Junior Section
Rooftop Studios, 47 Feeder Road,
John Griffin: 0788 7906075
Dan Masters: 0117 949 2738
Fri 7.30pm-9.45pm
Annual membership £25
11-18yrs

Membership is by audition, held before rehearsals start. There are currently about 50 members, boys are particularly welcome! The group's main annual production, a musical, is performed at The Redgrave Theatre in October. A revue takes place at The Newman Hall in May.

Bristol Amateur Operatic Society Senior Section
Address as above
Anne Rees: 01454 772167
Thu eve
16+yrs, annual membership £50

Their main show is performed at The Victoria Rooms in the spring. Other shows during the year are performed at various venues, including the society's own 70 seat theatre.

Bristol Musical Youth Productions (BMYP)

St Ursula's School, Brecon Road, Henleaze, Bristol
Bernadette Tucker: 01275 842563
Fri 7.30pm–10pm
12–18yrs, Annual membership £50

Auditions are held in December. A high level of parental input is expected (costume making/scenery building/painting and selling the 25 tickets allocated to each member for each production). All to ensure that the show goes on! The main show, a musical, is performed in October at The Redgrave Theatre, with a lower key production in the spring which is performed at various venues. This is a high profile, sociable group.

Bristol School of Performing Arts

The Elmgrove Centre, Redland Rd,
John Redgrave; 01278 434080/081
£75 per term

Open to all. Another high profile group, providing extras for shows at the Hippodrome and for TV. LAMDA exams may also be taken. The group has close links with Bristol School of Dancing, listed above.

HTV television workshops

The TV Centre, Bath Road, Bristol
0117 972 2497
Contact: Lisa Ruthven
lisa.ruthven@htv-west.co.uk
www.htvwest.co.uk (click on 'htvworkshop')
9-26yrs

Workshops provide experience to young people in front of and behind the scenes in film, TV, radio and theatre.

Drama workshop

Workshops run throughout the year teaching skills required to work in theatre, radio, TV and film. They regularly cast members in programmes and films.

Production

The production side of the workshop meets on a weekly and project basis. Members learn about all aspects of putting film together from writing, to directing, producing, camerawork, lighting and sound ... and will produce short films with actors from the Drama Workshop. Workshops meet in term time as follows:

Monday (Production Skills) 16+	6 – 8pm
Tuesday/Wednesday 13–16yrs	5 – 7pm
16–18yrs	7 – 9pm
Thursday 18–26yrs	6 – 8pm

The cost is £60 per term payable in advance to secure your place. Not surprisingly there is a waiting list!

QEH Youth Theatre

0117 939 6918
Contact: Debi Temple
Sat 10.30am-12.30pm (term time)
11-16yrs, £5 per session

Open to anyone.

The Tobacco Factory

Raleigh Road, Southville, Bristol, BS3 1TF

The Tobacco Factory is home to a number of dance and theatre groups:

Bristol Academy of Performing Arts (BAPA)

0117 902 6606
www.baparts.org.uk
16+yrs, £4 per session

Holds open classes on Mondays (term time). Practical sessions in musical theatre styles, dance and ensemble singing. The dance and ensemble classes use linked material for the benefit of those attending both, but they work equally well as standalone sessions.

Dance	4.15 – 5.15pm
	5.15 – 6.15pm
Ensemble	5.15 – 6.15pm
	6.15 – 7.15pm

A full time Music Theatre HND course is available for 18+yrs.

Danceblast (formerly Rocktap)

The Teenage Workshop
Mirrored Studio
Anne Taylor: 0117 964 6195
Sun 2-5pm
14+yrs, £5 per session

This workshop, which includes hip-hop,attracts boys and girls. You do not have to attend the whole session. An annual performance takes place, usually at QEH Theatre.

Middle Eastern dance classes

Monday Classes
Karine Butchart: 01373 466015
14+yrs, £4-6 per session

Beginners	6.30pm
Improvers/Intermediates	7.30pm
Intermediate/Advanced	8.45pm

Wednesday Classes
Medea Mahdavi: 0117 963 329
14+yrs, £4.50 per session

Beginners   7pm
Advanced   8pm

Teenagers welcome at these classes please
contact the teachers prior to attending.

USEFUL CONTACTS AND WEB SITES

The National Association of Youth Theatres
01325 363330, www.nayt.org.uk
Information on drama clubs and regional
youth theatres.

National Youth Music Theatre
0207 734 7478, www.nymt.org.uk
The UK's leading youth music theatre
company.

The National Youth Theatre
0207 281 3863, www.nyt.org.uk
Open to all young people, 13-21yrs, subject
to audition.

See Activities 0-12 Years chapter for other
dance & drama classes

MUSIC
Local authorities in and around Bristol have
music services providing music tuition in
schools and supporting many instrumental
and choral ensembles.

BRISTOL SCHOOLS MUSIC SERVICE
0117 903 1370
Informal auditions are held in June and July
at various locations across the city. Successful
musicians and singers will join one of the five
centres.

West Music Centre
Portway School
Mon 7.30pm–9pm
West Bristol Concert Band and Big Band,
Grade 5 and over.

South Music Centre
Hengrove School
Sat 9.30am-12.30pm
Wind and String Orchestra Band and
ensembles for Grades1-2+.

Choral Centre
Redland Park United Reform Church, Whiteladies Rd
Fri 6–8pm   Snr Girls Chamber Choir, 12–18yrs
Fri 7.30–8.30pm   Boys 'Changed Voice' Choir, U18's
Open to all interested singers with enthusiasm
and commitment.

Senior Music Centre
Henbury School
Sat 9.30am–12.30pm
Bands and orchestras for Grade 1+.
Chamber Orchestra for advanced string
players Grade 7+.

Percussion Centre
Henbury School
Wed 5pm–8pm
Individual lessons for senior pupils.

NORTH SOMERSET MUSIC SERVICE
01934 832 395
Operates the North Somerset Centre for
Young Musicians and co-ordinates the West
of England Schools' Symphony Orchestra and
West of England Schools' Symphonic Wind
Band.

North Somerset Centre for Young Musicians
Junior Centre
St Andrew's Junior School, Congresbury
Sat 9.15am–12.15pm
Venue for a variety of string and wind
ensembles for all ranges of ability, and a
Gospel Choir.

Senior Centre
Clevedon Community School
Sat 9am-12pm
Various orchestral groups Grade 5+ including
the Symphony Orchestra, Concert Band and
Swing Band.

Evening Ensembles
01934 832395
Jazz Orchestra and various other ensembles
for guitar, percussion, clarinet, brass and flute.

SOUTH GLOUCESTERSHIRE MUSIC SERVICE
01454 863147

Kingswood Area Music Centre
Kingsfield School

Sat 9.30am–12pm	Strings and Concert Band
Mon 7.30pm–9.15pm	Big Band
Wed 4pm	Junior Choir

Thornbury Area Music Service
Marlwood School
Saturday 9.30pm–12pm
String Group, Wind Band and Orchestra

Yate Area Music Centre
Brimsham Green School

Sat 9.30am–12pm	String Groups and Band
Wed 4pm	Junior Choir

CONTEMPORY BANDS

If you've got a rock band but need a vocalist or place to play, or you play lead guitar and are looking for a band, most musical instrument shops have notice boards where you can advertise.

Please remember when reponding to or placing an advertisement you should ensure that the advertiser/responders are genuine. You can do this by obtaining references prior to meeting in a public place. Take a friend with you and always let your parent/guardian know of the meeting.

See Music Shops in Shopping chapter.

NIGHT LIFE

Bristol with its huge student population, has a lively night life and music scene, but there's plenty out there for under 18's too.

CLUB SCENE

Bristol Academy
Frogmore Street, Bristol
0117 927 9227
Under 18's allowed in only on gig nights, which are generally once a week. A wide

variety of bands and solo artists perform on a huge stage and there is a large dance floor which can get very crowded. A crew of stewards ensure a strict door policy. Alcohol is sold only with photo ID.

The Works
15 Nelson Street, Bristol
0117 929 2658
£6 in advance
Once a month this club holds a 13-17's night from 7pm-12am (or 10.30/11pm school nights). The night features R&B, pop and chart music, plus a live act. Their special foam parties are particularly popular, if messy, affairs! The club operates a strict door policy including breath checks. No alcohol on sale, just soft drinks.

CONCERT/MUSIC VENUES

Anson Rooms
Bristol University Students' Union, Queens Road, Clifton, Bristol
0117 954 5830, www.ansonrooms.co.uk
This great venue has a wide range of live acts and is open to 14's and over.

Colston Hall
Colston Street, Bristol
0117 922 3686, www.colstonhall.org
The place to see big bands who come to the city, as well as big name comedy acts.

Hippodrome
St Augustine's Parade, Bristol
0870 607 7500
The place to see bands and West End musicals, ballet and opera.

The Prom
26 Gloucester Road, Bishopston, Bristol
0117 942 7319, www.theprom.co.uk
This music bar and café is a popular venue for teenagers after school or at weekends before 8pm only. Live bands sadly don't come on until 9pm.

SHOPPING

There is a chapter dedicated to shopping which will provide you with loads of useful information. The listings, below, have particular teen appeal.

CLOTHING

The Galleries, Broadmead

Cassidy,
Union Gallery, 0117 929 3273
Surf, skate and urban fashion. Clothes, accessories, watches, jewellery, hats, belts and shoes.

Legends Surf Shop plc
53 Union Street, 0117 933 8500
Skate clothes (particularly for boys) and equipment (decks, trucks etc), girlswear is not so skatey. Beachwear in season. Accessories include watches, badges, patches, key chains, sunglasses and hats.

Quiksilver
Union Gallery, 0117 929 2114
Surf, snow and skate clothing.

TMS
Union Gallery, 0117 922 7990
Surf, snow, skate and fashion clothes. Large selection of accessories including snowboards, boots and bindings.

Park Street

BS8
Park Street, 0117 930 4836
A large, funky store selling everything from corsets and basques to petticoated polka dot skirts. The wide range of trousers can be altered at a tailor across the road (for a small fee). Upstairs you'll find boys' clothes and a small area devoted to prom dresses. A dressmaker is on hand all year round to assist and alter the dress of your dreams for that all important prom night.

The Clothing Federation
56 Park Street, 0117 929 9889
This shop with its dimmed lighting is packed with accessories and clothes. Check out the jewellery, plastic and metal rings, earrings, necklaces, bracelets and bandannas.

Dna
24 Park Street, 0117 934 9173
If you like all things pink and feminine then this girly shop is for you. Inexpensive skirts, strappy tops and boob tubes. Check out their interesting fitting rooms and good sales.

Fat Face
86 Park Street, 0117 930 4357
Also at: 4-5 Green Street, Bath
www.fatface.co.uk
A surfer sanctuary and for those who just like wearing surf clothes. Quality clothes and great sales!

50:50
16 Park Row, Clifton, 0117 914 7783
www.fiftyfiftyskateboardsupplies.co.uk
"A skater's paradise", everything for the bona fide skater or wannabes. Clothing and footwear, to boards and accessories.

Rollermania
62 Park Row, Clifton, 0117 927 9981
Skate clothes and skating equipment.

Shark Bite Surf Shop
68 Park Row, 0117 929 9211
Surf kit for on and off the beach, and jewellery too.

White Stuff
64 Queens Road, 0117 929 0100
www.whitestuff.com
Unisex ski and surf clothing. Quite expensive but all well made, hard wearing, funky and fashionable. Great sales. Mail order also available.

The Mall

Cribbs Causeway
If it's fashion clothes you're looking for, then there are plenty of shops here for you including H&M, Miss Selfridge, New Look, Tammy, Top Shop/Top Man. Don't forget John Lewis sells skate, surf, snow and fashionwear and Per Una at Marks and Spencer is worth a look.

Free Spirit
0117 950 2575
Surf, snow and skate fashion, plus a full range of accessories and equipment. Beach and ski wear available in season. Adult sizes only, but the slim fit should fit those aged 14+ yrs.

Route One
0117 959 2696
Also at: 9 Broad Street & 20 Wansdyke Bsns Centre, Bath
Small, but packed with skate clothes, equipment and accessories.

Henleaze

Crazy Octopus
16 Kellaway Avenue, 0117 923 2255
www.beachshack.co.uk
Surf, beachwear and water sports specialists. Wide range of wet suits, surfboards and watersport accessories.

Bargains
For the individualists among you, there are bargains to be had. Charity shops found all over the region are a great source of good clothes at bargain prices. With a careful eye and a lot of patience, you should be able to kit yourself out without spending a fortune. See St Nicholas' Market in Shopping & Services chapter.

SPORT ACCESSORIES

Bike
Queens Avenue, BS8, 0117 929 3500
Bike heaven. Enough said.

Easy Runner
6 Horfield Road, 0117 929 7787
If it's running shoes you're after, then make sure you check this shop out.

Gilesports
The Mall, Cribbs Causeway
0117 950 9445
12-14 Merchant Street, Broadmead, Bristol
0117 925 1321
Sovereign Centre, Weston-super-Mare
01934 644641
Sports clothing, equipment, footwear and swim and leisure wear.

Outdoors
9-10 Transom House, Victoria Street, Bristol
0117 926 4892
www.outdoors.ltd.uk
Owned by the Scout Association. Sells a wide selection of outdoor equipment, gadgets and clothes along with Scout uniforms and equipment.

Quip U For Leisure
60 West Street, Old Market, Bristol
0117 955 8054
A mecca for canoe enthusiasts. Sells a wide selection of outdoor clothing along with climbing, caving, walking and mountaineering equipment.

Skate and Ski
104 High Street, Staple Hill
0117 970 1356
Sells everything connected with skiing, skateboarding and skating. Leisure clothing and accessories. Also hires out ski gear.

Snow and Rock Sports Ltd
Units 1-3 Gloucester Road North, Filton
0117 914 3000
Stocks ski and snow boarding clothing and equipment, and in the summer climbing equipment and walking gear.

See also the shops listed in Clothing, above as many of them stock equipment too.

BOOKS

Borders
Queens Rd, Clifton, 0117 922 6959
This was mentioned in many questionnaires. It is one of the newest and would appear to be a favourite among Bristol's teenagers. It is a large and peaceful place with a huge selection of books. Staff are reported as helpful, knowledgeable and un-pushy. Within the store are Paperchase and Starbucks.

CDS AND MUSIC

Fopp Ltd
1 Eldon Way, Bristol, 0117 972 7130
43 Park Street Bristol, 0117 945 0685
8 The Corridor, Bath, 01225 481949
Stock covers most musical tastes. Upstairs at the Park Street branch is given over to rock, pop, books and DVDs, while the selection downstairs is more specialist, jazz, hip hop,

R&B, drum and base. They also sell Vinyl 12" and LPs.

HMV
Broadmead, 0117 929 7467
The Mall, 0117 950 6581
13-15 Stall Street, Bath, 01225 466681
CDs, videos, DVDs covering a whole range of tastes.

Record Fair
The Folk House Park Street, (opposite Fopp Ltd)
0117 926 2987
3rd Sat in the month
LPs, CDs, DVDs, rarities and new releases.

Replay Records
Haymarket, 0117 904 1133
73 Park Street, Bristol, 0117 904 1134
CDs, vinyl and DJ gear. Also buys unwanted CDs.

Virgin Megastores
Broadmead, 0117 950 9600
The Mall, Cribbs Causeway, 0117 929 7798
Singles, albums, DVDs, videos, game consoles and games. Music to suit most tastes.

PCS AND GAMES
There are lots of outlets to choose from, some of which buy and sell second hand games. See also branches of Comet, Currys, PC World, Virgin and John Lewis.

Game
30 Merchant St, Bristol, 0117 929 8626
Debenhams, Broadmead 0117 921 1661
The Galleries, Broadmead, 0117 925 8180
The Mall, Cribbs Causeway, 0117 950 9292
12 Southgate, Bath, 01225 464164
85 High Street, Weston-s-Mare, 01934 416345

Eplay Ltd
22 Merchant Street, Bristol, 0117 927 6060
3 Lower Borough Walls, Bath, 01225 444101

Special Reserve
351 Gloucester Road, Horfield, 0117 924 5000

MUSICAL INSTRUMENTS AND SHEET MUSIC

Bristol Music Shop/Hobgoblin
30 College Green, Bristol, 0117 929 0390
A wide range of musical instruments, accessories and sheet music.

Drumbank Music Drum Centre
203 Gloucester Road, Bristol, 0117 975 5366
www.drumbankmusic.co.uk

Drumbank Music Guitar Centre
235 Gloucester Road, Bristol, 0117 924 7222

Mickleburgh
1-9 Stokes Croft, Bristol, 0117 924 1151
Guitars, amps, keyboards and all kinds of music books and accessories.

Sound Control
5 Rupert Street, Bristol, 0117 934 9955
Guitars, synthesisers, keyboards and accessories.

The Drum Store
125 St George's Road, Hotwells, 0117 929 8540
www.bristoldrumstore.co.uk

STATIONERY

Harold Hockey
174 Whiteladies Road, Bristol, 0117 973 5988
Packed with all things artistic, from easels to sketch and notebooks, cards and picture frames.

Paperchase
Borders, 0117 922 6959
House of Fraser, 0117 929 1021
31 Milsom Street, Bath, 01225 446824
Large selection of brightly coloured notebooks and matching pens.

COSMETICS AND SMELLIES

Lush
13 Union Street, Bath, 01225 428271
Mail order 01202 668 545
Soaps, bath bombs geared to relax and unwind you.

JEWELLERY/ACCESSORIES/ CRAFT

B'delicious
2 Triangle South, Bristol, 0117 929 1789
Creative fun with beads and feathers, ready made, made to order or even made by you!

The Silver Store
The Galleries
Stall selling rings, earrings, bracelets and necklaces.

Creativity
7-9 Worrall Road, Clifton, 0117 973 1710
The name says it. If you're feeling creative but need supplies or inspiration, this shop is for you.

CAFES

Boston Tea Party
75 Park Street, Clifton, 0117 929 8601
With its comfy décor, garden (with heaters for those chilly days), friendly staff and food that tastes so good it's hard to believe it's healthy, it's easy to see why this café is so popular.

Subway
The Berkeley Centre, Queens Rd, 0117 925 6164
This relative newcomer has found a niche for itself and spawned many branches in Bristol's busy café scene. The Park Street branch in particular is popular with skaters and students who love their trademark man-sized deli subs. Healthy, freshly prepared food that's reasonably priced and tastes delicious.

Woodes
18 Park Street, Clifton, 0117 926 4041
A popular café with a few tables outside on the pavement where you can watch the world go by (but watch out for long lunchtime queues that may spoil your view).

BEYOND SCHOOL

Practical and academic options

Connexions
4 Colston Avenue, Bristol
0800 923 0323 Helpline
www.connexionswest.org.uk
Provide advice on university and college applications, along with modern apprenticeship courses.

Bristol Academy of Performing Arts
0117 902 6606
Runs a full time Music Theatre HND for 18+. The course includes acting, dance and musicianship.

For further post 16 choices see Schools & Educational Support chapter.

Working holidays

BUNAC (British Universities North America Club)
16 Bowling Green Lane, London, EC1R 0QH
020 7251 3472, www.bunac.org

Camp America
37a Queen's Gate, London, SW7 5HR
020 7581 7373
www.campamerica.co.uk

Voluntary work in UK and overseas

BUNAC
Has volunteer programmes abroad. To find out more see the contact details above.

Raleigh International Volunteers
27 Parsons Green Lane, London, SW6 4HZ
020 7371 8585, www.raleighinternational.org
17-25yrs
Expeditions in locations all over the world.

VSO (Voluntary Service Overseas)
Youth For Development, 317 Putney Bridge Road, London, SW15 2PN 020 8780 7212
www.vso.org.uk

Archaeology
www.archaeovolunteers.org
See Specific Interest Groups, above.

Bristol International Twinning Association
0117 344 4450
www.bristol-city.gov.uk/twinning
Help and advice if you are looking to work in any one of the towns Bristol is twinned with.

Volunteer Reading Help
www.volunteer-reading-help.co.uk

The Guardian newspaper
Features a selection of voluntary opportunities most Wednesdays in the Society section. Also see Voluntary & Specific Interest Groups, above.

FAMILY HOLIDAYS & WEEKENDS AWAY

Elspeth Pontin

CHAPTER 6

INTRODUCTION

I, like many other parents before me, have found that having a baby or toddler (or both!), can sometimes mean that holidaying is harder work than staying at home. It can feel like there is endless paraphernalia that you need to pack, as well as worries that your little one will throw a tantrum on the train or plane. And for those parents who have an older child or teenager, trying to accommodate their and your needs on a family holiday can seem like a logistical nightmare. But it doesn't have to be that way. This chapter tries to take some of the stress out of planning your holidays by giving a few tips and suggestions whilst recognising that individual families have different budgets and enjoy different sorts of holidays. We have taken recommendations from many parents about family-friendly holidays, from getting there to the choice of accommodation on offer. Regardless of facilities, all the places that are listed are truly family-friendly.

Travel Tips

1. Sharing a holiday with relatives or friends may provide you with child-free time. Alternatively, you could choose a hotel or holiday village with childcare facilities e.g. baby sitting in the evening, child minder in the day.

2. Investigate your destination e.g. is there a beach, is it sandy, does it have shade, is the swimming safe, are there changing facilities, refreshments near by?

3. Is there much to do at the accommodation and in the surrounding area? Teenagers might not appreciate being miles from any activities, and parents with small children might want onsite facilities for after the children go to bed.

4. Check your accomodation covers your needs e.g. high chair, cot, space to run around, access to a fridge for storage, bottle warming facilities.

Have Toddler Will Travel
Published by Hodder and Stoughton
Sarah Tucker
This book gives good advice about travelling with your children.

Family Holiday Association
16 Mortimer Street, London, W1T 3JL
020 7436 3304, www.fhaonline.org.uk
The Family Holiday Association helps provide access to holidays for families in need. Applications are accepted from referring agencies (social workers, health visitors, etc) on behalf of families. Families have to be on low income, have at least one child of 3+yrs and not have had a holiday in the last four years.

WEST COUNTRY HOLIDAYS & WEEKENDS AWAY

With limited travel for restless toddlers, some of the cleanest beaches in the UK, and lots to see and do for all ages, holidaying in the West Country is proving to be an extremely attractive option.

All places listed in this section are roughly within a 2 to 2½ hour car, bus or rail journey from Bristol, and all have been recommended to us by parents. There is also a shortlist of accommodation, these are places that were suggested to us but have not yet been fully researched. We welcome your feedback.

B&B'S

Despite the fact that the West Country is overflowing with bed and breakfasts, at the time of going to print, we only had one recommendation of a truly family-friendly place. The reason for this seems to be that B&B's, although favourably priced in comparison to hotels, do have drawbacks for families with young children. Unlike hotels they generally do not offer evening meals, snacks for hungry toddlers at 5am, baby sitting services or evening entertainment.

Stoke Barton Farm
Stoke, Hartland, Bideford, Devon, EX39 6DU
Colin and Helen Davey: 01237 441238
£19 pp per night, £17 longer stays, £8 U5's, £10 6-13yrs
A family-friendly B&B on the North Devon coast. Prices include full English breakfast, and babysitting can be arranged free of charge. Also offers cream teas, morning coffee and light lunches.

CAMPING

Camping with children of all ages can be enormous fun and a great and affordable way to get away from it all. Camping no longer needs to equate to roughing it either as many campsites have excellent facilities - should you want them! The many benefits of camping include lots of freedom for children to run around or make a mess, and you can cook your own food.

Possible disadvantages include: no baby sitting services, the noise of campsites, worries about the noise of your own children, and of course ... the rain!

Brokerswood Country Park
Brokerswood, Westbury, Wiltshire, BA13 4EH
01373 822238
park@brokerswood.co.uk, www.brokerswood.co.uk
Open all year
£8-£17 per pitch per night

A36, 12 miles south of Bath, follow brown tourist signs

A Gold Conservation Award winning site, well located for visiting Bath, Salisbury, Stonehenge, Longleat and beyond. The site offers generously sized pitches on a flat, open field. There is a centrally heated shower block ensuring a comfortable stay all year round. There is no additional charge for awnings or showers. Pitch prices are based on 2 adults and up to 2 children and include access to the Country Park.

Christchurch Caravanning and Camping Site
Bracelands Drive, Christchurch, Coleford, GL16 7NN
0131 314 6505
info@forestholidays.co.uk, www.forestholidays.co.uk
Apr-Oct, Mid Dec-early Jan
£6.40-£11.80 per pitch per night

Excellent for families, a gently sloping site high above the beautiful Wye Valley, with waymarked walking routes down to the river through the surrounding woodland. Nearby are the Clearwell Caves ancient iron mines. Hot showers/water.

Croft Farm Leisure & Waterpark
Bredons Hardwick, Tewkesbury, Glos, GL20 7EE
Alan Newell: 01684 772321
alan@croftfarmleisure.co.uk
www.croftfarmleisure.co.uk
Mar-Oct
1 mile north of Tewkesbury on B4080

Lakeside camping and caravan park with sailing, windsurfing and canoeing; tuition and equipment hire.

Hoburne Cotswold Water Park
Broadway Lane, South Cerney, Cirencester, Glos, GL7 5UQ
01285 860216
www.hoburne.com
Please contact the park for availability and pricing

Hoburne Cotswold Water Park consists of holiday caravans, lodges and chalets, in addition to touring pitches. The accommodation surrounds four lakes teeming with wildlife, and a huge range of facilities in

and around the Lakeside Club. See Cotswold Water Park, Out & About in the West Country chapter.

Lundy Island Camp Site
Bristol Channel, North Devon, EX39 2LY
01271 863636
info@lundyisland.co.uk, www.lundyisland.co.uk
From £5 pp, per night
Boat crossing from Bideford or Ilfracombe or winter helicopter service from Hartland Point

After a short boat trip from Ilfracombe on the MS Oldenburg, visitors can camp or stay in one of the many Landmark Trust properties on the island. Booking in advance is essential. Campsite facilities include washrooms and showers. A haven for birdwatchers, climbers, canoeists and divers, Lundy is a very popular with people who love the great outdoors. Described as a child's 1000-acre playground, there is something for everyone.

Newton Mill Camping
Newton Road, Bath, BA2 9JF
Keith and Louise Davies: 01225 333909
newtonmill@hotmail.com
www.campinginbath.co.uk
Open all year
£10-£13.50 per pitch, £11-£16.85 caravans/motorhomes, free U3's, £1.50 3-16yrs

Located in a hidden valley close to the centre of Bath. There is a children's playground, free fishing, café, bar and restaurant, and hot showers/water. Nearby is the level traffic-free Bath-Bristol cycle path and frequent bus services.

Porthclais Farm
St Davids, Pembrokeshire, Wales, SA62 6RR
01437 720256
www.porthclais-campsite.co.uk
Easter-Oct
£5 adults, £2 child, pp per night

A family run campsite set within the Pembrokeshire National Park. With acres of space to camp, the site has basic but adequate facilities (toilets, washbasins, showers, washing up area, and drinking water). Located right on the sea front, close to Caerfai, Porthsele and Whitesands beaches and just one mile from St David's (the smallest city in the UK). It will take a little over 2½ hours to reach, but it is an area of such oustanding natural beauty that it is worth the extra stretch.

Ruda Holiday Park

Croyde Bay, North Devon, EX33 1NY
0870 220 4600
enquiries@parkdeanholidays.co.uk
www.ruda.co.uk
From £7 per pitch per night
For full details see entry under self-catering.

Sandy Balls Holiday Centre

Godshill, Fordingbridge, Hampshire, SP6 2JY
01425 653042
post@sandy-balls.co.uk, www.sandy-balls.co.uk
Open all year
Touring/camping £12.75-£28.50 per night
From the West - follow A31 to Ringwood, then A338 to Fordingbridge, then B3078 to Godshill

Situated in the New Forest, bordered by the river Avon and set in 120 acres of woods and parklands. The centre consists of forest lodges, holiday homes, touring and camping sites. There are first class facilities including a swimming pool, riding stables, bar, restaurant and activities for children. Cots are provided.

Stoke Barton Farm

Stoke, Hartland, Bideford, Devon, EX39 6DU
Colin and Helen Davey: 01237 441238
Easter-Oct
£3.50 adults, £2 child pp per night, free U5's
Situated in a beautiful spot on the North Devon Coast. There is ample space for camping and for children to run around safely. With basic but adequate facilities, the campsite commands wonderful views down to Hartland Quay.

"Stoke Barton farm is quite simply a wonderful, peaceful place to stay. A welcome change from busy, commercial campsites."

HOTELS

Staying in hotels, though it may not come cheap, has never been better for parents and children. The choice, from basic to luxury, is increasing, the facilities for children improving, and the possibility to rest and relax inviting. Things to ask:

- Lifts and pram access to rooms
- Baby listening and baby sitting

- The size of rooms (if you need cots, extra beds)
- Children's menu/portions and prices

All the hotels we feature in this guide come highly recommended. This means they not only have many facilities that make your stay, not to mention your packing, easier but they are truly welcoming of children and there will be lots for your children to do once you are there. As with all types of accommodation, however, if you need something specific for your stay, make sure that you confirm it is available prior to booking.

Babington House

Babington, Nr Frome, Somerset, BA11 3RW
01373 812266
enquiries@babingtonhouse.co.uk
www.babingtonhouse.co.uk
£215-£370 per night

A beautiful old house set in spectacular countryside, with large, very luxurious, contemporary rooms. There is a supervised play room for children from 12mths upwards, lots of activities for older children (ponies, scalextric, computer games), indoor and outdoor pools, baby sitters, baby massage, cinema, organic garden, and tennis courts. All rooms include a toaster, kettle and mini bar. Some include hotplates, microwaves, sterilisers and baby baths.

Calcot Manor Hotel

Nr Tetbury, Gloucestershire, GL8 8YJ
01666 890391
reception@calcotmanor.co.uk
www.calcotmanor.co.uk
Open all year
£205-£276 for B&B, child supplement £20 U12's, £25 over 12's, includes high tea and use of the playzone (or Mez for older children)
Three miles west of Tetbury, on the A4135, just before the crossroads with the A46

A charming Cotswold farmhouse, elegantly converted into a stylish hotel with a luxury spa. Calcot offers many facilities for families and children. There are family rooms, cots, baby listening and baby sitting.

"So geared up for children you don't notice they're there!"

Gara Rock Hotel

East Portlemouth, Nr Salcombe, Devon, TQ8 8PH
01548 842342
gara@gara.co.uk, www.gara.co.uk
From £31 adult, £17 child (3-12yrs) per night

Overlooking clean, sandy beaches and surrounded by National Trust Land. The accommodation is extremely versatile, with many different room options. There is a swimming pool, children's restaurant, tennis, and many high season facilities. There are playgroups for 3-12yrs run during the summer and school holidays. Cots and other baby equipment available, baby listening, laundry and drying room facilities.

Saunton Sands Hotel

Braunton, Devon, EX33 1LQ
01271 890212
www.sauntonsands.co.uk
From £73 (double) per night
M5 to junction 27, A361 (Barnstaple) to Braunton

The hotel has a range of rooms and self catering apartments to suit the particular needs of your family. The special facilities for children include a children's pool, games room, junior putting green, adventure area, nursery with toys (recently refurbished and governed by Ofsted), baby sitting and baby listening. There is also a full programme of children's activities during school holidays (5-a-side football, cricket, swimming galas, bouncy castle etc.) Staff are happy to heat up food and bottles (and will even supply bottles if you arrive without them). Special diets are also willingly catered for. Other facilities include indoor and outdoor heated swimming pools, table tennis, pool tables, tennis, squash, gym, sauna, solarium, hair salon and beauty treatments. Cots are provided.

The Bulstone

Higher Bulstone, Branscombe, EX12 3BL
01297 680446
stay@childfriendlyhotels.com
www.childfriendlyhotels.com
From £54 per room per night (B&B for 2 adults and 2 children under 11 yrs)

Set in the heart of the countryside and designed with children in mind. The aim of this small family run hotel is for it to be a home from home experience without all the hard work. There are a variety of child-friendly rooms with changing mats, cots, nappy buckets and baby listening devices. All bedding is provided, including spare. There is a kitchen for your use, with bottle steriliser, fridge, milk, microwave, ironing equipment. Fresh milk is always available for children. Washer and dryer available along with laundry service. Other facilities include a large playroom with toys, games and books, an outdoor play area with tractors, swings, slides, climbing frames and cars. Also guinea pigs and cats that the children can make friends with. Children's tea is served at 5pm. Baby sitting can be arranged.

The Sandbanks Hotel

Sandbanks, Poole, BH13 7PS
01202 707377
reservations@sandbankshotel.co.uk,
www.sandbankshotel.co.uk
Open all year.
From £70 B&B pp per night, phone for child rates

Located on a Blue Flag award beach. Most bedrooms have a sea or harbour view and a balcony. The hotel has an AA red rosette for the beachside brasserie and many leisure facilities. For the children there is a restaurant, Ofsted registered crèche on site (extra), many activities for all ages (soft play, games, discos, karaoke), and indoor pool with fun flume. There are many family rooms with cots provided and baby listening. Baby sitting available.

Woolley Grange

Woolley Green, Bradford-on-Avon, BA15 1TX
01225 864705
info@woolleygrange.com, www.woolleygrange.com
From £135 per room per night

Jacobean Manor House set in open countryside on the outskirts of Bradford-on-Avon, 8 miles from Bath. Facilities include the Woolley Bears' Den, an outdoor play area, children's croquet, bikes, football, play stations and an outdoor heated swimming pool. Cots are provided and there is a baby listening/sitting service. Nappy buckets, nappy sacks and changing mats available. Bottles and food items for babies can also be stored; there is a steriliser and microwave in the Den.

SELF-CATERING

Self-catering in this country ranges from cottages in remote locations to houseswaps, to chalets and lodges in holiday parks. Self-catering is arguably the most home from home situation that you will get with a holiday, which may be a blessing or a curse depending on your situation. If you self-cater you can cook for varied diets and keep to a budget. There are also often washing facilities, and usually there is more privacy than other holiday options.

Many of the places that we mention below allow you to have the flexibility of self-catering with the convenience of on-site restaurants and facilities. Many also have baby sitting services.

If you choose to do a houseswap, exchanging with a family with similar aged children can be advantageous particularly if you have access to their toys, games and existing babysitting arrangements.

Center Parcs

Longleat Forest, Warminster, Wiltshire, BA12 7PU
0870 520 0300
www.centerparcs.co.uk
Open all year

With nature on your doorstep and over 100 activities to choose from, it's a popular place to take a short break. You can choose to do as much or as little as you like. Cots, baby sitting service and children's activities provided.

Gara Rock Hotel

East Portlemouth, Nr Salcombe, Devon, TQ8 8PH
01548 842342
gara@gara.co.uk, www.gara.co.uk
Wide range of self-catering accommodation to suit your families needs. See Hotels above.

Hoburne Cotswold Water Park

Broadway Lane, South Cerney, Glos, GL7 5UQ
01285 860216
www.hoburne.com
From £145-£510 pw caravans, £190 pw chalets & lodges (prices seasonal)

See Camping above.

Lundy Island

Bristol Channel, North Devon, EX39 2LY
01271 863636
info@lundyisland.co.uk, www.lundyisland.co.uk
Contact Lundy Island Shore Office for prices

Lundy offers visitors a wide range of buildings in which to stay, including a castle, lighthouse and gentleman's villa. For more details on Lundy itself see Camping.

NCT Houseswap

Denise Tupman: 01626 355066
thetupmans@yahoo.co.uk
Annual: £29.99

The houseswap register is a list of over 257 families who are willing to swap houses with each other in order to have free accommodation. The register is a list by county of members' homes, so you can match up with someone whose home is suitable for your age of children, where there will be similar equipment and toys etc. At least one child must be under 13 years old.

Ruda Holiday Park

Croyde Bay, North Devon, EX33 1NY
0870 220 4600
enquiries@parkdeanholidays.co.uk, www.ruda.co.uk
Closed mid Nov-Feb
£175-£865 pw caravans, £215-£1265 pw lodges, £195-£1265 pw cottages/apartments
A361 to Braunton. B3231 to Croyde Village

A short walk from a Blue Flag beach. Activities include surf lessons, mountain biking, tennis, fishing, horse riding and swimming in an adventure pool (230ft waterslide and jacuzzi)). 3 children's clubs (U5's, 5-10yrs, 11-15yrs). There is also an entertainment lounge, bar, café and take away, supermarket and gift shop. Highchairs and cots £10 pw each.

Sandy Balls Holiday Centre

Godshill, Fordingbridge, Hampshire, SP6 2JY
01425 653042
post@sandy-balls.co.uk, www.sandy-balls.co.uk
See Camping above.

Saunton Sands Hotel
Braunton, Devon, EX33 1LQ
01271 890212
www.sauntonsands.co.uk
See Hotels above.

Torridge House Cottages
Little Torrington, North Devon, EX38 8PS
Barbara Terry: 01805 622542
info@torridgehouse.co.uk, www.torridgehouse.co.uk
www.southwoodcottage.co.uk
Open all year
£261-£945 pw & £513-£1230 pw

P ⌷ ⌂ ♥ ↾ ⌗ ⌸ ⊞ ⊢ ♿ ▤

Family farm holidays, under 7's especially welcome. Help feed the pigs, lambs, chickens, rabbits, ducklings etc. Outdoor heated pool. 10 lovely cottages, cots provided, baby sitting available, activities for children.

SHORTLIST
The following shortlist comprises places suggested shortly before the book was due to go to print. THG have not yet thoroughly researched but should you - let us know your views.

Alastair Sawday's Special Places to Stay
01275 464891, www.specialplacestostay.com

Beverley Park, Paignton, Devon
01803 843887, www.ukparks.com

Braddon Cottages, Ashwater, Devon
01409 211350, www.braddoncottages.co.uk

Chine Hotel, Bournemouth, Dorset
01202 396234, www.chinehotel.co.uk

Glencot House, Wookey Hole
01749 677160, www.glencothouse.co.uk

Higher Bowden Cottages, Dartmouth, Devon
01803 770745, www.higherbowden.com

Holiday Resort Unity, Brean, Somerset
01278 751235, www.hru.co.uk

Knoll House, Studland Bay Dorset
01929 450450, www.knollhouse.co.uk

Lady's Mile Holiday Park, Dawlish Devon
01626 863411, www.ladysmile.co.uk

Lydstep Beach Holiday Park, Tenby Pembrokeshire
01834 871871, www.ukparks.com

Moonfleet Manor, Weymouth
01305 786948, www.luxuryfamilyhotels.com

Old Bell Hotel, Malmesbury, Cotswolds
01666 822344, www.oldbellhotel.com

Symonds Yat Caravan & Camping Park, Forest of Dean
01600 890883, www.canoehire.com/symyat.htm

The Cottage, Hope Cove, Devon
01548 561555, www.hopecove.com

Watersplash, Brockenhurst
01590 622344
www.newforest-online.co.uk/watersplash

Woolacombe Bay Hotel, Woolacombe, Devon
01271 870388
www.woolacombe-bay-hotel.co.uk

Youth Hostel Association
0870 770 8868, www.yha.org.uk

HOLIDAYS FURTHER AFIELD

Introduction
Bristol and the West Country are well served for travelling further afield as, in addition to Bristol International Airport (BIA), which has scheduled and charter flights to many destinations, there are several ferry ports within easy reach.

Should you not find the flight that you require from BIA, Cardiff, Birmingham and Exeter airports are not far away.

AIRPORTS AND AIRLINES

Bristol Airport
0870 121 2747
www.bristolairport.com
There are many bonuses to starting your family holiday from your home airport, particularly when it is an airport like BIA. Not

having to travel for miles to get to the airport means that children will still be fresh for the flight.

One of the best things about BIA is that it is a small airport and this means that, unlike some of its London contemporaries, everything is within easy walking distance for parents with children in tow, and there are rarely long queues either on arrival or departure. Facilities that BIA has at present include baby changing on all floors, land and airside, lifts, shops and restaurants (all have high chairs).

For details of scheduled flights and tour operators see below.

Bristol Airport Tips

- Cars cannot be left unattended outside the terminal. There is a passenger pick up car park near to the entrance.

- You can drop small children and an accompanying adult at the passenger drop-off point near the entrance prior to parking in the long stay car park. This will save you negotiating the courtesy bus with bags, prams, and small children.

- There is an area in The Food Village (on the landside mezzanine floor) for young children to do colouring. From here you can watch the planes taking off and landing.

- The shops sell nappies and baby food, and the restaurant will warm bottles if needed. If your flight is seriously delayed and you have a young child, the airport has travel cots, bottles and nappies on stand-by.

- If travelling with small children on your own, or if you need extra assistance, there are always BIA hosts available to help you to and from the plane.

Flying Tips

When booking flights with babies or toddlers:

How much leg room is there on the plane? A child on your knees can get very cramped after a few hours. (Infants on a parent's lap do not have a baggage allowance.)

Is there priority infant boarding? (Useful when travelling on low cost airlines which do not always allocate seat numbers.)

Are there blankets, pillows, food and drink on board?

Will the airline heat bottles or baby food?

Does the airline have policies about how many infants can travel in each row, or where they want the infants to be placed in the row?

Can you pre-book seats?

Can you take your pushchair to the steps of the plane?

Can you book a flight time when your child may have their routine nap?

Other tips for on board:

Breastfeed or give your child something to suck or swallow to help prevent ears popping.

Wrap small inexpensive items eg sellotape, crayons, novelty toys.

Drape a blanket between the seat back table and the back of your child's seat to create an atmosphere for them to sleep.

Airlines

All the following airlines operate direct, scheduled flights from Bristol International Airport:

Aerarann - Cork
0800 587 2324, www.aerarann.com

Air France - Paris
0845 084 5111, www.airfrance.co.uk

Air Southwest - Jersey, Manchester, Plymouth
0870 241 8202, www.airsouthwest.com

Aurigny Airlines - Guernsey
0871 871 0717, www.aurigny.com

British Airways - Aberdeen, Dublin, Edinburgh, Frankfurt, Glasgow, Jersey, Munich, Newcastle, Paris, Plymouth
0845 773 3377, www.britishairways.com

Easyjet - Alicante, Amsterdam, Barcelona, Belfast, Berlin, Bilbao, Copenhagen, Edinburgh, Faro, Glasgow, Malaga, Newcastle, Nice, Palma, Prague, Venice
0870 600 0000, www.easyjet.com

Flybe - Belfast, Bergerac, Bordeaux, Isle of Man, Jersey, Toulouse, Paris
0871 700 0123, www.flybe.com

KLM - Amsterdam
0870 507 4074, www.klm.com

Ryanair - Dublin
0871 246 0000, www.ryanair.com

Skybus - Newquay, Scilly Isles
0845 710 5555, www.skybus.co.uk

SNBrussels - Brussels
0870 735 2345, www.flysn.com

Tour operators

Many tour operators are now including Bristol in their list of departure airports.
Family tour operators using BIA include:

Thomson
0870 514 3499; www.thomson.co.uk

Crystal
0870 888 0023, www.crystalholidays.co.uk

First Choice
0870 750 0001, www.firstchoice.co.uk

Simply Travel
020 8541 2222, www.simply-travel.co.uk

Airtours
0870 241 2572, www.airtours.co.uk

Cosmos
01233 211303, www.cosmos-holidays.co.uk

Neilson
0870 909 9099, www.neilson.com

Esprit
01252 618300, www.esprit-holidays.co.uk

JMC
0870 758 0194, www.jmc.com

TAXI HIRE

If you need a taxi from the airport you must go to the taxi desk in the arrivals area. You book and pay for the taxi there and pick it up directly outside the terminal.

Airportcarz

Bristol International Airport, Lulsgate Bottom, Bristol, BS48 3DY
01275 474888
Located opposite International arrivals.

Private hire taxis based at UK airports. Provide rear facing car seats (suitable for babies), in addition to forward facing car seats. Have large vehicles suitable for larger families.

WEST COUNTRY FERRY COMPANIES

Travelling by ferry can be one of the least stressful ways to do long journeys particularly with young children, (although there may be a long journey from your arrival port).
Many ferry companies now have play areas, and for the older children there are often cinemas and televisions. Booking a cabin on longer crossings can also have its advantages.

Brittany Ferries
08703 665333
www.brittany-ferries.co.uk
Operate on a number of routes, the closest for the West being from Plymouth, to Roscoff and Santander; Poole to Cherbourg. Facilities vary from children's play areas to swimming pools. Ask staff at the information points if you wish to have baby food or milk heated.

Condor Ferries Limited
0845 345 2000
www.condorferries.co.uk
Operate services from Weymouth and Poole to Guernsey, Jersey and St Malo. There are children's areas on some of the ferries.

Irish Ferries
08705 171717
www.irishferries.com
Operates a service from Pembroke to Rosslare. Facilities onboard for small children include films, games, and adventure tunnels. These are conveniently located beside a tea and coffee bar, so that parents can relax while their children play. For older children there is the Cyber Zone, which includes arcade games and simulators.

Stena Line
08705 707070
www.stenaline.co.uk
Operates routes between Fishguard and Rosslare. On board there are baby changing facilities, children's menus, family and play area. Children under 4yrs travel free.

Swansea Cork Ferries
01792 456116
www.swansea-cork.ie
Operates between Swansea and Cork. The majority of the sailings depart at 9pm and arrive in Ringaskiddy at about 7am. Onboard there are restaurants, bars, shops, cinema, and children's play area. All cabins are ensuite.

WEST COUNTRY FERRY PORTS

Poole Ferry Port
2 hrs from Bristol, 01202 207215
The Terminal offers a summer café for meals & refreshemnts, a Bureau de Change, and a left luggage locker facility.

Port of Fishguard
2¾ hrs from Bristol, 08705 707070
Buffet Bar serving snacks & hot & cold drinks, a further Cuppacabana bar, and various drink vending machines. Other facilities include disabled toilets & a baby changing room.

Port of Pembroke Dock
2½ hrs from Bristol, 08705 329543
The Passenger Terminal offers a spacious lounge with TV, as well as vending machines for refreshments.

Port of Plymouth
2¼ hrs from Bristol, 01752 662191
The Terminal offers a café for meals & refreshments, and a Bureau de Change.

Swansea Ferry Port
1½ hrs from Bristol, 01792 456116

Weymouth Ferry Port
2 hrs from Bristol, 01305 761551

FAMILY ACCOMMODATION IN BRISTOL

The new arrival of children in the family often means lots of visitors. If they need to stay over night and you are limited for space there is plenty of accommodation in Bristol to choose from. However if your visitors have small children, trying to find suitable accommodation can be a very different story. This part of the chapter lists a selection of places to stay that make visiting family and friends with small children feel truly welcome and accommodated.

B&BS

Westbury Park Hotel
37 Westbury Road, Bristol, BS9 3AU
Mr & Mrs Everett: 0117 962 0465
www.westburypark-hotel.co.uk
From £60 double, £70 family room, cot and bedding £5 per night (pre-book if needed)

A detached Victorian house on the edge of Bristol's famous Durdham Down. It is an AA four diamond rated hotel and has the English Tourist Board Silver Award. There are 2 large rooms accommodating 2 adults and 2 children, and also a large twin interconnecting with a large double. Bottles can be heated and baby food stored in a refrigerator.

CAMPSITES

Brook Lodge Farm Camping & Caravan Park
Cowslip Green, Bristol, BS40 5RB
Janet House, 01934 862 311
brooklodgefarm@aol.com, www.brooklodgefarm.com

A family run country touring park, based in the private grounds of a small farm. It is situated 12 miles from Bristol City Centre, and consequently makes an ideal place to stay if you want to camp when you visit family and friends in Bristol. Among its many charms, is an abundance of wildlife, a stream, and natural play areas for children. There is also an outdoor swimming pool (parental supervision essential).

HOTELS

Henbury Lodge
Station Road, Henbury, BS10 7QQ
Jonathon Pearce, 0117 950 2615
www.henburylodge.com

A luxury Georgian country hotel in Bristol extremely welcoming of children. It has very large family rooms which accommodate up to 5 individuals (for example, one double, 2 singles and a cot). The hotel chefs are more than willing to accommodate children's varying diets in the restaurant. Cots are provided and baby sitting can be arranged. There are toys and books for children provided in the hotel lounge. Ground floor rooms are available. And for those of you planning large family celebrations, parties can also be catered for (the dining room seats 34).

Long Reach House Hotel

321 Bath Road, Saltford, Bristol, BS31 3TJ
Jill Coles, 01225 400500/ 400600
reservations@longreach-househotel, www.longreach-house-hotel.com
Open all year.
£75+ per room, £10 for extra bed per night

P ⚹ 🚭 CP 🐾 🔥 🚫 🍳 🍴 ♿ 👶

A large country house on the outskirts of Bristol. The hotel itself is set in almost 2 acres of land, with lovely views. There is secure parking, and child-friendly lawns. Easy access for Bristol, Bath and Avon Valley Country Park. 2 stars. 2 ensuite family ground floor rooms, one with garden access. Rooms suitable for 4 adults, or 2 adults and 2-3 children. Cots provided. Baby listening and baby sitting can be arranged. Restaurant.

SELF-CATERING

Days Serviced Apartments

30 - 38 St Thomas Street, Redcliffe, Bristol, BS1 6JZ
0117 954 4800
sales@bristol.premgroup.com, www.daysinn.co.uk
£45-£140 per unit per night

P ⚹ 🔥 🚫 🍳 ♿

These centrally based, luxury, one or two bedroom serviced apartments are located a minutes walk from St Mary Redcliffe Church. Each apartment has a fully equipped kitchen with cooker, refrigerator, freezer, dishwasher, washing machine and microwave. There is also secure car parking on request (chargable at a daily rate). Bed linen, towels, cots are provided. No high chairs. There is an on call manager, and a shopping service.

PLAY DOUGH RECIPES

When all the bought playdough has gone hard, try making your own:

Play Dough - long life

You will need:

1 cup of flour, half a cup of salt, 2 teaspoons cream of tartar, 1 tablespoon cooking oil, 1 cup of water with food colouring added.

Mix all ingredients together in a saucepan and cook over a medium heat stirring all the time. As it becomes lumpy, continue to stir until it forms a ball. Leave to cool then knead until smooth. It is now ready to use. Store in an airtight container for a long life.

Modelling Dough

Why not try this recipe for children who want to keep their masterpieces!

You will need:

2 cups flour, 1 cup salt, 1 tablespoon cooking oil, 1 cup water with food colouring if required.

Mix together flour, salt and oil. Add water until mixture forms a ball. Knead. Make your model or roll out and use cutters to make hanging decorations. Bake at 180°c for approx. 35-40 minutes. Cool, paint and varnish if required.

CHILDCARE 0-4 YEARS

Diana Beavon

CHAPTER 7

INTRODUCTION

There are so many different options available for paid childcare, from using a day nursery, crèche or employing a nanny. This chapter aims to highlight what childcare facilities Bristol offers.

Finding the right solution to suit your family can be a lenghty exercise. It is advised that you investigate your options thoroughly, listen to other parent's recommendations, check up on references (including calling Ofsted) and ask lots of questions along the way.

There are several departments/charities listed below who can help you with this venture.

Children's Information Service

Unit 40 Easton Business Centre, Felix Road, Easton, BS5 OHE
0845 129 7217,
Minicom : 0117 941 3777
enquiries@cisbristol.co.uk, www.childcarelink.gov.uk
Mon-Fri: 9.30am-4pm, 8pm Tue & Wed

Provides free, impartial and confidential information or guidance on a full range of childcare, children's services and resources in Bristol.

Bath & North East Somerset Family Information Service

01225 395343
fis@bathnes.gov.uk, www.childcarelink.gov.uk
Free advice and information on choosing childcare provision and early years education.

Daycare Trust

020 7840 3350
Produce a useful booklet, free of charge, entitled "Choosing Childcare, Your Sure Start Guide to Childcare and Early Education".

The Office for Standards in Education (Ofsted)

Early Years Regional Centre: 0845601 4772
Responsible for the registration and inspection of nurseries, playgroups, pre-schools, crèches, out-of-school care and childminders for children up to the age of eight. You can either request Ofsted reports from establishments and child minders or from your Ofsted Early Years regional centre. Ofsted will also investigate complaints about providers and take action to close facilities down if necessary.

DAY NURSERIES

Open all year round, Monday to Friday, from early in the morning to at least 6pm at night, providing full time care from birth up to 5 years old. They must meet national daycare standards, be Ofsted inspected and adhere to specific staff and qualified staff to child ratios.
Many will take children on a part time basis, some for just a morning a week.
Children will be split according to age, some even have separate rooms for crawlers and walkers under 1.
Expect to pay from £30/day.

Advantages:

- Stability provided from attending regular sessions (closed only for bank holidays)
- All areas of development are encouraged
- Child benefits from different personalities of staff
- Opportunities for wide variety of equipment and other resources

- Child mixes with peers

Disadvantages:

- A young child may need more individual attention and some may have to compete for attention
- You have to get yourself and your child ready in the mornings
- May have to commit financially to secure a place and pay full price when on holiday
- Nurseries cannot accept ill children but you will still have to pay for the session

Questions you may want to ask on viewing:

What provisions are made for day time naps?
Do they provide a breakfast?
Who will be your child's key worker? What are the staff to child ratios?
Is there an outside play area or do staff take children out?
How long is the settling in period?
What do you need to provide for your child, i.e extra clothing, nappies?
Opening times and charges for late pick ups?
What is their sickness policy? (most nurseries exclude chicken pox, prolonged case of diarrhoea, conjunctivitis, weeping ears or hand, foot and mouth)

NEIGHBOURHOOD NURSERIES

A number of local authority and private nurseries are setting up 'Neighbourhood Nursery Places' for working/training parents living within specific areas of Bristol. There will be a limited number of places available and parents may be able to claim tax credits to offset some of the cost of fees which the nursery will be able to assist with. To find out if you qualify for a place contact the Children's Information Service, see Introduction.

NURSERIES

Nurseries are listed by geographical area starting in central Bristol, then north, north east, east ... clockwise around the centre.

CENTRAL BRISTOL

Amberley Hall
21 Richmond Dale, Clifton, BS8 2UB
Mary Butler: 0117 974 1550
Mon-Fri: 8am-6pm

Accepts children from 3mths-5yrs. Qualified teacher, plus teachers for dancing.

Bristol University Day Nursery
34 St Michael's Park, Kingsdown, Bristol
Sue Alexander: 0117 927 6077
www.bris.ac.uk/Depts/Nursery
Mon-Fri: 8.30am-5.30pm

Accepts children from 3mths-5yrs. Long waiting list, priority given to students and staff of the University.

Little Friends Nursery
City of Bristol College, Marksbury Road, Bedminster, BS3 5JL
Sally Frampton: 0117 904 5419
Mon-Fri: 8am-5.30pm

Accepts children from 18mths-5yrs.

Magic Roundabout Nursery
141 Coronation Road, Southville, Bristol, BS3 1RE
0117 963 9800
Mon- Fri: 7.30am - 7pm

Open 52 weeks of the year.

Mornington House Day Nursery
Mornington Road, Clifton, BS8
Mrs Farr: 0117 973 3414
Mon-Fri: 8am-6pm

Accepts children from 6wks-5yrs.

Redcliffe Early Years Centre
Spencer House, Ship Lane, Redcliffe, BS1 6RR
Mrs FM Blight: 0117 903 0334
redcliffe_n@bristol-city.gov.uk

Designated childrens centre will be running a neighbourhood nursery with places for children 0-5yrs. Call for an application form.

South Street Family Unit
British Road, Bedminster, BS3 3AU
The Manager: 0117 903 9941
south_street_day_n@bristol-city.gov.uk

Part of social services facilities, all children are referred by health visitors, practitioners etc and places allocated by a panel.

St Pauls Day Nursery
Little Bishop St, St Pauls, BS2 9JF
The Manager: 0117 377 2278
st_pauls_day_n@bristol-city.gov.uk
www.education.bcc.lan/
Mon-Thu: 9.30-4pm

State nursery providing sessional daycare for 2-4yrs. Children referred to a panel through health visitors or social worker.

The Rocking Horse Day Nursery
1 Woodland Road, Clifton, BS8 1AU
0117 946 7145
www.rockinghorsebristol.co.uk
Mon-Fri: 7am-6pm

Accepts children from 3mths to 5yrs.

NORTH BRISTOL

Abbeywood Tots Day Nursery
97 Station Road, Filton, Bristol
Amanda Fry: 0117 969 3990
Mon-Fri: 8am-6pm

Accepts children 0-5yrs.

Academy Day Nursery & Childcare Club
c/o Next Generation Health Club, Greystoke Avenue, Bristol, BS10 6AZ
Alexandra Morfaki: 0117 950 2550
www.academychildcare.co.uk
Mon-Fri 8am-6pm

Attached to Next Generation Health Club, offers full time care from 3mths-5yrs in three separate rooms. Members of Next Generation can book hourly sessions whilst using club facilities.

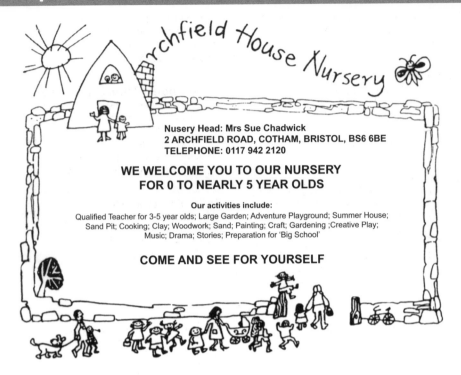

Nusery Head: Mrs Sue Chadwick
2 ARCHFIELD ROAD, COTHAM, BRISTOL, BS6 6BE
TELEPHONE: 0117 942 2120

WE WELCOME YOU TO OUR NURSERY
FOR 0 TO NEARLY 5 YEAR OLDS

Our activities include:
Qualified Teacher for 3-5 year olds; Large Garden; Adventure Playground; Summer House;
Sand Pit; Cooking; Clay; Woodwork; Sand; Painting; Craft; Gardening ;Creative Play;
Music; Drama; Stories; Preparation for 'Big School'

COME AND SEE FOR YOURSELF

Acorns Nursery

Henbury Hill House, College Park Drive,
Bristol, BS10 7AN
Becky Rowland: 0117 950 5885
www.acornsnurseries.co.uk
Mon-Fri 8am-6pm

Full and part time care offered for children from 6wks-5yrs. Located in large house, under ones are upstairs, whilst under twos rotate between six different rooms downstairs.

Archfield House Nursery

2 Archfield Road, Cotham, BS6 6BE
Mrs Sue Chadwick: 0117 942 2120
Mon-Fri 8am-6pm

Cares for children from 0-5yrs. Wonderful large garden with pets, summer house etc. Qualified teacher employed and visiting french teacher.

Art Raft Piglets Nursery

St Saviours Hall, Woodfield Road, Redland, Bristol, BS6 6JQ
Barbara Ramsey: 0117 904 6358
pigletsnursery@artraft.com, www.artraft.com
Mon-Fri 8-6pm

Self contained day nursery with a strong arts focus for children 12mths-5yrs.

Ashgrove Park Day Nursey

60 Ashgrove Road, Ashley Down, BS7 9LQ
Miss Winkworth: 0117 951 3123
Mon-Fri 8.15am-5.45pm

Open for children 6wks-5yrs, been established 14 years.

Brunel Nursery

City of Bristol College, Ashley Down, BS7 9BU
Sue Cowell: 07977 926346
Mon-Fri 8am-6pm

Students on low income or benefit with children from 3mths-5yrs can apply to the

'Learner Support Fund'. Nursery also has an after school collection from Sefton Park and runs a playscheme in the holidays.

Clyde House Day Nursery
1 Nevil Road, Bishopston, BS7 9EG
Mrs Tiley: 0117 924 7488
Mon-Fri 8.15am-5.45pm

Accepts children from 6wks-5yrs. Established 1988.

Daisychain Children's Day Nursery
Vining Hall, Etloe Road, Westbury Park, BS6 7PB
Vicky Morris: 0117 970 6828
Mon-Fri 8am-6pm

Aimed at children 2-5yrs offering a bright, cheerful and well equipped nursery close to Durdham Downs. Friendly, dedicated, qualified staff with full-time qualified teacher.

Downs Park Day Nursery
46 Downs Park West, Westbury Park, BS6 7QL
Mrs D Munk: 0117 962 8526
Mon-Fri 8.15am-5.45pm

Cares from birth to 5yrs.

Hampton Road Day Nursery
118-120 Hampton Road, Redland, Bristol
Miss J Watts: 0117 946 7054
Mon-Fri 8am-6pm

'Home from home' for babies from 0-4yrs.

Lake House Day Nursery
2 Lake Road, Westbury-on-Trym, BS10 5DL
Mrs Gillian Jones: 0117 962 2948
Mon-Fri 8am-5.45pm

Offers full time care from birth to 5yrs, with Montessori practical life section, French and pre-school group.

Manor House Day Nursery
145 Southmead Road, Westbury on Trym, Bristol
Shirley Whawell: 117 962 9620
www.themanorhousenursery.co.uk
Mon-Fri 8am-6pm

Housed in a large manor house with lots of space, it aims to meet needs of individual children. Facilities include sensory garden and separate craft rooms.

Once Upon a Time Day Nursery
2&4 Downs Cote Drive, Westbury-on-Trym, BS9 3TP
Ms. H. O'Neill: 0117 962 5203
Mon-Fri 8am-6pm.

Cares from 6wks to 5yrs in a home environment, offering excellent meals.

Peter Pan Nursery
1 Churchways Crescent, Horfield, BS7 8SW
Mrs Ellen Dunk: 0117 935 5410
ellen@ppan.fsbusiness.co.uk
Mon-Fri 8am-6pm

Pre-school teacher offering full time care for children 3-5yrs.

Pooh Corner Day Nursery
46 Lower Redland Rd, Redland, BS6 6ST
Mary Regan: 0117 946 6178
poohcorner.redland@virgin.net
www.poohcornernursery.co.uk
Mon-Fri 8am-6pm

Friendly caring environment for 3mths-5yrs. Separate floors for under and over 2's. 'Excellent' facilities. See advertisement.

Priory Day Nursery
99 Gloucester Road North, Bristol, BS34 7PT
Sue Farr: 0117 969 2503
Mon-Fri 7.30am-6pm

Friendly, safe nursery with caring staff for 6wks-5yrs offering learning through play.

The Red House Children's Centre
1 Cossins Rd, Westbury Park, BS6 7LY
0117 942 8293
www.redhouse-nursery.org.uk
Mon-Fri 8am-6pm

Formerly The Red House Nursery. Cares for children from 2-5yrs. See advertisement.

We Care For Children
Aged 3 Months - 5 Years
8am - 6pm
Monday to Friday

Information
Mary Regan or Sarah Bradley
46 Lower Redland Road, Bristol

0117 946 6178
www.poohcornernursery.co.uk

Toybox
11 The Drive, Henleaze, Bristol
Jan Johnson: 0117 962 3010
Mon-Fri 8am-6pm

Homely environment, caring for children from
3mths-5yrs.

Zebedees Day Nursery
26-28 Walsingham Road, St Andrews, Bristol,
BS6 5BT
Jane Galpin: 0117 985 3389
Mon-Fri 8am-6pm
near St Andrews Park

Friendly nursery open 52 weeks of the year
for 3mths-4yrs, with excellent facilities incl.
soft play, a security system. Nursery nurses
and early years teacher employed.

NORTH EAST BRISTOL

Barn Owl Nursery
Old Gloucester Rd, Hambrook, BS16 1RS
Dee Ireland: 0117 956 2222
Mon-Fri 8am-6pm

Small village nursery catering for children
from 2-5yrs with experienced staff.

Bambinos Day Nursery
The Old Vicarage, 63 Downend Road, Downend,
BS16 5UF
Sarah Gay: 0117 330 5300
bambinosdaynursery@hotmail.com
Mon-Fri 8.00am-6pm

Accepts children from 2-5yrs.

Fledglings Day Nursery
25 Oldbury Court Road, Fishponds, BS16 2HH
Mrs Lynne Slater: 0117 939 3398
Mon-Fri 8am-5.30pm

Accepts children from birth-5yrs.

The Red House Children's Centre
formerly - The Red House Nursery

Established in 1988 by Neville and
Maggie Kirby

1 Cossins Road,
Westbury Park,
Bristol BS6 7LY
Tel: 0117 942 8293
Email: info@redhouse-nursery.org.uk
www.redhouse-nursery.org.uk

Offers an exciting early years
curriculum for children
from 2 - 5 years

Jigsaw Day Nursery
Hunts Ground Road, Stoke Gifford, BS34 8HN
Mary Mahoney: 0117 979 9977
Mon-Fri 7.30am-6pm

Accepts children from 3mths-5yrs.

Stepping Stones Day Nursery
1 Hawkesbury Rd, Fishponds, BS16 2AP
Christine Williams: 0117 965 7269
Mon-Fri 8am-6pm

Est 1975 for children 2-5yrs. Stimulating but
very cosy environment.

UWE Students' Union Halley Nursery
St Matthias Campus, College Road, Fishponds,
BS16 2JP
Jackie Lewis: 0117 344 4452
nursery@uwe.ac.uk
Mon-Fri 8.30am-5.30pm

DAY NURSERY SCHOOL

Providing excellent care and early education

Our philosophy at The Rocking Horse Day Nursery is to enhance each child's curiosity, motivation and independence through sensitive support of qualified and experienced early years practitioners and to ensure all children feel included, secure and valued. We embrace active learning through play both indoors and outdoors.

Each nursery has received very good grades during OFSTED inspections. Please view the OFSTED website at www.ofsted.gov.uk/reports

For further information please ring the nearest nursery and arrange a visit.

We are at:

- **34 Northumberland Road, Redland, Bristol, BS6 7BD ☎ 0117 9240431**
- **C/O The Grange School, Tower Road North, Warmley, BS30 8XQ ☎ 0117 9476218**
- **1 Woodland Road, Clifton, Bristol, BS8 1AU ☎ 0117 9467145**

Accepts children from 6mths-5yrs, priority given to students of UWE, can accept children from the community.

EAST BRISTOL

Easton Community Children's Centre
Russell Town Ave, Upper Easton, Bristol, BS5 9JF
Amanda Rundle: 0117 939 2550
easton-childrens-centre@yahoo.co.uk
Mon-Fri: 8am-6pm

Centre offers day care facility for those living within the Easton and Lawrence Hill area for children 6mths-5yrs.

Hillside Day Nursery
20 Waters Rd, Kingswood, BS15 8EB
Yvonne Weaver: 0117 949 4466
www.hillsidedaynursery.co.uk
Mon-Fri: 8am-6pm

Family run nursery caring for 0-5yrs, 10% discount for siblings.

Kingswood Foundation Nursery
43, Britannia Road, Kingswood, Bristol, BS15 8DB
Sarah Johnston: 0117 935 2222
Mon-Fri 8am - 5.30pm (6pm on request)

Day nursery accepts children from 6wks to 5yrs. Part of Kingswood Gymnastics and Trampolining Centre, giving children access to all facilities. Staff will also take children on walks or swimming lessons, with parent authority.

Leapfrog Day Nursery
St Lukes Close, Emersons Green, BS16 7AL
Deborah Cottle: 0117 956 8222
www.leapfrogdaynurseries.co.uk
Mon-Fri: 7am-7pm

Accepts children from 0-5yrs.

Little Haven Day Nursery
261 Crews Hole Road, St George, Bristol
0117 941 4484
Mon- Fri 8am-6pm

Friendly pre-school nursery with baby unit. Excellent facilities with full day and half day sessions.

Redroofs Nursery
227 Kingsway, St George, BS5 8AH
Miss Jo Bates: 0117 949 2600
www.redroofsnursery.co.uk
Mon-Fri 8am-5.30pm

Personal profiles are kept by key workers who are all nursery nurses. During summer months children have access to swimming pool.

Redroofs Nursery
24 Poplar Road, North Common, Warmley, BS30 5JU
Lesley Bates: 0117 949 7200
Mon-Fri 8-5.30pm

Accepts children from 0-5yrs. During summer months children can enjoy swimming lessons.

The Rocking Horse Day Nursery
The Grange School, Tower Road North, Warmley, BS30 8XQ
Caroline Howe: 0117 947 6218
www.rockinghorsebristol.co.uk
Mon-Fri: 8am-6pm.

Cares from 6wks to 5yrs. All qualified staff.

Tiny Tots Day Nursery
130 High Street, Hanham, BS15 3EJ
0117 947 5436
Mon-Fri: 7.30am-6pm

Full and p/t day care for 0-8 yrs, including holiday club, before and after school care.

SOUTH EAST BRISTOL

Abacus Day Nursery
6-8 Emery Rd, Brislington, BS4 5PF
0117 977 2868
Mon-Fri 8am-6pm

Accepts children 3mths-5yrs.

Busy Bee Day Nursery
268 Wells Road, Knowle, BS4 2PN
Mrs Parker: 0117 977 5357
busy-bee@btconnect.com
Mon-Fri 8am-5.30pm

15mths-5yrs. Separate pre-school section, pets. Creative activities, visits to library & themed activities.

Court House Day Nursey
270 Wells Road, Knowle, BS4 2PU
Jenny Nott: 01454 614985
Mon-Fri 7.30am-6pm

Cheerful nursery for 6wks-5yrs with a high staff ratio & well planned curriculum.

SOUTH BRISTOL

Four Acres Family Unit
C/o Four Acres Primary School, Withywood, Bristol, BS13 8RB
0117 903 0476
four_acres_day_n@bristol-city.gov.uk
Mon-Fri 8am-6pm

Neighbourhood nursery opening from April 04, offering places to those training or working who live within the catchment area.

SOUTH WEST BRISTOL

Asquith Court Nursery
C/o David Lloyd Tennis Club, Ashton Road, Bristol, BS3 2HB
Wendy Palmer: 0117 953 2830
Mon-Fri 8am-6pm

Full day care offered for children 3mths-5years in a safe, stimulating environment. Also able to offer a pre-school curriculum.

Teddies Nursery
Clanage Road, Bower Ashton, Bristol, BS3 2JX
Lisa Prescott: 0117 953 1246
Mon-Fri 8am-6pm

Part of the BUPA Group, Teddies accepts children from 3mths-5yrs, offering nutured play and learning activities to help develop confidence and social skills.

NORTH WEST BRISTOL

Step Ahead Day Nursery
City of Bristol College, Broadlands Dr, Lawrence Weston, BS11 0NT
Pru Silverthorne: 0117 904 5695
Mon-Thu 8am-5.00pm, Fri: 8-4.30pm

P 🖊 WC ♿ 🔔 ☂ 🚭 🎦

Takes children from 2-5yrs.

CHILDMINDERS
All childminders must now be registered with Ofsted to look after children in their home. Registration includes a criminal records check of all persons involved (and anyone else living with them), inspection of the premises to look at health and safety, plus educational welfare issues.

Registration certificates state the number of children they are allowed to look after - the maximum being 6 under 5yrs (no more than 3 under 3 yrs) including any of their own children. Contracts are usually signed setting out the hours, fees, arrangements for provisions of nappies, food, playgroup fees etc. References and registration should be checked.

Advantages:
- A domestic setting with one primary carer may be more familiar and settling, especially for a very young child
- Economical, £2-4/hr per child with no tax and NI to pay
- May accommodate irregular, part time or unsociable hours
- May pick up children from school

Disadvantages:
- Alternative cover will need to be arranged if your child or the childminder is ill
- Your child's routine is determined by the childminder
- Time and patience to find the childminder to best suit you and your child's needs. You may need to visit several to make a comparison (even if the first one seems right)

National Childminding Association
8 Masons Hill, Bromley, Kent, BR2 9EY
The Manager: 020 8464 6164
info@ncma.org.uk, www.ncma.org.uk
The NCMA "Guide to choosing the right childminder" is free with a SAE.

NANNIES
A nanny is someone who cares for your child in your home with their undivided attention. Most hold an appropriate childcare qualification, such as an NNEB, B-Tec or NVQ3, although some have earned the nanny status by extensive experience and excellent references.

The best way to find a good nanny is to go through an agency, see those listed or look in 'The Lady' or the 'Nursery World' magazine (which includes a supplement called the 'Professional Nanny'). For a step-by-step guide to help you recruit good nannies and au pairs try 'The Nanny Handbook' by Karen House & Louise Sheppard.

Advantages:
- Can be flexible working part or full -time, living in or out
- No early or late journeys to and from nurseries/childminders
- Individual care provided in the secure and familiar environment of your home
- You are in control of the environment & rules that may apply
- Children still cared for when ill
- Nannies will do everything to do with the children e.g. sort out laundry, prepare meals, clean and tidy their bedroom/ playroom etc.
- Most nannies will prepare and organise activities and outings to stimulate all areas of a child's development. Particularly effective if care required for more than one child

Disadvantages:

- They are not subject to the requirements of The Children Act 1989 so are not registered or police checked. Nanny agencies will vet candidates although it is the parent's responsibility to research and check a nanny's background and references
- Can be quite expensive at £5.00-7.50/hr+ if required full-time for one child. You will need to sort out their tax and NI
- You will pay 4wks holiday and some parents make up wages on top of statutory sick pay
- Expect bigger household bills e.g. food, heating, lighting, telephone etc
- You may also have to pay for the use of the nanny's car
- May be issues of friends visiting during the day or evening

CHILDCARE AGENCIES

Able Nannies
18 Mivart Street, Eastville, BS5 6JF
The Manager: 0117 935 5030
Supplies nannies throughout the West Country.

Alphabet Childcare
46b High Street, Westbury-on-Trym, BS9 3DZ
Alison Hooper: 0117 959 1161
alphabet@btconnect.com, alphabet-childcare.co.uk
Long established agency with a register of nannies, nursery nurses and baby sitters. See advertisement.

Bristol Nannies
29 Royal Victoria Park, Bristol, BS10 6TD
Geraldine Hartnoll: 0117 950 5526
dina.hartnolll@btopenworld.com
Specialists in finding the most appropriate, quality childcare.

Park Lane Nannies
51 Knowleworth Crescent, Bristol, BS15 6RZ
The Manager: 0117 373 0003
www.parklanenannies.com

Established 1988, able to provide a variety of help from nannies, housekeepers and maternity nurses. Not only in the the West Country but nationwide.

Star Nannies
67 Sheldons Court, Winchcombe Street, Cheltenham, GL52 2NR
The Manager: 01242 512 636
tracey@starnannies.co.uk, www.starnannies.co.uk
Agency placing nannies throughout the UK and overseas.

Tinies Childcare
64 Nightingale Rise, Portishead, BS20 8LN
The Manager: 01275 849 608
bristol@tinieschildcare.co.uk, www.tinieschildcare.co.uk
Part of established national agency providing nannies and maternity nurses.

EMERGENCY COVER
What happens when your carefully arranged childcare provision falls apart due to illness of your child, nanny or childminder? Employment agencies for nannies and nursery nurses can provide temporary carers at short notice.

MATERNITY NURSES
Usually employed just before and immediately after you have a baby. May be a qualified nanny with experience with young babies, a qualified nurse, midwife or health visitor. Usually working on a short-term contract (2 wks-6mths) living with the family. Need to be booked well in advance.

They are on call 24 hours a day up to 6 days a week, helping with all aspects of new born care, even during the night. Sleeping and feeding routines are encouraged. See agencies listed.

133

NANNY TAX & NI

Nannytax
PO Box 988, Brighton, BN1 1NT
The Manager: 0845 2262203
mailbox@nannytax.co.uk, www.nannytax.co.uk
Nannytax is the original and inexpensive countrywide payroll service, designed to look after your nanny's tax and national insurance contributions.

The Alphabet Childcare Tax & NI
46b High Street, Westbury on Trym, Bristol, BS9 3DZ
Tara Parsons: 0117 959 1161
alphabet@btconnect.com
Free advice to nannies, service can also set up pay and deduction records for employers for an annual fee.

AU PAIRS
Aged between 18-27, an au pair comes to live with a host family to study in this country. Assisting with household chores and children, up to 5hrs/day (25 hrs/wk), 2 evenings babysitting, costing approx £45/wk. They are unqualified therefore best suited to care for school age children.

You should expect to enrol them in a class and will need to negotiate whether you will pay for their study. There are regulations laid down by the Home Office about appointing an au pair. Those from the EU do not need a work permit and have no time limit whilst restrictions apply to those outside the EU and they have to be formally invited by the host family. Details can be obtained from the Home Office.

Advantages:
- Helping hand with children and light housework.

- Flexible hours to suit you such as after school and evenings.
- Inexpensive option.
- Older children enjoy learning about the au pair's language and culture.
- Can be like an older sibling integrating into family life.

Disadvantages:

- Unlikely to meet them beforehand.
- Unqualified therefore should not have sole charge of young children.
- If no terms are agreed beforehand the au pair can leave at any time.
- May not be able to speak good English or have a driver's licence.
- You may need to provide specific guidance on certain jobs.
- Little continuity of care as they usually only stay for 6mths-1yr.
- Living with you as part of the family may encroach on your space.

The Au Pair Answer

27 Oakfield Road, Clifton, BS8 2AT
The Manager: 0117 974 4779
info@languageproject.co.uk
www.languageproject.co.uk
Specialists in au pairs placed throughout the UK both long and short term (from 2+mths).

BABYSITTERS

Having time to yourself in the evenings is important, but it can be difficult finding someone you can trust to look after your children. Expect to pay about £3-5 per hour for their services.

Babysitters can be quite young therefore you need to check their experience with children, references and any babysitting or childcare training completed. The agencies below can help or try advertising at local colleges for student nannies, or at local nurseries for nursery nurses.

Bristol Babysitting Agency

32 Bishop Rd, Bishopston, BS7 9LT
0117 940 5417
Evening babysitting within Bristol.

Featherbed Nannies

Buckingham Lodge, Station Road, Keynsham, BS31 2BN
0117 986 0710
Able to provide ad hoc babysitting services.

Time to Share

Unit 55, Easton Business Centre, Felix Road, Easton, BS5 0HE
The Manager: 0117 941 5868
info@time2share.org.uk, www.time2share.org.uk
For children with learning difficulties, this organisation provides sitters and caters for individual needs. Families are matched on a one-to-one basis with a volunteer.

See also

Able Nannies
18 Mivart Street, Eastville, BS5 6JF
The Manager: 0117 935 5030 (tel/fax)

Alphabet Childcare
46b High Street, Westbury-on-Trym, BS9 3DZ
Alison Hooper: 0117 959 1161
alphabet@btconnect.com, alphabet-childcare.co.uk

MOTHERS' HELPS

Usually assisting parents at home, mothers' helps are not normally trained in childcare although they may have lots of experience and completed relevant courses/first aid. Cost from £4/hr, they can work full/part time, living in or out.

Advantages:

- Flexible helping hand with children and light housework
- Ideal part time option if children at school

Disadvantages:

- Unqualified therefore should not be left in sole charge of young children
- As an employer you will have to sort out their tax and NI contributions
- Most nanny agencies have mother's helps on their books

City of Bristol College

5.E.5 College Green Centre, Saint Georges Road, Bristol, BS1 5UA
0117 904 5278
Contact; Works Placement Officer, Health & Education Dept.
Family placements needed for students on childcare courses. Families need to have a baby under one year old and students must be supervised. Families need public liability insurance. Police checks will be carried out. Ask for the Work Placement Officer in the Health and Education Dept.

CRÈCHES

Crèches are available in shopping, community and leisure centres as well as colleges of further education, see relevant chapters for listings. Most require you to stay on the premises.

MOBILE CRÈCHES

Crèches with qualified staff and appropriate equipment can be hired for short periods of time to look after a set number of children during a special occasion such as a wedding or company fun day.

ABC Childcare Crew

46b High Street, Westbury-on-Trym, BS9 3DZ
Alison Hooper: 0117 959 1161
alphabet@btconnect.com, alphabet-childcare.co.uk
🔳
Able to provide a mobile crèche facility.

Barton Hill Family Playcentre

Barton Hill Settlement, 43 Ducie Road, BS5 0AX
Vadna Chauhan: 0117 955 6971
Mon-Fri: 9.45-11.45am, 1-3pm
£1.50 for first child, 75p for second
🔳 🔳 🔳
Crèche for children 0-5yrs available for people using the Settlement.

Easton Community Children's Centre

Russell Town Ave, Bristol, BS5 9JF
Michelle Boyd: 0117 939 2550
easton-childrens-centre@yahoo.co.uk
Centre can provide an on site creche facility for individuals or organisations, alternatively, carers can be sought for a mobile creche at any location, day or night. Call to confirm costings.

Icon	meaning

General

	nearby public transport
P	parking
WC	toilets
	lift
	disabled facilities
	buggy friendly
	double buggy friendly
	no smoking
	nappy changing
	feeding room
	crèche
	indoor play area
	outdoor play area
	garden
	picnic area
	dogs allowed
	nearby public transport
	dogs allowed
	café
	shop

REFERENCE SECTION

ICON KEY

Icon	meaning

Pre-School

Pp	parent participation
	waiting list

Eating Out

	high chair
	toys/crayons
V	vegetarian option
CP	children's portions/meals

ALTERNATIVE SOURCES OF INFORMATION

www.titchhikers.co.uk
See our new website for new listings and changes to existing listings, feedback from readers, etc.

Bristol Tourism & Conference Bureau
www.visitbristol.co.uk

Venue Magazine
www.venue.co.uk
The 'what's-on guide' covering Bristol and Bath, for sale at newsagents throughout the region. Has regular Family sections with information on days out and activities for children.

Primary Times (in Avon)
Distrubuted, free, throughout primary schools in and around Bristol. Lots of seasonal information on services and activities for children aged 4-11yrs.

Local papers and their websites will also help you keep your finger on the pulse.

Bristol Evening Post
www.epost.co.uk

Bath Evening Chronicle
www.thisisbath.co.uk

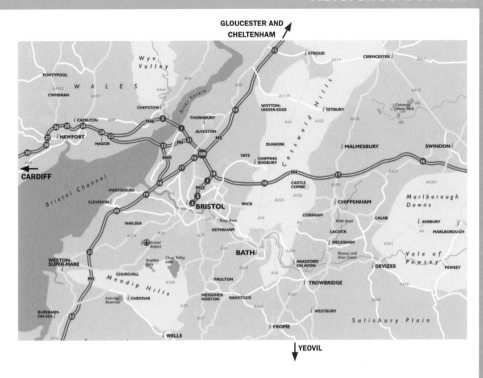

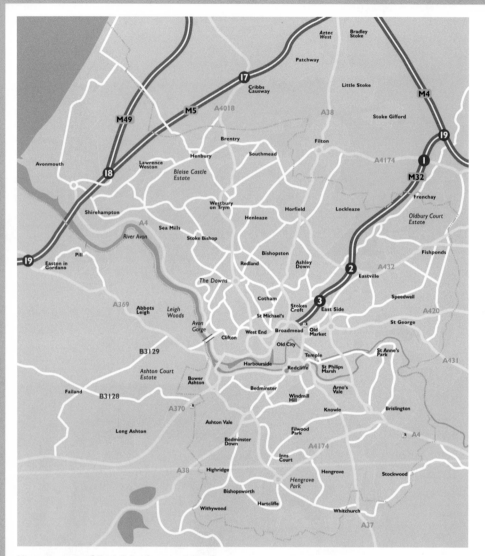

Maps courtesy of Bristol Conference & Tourism
www.visitbristol.co.uk

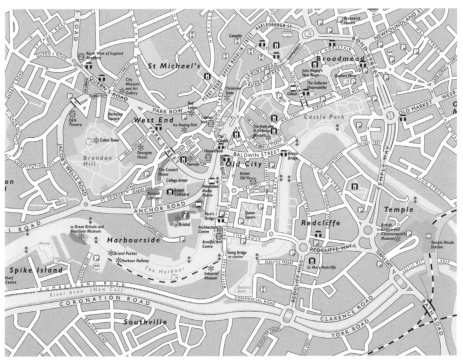

Reference Section

BRISTOL LEISURE CENTRES

All details for Bristol leisure centres at: www.bcsport.co.uk except Filton Sports and Leisure Centre at: www.filton-town-council.co.uk/html/leisure.html

Leisure Centres	Address and Phone Number	Opening Times	Softplay	Crèche	Swimming Pool	Gymnasium	Outdoor Facilities	Aerobics	Martial Arts	Netball	Basketball for under 12s	Badminton	Cricket Nets	Volley Ball	Football for under 12s	Squash Courts	Café	Holiday Timetable	Parties	Trampolining	Gymnastics	Disabled Facilities	Public Transport	Parking
Easton Leisure Centre 0117 955 8840	Thrissell Street, Easton, BS5 0SW	Mon-Sat 0700-2230, Sun 0800-2200	✓	✓	✓	✓	✓		✓		✓	✓		✓	✓	✓	✓	✓	✓		✓	✓	✓	✓
Horfield Sports Centre 0117 952 1650	Dorian Road, Horfield, BS7 0XW	Mon-Fri 0900-2230, Sat 0900-2200, Sun 0900-2230	✓	✓		✓		✓	✓			✓				✓		✓	✓	✓	✓		✓	✓
Kingsdown Sports Centre 0117 942 6582	Portland St, Kingsdown, BS2 8HL	Mon-Fri 0900-2300, Sat 0900-1900, Sun 0900-2300	✓			✓			✓							✓		✓	✓				✓	✓
Robin Cousins Sport Centre 0117 982 3514	Off West Town Rd, Avonmouth, BS11 9GB	Mon-Fri 0900-2300, Sat 0900-1730, Sun 0900-2300	✓	✓		✓		✓	✓		✓				✓			✓	✓	✓	✓		✓	✓
Whitchurch Sports Centre 01275 833911	Bamfield, Whitchurch, BS14 0XA	Daily 0900-2300	✓	✓		✓	✓	✓	✓	✓		✓	✓	✓	✓	✓		✓	✓	✓	✓		✓	✓
St Paul's Community Sports Academy 0117 377 3405	Newfoundland Road, St Paul's, BS2 9NH	Daily 0900-2230	✓	✓		✓	✓	✓	✓	✓	✓								✓			✓	✓	
Filton Sports and Leisure Centre (formerly known as the Dolphin Pool) 01454 866686	Elm Park, Filton, BS34 7PS	0900-2000 Mon-Fri, 0900-1800			✓	✓			✓		✓	✓						✓	✓			✓	✓	✓

*See Activities 0-12Years chapter for outdoor pools and themed pools

BRISTOL SWIMMING POOLS

All details for Bristol swimming pools at: www.bcsport.co.uk

Leisure Centres	Address and Phone Number	Pool Size	Outdoor Facilities	Aquafit classes	Swimming sessions for under 5's	Lessons	Swimming Club	Learner Pool	Off poolside changing rooms	Playpen and baby changing tables	Disabled facilities	Parking	Public Transport	Other swimming activities	Comments
Easton Leisure Centre 0117 955 8840	Thrissell Street, Easton, BS5 0SW	25m		✓	✓	✓	✓		✓	✓	✓	✓	✓		recently refurbished
Bishopworth 0117 964 0258	Whitchurch Lane, Bishopworth, BS13 7RW	25m		✓	✓	✓	✓		✓	✓	✓	✓	✓	sub-aqua	
Bristol North 0117 924 3548	Gloucester Road, Bishopston, BS7 8BN	23m		✓	✓	✓	✓		✓	✓	✓	✓	✓	water polo	
Bristol South 0117 966 3131	Dean Lane, Bedminster, BS3 1BS	30m		✓	✓	✓	✓			✓			✓		
Filwood 0117 966 2823	Filwood Broadway, Filwood, BS4 1JL	33m	✓	✓	✓		✓		✓	✓	✓		✓	canoeing, sub-aqua	
Henbury 0117 950 0141	Crow Lane, Henbury, BS10 7EN	25m	✓	✓	✓	✓	✓		✓	✓	✓	✓	✓		
Jubilee 0117 977 7900	Jubilee Rd, Knowle, BS4 2LP	22m		✓	✓		✓	✓	✓	✓			✓		
Shirehampton 0117 982 2627	Park Rd, Shirehampton, BS11 0EF	22m		✓	✓	✓	✓	✓	✓	✓		✓	✓	canoeing	
Speedwell 0117 967 4778	Whitfield Rd, Speedwell, BS5 7TS	22m			✓					✓			✓		

*See Activities 0-12Years chapter for outdoor pools and themed pools

BATH AND NORTH EAST SOMERSET LEISURE CENTRES

All details for Bath and North East Somerset leisure centres at: www.bathnes.gov.uk/atoz/comservs/sportsleisurecentres.htm

Leisure Centres	Address and Phone Number	Opening Times	Softplay	Crèche	Swimming Pool	Gymnasium	Outdoor Facilities	Aerobics	Martial Arts	Netball	Basketball	Badminton	Tennis	Football 5 a side	Squash courts	Café	Holiday Timetable	Parties	Trampolining	Gymnastics	Disabled Facilities	Parking
Bath Sports and Leisure Centre 01225 462565	North Parade Road, Bath, BA2 4ET	Daily	✓	Tues am	✓	✓	✓	✓			✓	✓	✓	✓	✓	✓	✓	✓				
Culverhay Sports Centre 01225 462565 Mon-Fri 01225 480882 Eve/WE's	Rush Hill, Bath, BA2 2QI	Out of school hours			✓				✓			✓		✓			✓	✓				
Keynsham Leisure Centre 01225 395161	Temple St, Keynsham, BS31 1HE	Daily	Wed am	Thurs am	✓	✓		✓				✓		✓	✓	✓	✓	✓				
South Wansdyke Sports Centre 01225 395161	Rackvernal Rd, Midsomer Norton, BA3 2UC	Daily	✓		✓	✓	✓	✓		✓				✓	✓		✓	✓	✓	✓		✓

*See Activities 0-12Years chapter for outdoor pools and themed pools

All details for South Gloucestershire leisure centres at: www.southglos.gov.uk/leisurecentres

Leisure Centres	Address and Phone Number	Opening Times	Softplay	Crèche	Swimming Pool	Gymnasium	Outdoor Facilities	Aerobics	Martial Arts	Netball	Basketball	Badminton	Tennis	Cricket Nets	Volley Ball	Football for under 12s	Squash courts	Café	Holiday Timetable	Parties	Trampolining	Gymnastics	Disabled Facilities	Public Transport	Parking
Bradley Stoke Leisure Centre 01454 867050	Fiddlers Wood Lane, Bradley Stoke, S.Glos, BS32 9BS	Mon-Fri 0715-2330, Sat/Sun 0730-2330	✓	✓	✓	✓	✓	✓	✓		✓	✓	✓		✓	✓	✓	✓	✓	✓	✓		✓	✓	✓
Kingswood Leisure Centre 01454 865700	Church Rd, Staple Hill, S.Glos, BS16 4RH	Mon/Wed/Fri 0700-2300, Tue/Thu/Sat 0800-2300, Sun 0800-2000	✓	✓	✓	✓	✓	✓	✓		✓	✓				✓	✓	✓	✓	✓				✓	✓
Thornbury Leisure Centre 01454 865777	Alveston Hill, Thornbury, S.Glos, BS35 3JB	Mon-Fri 0700-2330, Sat/Sun 0730-2330	✓	✓	✓	✓	✓	✓	✓		✓	✓			✓	✓	✓	✓	✓	✓				✓	✓
Yate Leisure Centre 01454 865800	Kennedy Way, Yate, S. Glos, BS37 4DQ	Mon-Fri 0700-2300, Sat/Sun 0730-2200	✓	✓	✓	✓		✓	✓		✓	✓	✓		✓	✓	✓	✓	✓	✓	✓	✓	✓	✓	✓
Downend Sports Centre 0117 9560688	Garnett Place, Downend, S.Glos	Mon-Fri 0600-2200, Sat/Sun 0915-2200																		✓			✓		
Patchway Sports Centre 01454 865890	Patchway High School, Hempton Lane, Almondsbury, S. Glos BS32 4AJ	Mon-Fri 0600-2200, Sat 0900-1800, Sun 0900-1930				✓	✓		✓	✓	✓	✓	✓	✓	✓	✓	✓		✓		✓		✓	✓	
Yate (Outdoor) Sports Complex 01454 865820	behind Brinsham Green School, Yate, S.Glos, BS37 7PN	Mon-Thu 0600-2200, Fri 0600-2100, Sat 0930-2000, Sun 0930-1830					✓											✓		✓				✓	✓

*See Activities 0-12Years chapter for outdoor pools and themed pools

NORTH SOMERSET LEISURE CENTRES

All details for North Somerset leisure centres at: www.n-somerset.gov.uk/enjoying/sports+and+leisure/index.asp

Leisure Centres	Address and Phone Number	Opening Times	Softplay	Créche	Swimming Pool	Gymnasium	Outdoor Facilities	Aerobics	Martial Arts	Netball	Basketball for under 12s	Badminton	Tennis	Cricket Nets	Volley Ball	Football for under 12s	Squash courts	Café	Holiday Timetable	Parties	Trampolining	Gymnastics	Disabled Facilities	Public Transport	Parking
Backwell Leisure Centre 01275 463726	Farleigh Rd, Backwell, BS48 3PB	Mon-Fri 0700-2200, Sat 0830-2000, Sun 0800-2000			✓				✓								✓	✓	✓	✓				✓	✓
Gordano Sports Centre 01275 843942	Portishead, BS20 7QR	Mon-Fri during term time 1730-2200, Sat and Sun 1000-variable closing time					✓	✓	✓	✓		✓	✓			✓			✓	✓	✓			✓	✓
Parish Wharf Leisure Centre 01275 848494	Harbour Road, Portishead, BS20 9DD	Mon-Fri 0700-2200, Sat and Sun 0800-2100	✓	✓	✓	✓	✓	✓	✓		✓	✓	✓		✓	✓		✓	✓	✓			✓	✓	✓
Portishead Open Air Pool 01275 843454	The Esplanade, Portishead, BS20 7HD	May and Sept 1400-1800, July and Aug 1000-1800			✓		✓											✓						✓	✓
Scotch Horn Leisure Centre 01275 856965	Brockway, Nailsea, BS48 1BZ	Mon-Fri, Sun 0900-2200, Sat 0900-2000	✓	✓		✓	✓			✓		✓				✓	✓	✓	✓	✓				✓	✓
Strode Leisure Centre 01275 879242	Strode Way, Clevedon, BS21 6QG	Mon and Fri 0700-2200, Tue -Thu 0730-2200, Sat and Sun 0830-2200	✓	✓	✓		✓	✓	✓	✓	✓	✓			✓	✓			✓	✓		✓		✓	✓
Swiss Valley Sport Centre 01934 877 182	Clevedon School, Clevedon, BS21 6AH	Mon-Fri 1730-2230, Sat and Sun 0900 -2200				✓	✓	✓	✓	✓	✓	✓		✓			✓							✓	✓

*See Activities 0-12Years chapter for outdoor pools and themed pools

PLAYGROUPS & EARLY EDUCATION 0-4 YEARS

Diana Beavon

CHAPTER 8

INTRODUCTION

Socialising with your child is a great way to meet other parents, but also a vital part of your child's education. This chapter looks at weekly groups held specifically for children prior to pre-school. It then highlights the various options available for pre-school education before your child heads off to primary school rising 5.

Also see Schools & Educational Support and Activities 0-12 Years chapters.

There are several government initiatives worth a mention:

Sure Start and Early Excellence Centres

These government initiatives pioneer ways to improve support for families and children. Their aim is to work with parents and children to promote the developmment of pre-school children, particularly those who are disadvantaged, to ensure that they are ready to thrive when they get to school. There are a number of centres in Bristol, providing a range of services from informal drop-in sessions for parents with their children to parenting classes. There are also crèche facilities to allow parents to learn a new skill.

Knowle West Sure Start	0117 9039781
Easton Sure Start	0117 9413400
Hartcliffe, Highridge & Withywood	0117 9030460
Kingsweston Sure Start	0117 9824578

Early Years Partnership
This has been set up to represent all the different sectors providing early years education and day care. It holds general open meetings, which parents are welcome to attend, to discuss key issues affecting young children. For details contact:

The Children's Information Service
0845 129 7217
www.childcarelink.gov.uk
See Childcare 0-4 Years chapter and advertisement.

UNDER 1'S & TODDLER GROUPS

We have listed all the toddler groups by the day the group meets each week.

If you are unable to find a group in your area keep an eye on notice boards in libraries, churches and doctors' surgeries where they might be advertised or call the Children's Information Service, see above. Let us know if you find one that should be listed here.

Unless otherwise stated, toddler groups are held once a week, during the school terms, stopping for the holidays, for children under 4 years. They are a good way for parents to meet up informally and for your child to socialise and try new skills under your supervision. Most groups charge a small fee for a drink and biscuit – for both adults and children.

Postnatal Group
Horfield Health Centre, Lockleaze Rd,
Horfield, BS7 9RR
0117 373 7133
Please phone for times

Free weekly group organised by Health Visitors for parents of babies up to 9 months. Phone in advance for times and details.

NCT Open Houses
31, Walsingham Rd, St Andrews, Bristol
Janet Bremner: 0117 942 2067
janet.bremner@btinternet.com
The National Childbirth Trust (NCT) offers a way of meeting other parents and their children through open houses. Parents open their house (providing a drink and biscuit) for parents and their babies/children. Details are published in the quarterly NCT Bristol newsletters. Open houses are a useful way of meeting other parents, especially if you are new to the area, and can provide social contact through the baby and pre-school years. You do not have to be a member of the NCT to attend.

MONDAY

Barton Hill Family Playcentre
Barton Hill Settlement, 43 Ducie Road, BS5 0AX
Vadna Chauhan: 0117 955 6971
Mon: 9.15am-11.45am, 75p

Structured group for pre-school children with art activity, construction toys, home/fantasy corner, sand & water play. Separate soft play area for babies. Dads welcome.

Bristol Children's Playhouse
Berkeley Green Rd, Eastville, BS5 6LU
Jackie Cutmore: 0117 951 0037
Mon-Fri 9am-3.15pm
£10 membership per year

Informal drop-in for parents/carers open to all, every day with extensive play equipment and playgrounds outside. Friendly, qualified, welcoming staff. Summer trips organised.

Child's Play Toddler Group
Easton Christian Family Centre, Beaufort Street,
Easton, BS5 0SQ
Gill Miles: 0117 955 4255
Mon 1pm-3pm, 75p

Children's Information Service for Bristol
ARE YOU LOOKING FOR CHILDCARE?

CIS provides free impartial information and guidance on a full range of childcare and children's services and resources in Bristol

Helpline Telephone Number 0845 129 7217
Email enquiries@cisbristol.co.uk

□ Childminders □ Pre-school Playgroups □ Day Nurseries
□ Afterschool Clubs □ Holiday Playschemes □ Leisure Activities
□ Parent & Toddler Groups □ Working Tax Credit
□ Nursery Education Grant □ Family Support Groups

Registered Charity No 105 3854   Registered Company No 316 8713

Structured play session runs four times a week for under 4's giving parents a chance to have a break and participate in another activity or stay with child.

Cotham Drop-in Playcentre
Cotham Parish Church, Cotham Road, BS6 6DP
Drew Esam: 0117 973 3395
Mon 1.30pm-3.30pm
£1 per family

Suitable from birth up to pre-school. Two halls, one for older and more mobile children. Sing song to finish.

Filton Avenue Nursery School
Blakeney Road, Horfield, Bristol, BS7 0DL
Sue Evans: 0117 377 2680
filton_avenue_n@bristol-city.gov.uk
Mon 9am-11.30am, Free

Free drop-in sessions for parents/carers with 20mths-3yrs.

Fulford Family Centre
237-239 Gatehouse Ave, Withywood, Bristol
Jenny Lewis: 0117 978 2441
Mon 9.30am-11.30pm, Free
BS13 9AQ

Free drop-in sessions for under 5's for parents/carers living in the Hartcliffe, Bishopworth and Withywood areas. Crèche also provided.

Gay Elms Sure Start
Gay Elms Primary School, Withywood Road, Bristol, BS13 9AX
07900 497740
Mon: 12.45pm-2.30pm, Free

Weekly informal drop-in for 0-4yrs.

Highridge Sure Start
Lakemead Grove, Highridge, Bristol, BS13 8EA
0117 978 1028
Mon 10am-12noon, Free

Informal baby breakfast run weekly for 0-1yrs. Crèche available for older children.

Hope Centre Parent and Toddlers
Hope Centre, Hotwells, BS8
Sue Michel: 0117 377 2270
Mon 2pm-3.30pm, Free
[✎] [WC] [👶] [♿]

Suitable from 0-5yrs. Group run by nursery nurses from Oakfield Day Nursery, with a baby clinic.

Mother & Child Playgroup
Charlotte Keel Health Centre, Seymour Road, Easton, BS5 0UA
0117 951 2244
Mon: 11am-1pm, 20p
[✎] [WC] [👶] [♿]

Drop-in group for approx 8-12 children. Restricted area with stimulating toys, good for a chat with new mothers. Open to local parents and carers with children under 5yrs.

Parkway Parent and Child Project
Parkway Methodist Church, Conduit Place, St Werburghs, BS2 9RU
Sue Dowd: 0117 935 0205
Mon 9.30am-12pm
£1 per family
[✎] [👶] [♿] [🚲] [📷] [🚌] [♿] [Pp]

Parent and toddler drop-in sessions run throughout the year in a safe, stimulating and supportive environment with separate area for older children to ride bikes.

Rainbow Tots
Kensington Baptist Church Hall, Seymour Road, Easton
Amanda Pearce: 0117 955 7768
Mon 10am -12pm, 60p
[✎] [WC] [📷] [Pp]

Friendly Church run group meets three times a week for 0-4yrs. Offers a craft activity every week, lots of toys plus baby area.

Southmead Day Nursery
Doncaster Road, Southmead, Bristol, BS10 5PW
Fiona Townsend: 0117 377 2343
Mon 9.15-11.15am, Free
[P] [✎] [WC] [👶] [♿] [🚲] [🚌] [♿] [Pp]

Informal drop-in sessions held at the nursery for children 0-4yrs. Parents can use the resource library or attend family learning activities whilst children use the Sensory Room and outdoor play area.

St Joseph's Toddlers
St Josephs Church Hall, Forest Road, Fishponds, BS16 3QT
Cathy Williamson: 0117 914 7173/0117 940 1782
Mon 1.45pm-3.15pm
£1 (2nd child 50p). Annual sub £2
[✎] [WC] [👶] [Pp]

Up to 4yrs. Variety of toys and activities, including baby area.

St Mary's Mother and Toddler Group
St Mary's Magdalene Church Hall, Mariners Drive, Stoke Bishop, Bristol
Jenny Williams: 0117 968 3892
Mon 1.30pm-3.30pm
70p per child, 30p additional children
[P] [✎] [👶] [♿] [📷] [Pp]

Informal drop-in group aimed at toddlers from 1-4yrs, creative activity every week, lots of toys and separate baby play area.

St Peter's Parent & Toddler Group
St Peter's Church Hall, The Drive, Henleaze, BS9 4LD
Parish Office
0117 962 3196
Mon 10am-12pm
50p per family per session, £1 per family per term
[P] [✎] [WC] [👶] [♿] [♿] [Pp]

Children from 'bumps' to nursery age, meets twice a week. Parents, grandparents, nannies are welcome to join. Action songs at the end.

Stepping Stones Toddlers
Salem Chapel, Trafalger Terrace, Bedminster Down, BS3 2SW
Karen Davis: 0117 985 4819
Mon: 9.30am-11.30am
£1 per family
Entrance to Chapel on Hardy Road
[P] [✎] [WC] [👶] [🚌] [Pp]

A chance to meet other mums and toddlers. Lots of toys with soft play area. All welcome.

Sydenham Road Under Fives Toddlers
Totterdown Baptist Church, Sydenham Road, Totterdown, BS4 3DF
Wendy McCarthy: 0117 907 4108

Mon 9.45-11.30am
£2.00, additional siblings £1

[✎] [WC] [👶] [♿]

"Toddle up" held twice a week for 2-3yrs. Refreshments included. Parent pack available.

The Roo Club
Filton Sports & Leisure Centre, Elm Park, Filton, BS34 7PS
Vicky Graham: 01454 866686
Mon 10.15am-11.15am, £2

[P] [✎] [👶] [♿] [Pp]

Pre-school activity club held in the Badminton Hall with bouncy castle, story and song time. Limited to 14 children per session.

The Salvation Army Candle Project Parent and Toddlers
6 Ashley Road, St Pauls, BS6 5NL
Maureen Baxter: 0117 942 4607
Mon: 10am-12pm, 50p

[✎] [WC] [👶] [♿]

Small group meets twice a week, with space for 12-15 children, offering a variety of educational toys, trikes, tunnel, slide, dolls prams etc. Fathers welcome.

Trinity Tots ABC Club
Holy Trinity Church, Hotwells Road, BS8 4ST
Vicki Wuss: 0117 929 0903
Mon 9.30am-11.30am
50p per adult incl. refreshments

[✎] [WC] [👶] [♿] [👶] [♿] [📖] [Pp]

Drop-in friendly group for pre-school children offering variety of toys for all ages.

Tyndale Baptist Church Baby & Toddler Group
Tyndale Baptist Church, Whiteladies Road, Clifton, BS8
Alison Lloyd: 0117 968 5289
Mon 2-3.30pm, 50p

[P] [✎] [WC] [👶]

Caters for children from baby to pre-school age.

Under One's Group
Charlotte Keel Health Centre, Seymour Road, Easton, BS5 0UA
Chloe Bodard-Williams: 0117 951 2244
Mon 11am-1pm (runs through holidays), 20p

[✎] [WC] [👶] [♿] [Pp]

Small informal drop-in group for 0-5yrs in restricted area with stimulating toys, good for a chat with new mothers. Open to local parents and carers.

Victoria Park Toddlers
Victoria Park Baptist Church, St Johns Lane, Bedminster
Sue Fortune: 0779 977 0619
Mon 9.30am-11.30am
£1 for one child, £1.50 for two or more

[✎] [WC] [⏰] [👶] [♿] [Pp]

Drop-in group for 0-4yrs, with baby area and toys for under ones. Variety of other toys, craft activities, sand etc. Fathers regularly attend. Outdoor area used.

Wessex Flyer Fun Factory
Hengrove Leisure Park, Hengrove Way, Hengrove, BS14 0HR
01275 834340
Mon 10.30-11.30am, £2

[P] [✎] [👶] [♿] [📖] [Pp]

Weekly drop-in Parent and Toddler sessions held in the Fun Factory, full use of all facilities for the under 5's. Price includes light refreshments.

Windmill Hill Children & Family Centre
Philip Street, Bedminster, Bristol, BS3 4EA
Mary Radley: 0117 963 3299
Tue 9.45am-11.45am
£1.50 members, £2.50 non members

[P] [✎] [👶] [♿] [♿] [📖] [♿] [♿] [Pp]

Toddler Group held three times a week for children 0-4yrs. Separate baby area, with indoor and outdoor toys for older children including art activities.

TUESDAY

Bib Club
Clifton Health Clinic, Mortimer Road, BS8 4EX
0117 973 5425
Tue 10.30am-12pm

[✎] [WC] [👶] [Pp]

Free drop-in facility for first time mums with babies under 4mths to meet for a chat . Organised by Health Visitors of the clinic.

Bristol Waldorf School Parent and Toddler Group

12d Cotham Rd, Cotham, BS6 6DR
Jan Coles: 0117 973 4399
Tue, Thu 9.30am-12noon, Tue 1pm-3.30pm
£2.50 per session

Part of Bristol Steiner Waldorf School's Kindergarten, weekly sessions are held for parents and toddlers in homely surroundings with natural play materials. Sessions include crafts, break time and circle time.

Chatter Tots

Soundwell Rd (entrance on Portland Street), Soundwell, Bristol, BS16 4QP
01454 613 305 Church Office
Tue 9.30-11am
75p session or £3 for half a term or £6 a term

Includes crafts, singing and storytime.

Counterslip Baptist Church

648 Wells Road, Whitchurch, Bristol, BS14 9HT
Margaret: 01275 833377
worship@counterslip.co.uk
Tue 10am-11.30am
£1, 50p for additional child

Parent and toddler group held in a large carpeted area with wide variety of toys appropriate to age range. Small waiting list, please phone before coming.

Emmanuel Toddler Group

Emmanuel Chapel, Satchfield Crescent, Henbury, BS10 7BL
Jayne Crocker: 0117 950 1951
emmanuelchap@supanet.com
Tue: 9.30-11.30am, £1

Meets twice a week. Large range of toys including ball pool tent, book corner, play kitchen area, bikes, trikes and baby toys. Quiet space. Newcomers welcomed.

Jumping Beans

St Francis Church, North Street (opposite Aldi), Ashton Gate

Tue 9.30-11.30am
£2 per session

Weekly group for childminders and their children.

Long Ashton Toddler Group

Long Ashton Village Hall, Keedwell Hill, Long Ashton
Sarah Leong
sarah@4mmaw.freeserve.co.uk
Tue 1.30-3.30pm
£1 first child, 60p for additional

Informal group held in Village Hall. Separate baby section and craft tables for toddlers. Entry includes light refreshments.

Noah's Ark Stay & Play

Cairns Rd Baptist Church, Cairns Road, BS6 7TH
Carol de Beger: 0117 944 6229
Tue 9.45am-11.45am (except 1st Tue of ev month)
£1 per session

Weekly group for children 2-3yrs plus carer. Offers a Bible story themed craft activity and story. Numbers limited to 30, please call for a place.

Parkway Parent and Child Project

Parkway Methodist Church, Conduit Place, St Werburghs, BS2 9RU
Sue Dowd: 0117 935 0205
Tue 1-3pm, £1 per family

Parent and toddler drop-in sessions run throughout the year in a safe, stimulating and supportive environment with separate area for older children to ride bikes.

Patacake Toddlers

Westbury on Trym Methodist Church Village Hall, Westbury Hill, Westbury on Trym
Linda Dunstan: 0117 962 2930
Tue 1.15pm-2.45pm
£1 per family

Informal drop-in for Mums with toddlers to have a chat and a coffee.

Philip Street Chapel Toddlers

Philip Street (entrance on Clarke St), Bedminster, BS3 4EA
Rhona Madden: 0117 951 8588

Tue 10-11.30am, £1.30 per family

P 🖉 WC 👶 👶

Well equipped group in large carpeted hall. Welcoming to new comers - users rate it very friendly.

Queen's Road Methodist Baby & Toddler Group

Queen's Road, Keynsham, BS31 2NN
Catherine Bennett: 0117 987 7753
Tue: 1.15pm-2.45pm
75p for one child, £1 for two

P 🖉 WC 🍼 👶 👶 🚼 🚻 Pp

Weekly organised group for children 0-5yrs for parents/carers. Weekly craft activity and lots of toys. Please call for a place.

Rainbow Tots

Kensington Baptist Church Hall, Seymour Rd, Easton
Amanda Pearce: 0117 955 7768
Tue 10am-12 noon, 60p

🖉 WC 👶 🚻 Pp

Friendly Church run group meets three times a week for the 0-4yrs. Offers a craft activity every week, lots of toys plus baby area.

Redland Toddlers

Redland Parish Church Hall, Redland Green Rd, BS6 7HE
Church Secretary: 0117 973 7423
Tue 10-11.30am, £1

🖉 WC

Spacious hall with good variety of toys and separate carpeted room for babies. Weekly craft activity. Very friendly and welcoming group, rated "Excellent" by users. Dads, Mums and carers attend. Organic refreshments included.

South Street Family Unit

British Rd, Bedminster, BS3 3AU
Jo & Lisa: 0117 903 9941
southstreetdayn@bristol-city.gov.uk
Tue 9.30am-12pm, 50p per child
Tue 1.30pm-3pm, 50p per child

WC 🚾 🚻 🚼 🦽 Pp

Morning, play and stay arranged in the centre for the under 5s. Afternoons, informal drop-in for parent/carers of babies.

St Matthews Church Toddler Group

Clare Road, Cotham, BS6 5TB
0117 944 1598
Tue 10am-11.30am

P 🖉 WC 🚾 Pp

Enjoyable group with good facilities, runs twice a week.

St. Michael All Angels Church "Piglets" Toddler Group

St. Michael All Angels Church Centre, 160a Gloucester Road, BS7 8NT
Jo Peters: 0117 924 1098
Tue: 9.45am-11.15am
£1 per family

🖉 WC 👶 🚻 🚼 Pp

Popular group for 0-4yrs, plenty of toys, separate area for babies. Runs three sessions a week.

Stockwood Free Church Toddler Group

Ladman Road, Stockwood, Bristol
Carol Ferris: 01275 541 908
Tue 1.30-3pm, £1

P 🖉 WC 👶 🚻 🚼 Pp

Toddler and baby group held in church hall. Climbing frame, carpeted area for babies. Activity table for jigsaws, Duplo or play dough.

Sunbeams

St Oswalds Church Village Hall, Cheddar Grove, Bedminster Down, BS13 7EN
John Lewis: 0117 964 2649
Tue: 9.30-am11.30am

P 🖉 WC 🍼 👶 🚻 🚼 🚼 🦽 🚼 Pp

Weekly group run for the under 4's.

Sydenham Road Under Fives Toddlers

Totterdown Baptist Church, Sydenham Rd, BS4 3DF
Wendy McCarthy: 0117 907 4108
Tue 9.45-11.30am
£2, additional siblings £1

🖉 WC 🚼 🚼

"Toddlers" held three times a week for 0-2yrs. Access is via some steps.

White Tree Parent and Toddler Group
Westbury Park Methodist Church, 4 North View, BS6 7QB
0117 973 1562
Tue 10am-11.30am, 75p, £1 for two
🖉 WC 👤 👶 Pp

Group held in 3 rooms with activities, slide & ride-on toys, plus toys for under 1yrs.

WEDNESDAY

Barton Hill Family Playcentre
Barton Hill Settlement, 43 Ducie Road, BS5 0AX
Vadna Chauhan: 0117 955 6971
Wed 1pm-3pm, Free
🖉 👤 👶 🏠 🚼 ♿ 📠 Pp

"Young Mums Group" for mums under 25yrs, with children under 5yrs.

Broomhill Playgroup
St Peter's Church, Allison Road, Brislington, Bristol
Pat Ashmead: 0117 977 8138
Wed & Thu 9am-11am, £3.50
P WC 👤 👶

Organised for children 3yrs+. Big indoor play area for trikes, etc, while art activities take place in a small side room.

Chatter Clatter Club
Bethesda Church, 29 Alma Road, BS8 2ES
Stuart/Karen: 0117 973 8776
Wed: 10-11.30am
75p for one child, £1 for two
🖉 WC 🍼 👤 👶 🚼 ♿ 📠

Friendly group, 0-3yrs, with lots of toys, videos, painting and singing. First time visitors welcome.

Child's Play Toddler Group
Easton Christian Family Centre, Beaufort Street, Easton, BS5 0SQ
Gill Miles: 0117 955 4255
Wed 10am-12pm, 75p
🖉 WC 🍼 👤 👶

Structured play session runs four times a week for under 4's giving parents a chance to have a break and participate in another activity or stay with child. Parenting courses, family support & English classes run alongside the Wednesday Child's Play session.

Counterslip Baptist Church
648 Wells Road, Whitchurch, Bristol, BS14 9HT
Margaret: 01275 833377
Wed 10am-11.30am
£1, 50p 2nd child
P 🖉 WC 👤 🏠 ♿ 📠 Pp

Drop-in baby group. Large space with mats and cushions for tiny babies as well as a good variety of floor toys, books and ride-on toys.

Wed 1.30pm-3pm
£1, 50p 2nd child
Parent and toddler group held in a large carpeted area with wide variety of toys appropriate to age range. Small waiting list, please phone before coming.

Elmgrove Centre Mums & Tots
Redland Road, Cotham, BS6 6AG
0117 924 3377
Wed 10am-12pm, 50p
P 🖉 WC

Drop-in group offering a variety of toys and activities including painting, games etc. Refreshments available. Use door at side which has no steps. Rumpus Room often open at this time and costs 50p per hour.

Filton Avenue Nursery School
Blakeney Road, Horfield, Bristol, BS7 0DL
Sue Evans: 0117 377 2680
Wed: 9-11.30am, free drop-in sessions for parents/carers with children 20mths-3yrs.
Wed: 12:45-3.15pm, free drop-in sessions for parents/carers with babies up to 20mths.
🖉 WC 👤 👶 🏠 🚼 ♿ 📠 Pp

Four Acres Sure Start
Four Acres Primary School, Four Acres, Withywood, BS13 8RB
0117 903 0460
Wed 9.30am-11.30am, Free
🖉 🏠 🚼 ♿

Informal drop-in for parents/carers with children 0-4yrs to stay and play.

Hanham Folk Centre Parent and Toddler Group

High Street, Hanham
0117 967 4439 (Folk Centre)
Wed 9.30am-11.30am
£1.50 one adult + child, 25p per extra child, plus £10 annual membership

P ✐ WC ⎷ ⎿ ◻ 🖬

Group runs throughout holidays with organised trips in Summer. Run by volunteers. Toys taken outside in good weather, plus weekly activities, refreshments included.

Highridge Sure Start

Lakemead Grove, Highridge, Bristol, BS13 8EA
0117 978 1028
Wed 1pm-3pm, Free

P ✐ ⎷ ⎿ ◻ 🖬 ⛟ ♿

Informal stay and play run weekly for 0-4yrs.

Horfield United Reformed Church

139 Muller Road, Horfield, Bristol
Alison Kinnersley: 0117 951 3321
dakin@btinternet.com
Wed 9.30am-11.30am

P ✐ WC ⎷ ⎿ ♿ Pₚ

Informal toddler group for 0-3yrs, singing at the end with craft activities lots of toys.

Imps

Henleaze & Westbury Community Church, Eastfield Road, Westbury-on-Trym, BS9 4AD
Jo Grover: 0117 962 3816
Cath Hickman: 0117 987 7829
Wed 9.45am-11.30am,£1.50

✐ WC ⎷ ⎿ ◻ 🖬 Pₚ

Friendly welcoming group for 0-3 yrs, with separate play areas, weekly craft activities and songs.

"Lobby" Café with toddler zone

Cairns Road Baptist Church, Cairns Road, Redland, BS6 7TH
Wed 9am-2pm, term time

No booking required. Soft play for toddlers and café serving drinks, cakes and lunches.

Mums and Tots

Leonard Hall, United Reformed Church, Waterford Rd, Henleaze
Sue Wright: 0117 962 4196
Wed 1.30pm-3.30pm, 50p

✐ WC ⎷ ⎿ ◻ Pₚ

Small, friendly and welcoming group with good range of toys.

Oakfield Road Nursery

17 Oakfield Road, Clifton, Bristol, BS8 2AW
Sue Michel: 0117 377 2270
oakfield_rd_day_n@bristol-city.gov.uk
Wed 2pm-3.30pm, Free

Stay and Play held weekly at the Nursery for babies 6-12mths.

Parent and Toddler Group

St George Baptist Church, Summerhill Rd,
St George, BS5 8HQ
Mary Weeks: 0117 955 0512
Wed 1.45pm-3.15pm
50p including refreshments

WC ⎷

Drop-in friendly group for 0-4yrs. Large hall to run around in. Everyone welcome.

Parkway Parent and Child Project

Parkway Methodist Church, Conduit Place,
St Werburghs, BS2 9RU
Sue Dowd: 0117 935 0205
Wed: 9.30am-12pm, £1 per family

✐ ⎷ ⎿ ⛟ ♿ Pₚ

Parent and toddler drop-in sessions run throughout the year in a safe, stimulating and supportive environment with separate area for older children to ride bikes.

Redcliffe Early Years Centre

Spencer House, Ship Lane, Redcliffe, BS1 6RR
Mrs FM Blight: 0117 903 0334
redcliffe_n@bristol-city.gov.uk
Wed 1pm-3pm, Free

P ✐ WC ⎷ ⎿ ◻ 🖬 ♿ Pₚ

Informal group for toddlers held weekly at the centre.

Rosemary Nursery School and Family Unit

Haviland House, St Jude's Flats, Bristol, BS2 0DT
Mrs Sarah Burns: 0117 377 3297
rosemaryn@bristol-city.gov.uk
Wed 9.30am-11.30am, Free

✐ WC ⛟

Informal stay and play for parents/carers with children up to 3yrs.

Southmead Day Nursery

Doncaster Road, Southmead, Bristol, BS10 5PW
Fiona Townsend: 0117 377 2343
southmead_day_n@bristol-city.gov.uk
Wed: 9.15-11.15am, Free

[icons]

Informal drop-in sessions held at the nursery for children 0-4yrs. Parents can use the resource library or attend family learning activities whilst children are allowed in the Sensory Room and outdoor playarea.

St Bernadette Playgroup

St Bernadette Church, Wells Road, Whitchurch, BS14 9UH
Mrs Panter: 01275 834311
Wed 9.45am-11am, £1 per family

[icons]

Informal parent and toddler group for 0-3yrs.

St Bonaventures Toddler Group

St Bonaventures Church, 7 Egerton Road, Bishopston
Elizabeth Molyneux: 0117 942 7849
Wed 2-3.30pm, £1 per family

[icons]

Plenty of space for wide range of ages (0-4yrs) with good variety of toys, crafts each week and singing at end. Very friendly group, ideal place to meet locals, organic refreshments served. Parents and childcarers attend.

St Francis Toddlers

St Francis Church, North Street (opposite Aldi), Ashton Gate
Wed 9.30am-11.30am, £2

[icons]

Weekly group for toddlers held in church hall.

St Patricks Toddler Group

St Patrick's Community Centre, Blacksworth Rd, St George
Mrs Hawkins: 0117 940 0482
Wed 8.30am-11am, £1
adjacent to St Patrick's School

[icons]

Toys suitable for children up to 5yrs. Includes painting, trains, bricks, play dough, jigsaws etc. Sometimes runs through half term holidays.

St. Michael All Angels Church "Piglets" Toddler Group

St. Michael All Angels Church Centre, 160a Gloucester Road, Bristol, BS7 8NT
Jo Peters: 0117 924 1098
Wed 9.30am-11am, £1 per family

[icons]

Popular group for 0-4yrs, plenty of toys, separate area for babies. Runs three sessions a week.

Sydenham Road Under Fives Toddlers

Totterdown Baptist Church, Sydenham Road, Totterdown, BS4 3DF
Wendy McCarthy: 0117 907 4108
Wed 9.45am-11.30am, £2, additional siblings £1

[icons]

"Toddle up" held twice a week for 2-3yrs. Refreshments included. Parent pack available.

Wessex Flyer Fun Factory

Hengrove Leisure Park, Hengrove Way, Hengrove, BS14 0HR
01275 834340
Wed 10.30am-11.30am, £2

Weekly drop-in Parent and Toddler sessions held in the Fun Factory, full use of all facilities for the under 5's. Price includes light refreshments.

Windmill Hill Children & Family Centre

Philip Street, Bedminster, Bristol, BS3 4EA
Mary Radley: 0117 963 3299
Wed 1.30pm-4pm
£1.50 members, £2.50 non members

[icons]

Toddler Group held three times a week for children 0-4yrs. Separate baby area, with indoor and outdoor toys for older children including art activities.

W-O-T Toddlers

Westbury on Trym Methodist Church
Helen Door: 0117 968 3398
Wed 9.30am-11.30am
50p, 25p 2nd child

[icons]

Popular group for 0-4yrs held in Church Hall. Large play area for older children with separate baby area. Weekly sing song.

THURSDAY

Barton Hill Family Playcentre
Barton Hill Settlement, 43 Ducie Road, BS5 0AX
Vadna Chauhan: 0117 955 6971
Thu 9.15am-11.45am, 75p, £1 2nd child
[icons]
Structured group for pre-school children, with art activity, construction toys, home/fantasy corner, sand & water play. Separate soft play area for babies. Dads welcome.

Chelsea Tots
Chelsea Gospel Hall, Devon Road, BS5 6ED
Jane Cox: 01275 830 059
Thu 10am-11.30am, 80p
[icons]
Happy, friendly and caring environment for 0-4yrs, with 10 mins singing each session. Occasional crafts. Open to all.

Child's Play Toddler Group
Easton Christian Family Centre, Beaufort Street, Easton, BS5 0SQ
Gill Miles: 0117 955 4255
Thu 1pm-3pm, 75p
[icons]
Structured play session runs four times a week for under 4's giving parents a chance to have a break and participate in another activity or stay with child.

Christchurch Clifton Toddlers
Christ Church Crypt, Clifton, BS8 4EE
Parish Office: 0117 973 6524
Thu 10.30am-12pm, 75p per family
[icons]
Suitable from 0-3yrs, friendly environment with blanket and toys for babies, wendy house and bikes for toddlers. Different weekly craft activity and singalongs.

Emmanuel Toddler Group
Emmanuel Chapel, Satchfield Crescent, Henbury, BS10 7BL
Jayne Crocker: 0117 950 1951
emmanuelchap@supanet.com
Thu 10am-11.30am, £1
[icons]

Meets twice a week. Large range of toys including ball pool tent, book corner, play kitchen area, bikes, trikes and baby toys. Quiet space in one room. Newcomers welcomed.

Filton Avenue Nursery School
Blakeney Road, Horfield, Bristol, BS7 0DL
Sue Evans: 0117 377 2680
filton_avenue_n@bristol-city.gov.uk
Thu 12.45pm-3.15pm, Free
Free drop-in sessions for parents/carers with 20mths-3yrs.

Gay Elms Sure Start
Gay Elms Primary School, Withywood Road, Bristol, BS13 9AX
07900 497740
[icons]
Thu 10am-12.30pm, 'Babes' a weekly support group for breast feeding Mums held with Midwife in attendance. Lunch is also provided. Free
Thu 12.45pm-2.30pm, Weekly informal drop-in for 0-4yrs, including family learning activities.

Highgrove Parents and Toddlers
High Grove Church, Highgrove, Sea Mills, BS9 2NL
Maria Stuart: 0117 946 6807
Thu 9.30am-11.30am, 80p per family
[icons]
Coffee & chat for parent/carers with children 0-4yrs, craft activity and singing/storytime. Lots of play equipment.

Horfield Methodist Church Thursday Morning Group
Horfield Methodist Church, Churchways Ave, Bristol, BS7 8NY
Lynne Richards: 0117 979 1010
Thu 9am-11.30am, Free
[icons]
Informal Church led fellowship group for adults with provision for children under four to play.

Horfield United Reformed Church
139 Muller Road, Horfield, Bristol
Alison Kinnersley: 0117 951 3321
dakin@btinternet.com
Thu 9.30am-11.30am

Informal toddler group for 0-3yrs, singing at the end with craft activities lots of toys.

Imps
Henleaze & Westbury Community Church, Eastfield Road, Westbury-on-Trym, BS9 4AD
Jo Grover: 0117 962 3816
Cath Hickman: 0117 987 7829
Thu 9.45am-11.30am, £1.50

Friendly welcoming group for 0-3yrs, with separate play areas, weekly craft activities and songs.

Jelly Beans
St Oswalds Church, Cheddar Grove, Bedminster Down, BS13 7EN
John Lewis: 0117 964 2649
Thu 9.30am-11am, £1

Weekly group run for the 0-4yrs, held in Church Hall.

Noah's Ark Playtime
Cairns Road Baptist Church, Cairns Road, BS6 7TQ
Carol de Beger: 0117 944 6229
Thu 10am-11.30am, voluntary donations

Weekly group for 0-3yrs held in two rooms offering variety of activities and toys inc. play dough, books, slide, and trampoline. Quieter carpeted area for babies. Weekly songs with instruments.

Oakfield Road Nursery
17 Oakfield Road, Clifton, Bristol, BS8 2AW
Jill Willoughby: 0117 377 2270
oakfield_rd_day_n@bristol-city.gov.uk
Thu 2-3.30pm, Free

Multiple birth group for babes up to 5yrs. Chance to meet other parents with twins and triplets, have a chat while children play.

Parent and Baby Group
Knowle Clinic, Broadfield Rd, BS4 2UH
0117 977 6292

Thu 10.30am-12 noon

Free weekly group (20p refreshments). Mats with toys for babies. Occasional speakers on health issues. Health visitor available.

Parkway Parent and Child Project
Parkway Methodist Church, Conduit Place, St Werburghs, BS2 9RU
Sue Dowd: 0117 935 0205
Thu 1pm-3pm, £1 per family

Parent and toddler drop-in sessions run throughout the year in a safe, stimulating and supportive environment with separate area for older children to ride bikes.

Rainbow Tots
Kensington Baptist Church Hall, Seymour Rd, Easton
Amanda Pearce:0117 955 7768
Thu 10am-12pm,60p

Friendly Church run group meets three times a week for the 0-4 yrs. Offers a craft activity every week, lots of toys plus baby area.

Redcliffe Early Years Centre
Spencer House, Ship Lane, Redcliffe, BS1 6RR
Mrs FM Blight: 0117 903 0334
Thu 1pm-3pm, Free

'Tums to Tots' held weekly at the centre. Access to health visitor.

Redland Park Church Baby & Toddler Group
Redland Park Church, 1 Redland Park, BS6 6SA
Viv Hayden: 01275 847692
Thu 10am-11.30am

Small friendly group for 0-4yrs. Money raised from the group is used to support orphans overseas.

Scramblers
St Francis Church, North Street (opposite Aldi), Ashton Gate
Margaret Bishop: 0117 966 7670
Thu 11am-12.30pm
£1 per family incl. drinks

Suitable for 0-3yrs. Access to church garden with good selection of toys, incl. bikes. Very welcoming - mothers/carers help run the group and also organise evening get-togethers. About 40 children attend. The Vicar runs a short "Play and Pray" session with songs once a month. Parking in Aldi.

St. Michael All Angels Church "Piglets" Toddler Group

St. Michael All Angels Church Centre,
160a Gloucester Road, Bristol, BS7 8NT
Jo Peters: 0117 924 1098
Thu 9.45am-11.15am, £1 per family

Popular group for 0-4yrs, plenty of toys, separate area for babies. Runs three sessions a week.

Stackpool Road and Methodist Church Parent and Toddlers

Stackpool Road Methodist Church, Southville, Bristol
corner of Stackpool Road and Howard Road
Margaret Baber: 0117 963 7607
Thu 10am-12pm, closed Aug, £1.15

Popular and well attended group with a caring and warm atmosphere for children 0-3yrs. Usually 60+ children, so can be quite boisterous held in two halls. Fathers welcomed.

Sticky Fingers

All Saints Church Hall, Grove Road, BS16
Jenny Emmett: 0117 907 9064
Thu 9.30am-11.30am
£2, £1 2nd child

Friendly, lively group for toddlers from 1-3yrs, with approx. 30 children offering a wide range of activities, including sand, craft activities and construction toys. Small waiting list, regular attendance expected.

Stockwood Free Church Toddler Group

Ladman Road, Stockwood, Bristol
Carol Ferris: 01275 541 908
Thu 1.15pm-2.45pm, £1

Toddler and baby group held in church hall. Climbing frame, carpeted area for babies.

Activity table for jigsaws, Duplo or play dough with sticking or painting.

Sydenham Road Under Fives Toddlers

Totterdown Baptist Church, Sydenham Rd, BS4 3DF
Wendy McCarthy: 0117 907 4108
Thu 9.45-11.30am
£2, £1 additional siblings

"Toddlers" held three times a week for 0-2yrs. Access is via some steps.

Victoria Park Toddlers

Victoria Park Baptist Church, St John Lane, Bedminster
Sue Fortune, 0779 977 0619
Thu 9.30-11.30am
£1, £1.50 for 2 or more

Drop-in group for 0-4yrs held twice a week, with baby area and toys for under ones. Variety of other toys, craft activities, sand etc. Fathers regularly attend.

Wessex Flyer Fun Factory

Hengrove Leisure Park, Hengrove Way, BS14 0HR
01275 834340
Thu 10.30am-11.30am, £2

Weekly drop-in Parent and Toddler sessions held in the Fun Factory, full use of all facilities for 0-5yrs. Price includes light refreshments.

FRIDAY

Chatterbox (Toddler Group)

Horfield Baptist Church (Brynland Road entrance),
279 Gloucester Road, Bristol, BS7 8NY
Roberta Johnson: 0117 924 3608
Thu 1pm-3pm, £1.50

Church based group for 0-4yrs, runs twice a week. Varied toys, craft table, climbing equipment and ride ons, with storytime at end. See also 'Mum's the Word!' for the under ones.

Child's Play Toddler Group

Easton Christian Family Centre, Beaufort Street,
Easton, BS5 0SQ
Gill Miles: 0117 955 4255
Fri 10am-12pm, 75p
[icons]

Structured play session runs four times a
week for under 4's giving parents a chance
to have a break and participate in another
activity or stay with child.

Fulford Family Centre

237-239 Gatehouse Ave, Withywood, BS13 9AQ
Jenny Lewis: 0117 978 2441
Fri 1pm-2.30pm, Free
[icons]

Free drop-in sessions for 0-5yrs for parents/
carers living in the Hartcliffe, Bishopworth and
Withywood areas.

Gay Elms Sure Start

Gay Elms Primary School, Withywood Rd, BS13 9AX
07900 497740
Fri 11am-1pm, Free

Weekly 'Baby Café' run for parents/carers to
meet up and chat over lunch.

Highridge Sure Start

Lakemead Grove, Highridge, BS13 8EA
0117 978 1028
Fri 10am-12pm, Free
[icons]

Informal stay and play run weekly for 0-4yrs.

Kings Tots Parent and Toddlers

Bristol Community Church, Bourne Chapel,
Waters Rd, BS15 8BE
Fran Puckett: 0117 947 8441
Fri 10am-11.30am
£1 incl. refreshments
[icons]

Children from 0-3yrs can play in a safe
environment. Possible waiting lists.

Mum's the Word!

Horfield Baptist Church (Brynland Road entrance),
279 Gloucester Road, Bristol, BS7 8NY
Katie Wilkinson: 0117 924 3608
Fri 2pm-3.30pm, 50p
[icons]

Weekly small club for new mums with babies
0-6mths, lots of toys and a chance to chat.

South Street Family Unit

British Road, Bedminster, Bristol, BS3 3AU
Jo or Lisa: 0117 903 9941
southstreetdayn@bristol-city.gov.uk
Fri 1pm-3pm, 50p per child
[icons]

Play and stay arranged in the centre for
0-5yrs.

Southmead Day Nursery

Doncaster Road, Southmead, Bristol, BS10 5PW
Fiona Townsend: 0117 377 2343
southmead_day_n@bristol-city.gov.uk
Fri 9.15am-11.15am, Free
[icons]

Informal drop-in sessions held at the nursery
for children 0-4yrs. Parents can use the
resource library or attend family learning
activities whilst children are allowed in the
Sensory Room and outdoor play area. Lunch
provided on Fridays.

St Matthews Church Toddler Group

Clare Road, Cotham, BS6 5TB
0117 944 1598
Fri 2pm-3.30pm
[icons]

Enjoyable group with good facilities, runs
twice a week.

St Pauls Day Nursery

Little Bishop St, St Pauls, Bristol, BS2 9JF
0117 377 2278
st_pauls_day_n@bristol-city.gov.uk
Fri 9.30am-12.30pm, Free
[icons]

Informal stay and play time for parents/carers
with children 0-5yrs.

St Peter's Parent & Toddler Group

St Peter's Church Hall, The Drive, Henleaze, BS9 4LD
Parish Office: 0117 962 3196
Fri 10.30am-12.15pm
50p per family, £1 per family per term
[icons]

Children from 'bumps' to nursery age, meets
twice a week. Parents, grandparents, nannies
are welcome to join. Action songs at the end.

Sydenham Road Under Fives Toddlers
Totterdown Baptist Church, Sydenham Rd, BS4 3DF
Wendy McCarthy: 0117 907 4108
Fri 9.45am-11.30am
£2, £1 additional siblings

"Toddlers" held three times a week for 0-2yrs. Access is via some steps.

The Salvation Army Candle Project Parent and Toddlers
6 Ashley Road, St Pauls, Bristol, BS6 5NL
Maureen Baxter: 0117 942 4607
Fri 10am-12pm, 50p

Small group, meets twice a week, with space for 12-15 children, offering a variety of educational toys, trikes, tunnel, slide, dolls prams etc. Fathers welcome.

White Tree Parent and Toddler Group
Westbury Park Methodist Church, 4 North View, Bristol, BS6 7QB
0117 973 1562
Fri 10am-11.30am
75p, £1 for 2

Group held in 3 rooms with activities, slide & ride on toys, plus toys for under 1yrs.

Windmill Hill Children & Family Centre
Philip Street, Bedminster, Bristol, BS3 4EA
Mary Radley: 0117 963 3299
Fri 9.45am-11.45am
£1.50 members, £2.50 non members

Toddler Group held three times a week for children 0-4yrs. Separate baby area, with indoor and outdoor toys for older children including art activities.

PLAYGROUPS
These groups require pre-booking and may require parent participation. Ideally suited to over 2's.

The Rowan Tree Kindergarten
12d Cotham Road, Cotham, Bristol, BS6 6DR
Janet Parsons: 0117 973 4399
Mon-Fri: 9.15am-12.15pm

Weekly playgroup for 3-6yrs, to introduce them to the Kindergarten's way of learning.

The Rowan Tree Kindergarten Parent & Toddler
Janet Parsons: 0117 973 4399
Mon, Tue, Thu & Fri: 9.30am-12noon
£4.50 per session

Part of Bristol Steiner Waldorf School's Kindergarten, weekly sessions are held for parents and toddlers in homely surroundings with natural play materials. Sessions include crafts, break time and circle time.

Ullswater Family Centre
52/54 Ullswater Road, Southmead, Bristol, BS10 6DP
Chris Lloyd: 0117 950 8334
Mon/Tue/Thu/Fri am & Tue/Thu pm
Free

Suitable for 2-4+ yrs. Also run parents' groups, afterschool group and parenting group. Application through health Visitor or social worker

Downend Baptist Church Toddlers
Salisbury Road, Downend, Bristol, BS16
Rachel Baker: 0117 956 1374
Tue, Wed & Thu: 10-11.30am & Wed: 1.30-3pm
£10 per term and £3 for siblings over 6mths

Weekly sessions for 0-5 yrs. Large variety of toys, weekly activity for older children, plus song time and refreshments. Please phone before attending.

Knowle West Play Centres

Mede Centre, 1 Marshall Walk, Knowle
Julie Shattock: 0117 963 1737
Mon, Wed & Fri: 9.30-11.30am
£2 per session

P WC ♿ ♿ 🏠 ✍

Three play sessions run for 2-5yrs, parents can leave children. Must book in advance.

Filwood Broadway, Knowle, Bristol, BS4 1JC
Julie Shattock: 0117 963 1737
Mon-Fri: 9.30-11.30am
£1.30

P WC ♿ ♿ ♿ 🏠 ✍

Daily play sessions run for 2-5yrs, parents can leave children. Must book in advance, minimum three sessions a week.

DIFFERENT LANGUAGE PLAYGROUPS

Clwb y Ddraig Goch (Welsh Club)

50 Richmond Street, Totterdown, Bristol, BS3 4TJ
Sioned Alexander: 0117 971 6478
sioned@alexanderthomas.co.uk

Structured sessions for 0-9yrs on the Welsh language and culture using games, songs etc. Held at Windmill Hill City Farm every third or fourth Sat of month. 'Phone Sioned Alexander for further details.

Cylch Ti a Fi (Welsh Toddler Group)

50 Richmond Street, Totterdown, Bristol, BS3 4TJ
Sioned Alexander: 0117 971 6478

P ✎ WC ♿

For pre-school children. Meets locally around Bristol weekly. Phone Sioned Alexander for further details.

Deutsche Spielgruppe

The Church Hall, St Matthews Church, Cotham, BS6
Astrid Pestell: 0117 962 0966
Mon: 3.15-5.15pm, £2.50 per session

P ✎ WC ♿ ♿ 🏠 🚻 PP

Group for German speaking parents and their pre-school children. Lots of toys, craft activities and songs. Meets at St. Matthews throughout the year except during the summer holidays when there are informal meetings at local parks. Phone for details.

Ecole Française de Bristol

C/o St Ursulas High School, Brecon Road, Westbury-on-Trym, BS9 4DT
Estelle Tenant: 0117 962 4154

WC ♿ 🚻

Nursery for bilingual and English children, also after school classes (5-12yrs). GCSE classes, adult classes and holiday activity weeks (5-12yrs).

La Casita Toddler Group

Quakers Society of Friends Building,
300 Gloucester Rd, Horfield, BS7 8PD
Rosabel Portela: 0117 914 6950
rosabel@bushinternet.com
Wed: 10am-1pm
£5 membership fee; £1.50 each visit

✎ WC ♿ ♿ ♿ 🚻 🏠 🚻 ♿ PP

Relaxed friendly group for Spanish speakers with children from 0-4yrs. Children use their knowledge of Spanish in play, songs and creative activities. Weekly summer outings.

EARLY EDUCATION IN BRISTOL

What is Pre-School Education?

The period from age 3 to the end of the reception year is described as the foundation stage. Children work through this initial stage of the national curriculum at a pre-school, playgroup or in a nursery class attached to a primary school, nursery school or day nursery. Most children transfer to the Reception year in a primary school in the September following their fourth birthday.

This pre-school learning is a distinct stage and important both in its own right and in preparing children for later schooling. The early learning goals set out six areas of learning which form the basis of the foundation stage curriculum. These areas are:

- Personal, social and emotional development
- Communication, language and literacy
- Mathematical development

- Knowledge and understanding of the world
- Physical development
- Creative development

Choosing the right Pre-school Facility

Only you as a parent can decide what is best for your child so we recommend that you visit as many as possible to see what care and facilities they offer. There are many pre-school groups held in Church Halls often called playgroups, whilst some primary schools also offer pre-school education in a nursery class. Whatever you choose, your child will normally spend a morning or afternoon on their own there for about 2½ hours up to five times a week. Most will follow the same term dates as a school.

All pre-schools, playgroups and nurseries, where children attend sessions of less than four hours, are now inspected by OFSTED (Office for Standards in Education) to ensure that they meet the national standards. When visiting you can request a copy of their Ofsted report, or call your Ofsted Early Years Regional centre on 0845 601 4772.

For a comprehensive list within your area you can contact the Children's Information Service on tel: 0845 129 7217 or the Pre-school Learning Alliance on tel: 0117 907 7073.

Nursery Education & Grants

All parents are entitled to claim assistance for the cost of pre-school education for their children once their child has reached 2years and 10mths, providing they attend a registered provider. Grants are claimed in the term following the child's third birthday up until the child reaches five years old. To access the grant parents will be asked by the provider to sign a Parental Registration form so that the pre-school can claim back the money and deduct it from the termly cost. In cases where the grant does not cover the entire cost of the pre-school session, parents will be asked to pay a top up fee.

LOCAL AUTHORITY NURSERY SCHOOLS

Local Authority Nursery Schools and classes

The Local Education Authority funds a number of early education places to allow children to spend a year in nursery provision before starting school. Places are available at some infant schools which have a Nursery Class attached to the school or at council run Nursery Schools.

Parents who wish to apply for a place should contact the school directly for details of their admission procedure. Attending the nursery attached to a primary school does not always guarantee your child a place at the school. To find out if there is an LEA nursery class or school in your area, contact the Children's

Information Service on tel: 0845 129 7217

Cashmore Nursery School
Cashmore House, Barton Hill, Bristol, BS5 9PR
Ms Hannah Hill: 0117 903 0253
cashmore_n@bristol-city.gov.uk
Mon-Fri: 9am-3pm
Wide range of learning opportunities for 3-4yrs.

Cheddar Grove Primary School
Cheddar Grove, Bedminster Down, Bristol, BS13 7EN
Miss Abbott: 0117 903 0418
Mon-Fri 9am-11.30am, 12.45-3.15pm
LEA funded nursery class attached to Primary School offering pre-school education for 3-5yrs; either morning or afternoon sessions.

Redcliffe Early Years Centre
Spencer House, Ship Lane, Redcliffe, BS1 6RR
Mrs FM Blight: 0117 903 0334
redcliffe_n@bristol-city.gov.uk
Mon-Fri 9am-11.30am & 12 noon-3.00pm

Foundation stage offered to children 3-5yrs living within catchment area. Parents must call for an application form.

Rosemary Nursery School and Family Unit
Haviland House, St Jude's Flats, Bristol, BS2 0DT
Mrs Sarah Burns: 0117 903 1467
rosemaryn@bristol-city.gov.uk
Mon-Fri 9am-3pm

Local authority nursery school for children 3-4yrs.

St James' & St Agnes' Nursery School
Halston Drive, St Paul's, Bristol, BS2 9JE
Ms L Watts: 0117 903 0337
Mon-Fri, term time, Free
Full and part time education places available for 3-4yrs.

St Phillips Marsh Nursery School
Albert Crescent, St Phillip's Marsh, Bristol, BS2 0SU
Mrs P S Willmott: 0117 977 6171
Mon-Fri: 9am-3pm

Local authority nursery which accepts children 3-4 years, providing a range of activities to promote and encourage children's independence and learning.

St Werburgh's Park Nursery School
Glenfrome Road, St Werburgh's Park, Bristol, BS2 9UX
Mrs S K Danvers: 0117 903 0323
Mon-Fri: 9am-3pm
Maintained nursery school offering nursery education and care.

NORTH BRISTOL

Filton Avenue Nursery School
Blakeney Road, Horfield, Bristol, BS7 0DL
Ms Sue Evans: 0117 377 2680
Mon-Fri 9-11.30am, or 12.45-3.15pm (term time only)
Free pre-school education for families in the North Bristol City Council area for children 3yrs. Children's names must be on waiting list either for five mornings or five afternoons a week.

NORTH EAST BRISTOL

Blaise Primary School
Clavel Road, Henbury, Bristol, BS10 7EJ
Mrs Yvonne Roberts: 0117 377 2424
Mon-Fri: 8.55am-11.30am, 1pm-3.30pm
Nursery class attached to Primary School offering pre-school education for rising 4yrs, ideal for those wishing to move on to the School.

Little Hayes Nursery School
Symington Road, Fishponds, Bristol, BS16 2LL
Mrs S Rolfe: 0117 903 0405
Mon-Fri: 9-11.30am, 12.30-3pm
Free
LEA run pre-school for 3-5yrs, phone for a place.

EAST BRISTOL

Speedwell Nursery School
Speedwell Road, Speedwell, Bristol, BS5 7SY
Mrs Ann Paterson: 0117 903 0329
speedwell_n@bristol-city.gov.uk
Mon-Fri: 9.30-12pm, 1.00pm-3.30pm

🖉 🚾 🕴 🔟 🏢 🖶 📖 🅟🅿

Local authority nursery school for children 3-4yrs.

Spring Woods Nursery School
Bannerman Road, Easton, Bristol, BS5 0HL
Mr Stephen Cummings: 0117 903 0269
springwoodsn@bristol-city.gov.uk
Mon-Fri: 9am- 3.15pm

🕴 🔟 🏢 🖶 📖

LEA funded pre-school with three sessions; full time, part morning or part time afternoons.

SOUTH EAST BRISTOL

Waycroft Primary School
Selden Road, Stockwood, Bristol, BS14 8PS
Simon Rowe: 0117 377 2198
waycroft_p@bristol-city.gov.uk
Mon-Fri: 9-11.30am, 12.45-3.10pm

LEA funded nursery school offers pre-school education for 3-5yrs attached to Primary School.

Burnbush Primary School
Whittock Road, Stockwood, Bristol, BS14 8DQ
Mr N Williams: 01275 832961
Mon-Fri: 9-11.30am, 12.45-3.15pm
no cost

LEA funded nursery class attached to Primary School offering pre-school education for 3-4yrs.

SOUTH BRISTOL

Fairfurlong Primary School
Vowell Close, Withywood, Bristol, BS13 9HX
Mr Peter Overton: 0117 377 2181
Mon-Fri: 8.55-11.30am, 1.00-3.15pm

Nursery class attached to Primary school offering pre-school education for 3-5yrs.

Four Acres Sure Start
Four Acres Primary School, Four Acres,
Withywood, BS13 8RB
0117 903 0460
Mon, Thurs, Fri: 9.30am-12 noon, Wed: 12.30-3pm
Free

🅿 🕴 🔟 🖶 🦽 📖

Free pre-school education for 2½-4yrs registered with Sure Start.

Gay Elms Primary School
Withywood Road, Withywood, Bristol, BS13 9AX
Annette Osbourne: 0117 903 0311
Mon-Fri: 8.55-11.30am, 12.40-3.15pm

Pre-school education offered for 3-5yrs, attached to Primary School.

Gay Elms Sure Start
Gay Elms Primary School, Withywood Road,
Bristol, BS13 9AX
07900 497740
Mon & Tue: 9.30am-12 noon
Free

🕴 🔟 🏢 🖶 📖

Free pre-school education for 2½-4yrs registered with Sure Start.

Highridge Infant School
Ellfield Close, Bishopworth, Bristol, BS13 8EF
Jill Hughes: 0117 377 2366
Mon-Fri: 9-11.15am, 12.45-3.15pm
no cost

Offers 'Foundation Stage', children from 3yrs accepted into Nursery class, moving to Reception at 4yrs.

Highridge Sure Start
Lakemead Grove, Highridge, Bristol, BS13 8EA
0117 978 1028
Tue & Thurs: 12.30-3pm

🅿 🕴 🔟 🏢 🖶 🦽 📖

Free pre-school education for 2½-5yrs registered with Sure Start.

Teyfant Community School
Teyfant Road, Hartcliffe, Bristol, BS13 ORG
Mr G Grimshaw: 0117 903 0356
Mon-Fri: 8.30-11.30am, 12 noon - 3.00pm

🅿 🕴 🔟

LEA funded pre-school for 3-5yrs attached to Primary School.

SOUTH WEST BRISTOL

Ashton Gate Primary School
Ashton Gate Road, Ashton Gate, Bristol, BS3 1SZ
Mrs A Johannson: 0117 903 0236
Mon-Fri: 9-11.30am, 12.45-3.15pm
no cost
LEA funded pre-school for 3-5yrs attached to Primary School. Must be 3yrs by 31 August. Please call to apply for a place.

NORTH WEST BRISTOL

Bluebell Valley Nursery School
Long Cross, Lawrence Weston, Bristol, BS11 0LP
Mrs Christine Menzies: 0117 903 1472

Early Education for children from 3-5 years. In addition the school has inclusive places for children 3-7 who have complex and severe learning difficulties. Contact the school for further information.

Henbury Court Primary School
Trevelyan Walk, Henbury, Bristol, BS10 7NY
Mrs Burkitt: 0117 377 2196
henbury_court_p@bristol-city.gov.uk
Mon-Fri: 8.50am-11.30am, 12.40pm-3.20pm

Nursery class for 3yrs, part time and full time places, phone to apply for a place.

PRE-SCHOOLS & PLAYGROUPS

Most pre-school groups are privately run, non profit making organisations often held in Church halls providing a fun learning environment through play for children 2½-5yrs. Under the Ofsted guidelines they must adhere to the correct adult to child ratio, have a first aider on site and all members be police checked.

Sessions last for 2-3hrs costing between £5-10. Each child normally attends 2-5 sessions a week. Popular pre-schools have waiting lists, so get your child's name down at least a year before they are due to start. 'Opportunity Playgroups' are set up for children with special needs, usually with trained staff. If your child has special needs a 'Statement of Needs' is required; your local education authority should be able to help you with obtaining this and advise you of local groups.

Advantages:
- Good first step, encouraging your child's learning and independence.
- Local, therefore your child will meet peers going on to the same school.

Disadvantages:
- Parent participation is sometimes required on a rota basis.
- Term time only with short sessions therefore usually not suitable for working parents.

PRE-SCHOOL - FEES

CENTRAL BRISTOL

Clifton High School Nursery Department
1 Clifton Park, Clifton, BS8 3BS
Tina Arthurs: 0117 973 0201
www.cliftonhigh.bristol.sch.uk
8.30am-12pm mornings, 8.30am-3.30pm all day, 3.30-5.30pm after school club for whole of lower school, rising 3-5yrs

Happy, lively and informal atmosphere for children from 3yrs, with a stimulating cirriculum offered in a spacious building and gardens.

Parkway Parent and Child Project
Parkway Methodist Church, Conduit Place, St Werburgh's, BS2 9RU
Sue Dowd: 0117 935 0205
Fri: 10am-12pm
£3.50

2's Group makes the transition from Crèche to the more formal environment of the Playgroup. Waiting list. Prefer potty trained.

Lunch club also available at extra cost, must be pre booked.

Parkway Parent and Child Project
Parkway Methodist Church, Conduit Place, St Werburgh's, BS2 9RU
Sue Dowd: 0117 935 0205
Mon-Thu: 9.30-12pm
£3.50p per session

Pre-school education for children 2½ to school age four times a week. Lunch club also available at extra cost, must be pre-booked.

Windmill Hill Children & Family Centre
Philip Street, Bedminster, Bristol, BS3 4EA
Mary Radley: 0117 963 3299
Mon: 9.30am-3pm, Wed: 9.30am-12 noon, Thu: 9.30am-12 noon, Fri: 12.30-3pm
on application

Pre-school held four times a week for 3-5yrs. From April 2004 more pre-school sessions available, phone for more information.

MAKE A DIFFERENCE
can you...
understand
listen
encourage
organise
educate
learn
challenge
FOSTER?
Tel: 0117 954 8545
Social Services and Health Family Placement Team
www.bristol-city.gov.uk/fostering

NORTH BRISTOL

Art Raft Piglets Nursery
St Saviours Hall, Woodfield Road, Redland, Bristol, BS6 6JQ
Barbara Ramsey: 0117 904 6358
pigletsnursery@artraft.com
Mon-Fri: 8am-6pm

Morning or afternoon pre-school sessions lasting 2½ hours are held within the friendly and secure nursery setting for 3-5yrs.

Bluebells Pre-school
Filton Community Centre, Elm Park, Filton, BS16
Jacquline Thinnock: 07855 645708
secretary@bluebellspre-school.co.uk
Mon-Fri: 9.15-12.45am
£6

Pre-school education offered for children from 2½-4yrs.

Busy Bees Pre-school
St Peters Church, The Drive, Henleaze, BS9 4LD
Sharon Penn: 07949 225350
Tue, Wed, Thu: 9.15-11.45am, Mon & Fri: 12.30-2.45pm
£6

Warm, caring and happy environment for 2½-5yrs, where each child feels valued.

Candle Project Playgroup
Salvation Army, 6 Ashley Rd, Ashley Down BS6 5NL
Christine Jones: 0117 942 4607
Mon-Fri: 9.30am - 12 noon
£2

Morning sessions for 2½+yrs held in large hall upstairs with spacious carpeted area and wet play area. Courtyard for outside play.

Eden Grove Playgroup
Eden Grove Methodist Church Hall, Eden Grove, BS7 0PQ
The Manager: 07792 013290
Mon-Fri: 9.30am-12pm
£3.75

2½-4+yrs. Friendly welcoming staff.

Harcourt Pre-school
Wells Room, St Albans Church, Bayswater Ave,
BS6 7NS
Mrs Christine Williams: 0117 942 5128
Mon-Fri: 9am-12pm
£6

Est. 1956 The Pre-school caters for 2½-5yrs in a happy, caring environment. Ensures children build up confidence to develop and learn through play.

Horfield Methodist Playgroup
Horfield Methodist Church, Churchways Ave,
BS7 8NY
Cherry Arnal: 07977 348850
Mon-Fri: 9-11.30am
£3

Church sponsored pre-school offering foundation stage eduction for children from 2½ to 5yrs.

Horfield Welly Playgroup
Wellington Hill West, Horfield, Bristol, BS7 8GT
Mrs L Seymour, 07712 643251
Tue - Fri: 9.30am-12pm
£5.50

2½-4yrs. Following Early Years guidelines.

Jack and Jill Pre-school
Northcote, Great Brockeridge, Westbury on Trym,
Bristol, BS9 3TY
Rita Dennehy: 0117 962 3382
Mon- Fri: 9am - 12 noon; 12.45pm - 2.45pm
AM - £10, PM - £10.50 per session

Small, friendly pre-school feeding Emlea Primary or Westbury on Trym C of E School. Children accepted from 2½yrs upwards for afternoon sessions, children 3+yrs stay five mornings a week.

Magic Dragon Pre-school
Church of the Good Shepherd Hall, Bishop Road,
Bishopston, BS7 8NA
Miriam Lord: 0117 924 3446
Mon-Thu: 9.30-11.45am term time
£5.75 a session

Children from 3-5yrs looked after in a friendly atmosphere, with stimulating activities and resources.

Noah's Ark Pre-school
Cairns Rd Baptist Church, Cairns Road,
Bristol, BS6 7TH
Carol de-Beger: 0117 944 6229 or 0117 950 3237
Mon- Fri: 9.15-11.45am, or 12.45-3.15pm
£6

Open to children of all faiths 2½yrs-5yrs. Christianity taught.

Pied Piper Playgroup
Bishopston Methodist Church, 245 Gloucester Road,
Bristol, BS7 8NY
Mrs Jenny McCaren: 0117 942 5104
Mon, Tue, Wed, Fri: 9.15am-12pm
£4

Playgroup for children 2yrs 10mths-5yrs, parent participation only required twice a term.

Redland High Nursery Class
1 Grove Park, Bristol, BS6 6PP
Judith Ashill: 0117 924 5796
admissions@redland.bristol.sch.uk
Mon-Fri: 8.30am-3.45pm

Accepts girls from 3-5yrs, also offers after school facilities until 6pm and holiday club scheme for 3-11yrs.

Redland Pre-school
Friends Meeting House, 126 Hampton Road,
Redland, Bristol, BS6 6JE
Louise Douglas: 0117 908 0455
Mon-Fri 9.15am-1.15pm
£7.50

Places for children between 3-5yrs, also offer lunchtime session for older ones at an additional cost. Please phone for a visit.

Silverhill School Nursery
Swan Lane, Winterbourne, BS36 1RL
Ian Philipson-Masters: 01454 772 156
Mon-Fri: 8am-6pm

Independent Nursery and Prep-school for 2½yrs. up to 11yrs. Holiday activity scheme available to pupils.

St Bonaventures Pre-school

The Parish Hall, Egerton Road, Bishopston, BS7 8HN
Jane Nelson: 0117 924 9379
Mon, Tue, Wed, Thurs: 9.00-11.30am
£5 a session

[P] [WC] [⚐] [⚑] [⊟] [WC] [⚑] [Pp]

Pre-school education for 3-4yrs.

St Matthews Church Playgroup

Clare Road, Cotham, Bristol, BS6 5TB
Sue Last: 0117 944 1598
Mon,Wed, Thurs & Fri: 9.15-11.45am, Mon & Wed: 12.30-3pm
£6.50 a session

[WC] [⚑] [♿] [⊟]

Community playgroup offering pre-school education to 2½-4yrs. Phone for a place.

The Lantern Playschool

Redland Parish Hall, Redland Green Road, Redland, BS6 7HE
Julie Cullum: 0117 973 7423
Mon, Tue, Thu & Fri: 9.15am-12.15pm
£10 a session (paid termly)

[⚐] [WC] [⚐] [⚑] [⚑] [⚑] [⊟]

A Christian pre-school aimed at 3-5yrs offering a high quality pre-school education.

The Red House Children's Centre

1 Cossins Rd, Westbury Park, BS6 7LY
0117 942 8293
www.redhouse-nursery.org.uk
Mon-Fri variety of sessions

[P] [⚐] [WC] [⚐] [⚑] [⚑] [⚑]

Formerly The Red House Nursery. Pre-school education for 2-5yrs. See advertisement.

Torwood House School

27-29 Durdham Park, Redland, BS6 6XE
Samantha Packer: 0117 973 5620
www.torwoodhouse.bristol.sch.uk
Mon-Fri: 8am-6pm term & holiday time

[⚐] [WC] [⚐] [⚑] [⚑]

Independent nursery and preparatory school from 2-11yrs.

Westbury Baptist Pre-school

Reedley Road, Westbury on Trym, Bristol, BS9 3TD
Mary Hughes: 0117 962 9990
Mon-Fri: 9am-12 noon
£8 per session

[⚑] [⚑] [♿]

Caring pre-school run with a Christian ethos.

White Tree Pre-school

Westbury Park Methodist Church Hall, 4 North View, Bristol, BS6 7QB
Alwyn Leverton: 0117 924 9894
www.geocities.com/whitetreepreschool
Mon-Fri: 9.15am-12pm, Thurs 12.30-3pm
£6

[⚐] [WC] [⚑] [⚑] [⚑] [⊟] [⊟]

Pre-school education for 2½-5yrs, within the context of the Christian faith. Warm, caring environment. Variety of activities provided in a large, airy, carpeted hall encouraging all areas of child development. Very close to the Downns for walks (weather permitting).

Windsor Playgroup

Sefton Park Youth Centre, Ashley Down Road, Bristol
Maureen Walford: 0117 924 6291
Tue, Wed & Thu 9.15-11.45am
£4

[P] [WC] [⚑] [⚑] [⊟]

Start in the term child turns 3yrs.

NORTH EAST BRISTOL

Bristol Children's Playhouse

Berkeley Green Rd, Eastville, BS5 6LU
Jackie Cutmore: 0117 951 0037
Mon-Fri: 9am-12.45pm school term time
£1 per session under 3's, free for over 3's

Pre-school nursery run every morning for 2½-5yrs. Parent support.

St Josephs Pre-school
St Josephs Church Hall, Forest Road, Fishponds, BS16 3QT
Cathy Williamson: 0117 914 7173
Mon-Fri: 9-11.30am, Tue, Wed, Fri: 1-3.30pm
£3 a session

2yrs&10mths-4½yrs. Parent participation encouraged. Community based group.

Sticky Fish Pre-school
Fishponds Baptist Church, Downend Road, BS16 5AS
Rachel Betts: 0117 904 2768
Mon-Fri: 9.30am-12.15pm
£5.00

Preparation for school for 2½-5yrs by learning through play.

EAST BRISTOL

Barton Hill Family Playcentre
Barton Hill Settlement, 43 Ducie Road, BS5 0AX
Vadna Chauhan: 0117 955 6971
Thu & Fri: 1-3pm
£1.25

"Two's Group" for children 2-3yrs in preparation for the pre-school group.

Barton Hill Family Playcentre Pre-school
Barton Hill Settlement, 43 Ducie Road, BS5 0AX
Vadna Chauhan: 0117 955 6971
Mon 12.30-3pm, Tue/Wed/Fri 9.15-11.45am term time
£2.00

Pre-school run four times a week for 3-5yrs.

Kingswood Methodist Church Playgroup
Two Mile Hill Rd, Kingswood, BS15 1JR
Saskia French: 0117 961 3488
Mon, Tue, Wed & Fri: 9.30am-12 noon & Thu: 12.30-3.00pm
£3 per session, £5 annually

Offers a safe, stimulating environment for 3-5yrs with trained staff.

St George Pre-school Group
The Baptist Church, Cherry Orchard Lane, BS5
Mrs Sharon Carstairs: 0117 935 4534
Mon-Thu: 9-11.30am
£3.25
off Summerhill Road

Accepts children from 2½-4yrs.

Tiny Happy People
Easton Christian Family Centre, Beaufort Street, BS5 0SQ
Dawn Falconer: 0117 955 4255
Mon-Fri 9.30am-12pm, 12.30-3pm
£2.50

3-4yrs. Garden used frequently (weather permitting) which is an excellent source for growing plants, observing birds, snails etc. Special lunch time arrangements available.

SOUTH EAST BRISTOL

Hamilton Playgroup
Wick Road, Brislington, Bristol, BS4 4HP
The Manager: 0117 914 4471
Mon-Fri: 9am-11.30am, 12.30am-3pm
£3.75

Friendly atmosphere with stimulating activities.

Queen's Road Methodist Church Pre-school
Queen's Road Methodist Church, Queen's Road, Keynsham, BS31 2NN
Ginny Ireland: 0117 987 7753
Mon-Fri: 9.30am-12noon , Mon-Fri (excl Tue): 12.30-3pm
£4 per session

Accepts children from 2yrs/9mths-5yrs to the pre-school, offering quality care and education. Please call for a place.

Sunshine Under Fives Pre-school
St Gerard Majella Church Hall, Buller Road, BS4 2LN
Karon Nichol: 0117 977 4170
Mon-Fri: 9.15-11.45am or 12.15-2.45pm
£5

WC 人 人 凹 圓

A friendly well organised group with lots of things to do for children 2yrs/10mths-5yrs.

Sydenham Road Under Fives Playgroup
Totterdown Baptist Church, Sydenham Road, BS4 3DF
Wendy McCarthy: 0117 977 3246
Mon-Fri: 9-11.45am & Tue: 12.30-3.00pm
£3.80 incl. refreshments

WC 凹 圓 WC 豆 Pp

Stimulating, community based group for 3-5yrs. Lots of craft activities. Bikes used indoors and out. Run by voluntary committee.

The Village Pre-school
St Lukes Church Hall, Church Parade, BS4 5AZ
The Manager: 0117 971 5222
Mon-Fri: 9.15-11.45am
£3.50

P WC 豆 人 人 凹 圓

Friendly, caring environment for 3-4yrs. Very good OFSTED inspection. Long-serving experienced staff.

Waycroft Primary School
Seldon Road, Stockwood, Bristol, BS14 8PS
Simon Rowe: 0117 377 2198
waycroft_p@bristol-city.gov.uk
Mon: 9-10.30am, Wed: 1.30-3.00pm
£2 per session

WC 人 人 凹 圕 ♨ 凸 圓 Pp

'Play to Learn' session held at the school with qualified play leader for 2-3yrs. Must book into a morning or afternoon session

SOUTH BRISTOL

Christ Church Playgroup
Church Hall, Petherton Road, Hengrove, BS14 9BP
Mrs H Wayborn: 0117 975 4616
Mon, Tue, Thu: 9-11.30am
£3 + £1 a term registration fee

P 刀 WC 人 人 圕 ♨ 圓

Pre-school for children 2yrs/10mths - 5yrs. Occasional parent participation required.

Counterslip Baptist Church
648 Wells Road, Whitchurch, Bristol, BS14 9HT
Margaret: 01275 833377
worship@counterslip.co.uk
Mon-Fri: 9.30-12pm
£5 per seession

P 人 圕 凸 圓

Pre-school for children 3-5 yrs with a wide range of foundation stage activities.

Dundry Playgroup
Village Hall, Crab Tree Lane, Dundry
Victoria Cook: 0117 964 3431
Mon, Tue, Wed & Thurs: 9.15am-12noon
£5 per session

人 圕 凸

Traditional pre-school education for 3-5yrs held in Village Hall. Please phone to confirm a place.

St Bernadette Playgroup
St Bernadette Church, Wells Road, Whitchurch, BS14 9UH
Mrs Panter: 01275 834311
Mon, Tue, Thu & Fri: 9.30-11.25am
£3.50

P 刀 WC 人 人 圓

Playgroup for children from 2yrs&10 mths - 5yrs, different weekly activities.

MONTESSORI NURSERY SCHOOLS

Clevedon Montessori School
34 Albert Road, Clevedon, BS21 7RR
Maureen Burgoyne: 01275 877743
Mon-Fri: 9am-5pm
Morning Session: £11.75, Full Day: £23.70 (inc lunch)

P 豆 人 凹 圕 ♨ 圓

Children from 2½-5yrs. In first year children must do a min. of 2 morning sessions, whilst pre-schoolers a min. of 2 full days.

The Clifton Children's House
Est. 1989

where

"children enjoy learning through a broad range of interesting and varied activities"
Ofsted report 2003

- Homely and nurturing environment
- Experienced staff
- High quality nursery education

Principal: Rosamund Payne   **Tel: 0117 923 7578**

The Clifton Children's House
2 York Gardens, Clifton, BS8 4LL
Mrs Rosamund Payne: 0117 923 7578
www.bristolmontessori.co.uk
Mon-Fri: 9.15am-12pm or 1pm-3.15pm

Well established traditional Montessori Nursery School accepts children from 2½ to 4½ yrs. Younger children start in afternoons in small groups, progressing to mornings in their pre-school year. See advertisement

Stoke Bishop Montessori School
70 Parrys Lane, Stoke Bishop, Bristol
Sandra Harris: 0117 968 6960
Mon-Fri: 8am-6.15pm

Full and part-time places for children 2-5 yrs.

STEINER EDUCATION NURSERY SCHOOLS

Bristol Steiner Waldorf School
Rudolf Steiner Education, Redhill House,
Redland, BS6
0117 933 9990
Mon-Fri: 8.55am-3.30pm various sessions available for early years

Provides alternative, quality education for 3-14yrs.

The Rowan Tree Kindergarten
12d Cotham Rd, Cotham, BS6 6DR

Janet Parsons: 0117 973 4399
Mon-Fri: 9.00am-12.45pm
on application

Children from 4-6yrs can attend Kindergarten to learn in a homely environment and develop at their own pace.

DIFFERENT LANGUAGE PRE-SCHOOLS

Ecole Française de Bristol
C/O St Ursula's High School, Brecon Road, Westbury on Trym, BS9 4DT
Estelle Tenant: 0117 962 4154

Pre-school education for children 2¾-4½yrs. For French native speakers and speakers of other languages.

Ecole Française de Bristol
0117 962 4154

- * OFSTED registered nursery
- * After-school classes for children (with qualified teachers, native French speakers)
- * Children's French Holiday Activity Weeks / Themed Days
- * GCSE revision
- * Adult tuition (Daytime)
- * Bilingual/Francophone children: Maternelle / Primaire : cours assurés par des Professeurs des Ecoles qualifiés

SCHOOLS & EDUCATIONAL SUPPORT

Emma Woodworth

CHAPTER 9

INTRODUCTION

As a teacher and parent of a toddler I am very aware of how important it is to make the right educational choices for your child. Every child's needs are different and finding the right path for them is one of the most important decisions a parent can make.

When I first embarked on writing this chapter I was unaware what a minefield the whole subject was and the anxieties many parents must face.

This chapter will provide helpful information outlining the options available to you and your child throughout their education. There are many useful links to organisations and services which give advice and support.

STATE EDUCATION

Local Education Authorities (LEAs) are part of local councils, which have a duty to promote economic, environmental and social well-being in their areas. Within local councils, LEAs are accountable for early-years education, schools, adult education, and youth services. LEAs are also responsible for promoting high standards of education and work to improve standards and tackle failure. They provide support for special educational needs, access and school transport, pupil welfare and educating excluded pupils.

Schools in Bristol and its surrounding area fall under 4 different LEAs.

Bristol City Council Education Department
PO Box 57, The Council House, College Green, Bristol, BS99 7EB
0117 9037710, www.bristol-city.gov.uk

South Gloucestershire County Council Education Service
Bowling Hill, Chipping Sodbury,
South Gloucestershire, BS37 6JX
01454 863155, www.southglos.gov.uk

North Somerset County Council Education Department
PO Box 51, Town Hall, Weston-Super-Mare, BS23 1ZZ
01275 888328, www.n-somerset.gov.uk

Bath and North East Somerset County Council Education Department
PO Box 25, Riverside, Temple Street, Keynsham, BS31 1DN
01225 394312, www.bathnes.gov.uk

TYPES OF LEA SCHOOLS

All LEA run schools are self-managing and do not charge fees. They work in partnership with other schools and LEAs, and receive LEA funding. Each category has its own characteristics:

Community schools (Primary and Secondary)

Community schools are very similar to former county schools. The LEA employs the school's staff, owns the school's land and buildings and is the admissions authority.

Voluntary-aided schools (Primary and Secondary)

These are run either by the Church of England or Catholic Church in partnership with the LEA. The governing body determines the admission arrangements. For further details about admissions, contact individual schools.

Voluntary-controlled schools (Primary and Secondary)

Management for these is shared between the LEA and the Church of England. The LEA is responsible for admissions and allocating school places.

Within these categories, there are further ways in which schools can specialise to offer additional benefits and services:

City Technology Colleges (Secondary)

City Technology Colleges (CTCs) are independent all-ability, non fee-paying schools for pupils, 11-18yrs. Their purpose is to offer pupils of all abilities the opportunity to study successfully towards the world of work. All CTCs offer a wide range of vocational post -16 qualifications alongside A-Levels or equivalents.

Academies (Secondary)

Academies are publicly funded independent schools that will provide a first class free education for local pupils. Visit www.dfes.gov.uk/academies.

Special schools (Primary and Secondary)

LEAs provide these schools for certain children with special educational needs (SEN). The great majority, however, are educated in ordinary schools.

THE RED MAIDS' JUNIOR SCHOOL
Westbury-on-Trym
7-11 education for girls

We understand the importance of choosing the best education for your daughter.

At The Red Maids' Junior School there is something for everyone. The children are valued as individuals.

The Red Maids' Junior School
Grange Court Road
Westbury-on-Trym
Bristol BS9 4DP
juniors @redmaids.bristol.sch.uk
www.redmaids.bristol.sch.uk

Come and see us!
Call 0117 9629451

PRIMARY EDUCATION (5-11 YEARS)

Primary education is normally provided in primary schools, although in some areas, there are specific infant and junior schools. Children come of compulsory school age the term after their fifth birthday. However children usually attend school the September after their fourth birthday so that all children benefit from 3 years of infant education. Often admissions can be phased in up to the half term holiday in October either on a part-time or full time basis at the discretion of the head teacher. If you wish to delay admission beyond the beginning of the autumn term there is no guarantee that a place that has been offered will still be available. Children whose admission to school is delayed will start in their chronological age group.

SECONDARY EDUCATION (11-16 YEARS)

Children transfer to secondary school the September after their eleventh birthday.

A list of Primary and Secondary schools can be found in the Yellow Pages or from the LEA admissions department.

CHOOSING SCHOOLS

The most important thing you can do before choosing a school for your child is to do your research. Find as much information as possible about the school you are interested in.

Visit the school

One of the best ways to assess a school is by visiting it in person. This way, you will gain first-hand knowledge of where your child will be spending his/her day. You can learn a lot from touring the school and observing the children, the teachers and the way they work together. Things to consider:

- The location of the school. Is it nearby? Will you have to drive or take public transport? When your child is older, can they safely walk to school? Remember, a long journey to school may be tiring for your child.

- Observe the children's work and check the school's resources. Does it appear to be a happy school where everyone is serious about learning?
- Find out how the school involves parents.
- Was the school welcoming? Would it suit your child?

Most secondary and some primary schools hold open days and evenings, where you can meet the staff and view children's work. You could also make an appointment to visit the school and speak with the head teacher. Schools also have Parent Teacher Associations (PTAs) or Friends Associations which may be able to give you extra information.

Obtain the LEA booklets

Your Local Education Authority (LEA) produces a booklet, which lists all the schools in your area and has information:

- About the schools
- How many pupils they admit
- Admission arrangements and a form to complete by a given deadline
- How popular they are
- Where to find more information

This can be obtained from any school in the LEA or from the LEA admissions department. They are also made available to view in public libraries.

Obtain the school prospectus

Each year, every school publishes a brochure called a prospectus. The prospectus will usually tell you more about a particular school than the LEA booklet can, and contains the school's admissions policy in detail. You can obtain a copy of the prospectus from the school.

Check the performance tables

Every year the Department for Education and Skills (DfES) publishes performance tables for primary and secondary schools. Though they cannot give a complete picture of a school, performance tables provide a guide to how well a school or college is doing. Visit: www.dfes.gov.uk/performancetables

Research Ofsted reports

It is also helpful to read the Office for Standards in Education (Ofsted) reports, which are produced by the government's school inspectors. A report is available for every school in the country. For more information visit: www.ofsted.gov.uk/reports

ADMISSION & APPEAL PROCEDURES

You have the right to say which school you would prefer your child to attend, regardless of the school's location (even if it does not fall into the LEA in which you live). But your right to express a preference does not guarantee you a place at the school if it is oversubscribed.

Time your application

LEA booklets are usually available during the summer the year before the child is due to start school. The application form, which must be completed and returned by the given deadline, (usually in the autumn term for both primary and secondary schools) will be included in the booklet. Late applications will be processed last and you may not get your preferred choice of school.

Some LEAs display posters (in local post offices, doctors' surgeries, nurseries etc) advising parents when to apply for a school place. Arrangements vary in each area so contact your local LEA for advice.

Find out who handles admissions

Admissions are handled either by the local authority, or by the school itself. If you have not applied, **do not** assume your child will get a place at the school you want. This is true even if your child is at a nursery which is linked to an infant school, or at an infant school which is linked to a junior school. Remember also, that you need to apply for each of your children as they reach school age. Having one child at a school does not automatically mean a place for siblings.

When completing the application form it is important to state your second and third preferred school in case your first choice is unsuccessful. Completed forms must be returned to the LEA or school before the closing date (depending on who handles admissions).

If there are sufficient places available your child will be offered a place at your preferred school. However in schools which are oversubscribed, the LEA uses specific criteria when allocating places. These are usually:

* Siblings already attending the school
* Medical, psychological or special educational reason
* Geographical location to home

Appeals procedure

If you are not allocated a place at your preferred school you will be offered an alternative school. You have the right to accept the alternative place or formally appeal to an independent panel for a place at your preferred school. The letter you receive from the admission authority should also provide information about your right to appeal and how to go about it.

SERVICES PROVIDED BY LEA

Free transport

Free transport is provided if pupils:

* Attend the nearest appropriate school as determined by the city council and
* The distance between home and school is 2 miles or more for pupils under 8yrs or 3 miles or more for pupils 8-16 yrs

Free school meals

These are available if you are entitled to Income Support, Income Based Job-seeker's Allowance, support under Part VI of the Immigration and Asylum Act 1999 or Child Tax Credit with an annual income of below £13,230.

Milk in schools

The LEA provides a free carton of milk to all pupils under the age of 5, each day at school. Some schools run their own scheme for pupils over the age of 5.

Grants

The LEA may be able to help with costs for families who are in financial difficulty. Contact your LEA for further details.

Welfare

The welfare of children in schools is primarily the concern of the staff and head teacher of the school. Schools are also allocated a welfare officer to support schools and parents in ensuring full-time school attendance, promoting good home/school liaison, supporting excluded pupils, special educational needs, bullying and welfare benefits.

Educational psychology

Schools are allocated an educational psychologist who is involved if there are any concerns with children's learning and general development, behaviour and special educational needs.

School nurse

Each school has a named nurse who works in partnership with parents, teachers and children offering help and support with any emotional/behavioural or physical concerns parents may have. At school entry parents are offered hearing and sight tests and growth measurement for their child. The school nurse can be contacted about any health related problems.

Contact details

Admissions

Bristol	0117 9037710
South Gloucestershire	01454 863155
North Somerset	01275 888328
Bath & NE Somerset	01225 394312

Awards/Support/Funding

Bristol	0117 9036666
South Gloucestershire	01454 863377
North Somerset	01275 888328
Bath & NE Somerset	01225 394319

Transport

Bristol	0117 9037672
South Gloucestershire	01454 863155

| North Somerset | 01934 412255 |
| Bath & NE Somerset | 01225 394312 |

Special Educational Needs

Bristol	0117 9036515
South Gloucestershire	01454 863174
North Somerset	01275 888331
Bath & NE Somerset	01225 395206

Educational Welfare

Bristol Primary	0117 9037098
Bristol Secondary	0117 9031660/1
South Gloucestershire	01454 863377
North Somerset	01275 888303/10
Bath & NE Somerset	01225 394241

Educational Psychology

Bristol	0117 9031650
South Gloucestershire	01454 863167
North Somerset	01934 634854
Bath & NE Somerset	01225 394901

SCHOOL YEARS

Nursery/Reception	Foundation Stage 3-5 years
Year 1 & 2	Infants/Key Stage 1 5-7 years
Year 3-6	Juniors/Key Stage 2 7-11 years
Years 7-9	Secondary/Key Stage 3 11-14 years
Years 10 & 11	Secondary/Key Stage 4 14-16 years

ASSESSING CHILDREN'S LEARNING

Foundation stage

Each child is issued with a profile which charts their development across the Areas of Learning throughout the Foundation Stage.

National Testing

Currently at the end of Key Stages 1 (Yr 2), 2 (Yr 6) and 3 (Yr 9) pupil progress is assessed through Standard Attainment Tests (SATs) in English, Maths and Science.

Key Stage 4 qualifications

- Entry level certificates - These are for pupils who would find GCSEs difficult
- GCSEs - A General Certificate for Secondary Education is offered as a main way to get Key Stage 4 qualifications. They generally take two years and students complete coursework and take examinations. Some new vocational subjects are now offered
- GCSE short courses - These are like full GCSEs but cover fewer topics, so they only take half the time to do. You need to do two short courses to make up a full GCSE
- GNVQs - General National Vocational Qualifications are courses where broad work areas are studied, but they don't train pupils for a specific job
- NVQs - National Vocational Qualifications are designed to relate to real work and test how competent pupils are at carrying out a particular job
- VQs - Vocational qualifications are helpful for pupils who want to gain a qualification through a more practical work-based placement course. Pupils actually work in the workplace – usually half or one day a week

It would be unmanageable for schools to offer all types of qualifications in all subjects. When choosing a school make sure it suits your educational preferences.

EDUCATIONAL WEBSITES

General

Allkids, www.allkids.co.uk
Extensive parent/child directory. The kids' section is huge with tons of links to educational and safe fun sites.

BBC Learning
www.bbc.co.uk/education/home
Useful resources and interactive activities.

Bookstart, www.bookstart.co.uk
The Booktrust's national 'books for babies' programme. Offering free books to every child and advice to every parent.

For parents

DfES: The Parent Centre,
www.parentcentre.gov.uk
Information about schools and the curriculum, as well as a facility to search for local schools.
Educate the Children, www.educate.org.uk
Offers guidelines to understanding the education system and provides information about local schools.

Reading is Fundamental
www.rif.org.uk
Top tips to help children read.

Spelling it Right
www.spelling.hemscott.net

For children

Digger and the Gang
www.bbc.co.uk/education/schools/digger
A BBC website based on the National Curriculum for primary school children.
Granada Learning
www.granada-learning.com
Curriculum software, online resources and multimedia products for all ages and needs.
Science Line, www.sciencenet.org.uk/index

Homework

Homework Elephant
www.homeworkelephant.co.uk
Help for homework assignments and provides a font of all knowledge, the 'agony elephant'!
Homework High, www.homeworkhigh.com
Help with main subjects, answers emails.
Kidscape, www.kidscape.org.uk
Practical advice to help beat bullying.

Revision

GCSE Answers, www.gcse.com
Tutorials, tips and advice on GCSE coursework and exams.

GCSE Bitesize
www.bbc.co.uk/education/revision
Brush up on your GCSE skills.

S-Cool
www.s-cool.co.uk
Revision guides and exam hints.

SPECIAL EDUCATIONAL NEEDS

Children with special educational needs (SEN) have learning difficulties, or disabilities that make it harder for them to learn than most children of the same age. These children may need extra help or different help to that given to other children of the same age.
Special needs could include problems with: thinking and understanding, physical or sensory skills, behaviour and emotions or speech and language.
Help for children with SEN will usually be in the child's ordinary, mainstream early education setting or school, sometimes with help from outside specialists.

If you are worried your child may be having difficulties

Your child's early years are a very important time for physical, emotional, intellectual and social development. When your health visitor or doctor makes a routine check, they might suggest that there could be a problem and give you advice about the next steps to take.
If you think your child may have a special educational need, you should talk to either your child's class teacher, the SENCO (the SEN co-ordinator), the head teacher or head of year straight away.
The Independent Panel for Special Education Advice (IPSEA) offers free and independent advice on LEAs' legal duties to assess and provide for children with SEN. Visit www.ipsea.org.uk

EDUCATIONAL SUPPORT GROUPS

Also see Special Needs, Advice & Support chapter.

Advisory Centre for Education
Unit 1C, 22 Highbury Grove, London, N5 2EA
www.ace-ed.org.uk
0808 800 5793, 2pm-5pm

Support for ADD/ADHD
45 Vincent Close, Broadstairs, Kent, CT10 2ND

support@adders.org, www.adders.org
01843 851145, 24 hr

AFASIC
2nd Floor, 50-52 Great Sutton St, London, EC1V 0DJ
info@afasic.org.uk, www.afasic.org.uk
020 7490 9410, Mon-Fri 9am-5pm
Helpline 0845 3555577 Mon-Thu 11am-2pm
Association for All Speech Impaired Children.

Bristol Dyslexia Centre
10 Upper Belgrave Rd, BS8 2XH
www.dyslexiacentre.co.uk
0117 973 9405
Full time school for 7-12yrs, and specialist
teaching 5yrs-adult.

British Dyslexia Association
98 London Road, Reading, Berkshire RG1 5AU
www.bda-dyslexia.org.uk
0118 966 2677
Mon-Fri 10am-12.45pm & 2pm-5pm

The Dyslexia Institute
90a High Street, Staple Hill, Bristol
0117 910 9265
Advice and Assessments

Dyspraxia Foundation
8 West Alley, Hitchin, Herts, SG5 1EG
www.dyspraxiafoundation.org.uk
01462 454986

Education and Life Long Learning
PO Box 57, BS99 7EB
0117 903 7961

Advice on early years and child care services,
admissions to schools, child welfare,
complaints, special educational needs etc.

Parents for Inclusion
Unit 2, 70 South Lambeth Road, London SW8 1RL
020 7735 7735

Portage Service
Elmfield House, Greystoke Ave, Bristol, BS10 6AY
0117 903 8438
A home-visiting educational service for pre-
school children who have special needs.

**The National Association for Gifted
Children - NAGC**
Suite 14, Challenge House, Sherwood Drive,
Bletchley, MK3 6DP
www.nagcbritain.co.uk
0845 450 0221

**Supportive Parents for Special Children
(SPSC)**
3rd FLoor Royal Oak House, Royal Oak Ave, BS1 4GB
0117 989 7724 Admin

0117 989 7725 Helpline, Mon/Wed/Fri 10am-
12.30pm
Operates during term time. Offering support
and information to parents of children with
any level of special educational need.

EDUCATION FOR SICK CHILDREN

The LEA and schools must ensure that
children who are unable to attend school
because of medical needs have access
to as much education as their medical
condition allows. If a child is hospitalised
then staff need to liase with and involve the
school early on. Contact your LEA or visit
www.dfes.gov.uk/sickchildren

**National Association for the Education of
Sick Children**
Open School, 18 Victoria Park Square, E2 0PF
www.sickchildren.org.uk
020 8980 6263 or 020 8980 8523

POST 16 CHOICES

At 16 pupils can legally leave full time
education. If your child wishes to pursue a
college education bear in mind that some
courses fill up by the previous November,
although most applications and decisions will
be made after Christmas in Year 11.

POST 16 EDUCATION

School Sixth Form
Many secondary schools have a Sixth Form
centre attached, the courses they offer
depends on what best suits their pupils.

Sixth Form College
These are similar to schools and a student can
transfer to one at the age of 16.

College of Further Education

These usually offer a wider range of courses than sixth form colleges and provide education and training for student of all ages.

Modern Apprenticeship

This is a work based learning programme supporting young people through nationally recognised qualifications.

Post 16 Courses

- Entry level certificates, GCSEs, GNVQs, NVQs. See Key Stage 4 Qualifications above.
- AS and A levels - are usually offered in a variety of subjects to those students who have 5 or more GCSEs. Courses usually last 2 years and students complete coursework and examinations, which are graded and count towards University places.
- Vocational AS & A levels (or AVCEs) - courses designed to develop the skills needed for a wide range of jobs such as engineering, hospitality and catering, leisure and tourism.
- Key Skills - the essential skills you need to do well in education and training, to succeed at work and to get on in life.
- BTEC Nationals, City & Guilds qualifications etc - nationally recognised occupational qualifications offered in a number of subjects.
- Modern Apprenticeship - a work based learning programme supporting young people through nationally recognised NVQ and Key skills qualifications.

USEFUL WEBSITES

Assessment and Qualification Alliance
www.aqa.org.uk
AQA offers a range of qualifications and services.

City and Guilds
www.city-and-guilds.com.uk
City & Guilds is the leading provider of vocational qualifications in the UK.

Connexions - West of England
www.connexionswest.org.uk
Aims to give young people the best start in life by helping them make the transition to adulthood and working life. Connexions can advise on work, training and further education opportunities as well as drug abuse, sexual health and relationships, housing and money matters. There is a vacancy database of jobs with training for 16-19yrs.

Department for Education and Skills - key skills
www.dfes.gov.uk/keyskills

Edexcel
www.edexcel.org.uk
A qualifications site which includes GCSEs, AS and A levels, GNVQ and many more.

Popular Questions
www.dfes.gov.uk/popularquestions
Designed especially for students, providing information on issues such as careers, education and skills.

StudentZone
www.studentzone.org.uk
Provides information on issues such as careers, news, travel, legal and finance matters, sport and much more.

Cost

There are no tuition fees for students under 19, although some costs may be incurred as part of the course e.g.

- Textbooks, stationery, materials, etc
- Travel costs to and from college/work experience placements
- Educational visits and residential courses

Help with costs

Some students aged 16 and over may be eligible for financial help through the learner support fund. There are two types of fund:

School learner support funds
These are administered by the LEA for 6th form students in school. Pupils in financial need can apply to their LEA.

College learner support funds
Administered directly by further education colleges. Contact college Student Support Officer for details.

The support funds are means tested and are intended to help with the cost of equipment, books, travel and field trips.

Educational Maintenance Allowance
The EMA is part of the government's commitment to help young people fulfil their educational potential. Payments are means tested. Visit: www.dfes.gov.uk/ema

Care to Learn
www.dfes.gov.uk/caretolearn
0845 600 2809
This is a new childcare funding scheme to support young parents in education and training. All parents aged 16-18yrs who study could be eligible to claim for childcare and associated transport costs up to £5,000 per child p.a.

HOME SCHOOLING
School is not compulsory. However, parents have a responsibility to ensure their child has an effective education, which can be given at home.

The Bristol Home Education Group
Kathy Nott: 0117 966 82675
Carla MacGregor: 0117 935 4389
Local contact for Education Otherwise providing social contact and support to parents and children who have chosen home schooling.

Education Otherwise
PO Box 7420, London, N9 9SG
Tel: 0870 730 0074
www.educationotherwise.org.uk
A self-help group offering support and information on home education.

Home Education Advisory Service
www.heas.org.uk
Provides advice and practical support for families who wish to educate their children at home.

LANGUAGE SCHOOLS & CLASSES
Out of school sessions for bilingual children or those who would like to learn a different language.

Ecole Française de Bristol
c/o St Ursula High School, Brecon Road, BS9 4DT
0117 962 4154

Greek School
St Peter & St Paul, Lower Ashley Road, BS5 0YL
Classes held at the community centre
0117 973 9335

Punjabi Classes
Sikh Resource Centre, 114 St Marks Road, Easton, BS5 6JD
0117 952 5023

Arabic Classes
468-470 Stapleton Road, Easton
Classs held at the Mosque
0117 951 1491

Bengali Classes
35 Mivart Street, Easton, BS5 6JF
0117 951 9777

PRIVATE TUITION
There are many independent tutors or larger agencies that can find a tutor to match your child's needs. Tutors may teach on a one-to-one basis or in small groups and some will come to your home. Independent tutors and agencies often advertise in the Yellow Pages, educational publications (Primary Times, a free half-termly publication distributed to schools and libraries), newspapers, local libraries, schools and shop windows.
Check any tutor you find for your child has passed a police check.

PRIVATE EDUCATION

INDEPENDENT SCHOOLS

These are schools that are independent of local or central government control. Most of them have their own board of governors and a bursar who is responsible for financial and other aspects of school management. The head is responsible to the governors but has the freedom to appoint staff, admit pupils and take day-to-day decisions.

Independent schools include day and boarding schools, single-sex and co-educational schools.

Choosing a school

Most schools advertise in the Yellow Pages, local papers and educational publications. Having obtained a prospectus, arrange a visit. Most schools have open days for prospective parents, but also try to visit on a normal working day.

Curriculum

Independent schools are not required to follow the National Curriculum and therefore set their own. Some schools place emphasis on the arts and/or sciences whereas some are more sport orientated.

Admission and selection

Many junior schools and even some senior schools admit pupils on a first-come-first-served basis. Independent senior schools often set some form of entrance test. The difficulty of these tests and the standards required for admission vary and will be related to the type of school.

How much?

Basic fees vary widely depending on the age of the child, location, facilities etc. Approximate fee range per term as at September 2003:

Pre-Prep (age 2-7)	£500-£2200
Junior/Prep (age 7-13)	£1100-£2500
Senior (age 11/13-18)	£2000-£3700

Many schools include lunches in basic fees. Uniforms, trips and other incidental costs will add to the bill. You may have to pay for books, entries for public examinations, stationery and medical supplies.

Scholarships and bursaries

Scholarships are awarded to students who have shown academic or sporting excellence. They rarely cover the whole fees.

Many schools also have bursaries, grants from the school, to help you pay the fees. These are often means tested. Some schools offer grants to children of clergy, teachers and armed forces personnel. Some give concessions for siblings.

For more information contact:

The Independent Schools Council information service (ISCis)
01736 799250, www.iscis.uk.net.

The Independent Schools Guide
www.gabbitas.net
A complete directory of the UK's independent schools and special schools.

BUTCOMBE
Clifton College Pre-preparatory School & Nursery

OPEN MORNINGS & AFTERNOONS EVERY TERM
or arrange a visit to suit you & your family

Give your child the best start in life!

Butcombe, Guthrie Road
Clifton, Bristol BS8 3EZ
Tel: 0117 3157 000
www.cliftoncollegeuk.com
Registered Charity No. 311735

Clifton College is a boarding & day school for boys & girls aged 3 - 18 yrs

SHOPPING & SERVICES

Jo Smart

CHAPTER 10

INTRODUCTION

I loved shopping until I had my daughter and realised how difficult it can be to shop with a pushchair and child. After a year's experience, I now consider myself to be 'semi-skilled' at negotiating my way around shop displays and in locating the nearest nappy changing facilities, feeding rooms and lifts. Shopping with children can be challenging, but this chapter aims to give you the knowledge to make it a more enjoyable experience for you and your family.

Broadmead and the Mall at Cribbs Causeway provide Bristol with a wide selection of shops along with good facilities for parents with small children. This chapter includes listings of the major high street names, but it is our aim to focus on the wide range of independent retailers found across Bristol, who, as well as having good product knowledge and vast stock ranges, offer a personal service.

SHOPPING CENTRES

The Mall at Cribbs Causeway
0117 903 0303
www.mallcribbs.com
Mon-Fri 10am-9pm, Sat 9am-7pm, Sun 11am-5pm
Bank Holidays 10am-6pm
John Lewis opening hours vary
Jct 17, M5

P ✎ WC ⚗ 🛉 CP 🛒 ⬆ ✂ 🏧 ⛲
🍴 🛗 🚼 ♿

The Galleries
0117 929 0569
www.galleries-shopping.co.uk
Mon-Wed 8.30am-6pm, Thu 8.30am- 8pm, Fri-Sat 8.30am-6pm, Sun 11am-5pm

P ✎ WC 🛉 CP 🛒 ⬆ 🍴

Car park stays open for one hour after shops close.

DEPARTMENT & LARGER STORES

Most parents are aware of the quality, price and range of products sold at the major high street stores. Therefore in this book, their facilities and product ranges have been summarised.

Larger stores usually offer the widest range of facilities to make shopping with children easier, but if you still can't face it, many now offer mail order or internet shopping services. See table opposite.

SUPERMARKETS

Over recent years, supermarkets have increased their non-food ranges significantly. Many of them now offer a one-stop shop for all your needs, stocking maternity wear, nursery equipment, clothing, toys and books. Some stock food ranges specifically manufactured for children. See Supermarket table overleaf.

ONLINE SHOPPING
Several supermarkets offer an internet shopping and delivery service. Very useful during the last few weeks of pregnancy and early months with a newborn. Most currently charge around £5 for delivery, although some waive this charge if you spend above a certain amount.

The following tips may help you when ordering your groceries online:

*   Ordering online can take a while at first, so it is advisable to use it a few times before your baby arrives, or before you need it to save you time! Make a list before you start.
*   It is good for heavy items, particularly if you have enough storage to buy in bulk.
*   Know the weights/sizes of products that you want to buy.

After the initial order, it can be a hassle-free way to shop, particularly if you are ill, have small children, have had a caesarian or have no car.

CHILDREN'S CLOTHES

From basic vests to exclusive party wear, the shops listed have a wide selection of children's clothing to suit all budgets. It is also worth looking at our Factory Outlet, Markets and Nearly New listings, which can save you money.

Adams Childrenswear Ltd
The Galleries, Broadmead
0117 922 1034
For hours and facilities see chapter introduction
Good selection of reasonably priced clothes for babies and children up to 10yrs. Branches also in Weston-Super-Mare and Yate.

Baby Gap & Gap Kids
30-32 The Broadmead, BS1 3HA
0117 922 0657
Mon-Fri 9.30am-6pm, Sat 9am-6pm, Sun 11am-5pm

✎ WC 🛒 ⬆

DEPARTMENT AND LARGER STORES SUMMARY TABLE

For stores situated at The Mall or The Galleries, the facilities shown are in addition to those at the shopping centre. All stores have nearby parking and can accommodate single and double buggies.

Department Store	Mail Order	Internet Shopping	Branch Location	Facilities	Clothing (Age Range)	Shoes	Maternity Wear	Maternity Underwear	Children's Furniture	Nursery Equipment	Toys	Outdoor Toys	Computer Games	Books
BHS www.bhs.co.uk			The Mall 0117 950 9493	[WC][✎][✗][café][CP]	0-14	✓								
			Broadmead 0117 929 2261	[WC][✎][✗][café][CP]	0-14	✓								
Big W www.bigw.co.uk			Filton 0117 969 7303	[WC][✎][✗][café][CP]	0+	✓				✓	✓	✓	✓	✓
Boots (larger branches) www.boots.com		✓	The Mall 0117 950 9744		0-4					web	✓	✓	✓	
			Broadmead 0117 929 3631	[✎]	0-4					web	✓	✓	✓	
			Avon Meads 0117 972 8056	[WC][✎]	0-4					web	✓	✓	✓	
Debenhams www.debenhams.com	✓	✓	Broadmead 0117 929 1021	[WC][✎][✗][café][CP][icon][icon]	0-14	✓		✓			✓	✓	✓	✓
House of Fraser www.houseoffraser.co.uk			Broadmead 0117 944 5566	[WC][✎][✗][café][CP][icon]	0-10			✓						
Ikea www.ikea.co.uk			Eastville 0845 355 2264	[WC][✎][✗][café][CP][icon][icon][icon][icon][icon]					✓	✓				
John Lewis www.johnlewis.com		✓	The Mall 0117 959 1100	[WC][✎][✗][café][icon][icon][icon][icon]	0-14	✓		✓	✓	✓	✓	✓	✓	✓
Marks & Spencer www.mands.com	✓	✓	Broadmead 0117 927 2000	[WC][✎][✗][café][CP][icon][icon]	0-12	✓	✓	✓		✓			✓	✓
			The Mall 0117 904 4444	[WC][✎][✗][café][CP][icon][icon]	0-12	✓		✓	✓			✓		✓	✓
Mothercare World www.mothercare.com	✓	✓	Avon Meads 0117 971 9815	[WC][✎][icon]	0-8	✓	✓	✓	✓	✓	✓	✓		✓
			Eastville 0117 951 8200	[WC][✎][✗][café][CP][icon]	0-8	✓	✓	✓	✓	✓	✓	✓	✗	✓
TK Maxx www.tkmaxx.com			The Galleries 0117 930 4404		0+:	✓						✓	✓	✓
			Cribbs 0117 950 8081	[icon]	0+	✓						✓	✓	✓
Woolworths www.woolworths.co.uk	✓	✓	The Galleries 0117 922 7778		0-13	✓					✓	✓	✓	✓

SUPERMARKETS

Supermarket	Mail Order	Internet Shopping	Branch Location	Facilities	Clothing (Age Range)	Open 24 hrs?	Shoes	Maternity wear	Maternity Underwear	Nursery Equipment	Toys	Books	Computer Games
Asda www.asda.co.uk		✓	Cribbs Causeway 0117 969 3973	WC 🖊 🍴 🚼 CP	0-15	✓	✓	✓	✓	✓	✓	✓	✓
			Longwell Green 0117 960 3947	WC 🖊 🍴 🚼 CP	0-15	✓	✓	✓	✓	✓	✓	✓	✓
			Bedminster 0117 923 1563	WC 🖊 🍴 🚼 CP	0-15		✓	✓	✓		✓	✓	✓
			Whitchurch 01275 839 431	WC 🖊	0-15		✓				✓	✓	✓
Tesco www.tesco.com	✓	✓	Brislington 0117 991 7400	WC 🖊 🍴 🚼 CP	0-13	✓	✓	✓	✓		✓	✓	✓
			Eastgate Centre 0117 912 7400	WC 🖊 🍴 🚼 CP	0-13	✓	✓	✓			✓	✓	✓
Sainsburys www.sainsbury.co.uk		✓	Ashton Gate 0117 966 3064	WC 🖊 🍴 🚼 CP	0-10		✓				✓	✓	✓
			Castle Court 0117 977 4887	WC 🖊 ✎ 🍴 🚼 CP	0-10		✓				✓	✓	✓
			Filton 0117 923 6459	WC 🖊 🍴 🚼 CP	0-13		✓				✓	✓	✓

Gap Kids
The Mall, Cribbs Causeway
0117 950 9667

Baby Gap
The Mall, Cribbs Causeway
0117 950 9698
For hours and facilities see Shopping Centres
Good quality clothing and shoes (American sizes). Clothing is expensive, but stock is changed regularly so reductions are usually available. Baby Gap sizes from premature baby to 5 yrs, Gap Kids from 5-15yrs.

Be Wise Ltd
26-32 Regent St, Kingswood, BS16
0117 935 2239
Mon-Sat 9am-5.30pm, Sun 10am-4pm
🚹 🚼
48 East Street, Bedminster, BS3
0117 963 1652
🚹 🚼
Sells inexpensive clothes, 0-13yrs.

Bishopston Trading Company
193 Gloucester Rd, Bishopston
0117 924 5598
bishopstontradingco@supanet.com, www.bishopsto
ntrading.co.uk
Mon-Sat 9.30am-5.30pm

Workers Co-operative set up to create employment in South Indian village of KV Kuppam. Fair trade shop with play area. Specialises in natural fabrics and organic handloom cotton in a range of colours, 0-13yrs. Also see Mail Order below.

Born
64 Gloucester Rd, Bishopston, BS7 8BH
Eva Fernandes, 0117 924 5080
info@borndirect.com, www.borndirect.com
Mon-Sat 9.30am-5.30pm

Most of the products in this shop are natural/organic. They stock a large range of cotton nappies and accessories, organic cotton clothing, soft leather shoes, recycled PET fleece and a practical range of high quality outdoor wear.
Also see Nursery Equipment and Maternity Wear sections.

Claire's Accessories
The Mall, Cribbs Causeway
0117 959 4779
For hours & facilities see Shopping Centres
&
Unit G11a Broadmead Gallery, Broadmead
0117 922 6657
Mon-Sat 9am-5.30pm, Thu 7pm
A great selection of beauty and hair accessories for young children.

Gymboree
The Mall, Cribbs Causeway
0117 959 1777
For see introduction above

American designer clothes for boys and girls from newborn to age 7. They usually have ranges at reduced prices. There is a TV instore to keep children entertained!

H&M
The Mall, Cribbs Causeway
0117 950 9590
For hours and facilities see Shopping Centres

Fashionable but inexpensive children's clothing from birth to 14yrs. Also see Maternity Wear below.

Katze
55 Gloucester Rd, Bishopston, BS7 8AD
0117 942 5625
Mon-Sat 10.00am-5.30pm

Sells a small selection of good quality ethnic children's clothes.

Laura Ashley
The Galleries, Broadmead
0117 922 1011
For hours and facilities see Shopping Centres

Lovely range of girls clothes from 2-10yrs.

Mama's
184 Henleaze Rd, Henleaze, BS9 4NE
0117 962 8704
www.mamasmaternity.co.uk
Mon-Fri 9.30am-5.30pm, Sat 9.30am-5pm

Sells good quality baby wear, blankets, shawls, christening gowns, books, soft toys, aromatherapy and maternity wear. Also see Maternity below.

Marks
61 Henleaze Rd, Henleaze, BS9 4JT
0117 962 1365
Mon-Sat 9am-5pm

Small range of chainstore seconds with brands such as Next, M&S, Mothercare, Adams & George. Stock changes frequently, 0-11yrs.

Monsoon
Unit 7 New Broadmead, Union St, BS1 2DL
0117 929 0870, www.monsoon.co.uk
Mon-Sat 9.30am-5.30pm, Sun 11am-5pm

The Mall, Cribbs Causeway
0117 950 4175
For hours and facilities see Shopping Centres

Lovely range of clothing in both casual and smart ranges. Girls from 0-12yrs, and a new boys range from 0-8 yrs. 'Posh party clothes.

Mothercare World
The Eastgate Centre, Eastville, BS12
0117 951 8200
Mon-Fri 9.30am-8pm, Sat 9am-6pm, Sun 11am-5pm
[P] [✐] [WC] [⌂] [CP] [⟋] [⟋] [⟋] [✕] [⊞] [⟟]
Avon Meads, St Philips Causeway
0117 971 9815
[P] [✐] [WC] [⟋] [⟋] [⟋]

Large range of reasonably priced baby and children's wear in all the branches. Clothes from 0-8yrs, school wear to 11yrs. Also see Nursery Equipment, Toys and Maternity Wear.

Next
Broadmead (opposite H & M)
0117 922 6495
Mon-Sat 9am-6pm, Thu until 7pm, Sun 11am-5pm
[P] [⟋] [⟋] [⟟]
The Mall, Cribbs Causeway
0117 950 9033
www.next.co.uk
For hours and facilities see Shopping Centres

Good range of mid-priced children's clothing and shoes. Stores stock sizes from 0-10yrs, but clothes up to age 16 available to order in store or from the directory.

Next Clearance
Abbeywood Retail Park, Station Rd, Filton
0117 906 2280
Mon-Fri 9.30am-8pm, Sat 9am-6pm, Sun 11am-5pm
[P] [⟋] [⟋]

End of season and clearance stock from Next and Next Directory. Prices are up to 50% off original selling price. Children's clothing and shoes available from birth upwards.

Oranges and Lemons
20 Princess Victoria Street, Clifton, BS8 4BP
0117 973 7370
Mon-Sat 9am-5.30pm
[⊙] [⟋] [⟋]

Wide range of designer children's clothing, shoes and accessories, including Baby Dior, Diesel and O'Neill. Excellent quality clothes, 0-12 yrs. See advertisement, central colour section.

Peacocks
147 Gloucester Rd, Bishopston, BS7
0117 942 8155, www.peacocks.co.uk
Mon-Sat 9am-5.30pm
[⟋] [⟋]

Large selection of reasonably priced clothing, 0-15yrs.
Branches also at Weston-Super-Mare, Bedminster, Keynsham, Nailsea.

TinyTots Kids Shop
Abbotswood Shopping Centre, Yate
01454 314 174
Mon-Fri 9am-4pm, Wed 1pm, Sat 9am-12am
[⟋]

Sells designer and well known chainstore clothing, 0-8 yrs, £9.99 or less.

CHILDREN'S SHOES

There are a wide range of shoes available from birth, suited to each stage of your child's development. When learning to walk, children use the feel of the floor to balance, so it is best to wait until they are walking confidently before buying their first pair of 'proper walking shoes'. Children's shoes can be expensive, but it is very important to look after their developing feet. Once purchased, it is important to check they fit frequently and a good shoe shop will be happy to do this.

Besides the specialist shoe shops listed below, please also see Department Stores, Supermarkets and Factory Outlets.

Clarks Shoes Ltd
35 Broadmead, BS1 8EU
0117 929 0992
Mon-Sat 9.30am-5.30pm, Sun 11am-5pm
[WC] [⟋] [⟋]
The Mall, Cribbs Causeway
0117 959 2290
For hours and facilities see Shopping Centres
[⟋] [⟋]

Clarks at Mothercare World
The Eastgate Centre, Eastville, BS12
0117 952 5335
&
Avon Meads, St Philips Causeway, BS2 0SP
0117 971 9815

For Hours & Facilities see Children's Clothing section. Good range of shoes in width fittings starting from size 3. Also a range of crawling and cruising shoes for those early months. The staff are helpful and shops have a few toys. Photo provided of your child in their first pair of shoes!

Holbrooks
190 Henleaze Rd, Henleaze, BS9 4NE
0117 962 2478
holbrooksshoes@ukonline.co.uk
Mon-Sat 9am-5.30pm

Good range of Start-rite and Clarks shoes and trainers from size 4. Dance shoes for ballroom, latin, ballet, tap and jazz. Access is difficult with double buggies but the staff are very helpful. Discount available for twins.

John Lewis
The Mall, Cribbs Causeway
For hours and facilities see Shopping Centres
Shoe department on the first floor selling Clarks and Start-rite shoes from size 2½. Also stock trainers, slippers, sandals and wellies.

KBK Shoes
203 Cheltenham Road, Cotham, BS6 5QX
0117 924 3707
Mon-Fri 9.30am-6pm, Sat 9am-6pm

Sells Dr Martens and Caterpillar boots. Children's feet can be measured accurately in the store.

Kids at Clinks
At Charles Clinkard, The Mall, Cribbs Causeway
0117 959 2484
For hours and facilities see Shopping Centres
A good selection of shoes starting at size 2. Brands include Clarks, Start-Rite, Kickers, Elefanten, Hush Puppies, Timberland, Babybotte, Buckle My Shoe and many more. Trained shoe fitters.

one small step one giant leap
See Shops Outside Bristol.

Oranges and Lemons
20 Princess Victoria Street, Clifton, BS8 4BP

0117 973 7370
Mon-Sat 9am-5.30pm

Shoes stocked from newborn upwards, including O'Neill trainers and sandals.

The Handmade Shoe Company
64 Colston Street, BS1 5AZ
0117 924 4247
www.handmadeshoecompany.co.uk
Opening hours vary, please call shop for details.

Handmade shoes starting at size 4, available in standard sizes and made to measure. Baby shoes available (not handmade).

Thomas Ford
12 St Mary's Way, Thornbury, BS35 2BH
01454 419142
Mon-Sat 9am-5.30pm

17 Old Church Rd, Clevedon, BS21 6LU
01275 879512

The Clarks Shop, Kingschase Shopping Centre, Kingswood, BS15 2LP
0117 961 3807
Mon-Sat 9am-5.30pm

All stores stock a full range of Clarks shoes in width fittings including cruisers, trainers and slippers. All staff are trained Clarks shoes fitters. Kingschase also stock discounted children's shoes.

UNIFORMS
Most department stores and supermarkets sell school uniforms and offer good value ranges in trendy styles. Below are specialist stockists of school uniforms.

National School Wear Centres
22 Gloucester Rd Nth, Filton Park, BS7 0SF
0117 969 8551, www.n-sc.co.uk
Mon-Sat 9am-5pm

Sells both generic and some North Bristol State school uniforms. Also clothing for Cubs,

Brownies, ballet and sport. Orders can be placed via web.

School Togs Nailsea Ltd.
110 High St, Nailsea, BS48 1AH
01275 857 491
Mon-Fri 9am-5.30pm, Sat 9am-5pm

A comprehensive range of uniforms for local schools, along with school sports, Scouts, Guides & dance clothing, 4-11+yrs.

MATERNITY & BABY

MATERNITY WEAR
There are good ranges of maternity wear available at varying prices, at the outlets listed below. There are several fastenings designed to accommodate your growing bump and it is a good idea to try, before buying, to find the most comfortable one for you.
Well-fitting, comfortable maternity underwear is a necessary expense during your pregnancy, to support your changing shape. Your bra size can change dramatically during pregnancy and most stockists offer a measuring service.
Also see Department Stores, Supermarkets and Nearly New for maternity clothing.

Mail Order Maternity Wear
If you would like the privacy and convenience of trying your maternity clothes at home before buying, try some of the recommended companies listed below. All offer maternity wear ordering and delivery either via the internet or by phone from a catalogue.

Argos Additions
Tel: 0845 304 0008
www.additionsdirect.co.uk

JoJo Maman Bébé
Tel: 0870 241 0560
www.jojomamanbebe.co.uk

Next
Tel: 0845 600 7000
www.next.co.uk

Vertbaudet
Tel: 0845 270 0270
www.vertbaudet.co.uk

Asda
For Hours & Facilities see Supermarket Tables.
Recently introduced range of maternity wear within their George clothing brand. It is stocked at their Cribbs Causeway, Longwell Green and Bedminster branches.

Blooming Marvellous
5 Saracen Street, Bath, BA1 5BR
01225 442 777
Mon-Sat 9.30am-5.30pm, Sun 10.30am-4.30pm

Mail order maternity & baby wear, nursery equipment & toys. "Good range of maternity wear." See advertisement in Healthcare.

Born
64 Gloucester Rd, Bishopston, BS7 8BH
0117 924 5080
www.borndirect.com
Mon-Sat 9.30am-5.30pm

Bravado range of maternity and nursing bras and underwear. Also feeding tops.

Dorothy Perkins
62 Broadmead, Broadmead
0117 927 3790
Mon-Fri 9am-5.30pm, Sat 9am-6pm, Sun 11am-5pm

The Mall, Cribbs Causeway
0117 950 7665
For hours and facilities see Shopping Centres
Good range of trousers, jeans, dresses, cotton tops and seasonal swimwear in sizes 8 to 22. No underwear.

H&M
The Mall, Cribbs Causeway
0117 950 590
For hours and facilities see Shopping Centres

Good range of inexpensive maternity wear in sizes 8 to 20.

John Lewis
The Mall, Cribbs Causeway
For hours and facilities see Shopping Centres

A good range of maternity and feeding bras, with a measuring service available. Also see Department & Larger Stores.

Mama's
184 Henleaze Rd, Henleaze, BS9 4NE
0117 962 8704
www.mamasmaternity.co.uk
Mon-Fri 9.30am-5.30pm, Sat 9.30am-5pm
[WC] [⅃] [⅂]

Wide range of smart and casual maternity wear, swimsuits, bras and nightwear. See advertisement.

Mothercare World
For Hours & Facilities see Children's Clothing.
Both stores in Bristol have a wide range of maternity wear in sizes from 8 to 22. Swimming costumes and bras (measuring service available).

NCT - Maternity bra sales
0117 924 3849
Ruth Bolgar sells maternity bras on behalf of the NCT. She offers a free fitting service. Call her for further details.

Next Clearance
Abbeywood Retail Park, Station Rd, Filton
0117 906 2280
www.next.co.uk
Mon-Fri 9.30am-8pm, Sat 9am-6pm, Sun 11am-5pm
[P] [⅃] [⅂]

End of season and clearance maternity wear at up to 50% off original selling price in Next Directory.

Tesco
For Hours & Facilities see Supermarkets Table.
The Brislington branch of Tesco stock a range of reasonably priced maternity clothing and underwear.

MATERNITY EQUIPMENT HIRE
The following companies and individuals offer equipment hire services for use before, during or after labour.

Jill Glover
Jill Glover, 0117 942 6810

Birthing pool hire for a monthly rate of £200 plus a returnable deposit of £50.

Natural Babies
11 Bartletts Road, Bedminster, Bristol, BS3 3PL
0117 966 7311
A long established company that hires heated pools for birth and relaxation. Prices from £45 per week.

NCT - electric breast pump hire
Fiona Hunter: 0117 962 1176 (Westbury-on-Trym)
Haidee Baker: 0117 985 6251 (Knowle)
The NCT in Bristol have 'hospital standard', electric breast pumps for hire. Please call for current charges.

NCT - valley cushion hire
Carol Billinghurst: 0117 973 0813 (Cotham)
The NCT in Bristol have an agent who hires valley cushions for use in the first few weeks after birth. Please call for current charges.

ObTENS
53 Linden Rd, Westbury Park, BS6 7RW
0117 924 1982
ObTENS hire out TENS machines for drug-free pain relief during labour. Hire for a six week period around the baby's due date costs £19.

NAPPY INFORMATION & LAUNDRY SERVICES
After the move away from washable nappies to disposables, the trend is now reversing. Modern washable nappies are different from the old-fashioned Terry towelling ones and there are several different types to choose from.
Nappy Laundry Services deliver re-usable nappies to your home and once a week collect the soiled nappies, which are washed according to NHS guidelines. Users rate their service as excellent and you may be surprised to see how little it costs. Both companies offer a trial of their service.

The Real Nappy Project
0117 930 4355
www.recyclingconsortium.org.uk
Working with parents, health professionals and community projects of all kinds to raise awareness of the cost and environmental savings that parents can make by using the new modern types of washable nappies. The new styles have poppers and Velcro. They wash and dry really easily.

Cloth Bottom Babes
01761 439373
Mon-Sat 9am-5pm
A locally based small business which sells a range of re-usable washable nappies and accessories at affordable prices. They also offer information and practical advice to help you make your choice. Trials are available with the full range hired, delivered and demonstrated. Other nursery products available - slings, carriers, pillows, toiletries.

Dinky Diapers
Unit 2, 13 Wellsway, Keynsham, Bristol, BS31 1HS
0117 986 6167, www.dinkydiapers.co.uk
Nappies are delivered to homes in Bristol and Bath. A special lined bin for storing soiled nappies is provided. Weekly collection and delivery, including nappy rental. Costs £7.45 for all cotton or £8.45 for 'Duo' cotton and disposable option. A 4-week trial with demonstration is £28. Also sells Tushies and Ecover refillable products.

The Nappy Stash
Unit 2C, Olympia House, Beaconsfield Rd, St George, BS5 8ER
0117 941 4839, www.nappystash.co.uk
Nappies are delivered and collected on a weekly basis in Bristol and North Somerset. Deodorised, sealed bin provided. The 'full-time' weekly service costs £7.95, and a month's trial including demonstration is £32. A 'part-time' service costs £2.50 per week plus 17p per nappy. 'Very efficient service.'

NURSERY EQUIPMENT
The independent retailers listed in this section offer a great choice of nursery equipment including prams, car seats and cots. They often stock "more unusual" brands to the high street names and are usually able to order prams etc in specific colours or fabrics. Staff are usually very helpful and have great product knowledge. Also see Department & Larger Stores.

Born
64 Gloucester Rd, Bishopston, BS7 8BH
0117 924 5080, www.borndirect.com
Mon-Sat 9.30am-5.30pm
🔲 🔲

Stockist of the Stokke Children's furniture collection, Tripp Trapp high chair, Sleepi Cot, Sleepy Care changing table and the Xplory pushchair. Also stock slings and backpacks.

Buggies & Bikes
21 Temple Street, Keynsham, BS31 1HF
0117 986 8184
Mon-Sat 9am-5pm
🔲 🔲

Large range of prams, highchairs, cots, car seats and clothing up to 3 years.

E. Harding (Prams & Toys) Ltd
45 East Street, Bedminster, BS3 4HB
0117 966 3584
www.ehardingpramsandtoys.co.uk
Mon-Tue 9am-5.30pm, Wed 9am-4pm, Thu-Sat 9am-5.30pm
🔲 🔲

Large selection of prams, cots, moses baskets, car seats as well as some clothes and toys.

Hurwoods Nursery World
32 Old Market Street, Old Market, BS2 0HB
0117 926 2690
www.hurwoodsnurseryworld.co.uk
Mon-Fri 9.30am-5.30pm, Sat 9am-5.30pm
🅿 ✏ WC 🔲 🔲

Established in 1899, Hurwoods have a huge range of nursery equipment. They stock a large selection of prams, travel systems, three wheelers and buggies, all which are serviced for free within the first twelve months. Good choice of car seats with a 'try before you buy' policy. Nursery furniture, bedding and decor department. "Excellent range with good service from knowledgeable staff". See advertisement.

John Lewis
The Mall, Cribbs Causeway
For hours and facilities see Shopping Centres

Large range of nursery equipment including prams, cots, bedding, car seats, high chairs and nursery furniture. Very helpful staff with good product knowledge. They run Nursery Events and will fit car seats by appointment. Also see Department & Larger Stores.

TinyTots Kids Shop
Abbotswood Shopping Centre, Yate
01454 314 174
Mon-Fri 9am-4pm, Wed 1pm, Sat 9am-12am

This shop stocks a full range of nursery equipment and accessories including buggies, bedding, Grobags and buggy boards. They also stock a wide range of personalised gifts and clothing for the under 8's. "Try them for something different."
Also see Children's Clothing section.

CAR SEATS

Child safety whilst travelling is of the utmost importance and there is a wide variety of car safety seats to suit each stage of your child's growth.
Important points to remember:
- It is the weight of your child, not the age, which is the determining factor for buying the correct stage seat.
- Car seats should not be used after being involved in an accident, therefore, for safety reasons, think twice before purchasing second hand seats.
- Not all seats are suited to all models of car and it is important to check the fit is correct before purchasing an expensive seat.

Recent research by a leading manufacturer of car seats found that many child car seats were fitted incorrectly. Most of the retailers who sell car seats offer a fitting service, usually by appointment. However, for a

completely unbiased opinion, Bristol city council offer a 'try before you buy' scheme.

Bristol City Council
0117 922 4383
www.bristol-city.gov.uk

The road safety education team within Bristol City Council currently operate a 'try before you buy' car seat centre, based at Tollgate Car Park. They hold stock of 40 different models of car seats, which they place in your car to check for fit and safety. The service usually operates on a Wednesday and an appointment is usually required. The team are also willing to visit playgroups etc to do educational safety talks.

EQUIPMENT REPAIR

The companies listed here can repair prams and buggies. For problems with other baby equipment it is probably best to contact your supplier or go direct to the manufacturer. For

the safety of you and your child, car seats should be replaced and not repaired.
For address and opening hours see listings in Nursery Equipment.

Buggies & Bikes
The workshop, which is on the premises, can repair all major makes of prams/buggies and carries many spare parts. If available, buggies can be loaned to you.

E. Harding (Prams & Toys) Ltd
Repairs to all popular makes of prams and buggies. Replacements may be available for loan while you wait, but a deposit is required.

Hurwoods Nursery World
All major makes of prams and buggies can be repaired, mostly on site.

John Lewis
Will arrange for the repair of any pram or buggy bought at John Lewis.

Mothercare World
Eastgate Centre
Most types of prams and buggies can be repaired here. The repair man is in the store on Mon, Wed and Fri. You must book your repair in advance.

NEARLY NEW
Children grow so quickly that most clothes, toys and nursery equipment are outgrown before they are outworn. The shops listed in this section specialise in buying and selling good quality, nearly new children's items. This is an ideal way to recycle, save and generate some cash, whilst clearing some space for the next stage.
Remember to check all second hand goods for safety before you buy.

Car Boot Sales
0117 922 4014, www.bristol-city.gov.uk
Toys and other items can be bought cheaply at car boot sales, which are held across Bristol. Some are held regularly, others on an ad-hoc basis and most are advertised in the local press. Bristol City Council Markets

Department will also be able to advise you of when and where they are held.

NCT Sales
Jane Monaghan: 0117 942 5329
The Bristol branch of the NCT organise nearly new sales on a regular basis. They sell clothes, toys, books, nursery equipment, prams, washable nappies and maternity wear. In Bristol, the seller receives 70% commission on sales, with 30% going to the NCT. Sales are busy and you usually need to go early to get the bargains! Call for details.

As New Toys and Togs
99 High Street, Staple Hill, BS16 5FH
0117 940 1214, www.asnewtoys.co.uk
Mon-Sat 9am-5pm

An Aladdin's Cave stocking second hand toys (disinfected, tested for safety), children's clothes, maternity wear and equipment. Also has new equipment, toys and books. Buys selected items from clients - with 50% commission. 0-11yrs.

Caterpillars
8 Alexandra Rd, Clevedon
01275 876 966
Tue-Sat 10am-4.30pm

High quality second hand nursery equipment, toys & children's clothes. 0-10yrs.

Jack & Jill
192 Wells Road, Totterdown
0117 958 8860
Mon-Fri 9am-5pm, Sat 11am-4pm
$\boxed{P}$

Full range of second hand children's products; Clothing 0-11yrs, nursery equipment, prams, maternity wear, nappies, toys, books. Sellers receive 60% commission on products over £25, and either 40% cash or 50% credit to spend in shop for products under £25.

Punchinello
133 Gloucester Road, Bishopston, BS7 8AX
0117 944 5999
Mon-Sat 9.30am-5.30pm
$\boxed{\varnothing}$ $\boxed{WC}$ $\boxed{\lambda}$

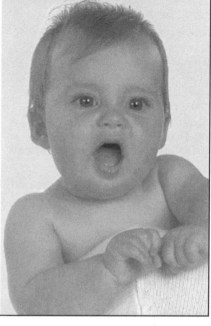
A large second hand shop selling good quality children's clothes, toys and equipment. If you wish to sell items, particularly equipment, it is best to ring to find out if they are in demand. Commission for items £30 and under is 50% and 60% for items over this amount. 0-8yrs.

Roundabout
14 North View, Westbury Park
0117 330 4941
Mon-Sat 9.30am-5pm

A small shop filled with second hand clothing for 0-12yrs, books, toys, nursery equipment and maternity wear. Commission is 50% on all sales. "Good quality second hand shop with friendly, helpful staff - well worth a visit."

Scallywags
121 Bell Hill Rd, St George
0117 947 7447
Mon-Sat 9am-4.30pm, closed Weds.

Sells good quality second-hand clothes for 0-15yrs, toys, books nursery equipment. 50% commission is given back to seller.

Zohara - The Little Used Clothing Company
Niki Williams: 0117 965 1319
Niki works from home selling good quality, pre-loved children's clothes for ages 0-5yrs. All items are £5 or less. She also takes stock to toddler groups / nurseries or to houses on a party plan basis.

BOOKSHOPS

There are some great bookshops in Bristol, all of which offer a good range of books from birth upwards. Many of the stores now offer good teenage ranges. Staff are usually very knowledgeable and helpful, with ordering services offered by the majority.

When the reading bug hits a child it can be costly Remember libraries and second hand books offer a cheaper alternative to keep them going!

Blackwell's
89 Park Street, Clifton, BS1 5PW
0117 927 6602
www.blackwell.co.uk
Mon-Sat 9am-7pm, Tue 9.30am, Sun 11.30am-5.30pm

Full range of books for all ages. Good children's selection, separated into suggested age groups.

Book Cupboard
361-363 Gloucester Road, Horfield, BS7 8TG
0117 942 8878
www.bookcupboard.co.uk
Mon-Sat 9am-5.30pm

A large area dedicated to children's books with an excellent range. There are easily defined sections displaying picture books, first readers and a reference section divided into topics for older readers. There is a separate section for teenage books, and a wide selection of books on parenting issues. Children are welcome to browse. Free 24 hour ordering service. "A book for everyone to be found here."

Borders Books
Clifton Promenade, 48-56 Queens Rd,
Clifton, BS8 1RE
0117 922 6959
Mon-Sat 9am-9pm, Sun 12am-6pm

A huge bookshop catering for all ages and tastes. There is a large, bright children's section with storytime (U8's) at 11am and 3.30pm on Saturdays and 2.30pm on Sundays. There is also a kid's club, contact store for details. This store is also very popular with teenagers as it has a Starbucks Coffee Shop which allows you to browse books while drinking coffee!

Family Books
3 Temple Court, Keynsham, BS31
0117 986 8747
david@familybooks.co.uk
Mon-Sat 9am-5pm

Children's books and Christian titles. Ordering service available.

Durdam Down Bookshop
39 North View, Westbury Park, BS6 7PY
0117 973 1995
Mon-Sat 9am-6pm

For a small bookshop it has a large section of children's books for all ages. Also books on parentnig, health and well-being. 24 hour ordering service.

Stanfords
29 Corn Street, BS1 1HT
0117 929 9966, www.stanfords.co.uk
Mon-Sat 9am-6pm, Tue 9.30am

This is a great shop for young explorers. Stanfords specialise in maps, but also stock a wide range of travel and guide books. There is a small children's section with soft baby globes and puzzles for the younger ones, and children's guide books for the young traveller. Online ordering is available.

The Clifton Bookshop
84 Whiteladies Rd, Clifton, BS8 2QP
0117 983 8989
Mon-Sat 9am-5.30pm

A large selection of children's books along with parenting and health sections. Staff are happy for children to look at the books whilst the adults browse. An ordering service is available. Staff will carry buggies upstairs, or watch them downstairs.

Waterstones
College Green, BS1 5TB
0117 925 0511, www.waterstones.co.uk
Mon-Sat 9am-6pm, Tue 9.30am-6pm, Sun 11am-5pm

The Mall, Cribbs Causeway
0117 950 9813
For hours and facilities see Shopping Centres

The Galleries, Broadmead, BS1 3XF
0117 925 2274
For hours and facilities see Shopping Centres

Full range of books available for children, teenagers and parents. Large children's sections where children are welcome to browse. Ordering service available.

West Country Travelling Books
Mike Wright: 0117 932 4173
www.booktime.co.uk
Run book fares, for nursery and primary age children in schools in the South West, as an aid to fundraising.

Westbury Bookshop
67 Westbury Hill, Westbury on Trym, BS9 3AD
0117 908 0810, www.westburybookshop.co.uk
Mon-Sat 9am-5.30pm, Sat 5pm

Full range of books for children, teenagers and adults. Good children's section with reading area. Children's audio books are stocked and there is an ordering service available.

WH Smith
The Mall, Cribbs Causeway, BS34
0117 950 9525
For hours and facilities see Shopping Centres
&
The Galleries, Broadmead
0117 925 2152
www.whsmith.co.uk
For hours and facilities see Shopping Centres
Range of books to suit all ages. Also stock stationery, CD's and toys. An ordering service is available.

TOYS
Toys can be bought from all sorts of places, from department stores to school fetes. Check that toys are safe for the age of the child you are buying for. Also try nearly new shops, car boot sales or 'Trade It', as many toys, particularly the plastic variety, can be cleaned easily and look brand new.

Bristol Guild of Applied Art Ltd

68-70 Park Street, BS1 5JY
0117 926 5548, www.bristolguild.com
Mon and Sat 9.30am-5.30pm, Tue-Fri 9am-5.30pm

Large store selling a wide variety of gifts and household goods. The toy department sells toys, games and puzzles for all ages. The store is not buggy friendly, as there are lots of stairs, but staff are happy to mind buggies on the ground floor. "Good quality, gifts and toys".

Early Learning Centre

The Galleries, Broadmead, BS1 3XJ
0117 926 8645
For hours and facilities see Shopping Centres

The Mall, Cribbs Causeway, BS34
0117 950 8775, www.elc.co.uk
For hours and facilities see Shopping Centres

A range of traditional and modern toys, with an emphasis on learning through play. The majority of stock is aimed at pre-school children, but some stock is suitable to age 8. Mail order and outdoor equipment is available.

Tuesday Playtime (2+yrs)

10am-11am, The Galleries
10am-11.30am, The Mall

Toys are brought out specifically for children's use - paints, crayons etc.

Formative Fun

58 High St, Staple Hill, BS16 5HN
0117 957 0948, www.formative-fun.com
Mon-Sat 9am-5pm, Wed 4.30pm

Stocks educational toys, games and puzzles supporting the National Curriculum and the Early Learning Goals, for ages 0-14 yrs and those with Special Needs. 10% discount cards for schools, nurseries and playgroups.

Just So Toys

Arch House, Boyces Ave, Clifton, BS8 4AA
0117 974 3600
Mon-Sat 9.30am-5.30pm

A traditional shop selling good quality toys and puppets. Also Tripp Trapp high chairs, soft shoes and blankets. 0-7 yrs. "Helpful staff."

Playfull

Upstairs at Rukantun, 87 Gloucester Rd, BS7 8AS
0117 944 6767
Mon-Tue 12.30pm-5.30pm, Wed-Sat 10am-5.30pm

This shop sells a wide range of natural toys, puzzles, gifts and some craft materials. They have handmade wooden toys suitable from birth, starting at £4.50. There is a small play area for children to test the toys! Mail order is also available. "A friendly place to buy special, handmade gifts". The shop is on the first floor, so pushchair access is difficult, but the staff downstairs will mind buggies.

The Entertainer

The Galleries, Broadmead, BS1
0117 934 9522, www.theentertainer.com
For hours and facilities see Shopping Centres, closed Sundays

Toys for all ages (up to adult!) - 6,000 lines. Also branches in Keynsham, Yate and Midsomer Norton. Mail (01494 737002) or internet ordering available.

Totally Toys

109 Gloucester Rd, Bishopston, BS7 8AT
0117 942 3833
Mon-Sat 9am-5.30pm

Friendly shop stocking major brands of toys including Brio, Lego, Play Mobil, Gault and TP (outdoor equipment). Good range of pocket money toys, party bag items etc. There are play tables available for children to use whilst you browse.

Toys R Us

Centaurus Road, Cribbs Causeway, BS12 5TQ
0117 959 1430
www.babiesrus.co.uk/www.toysrus.co.uk
Mon-Sat 9am-10pm, Sun 11am-5pm

A warehouse type shop with a huge range of indoor and outdoor toys, bikes, computers, nursery equipment, prams and car seats. Mail order and internet shopping available.

OUTSIDE ACTIVITY TOYS

Child's Play Activity Toys
The Close, Inglesbatch, Bath, BA2 9DZ
01225 314123
www.tptoys.co.uk
Opening hours vary, please call for details.

Stocks mainly TP Activity toys - wooden and galvanised metal frames. Also a range of pedal powered go-carts, equipment for table tennis, tennis, indoor play and giant garden games. Will deliver and large orders free. See advertisement below.

Eastermead Activity Toy Centre
Eastermead Farm, Eastermead Lane, Banwell, BS29 6PD
01934 823926
www.eastermead-activity-toys.co.uk
Mon-Sat 10am-5pm, Sun am by arrangement.

Stocks TP galvanised frames. Also has a wide range of wooden toddler toys including garages, castles, farms and dolls houses. Stocks sledges and ride-on tractors. Will deliver locally (free on orders over £100).

SJ Activity Toys
Mapleridge Farm, Mapleridge Lane, Yate, BS37 6PB
01454 294544
www.tptoys.co.uk
Sat open all day, by appointment at any other time
Situated off the B4060 between Wickwar and Chipping Sodbury

A stockist for TP equipment and Super Tramp Trampolines, with a garden display of toys to test. Free local delivery. 'Try before you buy.'

DANCEWEAR

Cavalier Dancewear
45 Deanery Rd, Warmley, BS15 9JB
0117 940 5677
Mon-Fri 10.30-5pm, Closed Wed, Sat 10am-4pm

Good range of clothing and shoes for Ballet, Tap and Jazz. Also stock fancy dress and party wear. Sizes from age 2 upwards.

Dance World
52 Bedminster Parade, Bedminster, BS3 4HS
0117 953 7941, www.danceworld.ltd.uk
Mon-Sat 9am-5.30pm, Thur 7.30pm during term time only.

Extensive range of dancewear and dance shoes for Ballet, Tap and Salsa from aged 3 upwards.

Dancewell
60 Cotham Hill, Bristol, BS6 6JX
0117 973 0120, www.dancewell.com
Mon-Sat 9am-5pm

Supplying Bristols' dancers for 40 years. Dancewear and shoes for all types of dance from aged 2 upwards.

Holbrooks
190 Henleaze Road, Henleaze, BS9 4NE
0117 962 2478
Mon-Sat 9am-5.30pm

Dance shoes available for Ballroom, Latin, Ballet, Tap and Jazz. Access is difficult with double buggies, but staff are very helpful. Adult shoes also available.

Kathy's Dancewear
Alexandra Park, Fishponds, BS16 2BG
0117 965 5660, www.344dance.freeserve.co.uk
Mon-Fri 9am-6pm, Sat 9am-5pm

Good range of Ballet, Tap, Modern & Jazz dance wear, plus shoes & leotards. 2-11+.

ARTS & CRAFT SHOPS

Children's Scrapstore
O Shed, Welshback, Bristol, BS1 4SL
0117 925 2229, www.childrensscrapstore.co.uk
Mon-Wed 1am-5pm, Thu 10am-8pm, Sat 10am-5pm

P WC 人 ♿

Registered charity who recycle safe waste for play purposes. There is a 'members only' warehouse and an art and craft shop, 'Artrageous', which is open to all (members receive 20% discount). Membership is open to any group working in creative play in an educational or therapeutic setting. Items sold include paper, plastic, thread, material, foam etc. Please note: For safety reasons, children under 11 are not allowed into the warehouse.

Craft Works

355-357 Gloucester Rd, Horfield, BS7 8TG
0117 942 1644
Mon-Fri 9am-6pm, Sat 9am-5pm

人 🚻

Everything for the craft lover including kids crafts, fine art, needle craft and creative craft. Daily demonstrations are held providing tips and ideas.

Creativity

7/9 Worrall Rd, Clifton, BS8 2UF
0117 973 1710
Mon-Sat 9am-5.30pm

人 🚻

Everything creative, decorative mirrors, paints, tapestries, beads, glass and silk paints, candle making kits, ribbons and a lot more.

Evangeline's

58-61 St Nicholas Market, Bristol, BS1 1LJ
0117 925 7170, www.evangelines.co.uk
Mon-Sat 9.30am-5pm

WC 人

Small arts and crafts shop stocking most things, glass paints, acetate sheets, beads, embroidery material, origami paper and much more. Postal service available.

Hobbycraft

Centaurus Road, Cribbs Causeway, BS34 5TS
0117 959 7100, www.hobbycraft.co.uk
Mon-Fri 9am-8pm, Sat 9am-6pm, Sun 10am-4pm

P 人 🚻

Superstore packed with craft and art materials for children through to professionals! Regular in-store demonstrations and activities for children.

HOBBY TOYS

Modelmania

13 Clouds Hill Rd, St George, BS5 7LD
0117 955 9819
Tue-Sat 9.30am-6pm

Stock die cast models, scalextric and plastic model kits, also new and second hand model railways, 5+yrs.

Nobby's Hobbies

40 Gloucester Rd, Bishopston, BS7
0117 942 4578
Tue-Sat 9.30am-5pm

P 人 🚻

For all hobby and modelling enthusiasts. Large stacks of balsa wood, building materials, paints, clay, brushes, model kits etc. 8+yrs.

KITE & SKATEBOARD SHOPS

50/50 Skateboard Supplies

16 Park Row, BS1 5LJ
0117 914 7783
Mon-Sat 9am-6pm

人

Skateboard specialists stocking hardware, footwear, clothing, accessories, videos, 4+yrs. Mail order available. 'Skateboarder owned and operated.'

Bristol Kite Store

39A Cotham Hill, Redland, BS6 6JY
0117 974 5010
info@kitestore.co.uk, www.kitestore.co.uk
Mon-Fri 10am-6pm, Sat 9.30am-5.30pm

人 🚻

Wide range of kites and kite surfing equipment, DIY Kites and spare parts. Also frisbees, yo-yos, juggling and circus equipment, books & videos, 3+yrs.

UFO Power Kites

See entry in Shopping Outside Bristol

MUSIC SHOPS

Clevedon Music Shop
19 Alexandra Rd, Clevedon, BS21 7QH
01275 342 090, www.thatmusicshop.com
Mon-Sat 9am-5.30pm
Road is opposite pier, café 'Scarlett's' on corner.

Great selection of instruments and accessories, particularly electric and acoustic guitars. Walls lined with sheet music. Ordering system.

Mickleburgh
1-9 Stokes Croft, Bristol, BS1 3PL
0117 924 1151, www.mickleburgh.co.uk
Mon-Sat 9am-5.30pm

Large selection of new and second hand upright and grand pianos. Also guitars, drums, violins, amplifiers, brass and woodwind instruments. Sheet music and accessories.

Music Room
30 College Green, Bristol, BS1 5TB
0117 929 0390
Mon-Sat 9.30am-5.30pm

A large range of printed sheet music. Also sell basic school recorders, percussion instruments, flutes, saxophones, clarinets and trumpets. There is an instrument hire scheme and mail order.

Saunders Recorders
205 Whiteladies Rd, Bristol, BS8 2XT
0117 973 5149, www.saundrecs.co.uk
Mon-Sat 9.30am-1.15pm & 2.30pm-5.30pm, closed Wed & Sat pm

International supplier of recorders, the walls are stacked - the smallest being a few centimetres, the largest 2 metres! Large range of sheet music for recorders.

SPORTS & OUTDOOR STORES

Gyles Bros Ltd
188 Whiteladies Rd, Clifton, BS8 2XU
0117 973 3143
Mon-Sat 9am-5.30pm

This is a long established family run business (1894), selling quality equipment for most major sports. They offer a racquet restringing service (next day) and an on the spot grip replacement. "Helpful and knowledgeable staff."

Marcruss Stores
177-181 Hotwells Rd, Hotwells, BS8 4RY
0117 929 7427
Mon-Sat 9am-5.30pm
Large range of camping equipment and accessories. Family ski and outdoor wear.

Outdoors
9-10 Transom House, Victoria Street, BS1 6AH
0117 926 4892, www.outdoors.ltd.uk
Mon-Sat 9am-5.30pm

Owned by the Scout Association, Outdoors sells a wide selection of outdoor equipment and clothes as well as Scout uniforms and equipment.

Quip-U for Leisure
60 West St, Old Market, BS2 0BL
0117 955 8054
Tue-Sat 9am-5pm

A mecca for canoe enthusiasts, Quip-U also sells a wide selection of outdoor clothing and equipment related to climbing, caving, walking and mountaineering. Small and friendly, the shop has a little play area for toddlers.

Snow & Rock Superstore
Shield Retail Centre, Filton, BS34 7BQ
0117 914 3000, www.snowandrock.com
Mon-Fri 10am-7pm, Thu 8pm, Sat 9am-6pm
Sun 11am-5pm

Packed full of stylish outdoor clothing for both adults and children, Snow & Rock stocks a huge selection of ski and rock climbing equipment as well as child carriers and rucksacks.

Taunton Leisure
38-42 Bedminster Parade, Bedminster, BS3 4HS
0117 963 7640, www.tauntonleisure.com
Mon-Sat 9am-5.30pm, Thu 9am-7pm

Stocks a broad range of outdoor clothing and camping equipment as well as climbing, cycling and walking gear. It also sells a selection of guidebooks and maps, rucksacks and baby carriers. There is a small play area for the children while you browse.

FANCY DRESS

Dauphine's of Bristol
34 Cloud Hill Rd, St George, BS5 6JF
0117 955 1700
Mon-Sat 9am-5pm

Adult/children's fancy dress hire and retail sales for face painting, hats and wigs. They also run 'make-up' children's birthday parties and teach face painting and theatre makeup.

Starlite Costumes
275-277 Lodge Causeway, Fishponds, BS16 3RA
0117 958 4668, www.starlitecostumes.co.uk
Mon-Sat 9am-5pm, closed Wed

Quality fancy dress hire, theatrical costumes and wigs. Costume sizes from 18 months to adult. Face paints and other novelties.

PET SHOPS

The recommended independent pet shops listed below stock smaller animals such as hamsters, rabbits, guinea pigs, fish and birds. It is not possible in the Bristol area to buy puppies and kittens from pet shops, please contact your local vet or rescue centre.

Mar-Pet
25 Highridge Rd, Bishopsworth, BS13 8HJ
0117 964 3416
Mon-Sat 9am-1pm & 2pm-5.30pm, closed Wed.

Specialises in birds, cold water fish and small animals. Sells cages, hutches, runs, tanks, food and accessories.

Pet & Poultry Stores
5 Worrall Rd, Clifton, BS8 2UF
0117 973 8617
Mon-Sat 9am-5.30pm, Wed 3.30pm

Friendly shop with range of small animals, birds, animal feed and accessories. Also specialises in garden bird food and feeders. Free deliveries.

Roxfords
155 Gloucester Road, Bishopston, BS7 8BA
0117 924 8397
Mon-Fri 8.30am-5.30pm, Sat 8am
P 人 人

Large range of small animals, rodents and fish. Pet toys, leads (can engrave discs), cages, etc Lodges animals for the holidays. Free local deliveries for £10 and over.

MARKETS

Bristol has its fair share of markets where bargains and quality produce can be bought. Crowded markets can make the manoeuvring of buggies and toddlers difficult, but children of any age can enjoy the atmosphere, colours and sounds. Non-regular markets and sales are usually advertised in the local press.

Craft Market
Corn St, BS1 1LJ
Fri 10am-5pm, Sat 10am-4pm
人

Crafts of all kinds including glass, clothing, jewellery etc.

Eastville Market
Eastgate House, Eastgate Shopping Centre, Eastgate Road, BS5 6XY
0117 935 4913/0117 934 9870
Fri and Sun until 2.30pm
P WC 人

Varied range of inexpensive goods, with an emphasis on clothes and fabrics. "Great for fancy dress/costume fabrics."

Quaker's Friars Market
Broad Weir, Broadmead
Thur 10am-4pm

Small market, clothing, fruit, vegetable and home wares.

Southmead Hospital Market
Dorian Road, Southmead, BS10
07050 236 682

Sat 9am-4pm
P WC 人

Good for general bargain hunting. Food, clothing, home wares. Bouncy castle in the summer.

St Nicholas' Market
St Nicholas St/Corn St, BS1 1LJ
0117 922 4017
Mon-Sat 9.30am-5pm

This is both an indoor and outdoor market, situated in the Glass Arcade and the Corn Exchange, selling a wide variety of goods.

The Farmers' Market
Corn St, BS1 1LJ
Wed 9.30am-2.30pm

Local farm produce including dairy, meat, fruit and vegetables along with local wines, preserves, etc.

The Sunday Market
Alberts Crescent, St Philips Marsh
Grenchurch, 01608 652556
Sun 9am-3pm
P WC 人

In the grounds of the Wholesale Fruit and Veg Market. Large market selling almost everything, including some inexpensive clothes for children and adults with some brand names.

Tollgate Big Boot
0117 922 4017
Sun 7am-1pm
P

A large car boot sale held weekly selling both second hand and new items.

ORGANIC & SPECIALIST FOODSTORES

In recent years, the demand for organic food has grown enormously and many parents are very keen to give their children organic food from weaning onwards. The companies listed below offer fantastic organic and specialist food, either from their premises or delivered

207

straight to your door. Nearly all supermarkets sell organic food, with some of them having large fruit and vegetable sections.

Soil Association
Bristol House, 40-56 Victoria Street, Bristol, BS1 6BY
0117 929 0661, www.soilassociation.org
The Soil Association have a wealth of information on organic food and healthy living. They produce a guide and have a website which lists places you can buy organic food.

Earthbound
8 Abbotsford Rd, Cotham, BS6 6HB
0117 904 2260
Mon-Sat 9am-6pm

Friendly store specialising in locally produced organic foods. Sells a wide range of fresh fruit and veg, basic and luxury organic groceries, wholefoods and fair trade products.

Harvests Natural Foods
11 Gloucester Road, Bishopston, BS7 8AA
0117 942 5997
Mon-Sat 9am-6pm

This workers co-operative (est. 30yrs ago) sells a wide range of organic products including bread, fresh fruit and veg, beers and wines (suitable for vegans). Gluten free products, delicatessen and self serve area.

Health Unlimited
248 North St, Bedminster, BS3 1JD
Nr Tobacco Factory
0117 962 0622, www.silver-gecko.com
Mon-Sat 9.30am-5.30pm

Run by nutritional therapist Patrick Graham. A wealth of natural products for all the family. Homoeopathic remedies, nutritional supplements, organic annd natural toiletries, aromatherapy oils, baby care and skincare products, herbal teas and gifts. "Always friendly with helpful informed advice."

Mobile Fishmongers
Roy Barnes: 0117 957 4747
Door to door in most areas, stocking a wide variety of fish and other foods including free

range eggs and locally produced vegetables. "Very friendly and very handy for when you can't get out of the house with a young baby."

Somerset Organics
Gilcombe Farm, Bruton, Somerset
01749 870919, www.somersetorganics.co.uk
Delivery of a wide range of fresh organic meat, cheese, fish, juices, chutneys & butter to your door. Minimum order £40, deliveries cost £7 to any UK address.

Southville Deli
262 North St, Bedminster, BS3 1JA
0117 966 4507, www.southvilledeli.com
Mon-Sat 9am-5.30pm

A good range of organic whole foods, ground coffee, herbal teas, preserves, goat milk, and a range of baby products including Tushies nappies. "A wonderful shop in the heart of South Bristol."

Stone Age Organics
01823 432 488, www.stoneageorganics.co.uk
Boxes of 100% organic vegetables priced from £5-£9. Also sells organic lamb. Delivery is free in Bristol, Clevedon, Weston, Shepton Mallet and Wells. Newsletter once a month with information and recipes.

Stoneground Health Foods
5 The Mall, Clifton Village, BS8 4DP
0117 974 1260
Mon-Fri 9am-5pm, Sat 9am-3pm
Combination of organic, GM free and natural products, 100% vegetarian. Sells fruit, veg, dairy products, dry goods; and sandwiches, home-made soup and jacket potatoes to take-away.

The Bay Tree
176 Henleaze Rd, Henleaze, BS9
0117 962 1115
Mon-Fri 9am-5pm, Sat 9.30am-5pm
A wide variety of natural and organic foods as well as supplements and natural toiletries. Bach Flower and homeopathic remedies, as

well as a wide range of organic, gluten-free and natural foods.

Viva Oliva
30 Oxford St, Totterdown, BS4
07967 202625
Mon-Sat 10am-6pm, Thurs 10am-8pm

Friendly delicatessen stocks a variety of Mediterranean delights including breads, olives, sun dried tomatoes, handmade sauces and pestos, authentic preserves, cheeses and meats. "The stuffed vine leaves are a must!"

SHOPS OUTSIDE BRISTOL

Bath and Weston-Super-Mare are great for a day trip from Bristol, see Out & About in the West Country chapter. Whilst you're visiting, why not check out some of the shops recommended below.

BATH

Bath Model Centre (The Modeller's Den)
2 Lower Borough Walls, Bath, BA1 1QR
01225 460115, www.bathmodelcentre.com
Mon-Fri 9.30am-5.30pm, Sat 9am-5.30pm

This store is crammed from floor to ceiling with all types of models. Ranges include Hornby Trains, Scalextric, die cast cars and pedal cars. Suitable for 4-99yrs. "For model loving kids and dads!"

Blooming Marvellous
5 Saracan Street, Bath, BA1 5BR
01225 442 777
Mon-Sat 9.30am-5.30pm, Sun 10.30am-4.30pm

Mail order maternity & baby wear, nursery equipment & toys. "Good range of maternity wear." See advertisement.

Eric Snooks, The Golden Cot
2 Abbeygate St, Bath, BA1 1NP
01225 463739, www.snooksonline.co.uk

Mon-Sat 9am-5.30pm

Wide range of toys on ground floor, including hobby toys (skateboards etc) for the older child. Upstairs wide range of nursery equipment and clothes (0-7yrs). There is no lift but staff will mind buggies. "A great range of good quality, modern and traditional toys."

one small step one giant leap
5-6 Cheap Street, Bath, BA1 1NE
01225 445345
Mon-Sat 9am-6pm, Sun 11am-5pm

Large shop with a huge range of children's shoes and trainers, from size 0. A large range of Start-Rite shoes in width fittings. Also stock Replay, Diesel, Timberland, Kickers and Birkenstock. More expensive but unusual ranges include Asster, Mod8, Pom D'api and Ricosta. "Shoe-tail therapy at its best!"

Paddington & Friends
1 Abbey St, Bath, BA1 1NN
01225 463598, www.charactergifts.com
Mon-Sat 9am-5.30pm, Sun 11am-5pm

Small store selling a huge range of character gifts. Ranges include Beatrix Potter, The Snowman, Paddington and Wallace & Gromit. Small step up to shop, but staff are helpful. Mail order available.

Roundabout
2-4 Prior Park Road, Bath, BA2 4NG
01225 316696
Mon-Sat 9am-5pm

One mile from city centre. Good quality nearly new and second hand nursery equipment, toys, maternity, adult and children's wear. (Clients given 50% commission after sale.)

Routeone
9 Broad Street, Bath, BA1 5LJ
Tarl, 01225 446710
www.routeone.co.uk
Mon-Sat 9.30am-6pm, Sun 11am-5pm

Skate boards and hardware, roller blades, inline skates, power kiting, frisbees and BMX.

They also have a range of clothing suitable for age 7 upwards.

The Faerie Shop
6 Lower Borough Walls, Bath, BA1 1QR
01225 427 773, www.fairyshop.co.uk
Mon-Sat 9am-5pm

Full of enchanting fairy items - costumes, fairy dolls, sparkly wings, magic dust, etc See website for products. They also host fairy parties, see Activities 0-12 yrs.

Tridias
124 Walcot Street, Bath, BA1 5BG
01225 314 730, www.tridias.co.uk
Mon-Sat 9am-5.30pm

Unusual and exciting selection of ideas for children's birthday presents and parties. They have a range of games, activities and 'made up' party bags suitable for different ages. Please call for a free mail order catalogue.

WESTON-SUPER-MARE

Adams Childrenswear Ltd
Sovereign Centre, High St, Weston-Super-Mare
01934 643 501
Mon-Fri 9am-5.30pm, Sun 11am-4pm

Good selection of reasonably priced clothes for 0-10yrs.

Model Masters
International House, Clifton Rd, Weston-Super-Mare, BS23 1BW
01934 629 717, www.modelmasters.co.uk
Mon-Sat 9am-5pm (Display closed between Christmas and Easter)

This shop sells model trains and railways sourced mainly from Germany, Switzerland and Austria. To the rear of the shop there is a model railway layout, for customers to see the products in operation. Products suitable for 5+yrs, layout suitable for all!

Ottakas
The Sovereign Centre, High Street, Weston-Super-Mare, BS23 1HL
01934 642588, www.ottakas.co.uk
Mon-Sat 9am-5.30pm, Tues 9.30am,
Sun 10.30am-4.30pm

Books to suit all ages. There is a large, bright, children's department stocking a wide range of books, which has a rocking horse for children to ride. Educational and young adult books available.

Peacocks
4-5 Regents St, Weston-Super-Mare, BS23 1SE
01934 632553, www.peacocks.co.uk
Mon-Sat 9am-5.30pm, Sun 12pm-4pm

Large selection of inexpensive baby, children's and teenager's clothing, 0-15yrs.

TJ Hughes
Fairfax House, 17-21 High Street, Weston-s-Mare
01934 414 466
Mon-Sat 9am-5.30pm, Sun 11am-5pm

Discount department store selling brand names at low prices. Children's clothes from birth upwards. Stock changes frequently.

UFO Power Kites
41 Alexandra Parade, (opp. Tesco), Weston-S-Mare,
01934 644 988
Mon-Sat 10am-5.30pm

Extended shop selling kites, kite surfing equipment, spare parts, skate boards, inline skates, frisbees, yo-yos, juggling equipment and clothing, 8+yrs.

Weston Dancewear
32a-34 Orchard St, Weston-Super-Mare, BS23 1RQ
01934 419818, www.westondancewear.co.uk
Mon-Sat 9am-5pm

Enlarged range of dancewear, gym leotards and shoes for ballet, tap, jazz and modern for 2+yrs.

Weston Park Raceway
25 Meadow Street, Weston-Super-Mare, BS23 1QQ
01934 429 812, www.westonparkraceway.co.uk
Mon-Sat 10.30am-7pm, Thu 9pm,
Sun 10.30am-4.30pm

Offers everything for the 'slot car' enthusiast including spares, servicing and repairs. There is a large track available for parties see Activities 0-12 yrs. "Dads will love this."

FACTORY OUTLETS

Factory outlet centres are great because you always feel like you're saving money - even if you're not! The three listed all have a diverse range of shops in their complexes, selling high street and designer labels at a fraction of their original cost. Each offer good facilities for children and can be a fun day out.

Clarks Village

Farm Rd, Street, Somerset, BA16 0BB
01458 840064, www.clarksvillage.co.uk
Apr-Oct: Mon-Sat 9am-6pm, Sun 10am-5pm
Nov-Mar: Mon-Sat 9am-5.30pm, Sun 10am-5pm
Jct 23 M5 or A37, excellent sign posting

P ✏ WC ♿ CP 🚻 ♿ ◪ ▱ 🍴 🎁 ⬚

Extended in 2003, there are now over 80 well known high street stores selling discontinued lines, last season's stock and factory seconds. "A good place to shop for and with children." Street centre also has several discount shoe shops and attractions worth visiting. See Out & About in the West Country chapter.

McArthurGlen Designer Outlet, Bridgend

The Derwen, Bridgend, South Wales, CF32 9SU
01656 665 700, www.mcarthurglen.com
Mon-Fri 10am-8pm, Sat 6pm, Sun 11am-5pm
Jct 36, M4

P ✏ WC ◪ 🚻 CP 🍴 ♿ ◪ 🎁 🍴 ⬚

McArthurGlen offers end of season and excess stock at discounts of up to 50%. There are more than 80 stores at Bridgend, with an on-site cinema. As at Swindon, there is a full programme of events during school holidays.

McArthurGlen Designer Outlet, Great Western

Kemble Drive, Swindon, SN2 2DY
01793 507600, www.mcarthurglen.com
Mon-Fri 10am-6pm, Thu 8pm,
Sat 9am-6pm, Sun 11am-5pm
Jct 16, M4 follow brown signs.

P ✏ WC ♿ 🚻 CP 🍴 ♿ ◪ ▱ 🍴 🎁 ⬚

McArthurGlen offers end of season and excess stock at discounts of up to 50%. It has over 100 shops including fashion, toys, home-wares & sport. They run an events programme, with children's fun workshops in the holidays (call for further details). It is situated in a restored grade II building that once housed the Great Western Railway works and is next door to the Museum of the Great Western Railway. See Out & About in the West Country chapter.

MAIL ORDER

A selection of locally based companies where you can order via the internet or by phoning for a catalogue. For further mail order companies, see Time Out for Adults.

Bishopston Trading Company

193 Gloucester Rd, Bristol, BS7 8BG
0117 924 5598, www.bishopstontrading.co.uk
Workers Co-operative set up to create employment in South Indian village of KV Kuppam. Catalogue includes children's clothing 0-13yrs, range of colours, mainly produced in organic handloom cloth. See Children's Clothes.

Blooming Marvellous

5 Saracen Street, Bath, BA1 5BR
0870 751 8944 (call for catalogue)
www.bloomingmarvellous.co.uk
Maternity & baby wear, nursery equipment & toys.

Coach House

Unit 2, 21 Broadway, Chilton Polden,
Bridgwater, TA7 9DR
08450 616262 (call for catalogue)
www.coach-house.co.uk
A great range of competitively priced, traditional wooden toys and games. "Traditional but trendy."

Ethos Baby Care Ltd

37 Chandos Rd, Redland, BS6 6PQ
0117 907 3320 (call for catalogue)

211

www.ethosbaby.com
Stocks natural products, for baby: 100% natural cotton nappies, organic cotton clothing, sleeping bags, natural baby care products and a range of wooden toys. For Mum: a range of books and maternity pillows.

Party Pieces

Childs Court Farm, Ashhampstead Common, West Berkshire, RG8 8QT
01635 201844, www.partypieces.co.uk
Mon-Fri 8.30am-6pm, Sat 9am-5pm

A mail order company selling a wide range of top quality products for children's parties. A range of themes are in stock, products are competitively priced with a nominal delivery charge.

Tridias (Mail Order)

The Buffer Depot, Badminton Rd, Acton Turville, Gloucs, GL9 1HE
0870 443 1300 (call for catalogue)
www.tridias.co.uk

Unusual and exciting selection of ideas for children's birthday presents and parties. They have a range of games, activities and 'made up' party bags suitable for different ages.

SERVICES

HAIRDRESSERS

The following are salons that offer staff experienced in cutting children's hair, plus they have a few tools for distracting the child whilst they do it. See also Mobile Hairdressers, in Time Out for Adults chapter.

Bonomini

22 Alma Vale Road, Clifton, BS8
0117 923 9169
£10 under 5's, £15 6-9yrs
[↑] [☺] [♀]

Despite being a sophisticated salon, Bonomini welcomes children and the staff are experienced in cutting children's hair. An appointment is not always needed.

Follicles

56 Gloucester Rd, Bishopston
0117 924 9098
Mon-Sat 9am-5pm
Prices vary
[WC] [↑]

Family-friendly salon, experienced at dealing with wriggly children! Books available.

Illusions Hair

22 Gloucester Road, The Promenade, Bishopston, Bristol, BS7 8AE
0117 907 7447
Tue-Fri 9am-5.30pm, Thu/Fri 7pm,
Sat 8.30am-5.30pm
From £7.35 under 4's, £11.55 4-8yrs, £13.65 8-14yrs
[WC] [☺]

Child seats and gowns. From 8yrs hair is washed and cut wet. Appointment usually necessary. Prices given are discretionary.

Pink Hair Designs

282 Gloucester Rd, Horfield
0117 944 4080
Mon & Thu 10am-8pm, Tue 10am-4pm,
Fri 10am-5pm, Sat 7.30am-2.30pm
From £3.50 depending on age
[↑] [↑] [☺]

Newly opened salon in January 2004, these people just love children! A selection of videos and often a treat for good behaviour. (Staff formerly at VK One, Kellaway Ave.)

Pride Hair and Beauty Salon

236 Stapleton Rd, Easton, BS5 0NT
0117 951 9518
Mon Closed, Tue-Wed 9am-5.30pm, Thu 10am-6pm,
Fri 11.30am-8pm, Sat 8.30am-4.30pm
£5.90 infants & boys under 12yrs, £10 girls
[WC] [↑]

Cuts all types of hair but specialises in Afro hair. An appointment is required.

Reflections

Branches: Clifton, Broadmead, Yate, Keynsham, Nailsea, Thornbury, Bedminster, Fishponds, Knowle and Kingswood
From £5 under 6yrs, £12.50 female 6-14yrs, £11.50 male 6-14yrs, trims priced at discretion of management
[WC] [☺] [↑] [↑]

All salons across Bristol welcome children, some with toys and lollipops. See Yellow Pages for details.

Supercuts

In-store at Asda Walmart, Highwood Lane, Cribbs Causeway
Mon-Fri 9am-6pm, Sat 8.30am-4.30pm
£6.95 under 8 yrs, £10.95 over 8's (& all children at weekends).

P ⬚ WC ⬚ CP ⬚ ⬚ ⬚

The Mall, Cribbs Causeway
0117 959 2437
Mon-Fri 10am-9pm, Sat 9am-7pm, Sun 11am-5pm

P ⬚ ⬚ ⬚

All part of a national chain of salons geared to cutting children's hair. You do not need an appointment.

The Business Hair Studio

69 Islington Road, Southville, BS8
0117 966 6618
Mon & Wed 9am-5pm, Tue closed,
Thu & Fri 9am-8pm, Sat 8.30am-4.30pm
£4.50 under 10 yrs

WC ⬚ ⬚

This is a child-friendly salon with toys. An appointment is usually required.

LATE NIGHT PHARMACIES

Pharmacies have a rota for opening outside normal retail hours. Details can be found in the Bristol Evening Post or displayed in your local pharmacy window, or by calling NHS Direct (number below). This section lists some of the pharmacies which are open after 5.30pm and on Sundays.

NHS Direct

NHS Direct will give you details of out of hours pharmacies available in your local area. Please call them on 0845 46 47.

Asda Walmart

Highwood Lane, Cribbs Causeway
0117 979 0426
Mon-Fri 9am-10pm, Sat 8.30am-10pm,
Sun 10am-4pm

Boots The Chemists

19 St Augustines Parade, (near to Hippodrome)

0117 927 6311
Mon-Fri 8am-7pm, Sat 8.30am-5.30pm
&
Upper Mall, Cribbs Causeway
0117 950 9744
For hours and facilities see Shopping Centres
&
59 Broadmead
0117 929 3631
Mon, Wed, Fri 8.45am-5.30pm, Tue 9am-5.30pm,
Thu 8.45am-7pm, Sat 8.45am-6pm, Sun 11am-5pm

Safeway (Fishponds)

688-718 Fishponds Road, Fishponds
0117 965 3014
Mon-Fri 9am-8.30pm, Sat 9am-8pm, Sun 10am-4pm

Sainsbury's

Winterstoke Road, Ashton
0117 953 7273
Mon-Fri 8am-10pm, Sat 7.30am-10pm,
Sun 10am-4pm
&
Fox Den Road, Stoke Gifford, S.Glos.
0117 923 6459
Mon-Sat 8am-8pm, Sun 10am-4pm

P WC ⬚ CP ⬚ ⬚ ⬚

Tesco

Callington Road, Brislington
0117 991 7400
Mon-Sat 8.30am-8pm, Sun 10am-4pm

P ⬚ WC ⬚ ⬚ ⬚

&
Eastgate Centre, Eastville
0117 951 1156
Mon-Sat 8am-9pm, Sun 10am-4pm

PORTRAITURE

Baby and Child Portraiture

32 Belmont Road, St Andrews, BS6 5AS
Phillippa Read: 07971 047509
From £40
Hand drawn portraits of your child. Either as a gift for grandparents or keepsake for you. Commissions also taken for adult and group work. See advertisement.

PHOTOGRAPHERS

The photographers listed here have been recommended for their expertise in children's photography.

James Owens Studios

Charlton Studio, 18 Charlton Road, Keynsham
James Owens: 0117 986 5114
www.jamesowens.co.uk
A 1 hr studio session costs £15, there is no minimum
order and prints start at £25

P WC

A family run photographic studio with 25
years' experience. Examples of previous work
are shown on the website.

Downend Portrait Studio

38 Downend Road, Downend, BS16 5UJ
0117 957 3301, www.downendportraits.com
Tue-Fri 9am-5.30pm

P WC

This studio specialises in portraits of babies
and children. Join the 'Cherubs' scheme for a
fee of £30. Three sittings in your baby's first
year, includes a print from eacth sitting.

James Nicholas Photography

27 Pool Road, Kingswood, Bristol
0117 985 9520
jnichphoto@lineone.net
www.jamesnicholasphotography.co.uk
From £13.50 for 7"x 5" print

P WC

Free studio fee, or £25 for a venue anywhere
in Bristol.

Mark Simmons

The Fire Station, 82-84 York Road, BS3 4AL
Mark Simmons: 0117 914 0999
www.marksimmonsphotography.co.uk
Appointment only
From £7 for a 7"x5" print, studio fee is £80,

P WC

An established Bristol portrait photographer
with a warm, spacious and comfortable
studio. He is friendly, relaxed and favours an
informal style of portraiture.

Michael Rich Studios

3 Prospect Lane, Frampton Cotterell, Bristol,
BS36 2DR
Michael Rich: 01454 778816
www.richphotos.com

P WC

Offers a free 'Little Angels' scheme for babies
up to one year old. Your child will have three
sittings, and a print from each sitting. Family
portraits in colour or back and white, for a

**Baby and Child
Portraiture**

07971 047 509 or
readphilippa@hotmail.com

Commissions also taken for
adult and group work

studio sitting fee from £25. An 8"x 6" print
costs £20.

Olan Mills Portrait Studio

393 Gloucester Rd, Horfield, BS7
0117 924 9611
Tue-Thu 11am-8pm, Fri 10am-5pm, Sat 9am-6pm

WC

This studio has a 'Watch Me Grow' scheme.
For £24.99 you get four family or individual
sittings over the year, with a free 10" x 8"
print from each. Additional photographs start
at £30 for a 7" x 5" print.

Phil McCheyne Photographers

5 St. Austell Close, Nailsea, Bristol, BS48 2US
Phil McCheyne: 01275 858 545
Flexible opening times

P WC

Friendly photographer specialising in school,
nursery and playgroup photography along
with portraits and passport photos (especially
for babies and children).

Portrait Place

Debenhams, 1-5 St James Barton, Broadmead
0117 922 5960
Opening hours same as Debenhams (see
Department Stores)

WC

Vouchers for free baby photo sessions are
found inside Bounty Packs. Otherwise a photo
session costs £10, which includes a 12" x 10"
portrait. Additional prints start at £20.

TIME OUT FOR ADULTS

Paula Brown

CHAPTER 11

INTRODUCTION

Finding time for yourself when you have a family is no mean feat. In this chapter we list hobbies, sports, relaxation facilities, new skills and retraining that you can undertake while your children are cared for (and a couple where they're not but are worth mentioning). We've also tried to include listings of things you can do from home. We hope they will give you some ideas of things you can do with limited time, money and often energy! If you think of more, let us know.

Crèche Information is given in several sections within this chapter. They are intended as temporary care and you are generally required to stay on the premises. Most crèches need to be booked in advance, some with long waiting lists.

BEFORE YOU START

There are other other chapters well worth looking at:

Family Holidays & Weekends Away

When many of us need time out most is on holiday but children can often be at their most demanding away from home. Loads of tips and ideas for family breaks.

Teen Guide

If having time out involves an unusual sport you will find it here, climbing, canoeing, scuba diving to name but a few.

Advice & Support

There are many support groups giving support, advice and respite care. Some offering crèche facilities whilst you learn a skill, see subchapter, Families & Individuals.

HOBBIES & DEVELOPING SKILLS

It can be very liberating to gain a new qualification, retrain or take up a new hobby. Many colleges have crèche facilities or courses that can be taken in the evenings. There are also numerous correspondence courses. Please note that 'Essential Skills' are literacy, numeracy, IT and English as a foreign language (where applicable).

Information on courses is split into three sections:
Adult Education
Community Education
Distance Learning

ADULT EDUCATION

City of Bristol College

College Green Centre, St Georges Road, BS1 5UA
0117 904 5000, www.cityofbristol.ac.uk

A large range of courses covering many topics with varying levels of accreditation. It is one of the UK's largest colleges, spread over 9 sites in Bedminster, Ashley Down, Hartcliffe,

Lawrence Weston, Soundwell, St Phillips, Downend, Parkway and College Green. The first five have day care nurseries and crèche facilities.

Filton College

Filton Avenue, Filton, BS34 7AT
0117 931 2121, www.filton-college.ac.uk

Comprehensive range of courses, see prospectus.

Filton College Nursery

0117 931 5072
Mon-Fri 8am-6pm, 0-5yrs

After school/playscheme during main holidays 0-8yrs. Usually a 2 month waiting list for babies.

Folk House Adult Education Centre

40A Park Street, Bristol, BS1 5JG
0117 926 2987, www.beehive.thisisbristol.co.uk

Languages, dance, music & fitness. Crèche not available though many of the courses are in the evening or at weekends.

Hartcliffe Health & Environmental Action Group Ltd

The Gate House Centre, Hareclive Road, BS13 0EE
0117 946 5285

Cooking and nutrition projects for families with children under 5yrs from the BS13 area, supported by a free crèche. Contact your health visitor for a referral.

Knowle West Health Association

Filwood Community Centre, Barnstaple Rd, BS4 1JP
0117 963 9569

Classes cover health, cooking and childcare.

Crèche

0117 963 6475
0-8yrs, 50p per session

Run to coincide with classes, times vary according to which projects are running.

Sikh Resource Centre

114 St Marks Road, Easton, Bristol BS5 6JD
0117 952 5023

Classes cover IT, sewing, English as a second language, first aid and design. Crèche organised on demand.

Silai For Skills
176-178 Easton Rd, Easton, Bristol BS5 0ES
www.silai.org.uk
0117 941 5180
Mon-Fri 10am-3pm (term-time only)
Provide courses in creative textiles, for women. Crèche available.

Southmead Development Trust
Greenway Centre, Doncaster Road, BS10 5PY
0117 950 3335, www.southmead.org
IT, karate training, trampolining and a Learndirect centre.

Crèche
9am-1pm, 3mth-5yrs, £2/hr

University of Bristol
34 St Michael's Park, Kingsdown, BS2 8BW
0117 928 9000, www.bris.ac.uk
Range of under/postgraduate courses and evening classes open to the public.

Nursery
0117 927 6077
8.30am-5.30pm, 3mth-5yrs
A long waiting list, giving priority to students and staff.

Workers Educational Association
7 York Court, Wilder Street, BS2 8QH
0117 916 6500, www.wea.org.uk
Basic skills, teaching qualifications, history, literature, creative writing. Limited childcare facilities but can arrange crèches for courses run for women's or community groups.

University of the West of England
Coldharbour Lane, Frenchay, BS16 1QY
0117 965 6261
www.uwe.ac.uk
Range of under/postgraduate courses and courses open to the public.

The Nursery at Coldharbour Lane
Coldharbour Lane, Frenchay, BS16 1QY
0117 344 2434
9am-5pm term time, 2-5yrs
£22 per day, ½ days available
A long waiting list, check for cancellations.

Halley Nursery at St Matthias Campus
St Matthias Campus, College Road, Fishponds, BS16
0117 344 4452
Mon-Fri 8.30am-5.30pm term time only, 6mths-5yrs

£12-14 ½ day
Availability varies, book prior to course, priority to students.

COMMUNITY EDUCATION

Bristol City Council, Community Education programme
0117 903 8844
www.bristol-lea.org.uk/lifelong/commed
Provides over 1000 vocational and leisure courses at a number of centres across Bristol. Prospectuses are available in supermarkets, libraries, job centres and community centres.

The Adult Learners' Framework
0800 923 0323
Enables you to accrue credits and certificates for courses taken across a range of education providers.

Barton Hill Workshop
43 Ducie Road, Barton Hill, BS5 0AX
0117 955 6971, www.bartonhillsettlement.org.uk
English, maths, computing, teaching, counselling, hobbies and healthy living.

Crèche
9.30am-11.45am, 12.30-3.30pm, 8wks-5yrs
Call for costs

East Bristol Adult Education Centre
Alexandra Park, Fishponds, BS16 2BG
0117 903 8822
GCSE's, A Levels, health & fitness and IT.

Nursery
0117 965 1116
9.00am-3.45pm, 2-5yrs, £12 ½ day

Fonthill Centre
Stanton Road, Southmead, BS10 5SJ
0117 903 0059
Crèche working, crafts, IT, essential skills and teaching.

Crèche
Runs informally, ask about availability when you book a course.

St Paul's Learning and Family Centre
94 Grosvenor Road, St Paul's, BS2 8XJ
0117 377 3405
IT, basic skills, English as a second language, crafts, languages, healthy living.

Crèche
Mon-Wed 10am-11am, 8wks-4yrs, £1.30 per child

The Gatehouse Centre
Hareclive Road, Hartcliffe, BS13 9JN
0117 903 8833
Counselling, sign language, English and Maths

Nursery
0117 978 1708
0-5yrs, £2.75/2hrs
Operates as a day nursery but there are a few crèche places.

The Old Co-op
38-42 Chelsea Road, Easton, BS5 6AS
0117 903 9893
English language, essential skills, Punjabi and crèche work.

Crèche
6mths-5yrs, free
Runs alongside classes, book when signing up for class.

The Park Centre
Daventry Road, Knowle, BS4 1QD
0117 903 9770
Basic skills, languages, childcare and crafts.

Crèche
0117 377 2664
Tues-Fri 10am-12pm, 1pm-3pm (subject to funding), 0-5yrs, free

DISTANCE LEARNING
Distance learning can combine well with family life. The following are two distance learning institutions which offer a variety of courses.

Learn Direct
0800 101901
www.learndirect.co.uk
An online learning network offering over 650 courses in self development, computer & office skills, many of which are free or subsidised, paced to suits. Courses available online and through Alexandra Park and Greenway Centre (see above).

Learn Direct Helpline
0800 100 900
Impartial advice to help you choose from over a million courses (many online) including Learn Direct courses as well as many others. Covers the whole of the UK.

Open University
0870 900 0310
www.open.ac.uk
Well-respected undergraduate and postgraduate courses including courses on Childhood and Youth Studies.

SPORTS CENTRES & SWIMMING POOLS
When you are physically exhausted from childcare the thought of exercise may be the furthest thing from your mind. Exercise can increase your stamina and Bristol City Sports has launched their Year of Sport 2004 to help us discover this! There is a huge amount on offer at your local leisure centre, many providing crèche facilities. Lookout for those swimming pools offering free swims in pregnancy.

View the Leisure Centre tables to see what is on offer and where there are crèche facilities. Some classes allow babies in their car seats/prams. Alternatively if you have childcare arrangements in the evening, there is often a good choice of classes at this time. Failing all this – there are always exercise and relaxation videos but they often require more motivation!

PRIVATE HEALTH & FITNESS CLUBS
Joining fees and monthly membership (often with minimum terms) can be very motivating! Those listed here have a variety of facilities.

Most have gym and spas, some have pools. A few are open to non-members off peak, unless stated otherwise, assume the clubs are members only. Those listed below provide crèches, most require pre-booking.

En Forma Health Club
Bath Hill, Keynsham, BS31 1EB
0117 987 3262
www.enforma.co.uk
Crèche: Mon-Fri 10am-12noon, from 6 wks
£3/hr non-members, free to members

Fitness classes, sauna and crèche are open to **non-members** during crèche hours. Crèche runs on a first-come basis.

David Lloyd Club
Ashton Road, Ashton
BS3 2HB
0117 953 1010
www.davidlloydleisure.co.uk
Crèche: Mon-Fri 9am-5pm (closed 12.30pm-1.30pm) Sat 9.30am-3.30pm, Sun 10am-2pm, 3mths-6yrs, £3/hr

You may need to book up to 8 days in advance. Babies can be left by the pool in car seats.

Esporta Health and Fitness Club
Hunts Ground Road, Stoke Gifford
BS34 8HN
0117 974 9740
www.esporta.com
Crèche: Mon-Fri 9am-3pm, exc Weds 9am-12.30pm & Fri 5pm-7pm, Sat-Sun 9.30am-12.30pm, 6wks-5yrs, £1.50/hr, 2 hrs max

Holiday activities and sports available for children aged 5-11yrs.

Redwood Lodge
Beggar Bush Lane, Failand, BS8 3TG
01275 395888
Crèche: Mon-Wed 9.15am-5pm, Thu/Fri 9.30am-2pm, Sat 9.45am-1pm, Sun 9.45am-12.45pm
5mths-5yrs, £3.50/hr

Holiday activities and sports available for children aged 5-11yrs.

Livingwell Health & Leisure Club
Cotham Gardens, 80 Redland Road, Redland
BS6 6AG
0117 942 5805, www.livingwell.co.uk
Crèche: Mon-Fri 9am-5pm,
0-5yrs, £6.50 per mth, plus £2/hr

Better Bodies
59 High St, Portishead, BS20 6AG
01275 845353
Crèche: Mon-Fri 9am-11am
0-5yrs, £1/hr, pre-booking required
Gym facilities only, **non-members** can use gym and crèche.

Fitness Factory
17 Broad Road, Kingswood, BS15 1HZ
0117 935 2060, www.fitnessfactoryltd.co.uk
Crèche: 0117 949 7748
Mon-Fri 9am-11am
6wks-4yrs, £1.50/hr members, £2/hr non-members
Non-members may use spa facilities and crèche.

Ambassadors Health and Fitness
Backwell Hill House, Backwell Hill, Chelvey Batch, Backwell, BS48 3DA
01275 464462
Crèche: Mon/Weds/Fri 10am-12pm, Tues/Thurs 9.30am-11.30pm
6wks-5yrs, £2.50/hr
Non-members can use beauty salon, spa and crèche.

Riverside Leisure Club (formerly Spring Health)
Station Road, Little Stoke, BS34 6HW
01454 888666
Crèche: Mon-Fri 9.30am-11.25am
3mths-8yrs, £1.15/hr, pre-booking required

Next Generation
Greystoke Avenue, Westbury-on-Trym, BS10 6AZ
0117 959 7140, www.ngclubs.co.uk
Crèche: 0117 950 2550
Daily 8am-6pm
3mths-5yrs, £3/hr, pre-booking required
Non members can use the privately run crèche but not facilities.

PERSONAL TRAINERS

Karen Hutchinson
07960 950858, £25/hr pp
Personal training, fitness plans, slimming, sports injuries, postnatal issues, working with groups or individuals in their homes. Flexible hours in west Bristol area.

Alison Merry
07973 565779, £30/hr
Fitness, lifestyle & nutrition support, particularly postnatal, working in school hours and covering the west Bristol area out to Nailsea.

Lucy Livingstone
0117 924 9455
Non-stylised dance and movement sessions, non-mobile babies welcomed (in your arms or pram/car seat).

RELAXATION

If going back to college or treadmills aren't your idea of relaxing, you might want to try a massage in the comfort of your own home or a sauna while the children are cared for in a crèche.

Some of the private gyms listed above offer spa, relaxation facilities and crèche to non-members (see individual listings). Some may offer one-off day rates. Alternatively student practitioners often offer free treatments. Contact: Filton College Health & Beauty department on 0117 909 2319.

The Massage Centre at Kingsdown Sports Centre
Portland Street, Kingsdown, BS2 8HL
0117 942 6582, www.bcsport.co.uk
A variety of treatments and spa.

Crèche: Mon/Fri 10.30am-11.30am, Tue/Thu 10am-11am
8wks-4yrs, £1.30 per child, 85p for extra child

Relaxation Centre
9 All Saints Road, Clifton BS8 2JG
0117 970 6616, www.relaxationcentre.co.uk
Mon-Thu 11am-10pm, Fri-Sun 9am-10pm
Offers a range of holistic treatments, spa facilities and gift vouchers; no membership required. Various sessions including women and men only. No crèche.

MOBILE THERAPY

Ashram 4 Body Harmony
07740 245890
Bharti will do various massage techniques, reflexology and beauty treatments, flexible with location and times.

Essential Health
0117 330 6443, www.sojam.com/essential
£18-30
Jo does reflexology, aromatherapy and Indian head massage and will travel within the north Bristol area, working evenings and weekends.

Helen Dix
0117 935 2564
£20-30
Practices shiatsu and will travel across the Bristol area.

Sole Relief
01454 615315 or 0781 479 2530
Rebecca practices reflexology or Indian head massage in the north Bristol area.

Stan Patrzalek
0117 952 2071
From £30
Thai yoga massage, Stan covers the wider Bristol area with flexible working hours.

MOBILE HAIRDRESSERS

All cover the Bristol area

Hair at Home
07899 921693
Thu & Fri & some eves
From £14
Kelly will colour, cut and perm hair.

Heidi Mobile Hairdresser
07770 234804 or 0117 961 5925
From £15
Mon-Fri, Wed & Thu eve, Sat am
Will colour, perm and cut adults and children's hair. Covers greater Bristol area.

Kreative Cuts
07762 014770 or 0117 983 8657
Mon-Fri, day & eve
From £15
Jane will do a variety of hair treatments and cuts using modern styling.

Tina Lombardi
0117 940 1294 or 07979 046001

Mon-Fri 8.30am-2.30pm, term time
From £10 adult, £5 child
Tina also works some Saturdays for bridal hair.

MOBILE NAIL TREATMENTS

Mobile Nail Technician
07779 877024 or 0117 377 8317
From £30
Ann does nail extensions, flexible working hours.

New Nails
07811 561476 or 0117 908 7086
Mahdi's work covers a range of nail treatments, working at evenings and weekends.

ALLOTMENTS
You may smile, many readers recommend having an allotment as a good way to relax, get fit and can keep the kids entertained.

Bristol City Council Allotments Dept
0117 922 3737

Windmill Hill City Farm
Philip Street, Bedminster, BS3 4EA
0117 963 3299
www.windmillcityfarm.org.uk

Crèche
Tue/Thu 12.45pm-2.45pm
1-5yrs, £2.50 members, £3 non-members
Allotments available and crèche if you'd rather not have your children dissecting worms while you dig! (Long waiting list.)

SHOPPING
Shopping can be relaxing but with small children in tow it is not always straightforward or enjoyable. For those of you who prefer to window shop from catalogues and web sites when you have 'quiet time' see Shopping & Services which covers supermarket online shopping, organic food boxes delivered to your door and West Country based mail order

companies. If you want more ideas from further afield, see below:

Next
0845 600 7000
www.next.co.uk
Classic designs for the whole family.

La Redoute
0500 777777
www.redoute.co.uk
French designs at reasonable prices.

Boden
0845 677 5000
www.boden.co.uk
Bright upmarket women's and children's clothes.

People Tree
020 7739 0660
www.peopletree.co.uk
Fair-trade clothes made in developing countries.

Freemans
0800 900 2000
www.freemans.com
Good value basics for the family including well-known brands.

Evans
0870 606 9666
www.evans.ltd.uk
Women's fashion sizes 14-30.

www.ebay.co.uk
Discover nearly new or second-hand items, from furniture to software.

www.amazon.co.uk
Click on Marketplace. Inexpensive second-hand books through to new electric toothbrushes!

ENTERTAINMENT
20th Century Flicks in Clifton
0117 974 2570
www.20thcenturyflicks.co.uk
Video hire for artier films

Also see Alternative Sources of Information

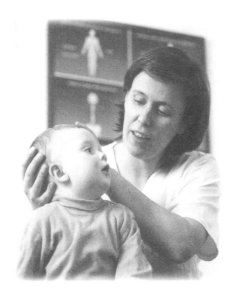

HEALTHCARE

Elspeth Pontin

GENERAL HEALTHCARE

We have taken recommendations and advice from parents in the Bristol area in order to compile our own specific healthcare directory. The directory covers general healthcare services with an emphasis on pregnancy and child health. It aims to cover all NHS services and organisations in addition to recommended complementary clinics and practitioners. For more detailed listings on medical conditions and special needs see Advice & Support chapter.

HEALTHCARE SERVICES

Avonweb
www.avon.nhs.uk

Contact and online site providing information about local NHS services such as GP's, dentists, hospitals, opticians, as well as NHS organisations.

Maternity and Health Links
Charlotte Keel Health Centre, Seymour Road, Easton
0117 951 2244
Information videos and bilingual scripts in many languages. Also interpreting and advocacy services available.

PRIMARY CARE TRUSTS (PCTS)
Provide information on healthcare services in your area.

North Somerset PCT
Waverley House, Old Church Road, Clevedon BS21 6NN
01275 546770, www.northsomerset.nhs.uk

Bristol North PCT
King Square House, King Square, Bristol, BS2 8EE
0117 976 6600, www.bristolnorthpct.nhs.uk

Bristol South and West PCT
King Square House, King Square, Bristol, BS2 8EE
0117 976 6600, www.bristolswpct.nhs.uk

Bath and North East Somerset PCT
St Martin's Hospital, Midford Road, Bath, BA2 5RP
01225 831800, www.banes-pct.nhs.uk

South Gloucestershire PCT
1 Monarch Court, Emerald Park, Emerson's Green, BS16 7FH
0117 330 2443, www.sglos-pct.nhs.uk

GP'S & NURSES

Family Doctor (GP)
If you or a member of your family are ill or have any health concerns, your first point of contact will probably be your family doctor (GP). If your problem occurs out of surgery hours, you can contact NHS Direct (see below). If you are not registered with a GP, you can find the telephone number of the nearest surgery in the Yellow Pages under

'Doctors', from NHS Direct, Avonweb or your local Primary Care Trust, see above.

Practice Nurses
Registered nurses, usually based in health centres or surgeries, they work closely with GP's and often run clinics in specialised areas (such as family planning, diabetes and asthma care).

NHS Direct
0845 46 47
www.nhsdirect.nhs.uk
A confidential advice line, staffed by nurses, offering healthcare advice 24 hours a day. After asking a series of questions they will assess your needs either giving over the phone advice or referring you to your out of hours GP service or hospital. NHS Direct can also give information about local NHS services, such as GPs and dentists.

HOSPITALS
The following hospitals all have accident and emergency departments.

Frenchay Hospital
Frenchay Park Road
0117 970 1212 (ext 3887)

Southmead Hospital
Monks Park Avenue Entrance
0117 950 5050

The Bristol Royal Hospital for Children
Upper Maudlin Street
0117 927 6998

The Bristol Royal Infirmary
Marlborough Street
0117 923 0000

LATE NIGHT PHARMACIES
In all chemist shops (or pharmacies) there is a pharmacist on duty who is able to give advice on the treatment of many health problems. There will always be a pharmacy in your area open outside normal shop hours. A list of these is published daily in the Bristol Evening Post or can be obtained by telephoning NHS Direct. For more details see SHOPPING & SERVICES.

WALK-IN CENTRES

NHS walk-in centres provide treatment for minor injuries and illnesses seven days a week. You don't need an appointment and will be seen by an experienced NHS nurse.

Bristol (City Gate) NHS Walk-in Centre
33 Broad Street, BS1 2EZ
0117 906 9600
www.nhs.uk
Daily 8am-8pm

South Bristol NHS Walk-in Centre
5 Knowle West Health Park, Downton Road, Knowle West, BS4 1WH
0117 903 0000
www.nhs.uk
Daily 9am-9pm

COMPLAINTS

If you are not happy with the care that you have received from any aspect of the NHS, you have every right to complain. For information about how to make a complaint, see www.nhs.uk/patientsvoice or contact your local PCT, see above.

COMPLEMENTARY MEDICINE

This section puts several branches of western medicine under the same umbrella as those medicines which are traditionally thought of as complementary. Some of these services can be received within the NHS but many are private; some offer reduced rates.

The clinics, practitioners, and complementary therapy governing associations listed below all offer their services to non-specific age groups or clients. If your needs are more specific, see the relevant subchapters below.

Institute of Complementary Medicine

PO Box 194, London, SE16 7QZ
0207 237 5165
www.icmedicine.co.uk
The Institute is a charity providing information on all complementary medicines.

The Chandos Clinic

21 Chandos Rd, Redland, BS6 6PG
0117 974 5084
Practitioners offering osteopathy, cranial osteopathy, homeopathy, Alexander technique, reflexology, massage and aromatherapy.

The Clifton Practice

8-10 Whiteladies Rd, Clifton, BS8 1PD
0117 946 6070
www.thecliftonpractice.co.uk
Offers all the main complementary and alternative therapies.

The Key Centre for Complementary Therapies

2 North Parade Passage, Bath, BA1 1NX
01225 420953
Wide range of therapies offered.

ACUPUNCTURE

Used in traditional Chinese medicine for around 4,000 years. It involves the painless insertion of fine needles into specific points on the body. Treatment is sometimes available on the NHS.

British Acupuncture Council

63 Jeddo Road, London, W12 9HQ
020 8735 0400
www.acupuncture.co.uk
Free information and lists of local practitioners. Look for letters such as Lic Ac, Dip Ac, M Ac, after a practitioner's name.

AROMATHERAPY

Aromatherapy is the holistic application of essential oils, often involving massage. Aromatherapy can be used on small children and can be beneficial during pregnancy, labour and postnatally.

The International Federation of Aromatherapists

182 Chiswick High Rd, London, W4 1PP
020 8742 2605
www.ifaroma.org

Lists of local practitioners (for a small fee). Look out for MIFA after a practitioner's name.

The Register of Qualified Aromatherapists

PO Box 3431, Danbury, Chelmsford, Essex
01245 227957
Look out for MRQA after the practitioner's name.

CHINESE MEDICINE

See Acupuncture and Chinese Medicine in Postnatal Healthcare and Child Health below.

CHIROPRACTORS

Chiropractors diagnose and treat conditions rising from the mechanical dysfunction of the joints and their effects on the nervous system. Chiropractors use their hands to adjust the joints of your spine and extremities where signs of restriction in movement are found.

The British Chiropractic Association

Blagrave House, 17 Blagrave Street,
Reading, RG1 1QB
0118 950 5950
enquiries@chiropractic-uk.co.uk, www.chiropractic-uk.co.uk
For information and lists of practitioners. Fully qualified practitioners carry the letters DC.

Vital Health Clinic

8 North View, Westbury Park, BS6 7QB
0117 973 0878
Nina Hollingsworth (chiropractor), Louise Bashall (chiropractor) and Christine Andrew (osteopath and chiropractor) have a particular interest in treating women pre-conceptually and throughout pregnancy, as well as treating babies and children for infantile colic, growing pains, headaches etc.

COUNSELLING

Counselling is sometimes available on the NHS; the BACP list indicates which counsellors work within the NHS.

The British Association of Counselling and Psychotherapy (BACP)

BACP House, 35-37 Albert St, Rugby, CV21 2SG
0870 4435252
bacp@bacp.co.uk, www.bacp.co.uk
Lists of therapists local to your area are available online or by sending an SAE. Look for BACP, UKCP, UKRC, BCP, or BPS after a counsellor's name.

CRANIAL OSTEOPATHS

Cranial osteopathy is a delicate form of manipulation to the skull and facial bones. Treatment can be helpful in pregnancy and for babies and young children with feeding difficulties, colic, sleep disturbances, behavioural problems, learning difficulties, asthma and ear infections. It is sometimes available on the NHS.

International Cranial Association

478 Baker St, Enfield, Middlesex, EN1 3QS
020 8367 5561
kbs07@dial.pipex.com
Publishes a directory of practitioners.

The Craniosacral Therapy Association of the UK

Monomark House, 27 Old Gloucester Street, London, WC1N 3XX
07000 784735
info@craniosacral.co.uk
Practitioner listing and information on craniosacral therapy.

The Centre for Whole Health

12 Victoria Place, Bedminster, BS3 3BP
Claire Howard, 0117 923 1138
Aims to make complementary therapies available to those on a limited income. Claire Howard and Jeni Briggs offer free initial consultation/treatment for babies up to 4 weeks. Toy box available.

DIETICIAN

Catherine Turner BSc MSc SRD

Clare Collins and Associates, 16B Chandos Road,
Redland, BS6 6PE
Catherine Turner, 0117 330 8672
ceturner@blueyonder.co.uk
Catherine is a state registered dietitian for
children and adults. Advice given on allergies,
food refusal, weight problems, fussy eating
etc.

HOMEOPATHY

Homeopathic medicines are derived from
a variety of plants, animal materials and
minerals.

The British Homeopathic Association

Hahnemann House, 29 Park Street West,
Luton, LU1 3BE
0870 444 3950
www.trusthomeopathy.org
Details of medically qualified homeopaths
available. Look for the letters MF Hom; FF
Hom.

The Society of Homeopaths

4a Artizan Road, Northampton, NN1 4HU
01604 621400
www.homeopathy-soh.org
Information about homeopathy, and register
of qualified homeopaths in your area.

Gordon Adam, DSH RSHom

0117 942 6810

Maddhu Anhes, DSH PCH RSHom

0117 977 8737
St Andrews and Totterdown.

Lesley Harris, DSH RSHom

30 Thingwall Park, Fishponds, BS16 2AE
Lesley Harris, 0117 902 8484

Claire Long

82 Richmond Road, Montpelier, BS6 5EW
Claire Long, 0117 942 9744

Works with babies, children and pregnant
women. Toy box available.

Diane Murray, RSHom

Neals Yard Remedies, 121 Whiteladies Road,
BS8 2RP
0117 946 6035 (Clinic of Natural Medicine)

Penny Stirling, DSH RSHom

7 York Gardens, Clifton, BS8 4LL
0117 973 0459

Jane Whitehead, DSH RSHom

56 Dunkerry Road, Windmill Hill, BS3 4LA
Jane Whitehead: 0117 963 6267/946 6035

Chris Wilkinson DSH RSHom

24 Dunkerry Rd, Windmill Hill, Bristol
0117 963 2306

Health and Healing

355-359 Two Mile Hill Road, Kingswood, BS15 1AF
0117 914 5590
Tue 12pm–4pm
Homeopathic sleep clinic and treatments
available for all conditions and ages. Toy box.

Bristol Natural Health Service

407 Gloucester Rd, Horfield, BS7 8TJ
0117 944 4448
Wide range of therapies and a special
children's clinic with reduced rates. Access via
wide steps. Toy box.

Montpelier Natural Health Clinic

26 Picton St, Montpelier, BS6 5QA
0117 924 9353
Offers a range of therapies including acupuncture, aromatherapy, massage, homeopathy
and cranial osteopathy for infants. Babies
under 6 weeks get a free initial session. Toy
box and concessions available.

Natural Health Clinic

39 Cotham Hill, Cotham, BS6 6JY
0117 974 1199
www.thenaturalhealthclinic.com
Wide selection of practitioners including
homeopathy and cranial osteopathy.
Concessions offered. Toy box available. Access
by steps but staff will help.

Clinic of Natural Medicine
126 Whiteladies Road (above Neal's Yard Remedies), Clifton, BS8 2RP
0117 946 6035
Offers a wide range of therapies and a free initial 15 minute consultation to select a suitable treatment. Reduced rates for children.

MASSAGE

The Massage Therapy Institute of Great Britain
PO Box 2726, London, NW2 3NR
www.cmhmassage.co.uk
An educational and professional organisation for massage therapists and others interested in the health sciences. Lists registered therapists in your area.

OSTEOPATHY
Osteopathy treats faults which occur in the musculo-skeletal system of the body due to stress, injury and sometimes disease. It can be beneficial during pregnancy and on small children. Osteopathy is sometimes available on the NHS.

General Osteopathic Council
Osteopathy House, 176 Tower Bridge Road, London, SE1 3LU
020 7357 6655
www.osteopathy.org.uk
List of registered osteopaths. Qualified Osteopaths will either have DO, BSc(Ost), MSc(Ost) or MLCOM (if they are also medically qualified) after their name. Under the Osteopaths Act 1993, all qualified Osteopaths have to be listed with the General Osteopathic Council.

REFLEXOLOGY
Reflexologists work on specific "reflex points" on the feet to treat imbalances in the whole body. It is drug free and can be used to treat many acute and chronic conditions. It can be beneficial during pregnancy.

British Reflexology Association
Monks Orchard, Whitbourne, Worcester, WR6 5RB
01886 821207
www.britreflex.co.uk
Lists registered reflexologists.

Henrietta Gibbs Dip BSR MIFR Reflexologist
0117 942 2769 mob. 07812 187730
henriettagibbs@onetel.net.uk
Tue-Thu 9am-3pm
Runs clinics in Redland and Westbury Park. Treats adults and children with various conditions, many hormonal. Works to leave the body healed, balanced and healthy.

SHIATSU
Practitioners use fingers, palms, elbows, knees and feet to apply pressure to the energy lines, to stimulate the body's energy flow. Treatment is helpful for pregnant women and can also benefit children.

Bristol School of Shiatsu
4 Brecknock Road, Knowle, BS4 2DD
0117 977 2809
shiatsubss@blueyonder.co.uk,
www.shiatsubristol.co.uk
Contact for details of practitioners in the area, registered with the Shiatsu Society UK.

The Shiatsu Society UK
Eastlands Court, St Peters Road, Rugby, CV21 3QP
0845 130 4560
www.shiatsu.org
The governing body for all Shiatsu practitioners. Look for the letters MRSS after the name. Contact for practitioner listing.

ANTENATAL CARE
Bristol has many services available to women during their pregnancy. The aim of this part of the chapter is to give information on pregnancy rights and services. For details of home and hospital births see Birth subchapter. For pre-conception support see Advice & Support Directory.

Health in Pregnancy

There are many books available about health in pregnancy, which you can find at your local library or book shop. Your midwife and GP will also give you advice on foods to avoid in pregnancy, exercise etc.

Taking regular and appropriate exercise is recommended whilst pregnant, and the Bristol area has many opportunities for different types of exercise to suit any budget. See also Time Out for Adults.

Many women will be apprehensive about the birth itself and especially the pain of labour. Taking parentcraft classes can help as it is a chance to discuss concerns, see Parentcraft below.

Antenatal Depression: Experienced by about 10% of women some who will never have been depressed before. The symptoms to look out for are similar to those for postnatal depression (see Postnatal below). If you think that you are suffering from antenatal depression seek medical advice. It is important to point out that it is not only mothers-to-be that suffer from depression but also fathers-to-be, and they too should seek support.

Aled Richards Trust
8-10 West St, Old Market, BS2 0BH
0117 955 1000
Mon-Fri 10am-4pm
Counselling for mothers who are HIV positive. See Advice & Support Directory for other support agencies.

MIDWIVES

Antenatal care has been designed to help ensure that expectant mothers and their babies remain healthy throughout the duration of the pregnancy. This is most commonly shared between your GP and midwife. In Bristol, there is the opportunity to go with a community or independent midwife for your antenatal care. Your first midwife appointment is usually between the 8th and 12th weeks of pregnancy. Some women, because of health problems or difficulties with previous pregnancies, may also want or need to see an obstetrician. Your midwife or GP will be able to advise you should this be the case.

Community Midwives

Working for the NHS and usually based at your local surgery or clinic. They provide care and advice during pregnancy and for the first ten days after birth. If you are planning a home birth, they will also deliver your baby. Community midwives in Bristol work in teams so you will probably see more than one midwife during your pregnancy.

Independent Midwives

Qualified midwives who have chosen to work outside the NHS in a self-employed capacity, whilst still supporting its aims and ideals. All independent midwives are regulated. They care for women during pregnancy, birth and afterwards and liaise with other healthcare professionals if necessary. In Bristol, bookings are only taken for planned homebirths although if necessary, midwives can accompany their client into any hospital. Contact lisitings for costs.

Bristol Birth Practice
Sally Randle & Jo Taylor
0117 909 0475, 0117 924 5375
landerandle@magic-tree.com
jomtaylor@lycos.co.uk, www.bristolbirth.co.uk
Offering a home birth service which includes your own midwife for pregnancy, birth and a month afterwards; informed support and 24 hour emergency contact. Covering Bristol, Bath and surrounding area.

Sue Learner
58 Bellevue Crescent, Cliftonwood, BS8 4TF
Sue Learner: 0117 927 6131
Covering central Bristol and occasionally further out, offering home-based antenatal birth preparation, intra partum and postnatal midwifery care. She has an information leaflet and sometimes gives advice by telephone.

SCANS & TESTS

In Bristol, antenatal scans and tests are carried out at St Michael's hospital, Southmead hospital, or the private BUPA hospital (the nuchal translucency scan is only available privately). Your midwife or GP will give you details of the various scans and tests that you may have. At 18-20 weeks an ultrasound scan checks your baby's growth and development, the position of the placenta, any abnormalities, and how many babies you are carrying. You may also wish to ask the sex of the baby! For a small fee you can purchase ultrasound pictures.

BUPA
The Glen, Redland Hill, Durdham Down, Bristol
0117 973 2562

Southmead Hospital
Southmead Road, Westbury-On-Trym, Bristol
0117 950 5050

St. Michael's Hospital
St. Michael's Hill, Southwell Street, Bristol
0117 921 5411

ARC (Antenatal Results and Choices)
020 7631 0285, www.arc-uk.org
Offers information and support throughout antenatal testing and when serious abnormalities are diagnosed in an unborn baby.

PARENTCRAFT
Parentcraft (antenatal) classes are specifically designed to prepare parents for the experience of birth and the task of looking after their new baby. They cover topics such as health in pregnancy, coping with labour, birth choices, pre and postnatal exercises, relaxation techniques, and how to care for and feed your new baby (many offer an optional session about breastfeeding). These classes provide an opportunity to meet other parents. Classes may be provided by your midwife or independent practitioners and the NCT, see below. If this is not your first pregnancy there are refresher courses which give you an opportunity to discuss concerns from your previous birth/s and meet others.

BIRTH PREPARATION

NCT Antenatal Classes
77 Leighton Road, Southville, Bristol, BS3 1NR
Sarah Baker: 0117 902 3811
nb007f0808@blueyonder.co.uk
www.nctpregnancyandbabycare.com
£80, £36 to join NCT (classes not complusory)
Antenatal classes for all parents-to-be run by the National Childbirth Trust (NCT), a charity that aims to help all parents have a life enriching experience of pregnancy, birth and early parenting.

Gay Elms Sure Start
Gay Elms Primary School, Withywood Road, Bristol, BS13 9AX
Tues 12.30pm-2.30pm

Pregnancy group meets once a week to have lunch and informal chat.

Chris Fielder
Avon Cottage, White Hart Steps, Clifton, BS8 4TQ
0117 929 4894
Runs a series of birth preparation sessions for women and their partners with "excellent" handouts, cost £52. Also see Yoga, below.

Dominique Ker
Dominque Ker: 0117 968 6030
sakoilsky@msn.com
Offers Active Birth Workshops on Saturdays over 6 weeks. These are for the pregnant woman and her birth attendant or partner, and are based on the work of Janet Balaskas.

Well Mother
24 Dunkerry Road, Windmill Hill, BS3 4LB
Suzanne Yates: 0117 963 2306
suzanne@wellmother.org, www.wellmother.org
1:1 sessions of massage and shiatsu for pregnancy, birth preparation and postnatal mother and baby. Sessions cover relaxation/shiatsu/yoga and physio-based exercise.

AROMATHERAPY

Anne Badger, MGCP
Anne Badger: 0117 963 6557
annebadger@madasafish.com
Offers aromatherapy pregnancy massages. She also prepares aromatherapy blends for use in labour.

BIRTHING POOLS

Birthing Pool Hire
Jill Glover: 0117 942 6810
For full details see Shopping and Services.

Natural Babies
See Shopping & services.

HYPNOTHERAPY

Bristol Hypnotherapy Clinic
The Courtyard, 11A Canford Lane, BS9 3DE
David Kato: 0117 968 6886
info@childbirth-bristol.co.uk
www.childbirth-bristol.co.uk
Using hypnosis in childbirth can allow you
to be in control of your mind and body,
reduces fear, anxiety and discomfort. During
pregnancy, back pain, nausea, hypertension
and insomnia can be reduced. Phobias, ante &
postnatal depression are specialities.

SWIMMING

Free swimming for pregnant women
Bristol Community Sport
0117 922 4416
www.bcsport.co.uk
SportsCard, £3.50
Bristol Community Sport have relaunched their
'Swim Free during Pregnancy' programme. To
qualify for free swims during pregnancy, you
will need to purchase a SportsCard, available
from Bristol Community Leisure Centres, see
tables, central colour section. Take your credit
card sized NHS Prescription Charge Maternity
Exemption Certificate (available from your
GP).

YOGA

Chris Fielder
Avon Cottage, White Hart Steps, Clifton, BS8 4TQ
Chris Fielder: 0117 929 4894
£25 for 5 sessions
Day (and some evening) yoga classes from
her home. Birth preparation sessions also
available (see above).

Dominique Ker
c/o Relaxation Centre, All Saints Rd, Clifton
Dominique Ker: 0117 968 6030
sakoilsky@msn.com
£7 per class.
Evening antenatal yoga classes.

MATERNITY RIGHTS

For details about maternity rights, please refer
to the Department of Trade and Industry,

or the Advisory Conciliation and Arbitration
Service (see below).

**Advisory, Conciliation and Arbitration
Service**
0117 946 9500
www.acas.org.uk
An independent and impartial service to
prevent and resolve disputes and to build
harmonious relationships at work.

Department of Trade and Industry
0870 1502500
www.dti.gov.uk/er/individual
www.dti.gov.uk/er/parental_leave
www.dti.gov.uk/er/maternity
Information about parental leave and
maternity rights.
Parental leave is available to employees
who have, or expect to have, parental
responsibility for a child, and have worked for
their current employer for at least a year.

Maternity Alliance
Third Floor West, 2-6 Northburgh Street, EC1V 0AY
020 7490 7638
www.maternityalliance.org.uk

Supports pregnant women and parents-to-be, working to ensure that all babies have the best possible start in life.

BIRTH HEALTHCARE

Choosing where you give birth should be about what is best for you, your family, and your individual circumstances. In Bristol, you have the choice of giving birth at home or in hospital. In both instances you will be attended by a midwife. Although birthing in hospital is still the more common option, there have been many moves by the Government to take birth back into the home. This is based on the premise that home birth is as safe as hospital birth for the majority of women.

If you choose to give birth in hospital, you can choose between the midwife-led birthing centre at St. Michael's or the hospital delivery suites at St. Michael's or Southmead.

If you book into St. Michael's hospital, you can choose a water birth, however it should be planned well in advance. It is possible that due to demand you may be unable to use the pool on the day.

It is hoped that choices for birth in Bristol will increase in the future with plans for community birthing centres and a midwife-led unit at Southmead hospital.

HOME BIRTH

Bristol Home Birth Group
Alison White: 0117 966 4148
pontinfamily@aol.com
£2 per person

Offering encouragement, information and support for parents and parents-to-be who would like their children born at home. A range of topics are discussed at meetings, with occasional guests invited to share specific expertise (an experienced midwife usually attends).

HOSPITAL BIRTH

Both these hospitals have Neonatal Intensive Care Units.

Southmead Hospital
Westbury-on-Trym, BS10 5NB
0117 950 5050

St. Michael's
St. Michael's Hill, BS2 8EG
0117 923 0000

REGISTERING THE BIRTH

Frenchay Hospital
Frenchay Park Rd, BS16 1LE
0117 975 3814

Southmead Hospital
Monks Park Lodge, BS10 5NB
0117 950 7959/0117 903 8888
Mon-Fri 10am-4pm appt only

St Michael's Hospital
Mon, Wed, Fri 9.30am-11am
Birth registration service, in-patients only.

Registration District: Bristol
Quakers Friars, BS1 3AR
0117 903 8888
Mon-Fri 9am-5pm (Wed 4pm)
Late nights & Sat by appt only

Subdistrict: Thornbury
Health Centre, Eastlands Road, Thornbury
Contact the Bristol office for an appointment.

POSTNATAL HEALTHCARE

Some women are fortunate, having straightforward births with bodies that bounce back very quickly. However, for some, things are not that straightforward. A difficult birth can leave mothers feeling drained and in discomfort. A new baby, particularly for first time parents, can also induce anxieties. Sometimes just getting out and involved with local parent groups, see Playgroups & Early Education, or taking some time out for yourself, see Time Out for Adults can help.

Postnatal Depression: Affects 10% of women who have recently had a baby. Some of the symptoms include anxiety/panic attacks, fatigue, feeling low, sleeplessness, and irritability, aches and pains and fears of unknown cause. Your health visitor will use a questionnaire/scale shortly after the birth to detect signs of postnatal depression, but it can occur at any time. It can also occur in fathers. See Advice & Support Directory. This part of the chapter lists people and places that you can contact for postnatal support, relaxation or other therapeutic approaches.

HELP AND SUPPORT

Health Visitors
These are nurses, based at local clinics, with further training in child development, health education and the social aspects of health. They visit you at home after your baby is ten days old and stay in touch with you to advise on any aspect of childcare including feeding, sleeping, crying, and behaviour problems. Your health visitor will perform your child's developmental checks.

Breast Feeding Counsellors
If you experience technical difficulties with breastfeeding when you first start, you might want to contact your midwife, health visitor or NCT breastfeeding counsellor for help and support.

NCT Breastfeeding Counsellors
0870 444 8708
www.nctpregnancyandbabycare.com
NCT Breastfeeding line gives details of local breastfeeding counsellors. Alternatively, see the quarterly NCT newsletter (available to members and in Bristol libraries).

NCT Postnatal Support
08704 448707
www.nctpregnancyandbabycare.com
If you are a member of the NCT, a local NCT member will contact you before or soon after your baby is born. The contact will not be a trained counsellor or offer professional advice, but a mother who knows what is happening locally and will be happy to chat.

COMPLEMENTARY MEDICINE

Acupuncture & Chinese Medicine
Jill Glover
Alma Vale Centre, 30 Alma Vale Road, Clifton
Jill Glover, 0117 377 1186
Acupuncture and chinese herbs for postnatal depression, exhaustion and menstrual difficulties.

Aromatherapy
Anne Badger, MGCP
Anne Badger, 0117 963 6557
annebadger@madasafish.com
Anne offers postnatal aromatherapy massage.

Baby Massage
There are many benefits of baby massage for both the baby and the mother. Some of the benefits include: strengthening and regulating the digestive, respiratory and circulatory systems; helping to relieve the symptoms of colic and gas; relaxation for both carer and baby; encouraging nurturing skills which may help alleviate postnatal depression.

Anne Badger, MGCP
0117 963 6557
annebadger@madasafish.com
Baby massage classes in Southville and mainly in South Bristol. Open to all babies and carers including babies with special needs.

Jayne Moffat, CIMI
01454 614390
Baby massage classes in NW Bristol - Pill, Almondsbury, Bradley Stoke areas.

Joanne Morgan, CIMI
0117 969 1664
Baby massage classes in Bishopston, central/ north Bristol.

Katie May, Health Visitor
Woodbine Cottage, Pye Corner, Hambrook, BS16 1SE
01454 776831
Katie has made a self-instructing baby massage video. Send a cheque for £11 payable to Katie May.

Melissa Carter-Taylor, CIMI
01225 859890
Baby massage covering Bath and Glastonbury

Teresa Bultitude, CIMI
0117 949 8428
pbultitude@blueyonder.co.uk
Baby massage in Kingswood, Fishponds, Hanham, outer North East Bristol.

Victoria Kubiak , CIMI
164 Old Church Rd, Clevedon, BS21 7TU
01275 876688

Baby massage instruction in Bristol areas.

Yoga & Relaxation

Buggy Club
22 Russell Road, Westbury Park, Bristol, BS6 7UB
Kate Humphries: 0117 904 8125
katehumphries@blueyonder.co.uk
£40.00, 4 x 1½ hour sessions
Course for mums to exercise with their babies. Also provides information regarding healthy eating, posture etc. A friendly group run by two personal trainers (and Mums) suitable for all levels.

Dominique Ker
c/o Relaxation Centre, All Saints Rd, Clifton
Dominique Ker: 0117 968 6030
sakoilsky@msn.com
Fortnightly yoga for mother and baby.

Postnatal Exercise and Relaxation Class for Mothers and Babies
St Barnabus Church, Daventry Road, Knowle, BS4
Sabine Mueller: 01373 467575
Monday 12.30pm-2pm, termtime
£4.50 per session
Small group with a very friendly atmosphere. Exercises are adjusted to individual needs.

Suzanne Yates
24 Dunkerry Road, Windmill Hill, BS3
0117 963 2306
suzanne@wellmother.org, www.wellmother.org
Tue 10am-11.30am, Windmill Hill City Farm
Ante & postnatal combined class. Also offers 1:1 session of massage and shiatsu. Crèche available.

CHILD HEALTHCARE

The following section focuses on healthcare for children of all ages and lists specific services both in Bristol and nationally. For more information on any aspect of

healthcare for children (special needs, medical conditions), you should contact your health visitor and see Advice & Support Directory.

First Aid for Children - Fast
1994, (2nd Edition), Dorling Kindersley
Produced in association with the British Red Cross. A guide to dealing with childhood emergencies.

The NCT Book of Child Health
NCT Sales
Dr Morag Martindale: 0870 112 1120
www.nctms.co.uk

DEVELOPMENT

For the first five years of your child's life, developmental reviews are held at your local clinic. They focus on your child's growth and development, checking their vision, hearing, speech and movement. You will be given a 'Personal Child Health Record' which contains charts used to monitor your child's progress and information about immunisations. This record should be taken with you to all your child's clinic and hospital visits.

IMMUNISATIONS

Immunisations protect your child against dangerous infectious diseases. They are given at your local clinic. Full details of which immunisations are given and when, are written in your 'Personal Child Health Record'. Should you have any questions about immunisations, discuss them with your health visitor.

EYES

Eye checks are carried out during your child's developmental reviews at 9 mths, 18 mths and 3 to 4 yrs. If any problems are noted then they may be referred to either an optician or a hospital clinic. Children are eligible for free eye tests at an optician from the ages of 1 to 16 yrs. A list of opticians can be found in the Yellow Pages, from Avonweb or your local PCT (see above).

Bristol Eye Hospital
Lower Maudlin Street, BS1 2LY

0117 923 0060
www.ubht.nhs.uk/eye

TEETH

Dentists advise that you should begin brushing your child's teeth as soon as they come through and you should also take them to the dentist regularly for check-ups. All children are entitled to free dental treatment at any NHS dentist, a list can be found in the Yellow Pages (listed under Dental Surgeons), from Avonweb or your local PCT.

British Dental Association
www.bda-dentistry.org.uk

Dentists
0117 976 6600
www.avon.nhs.uk

Dental Emergencies
You should call your own dentist if you need emergency dental care, as they should have an out-of-hours service. If you do not have a dentist, call NHS Direct on 0845 46 47.

Word of Mouth Helpline
0870 333 1188

AILMENTS AND CONDITIONS

There are many agencies offering information and support on medical conditions, see Advice & Support Directory.

ACCIDENTS

Accidents are the most common cause of death in children. There are many ways to prevent accidents and you can discuss these with your health visitor, or see our list of contacts below.

St. John Ambulance
The Harry Crook Centre, Raleigh Road, Bedminster, Bristol, BS3 1AP
0117 953 3880
courses@avon.sja.org.uk, www.avon.sja.org.uk
St John Ambulance run baby and small children first aid courses, for groups of 6 to 12 people. They can be run in your own home, place of work or other suitable venue.

Child Accident Prevention Trust
18-20 Farringdon Lane, London EC1R 3HA
020 7608 3828

www.capt.org.uk
Child Accident Prevention Trust is a national charity in the United Kingdom committed to reducing the number of children and young people killed, disabled and seriously injured as a result of accidents.

The Royal Society for the Prevention of Accidents
Birmingham, B5 7ST
0121 428 2000
www.rospa.co.uk

ALLERGY THERAPY

Allergy therapy looks specifically at food and chemicals in relation to health and the development of disease and symptoms. It can help to control and sometimes cure a very large range of common allergic ailments. A few examples include asthma and hyperactivity in children.

Catherine Cooke
The Clifton Practice, 8-10 Whiteladies Road, Bristol, BS8 1PD
0117 946 6070/973 3530
kramco@talk21.com, www.thecliftonpractice.co.uk
£30 per session
Victoria Kubiak
164 Old Church Road, Clevedon, BS21 7TU
01275 876688
£50 per session

Allergy UK
See Advice & Support Directory

COT DEATH & MENINGITIS
See Advice & Support Directory

COMPLEMENTARY MEDICINE
The following complementary health clinics offer a range of therapies for children.

Acupuncture & Chinese Medicine

AcuMedic Chinese Medical Centre
Manvers Chambers, Manvers Street, Bath, BA1 1PE
01225 483393
www.acumedic.com

Treatments for babies (6+mths) and children with skin conditions such as eczema and psoriasis. Reduced rates available. Staff help with buggies up steps at entrance.

Chinese Medicine and Skin Centre
51 Sandy Park Rd, Brislington, Bristol, BS4 3PG
Zhiqiang Zhu: 0117 972 4716
Qualified and registered consultant of Herbal Medicine and Acupuncture. Treatments offered can help most common and chronic disorders including baby and children's eczema, impetigo, scabies, flu, coughs, poor appetite and constipation.

Oriental Medicine Practice
35 North View, Westbury Park, BS6 7PY
0117 907 8890, www.swcom.org.uk
Offers acupuncture, shiatsu, Chinese herbs, nutritional consultation and allergy testing for babies and children. Helen Fielding will support pregnant women in pregnancy and during labour, both in hospital and for home births. Easy accesss and toy box available.

Chiropractors

Vital Health Clinic
8 North View, Westbury Park, BS6 7QB
0117 973 0878
For full details see General Healthcare above.

Cranial Osteopathy

Bristol Centre for Craniosacral Therapy
8 Cotham Grove, Cotham, BS6 6AL
0117 942 8647
cst.bristol@ic24.net, www.bristolcraniosacral.co.uk
A very gentle whole body therapy addressing structural problems and restrictions arising from the birth process. Also helpful with colic, digestive, respiratory, anxiety and stress difficulties. Mums encouraged to take sessions too. Young children with problems including glue ear, hyperactivity, dyslexia and cerebral palsy are treated. Children's rates.

Dominique Ker
c/o Bristol Centre for Craniosacral Therapy
0117 968 6030
Fri 9am-1pm
Craniosacral clinic for mother and baby, with two practitioners in attendance so that the mother may have treatment as well as the baby, if appropriate. Booking essential.

The Centre for Whole Health
12 Victoria Place, Bedminster, BS3 3BP
0117 923 1138

For full details see General Healthcare section of this chapter.

Bristol Children's Osteopathic Clinic
Chandos Clinic, 21 Chandos Road, Redland, BS6 6PG
0117 974 5084
Mon-Fri 9am-5pm
Cranial osteopathy treatment from 0-16yrs, conditions including glue ear, colic, feeding difficulties and asthma. Flexible appointment times.

Osteopathy

The Fishponds Practice
834 Fishponds Rd, Fishponds, Bristol, BS16 3XA
Martyn Morgan: 0117 949 1290
enquiries@fishpondspractice.co.uk
www.fishpondspractice.co.uk
£35 consultation £20 treatment
Child-friendly osteopathy for babies and children.

General

Clover House Children's Complementary Therapy Centre
447 Bath Road, Saltford, Bristol, BS31 3AZ
01225 344047
info@cloverhouse.org, www.cloverhouse.org
An appointment includes seeing 3 therapists covering aromatherapy, nutrition & imagery to help with fears surrounding illness. Ring for appointment. Payment by donation, £10 min.

Healing Centre
33 The Park, Kingswood, BS15 4BL
0117 967 3154
Dennis and Doreen Fare offer healing sessions by appointment. They work with children and payment is by donation. They are a useful point of contact for other healers in Bristol.
The following clinics offer children's therapies, see their full entry in General Healthcare, above.

Bristol Natural Health Service
407 Gloucester Rd, Horfield, BS7 8TJ
0117 944 4448

Clinic of Natural Medicine
126 Whiteladies Rd, Clifton, BS8 2RP
0117 946 6035

Montpelier Natural Health Clinic
26 Picton St. Montpelier, BS6 5QA
0117 924 9353

Natural Health Clinic
39 Cotham Hill, Cotham, BS6 6JY
0117 974 1199

The Chandos Clinic
21 Chandos Rd, Redland, BS6 6PJ
0117 974 5084

Health and Healing
355-359 Two Mile Hill Rd, Kingswood, BS15 1AF
0117 914 5590

Homeopathy

Children's Homeopathic Clinic
St Werburghs City Farm, Watercress Rd,
St Werburghs, BS2 9YJ
Jo Morgan: 0117 914 1694
jomorgan321@hotmail.com
Fri 9am-1pm, term time
Homeopathic treatment for 0-18 yrs. Low cost clinic.

CHILDREN'S WARDS

If your child needs to go into hospital, they will be admitted to a separate children's ward where they will be looked after by specially trained nurses, doctors and support staff in bright and friendly surroundings. You will be encouraged to stay with your child and take an active part in his or her care and if you wish, to sleep overnight with them.

Each of the hospitals also has 'Play Specialists' who help to make hospital life as normal as possible, by encouraging children to play as they would at home. They also have specific toys and games, designed to help children understand the treatments they are being given and distractions for some of the more unpleasant procedures that may be carried out e.g. blood taking. Older children, who are staying in hospital for long periods, may be disappointed to learn that the hospitals also have school teachers to help them with their studies!

Bristol Royal Hospital For Sick Children
Upper Maudlin Street, BS2 8HW
0117 923 0000

Frenchay Hospital
Frenchay, BS16 1LE
0117 970 1212

Southmead Hospital
Westbury-on-Trym, BS10 5NB
0117 950 5050

ADVICE & SUPPORT DIRECTORY

Alison Simmonds

CHAPTER 13

INTRODUCTION

Family life does not always run smoothly. At times of trouble we often find it difficult to know where to turn.

There is an incredible network of charities and support agencies out there, offering a huge range of services both regionally and nationally. In this chapter I have created a directory which is by no means an exhaustive list, but I hope the organisations and charities listed can either help you or advise you on where to find help.

Contact details change frequently and new support services are starting up all the time. Please let us know any updates via our website.

FAMILIES & INDIVIDUALS

GENERAL SUPPORT IN LIFE

Bristol City Council
Social Services and Health Department
Amelia Court, PO Box 30, Bristol BS99 7NB
Switchboard 0117 922 2000   Mon-Fri 8.30am-5pm
Emergencies out of hours 01454 615 165

Services include: Social workers, family support workers, special needs provision, respite care, adoption and fostering, child protection, services and support for disabled children and their families etc.

They also work closely with Children's Information Services, see Babies & Children section, below.

Easton Community Children's Centre
Russell Town Ave, Bristol BS5 9JF
easton-childrens-centre@yahoo.co.uk
0117 939 2550

Provides childcare services, information on learning opportunities and support for inner-city families.

Fulford Family Centre
237-239 Gatehouse Avenue, Bristol BS13 9AQ
0117 978 2441   Mon-Fri 9am-5pm

For families with pre-school children. Provides parent and toddler support groups, individual and family counselling, play therapy, welfare rights advice, holidays and outings.

Home-Start Bristol
St Matthews Rd, Kingsdown, Bristol BS6 5TT
staff@homestart.vispa.com, www.home-start.org.uk
0117 942 8399   Mon-Thu 9am-3pm
(answer phone out of hours)

Voluntary home-visiting scheme for families with children under five, where there are difficulties or stress.

Parentline Plus
520 Highgate Studios, 53-79 Highgate Road,
London NW5 1TL
centraloffice@parentlineplus.org.uk
www.parentlineplus.org.uk
Freephone 0808 800 2222
Textphone 0800 783 66783

Call centres run by parents, offering a listening ear and practical help. The lines are often busy so keep trying!

Totterdown office:
0117 9714 831

Offers a range of parenting courses.

Working Families
1-3 Berry Street, London EC1V 0AA
office@workingfamilies.org.uk
www.workingfamilies.org.uk
020 7253 7243
0800 013 0313 legal advice for low income families

Offering help to children, working parents/carers and their employers to find a better balance between responsibilities at home and work.

BABIES & CHILDREN

Educational Special Needs
See Schools & Educational Support chapter

Bristol City Council - Child Protection
The Telephone Directory provides a list of all local Child Protection offices, contact the one nearest to the child's home.
Citywide services are provided for:
Adoption 0117 954 8545
Disabled Children's Service 0117 903 8250

ChildLine
Childline, 45 Folgate Street, London E1 6GL
www.childline.org.uk
020 7650 3200
Helpline 0800 1111

UK's free helpline for children and young people. Telephone counselling service for any child with any problem, 24/7. It comforts, advises, protects. Correspondence address for children: Childline, Freepost NATN1111, London E1 6BR.

'The Line'

0800 884444	Mon-Fri 3.30-9.30pm
	Sat-Sun 2-8pm
Minicom 0800 400222	Mon-Fri 9.30am-9.30pm
	Sat-Sun 9.30am-8pm

A special helpline for children living away from home.

Children's Information Service

enquiries@cisbristol.co.uk, www.childcarelink.gov.uk
0845 129 7217
Minicom 0117 941 3777
Mon/Thu/Fri 9.30am-4pm, Tues/Wed 9.30am-8pm

Provides free, impartial and confidential information/guidance on a full range of childcare, children's services and resources in Bristol. See Childcare 0-4 Years.

Childtime

30A College Green, Bristol BS1 5TB
info@childtime.org.uk, www.childtime.org.uk
0117 929 1533 (answer phone out of hours)

Helps children who are experiencing emotional or psychological difficulties. Works in partnership with parents and relevant professionals. Fees on sliding scale.

CRY-SIS

BM Cry-sis, London WC1N 3XX
www.crysis.com
Helpline 0207 404 5011 24 hr

Emotional and practical support to parents whose babies cry excessively. Helpline gives local contacts, who are available 9am-10pm.

Little Saplings

Oakfield Road Day Nursery, 17 Oakfield Road, Clifton, Bristol BS8 2AW
0117 377 2270

For parents/carers of multiple births, offering activities, trips and qualified family support. Meets on Thu 2pm-3.30pm.

NSPCC (National Society for the Prevention of Cruelty to Children)

help@nspcc.org.uk, www.nspcc.org.uk
Helpline 0808 800 5000 24 hr
Child Protection Helpline 0808 800 5000 24hr
Textphone 0800 056 0566 24 hr

Offers advice and support to anyone who is concerned about a child.

NSPCC Asian Child Protection Helpline
0800 096 7719   Mon-Fri 11am-7pm

Sure Start Units

www.surestart.gov.uk

Bring together early education, better childcare, and health and family support in disadvantaged areas. It aims to deliver free early education for all 3 & 4yrs, affordable, quality childcare and after-school activities. Working with parents to build aspirations for employment and their children's education.

Four Acres Sure Start
Covering Hartcliffe, Highridge & Withywoods
Four Acres Primary School, Four Acres, Withywood, Bristol BS13 8RB
0117 903 0460   Thu 1pm-3pm

Weekly talk for families run by a speech therapist to help parents enhance their children's speech development.

Other SSU's in the Bristol area:
Knowle West Sure Start: 0117 903 9781
Easton Sure Start: 0117 941 3400
Kingsweston Sure Start: 0117 982 4578

Twins and Multiple Births Association (TAMBA)

2 The Willows, Gardner Road, Guildford GU1 4PG
enquiries@tamba.org.uk, www.tamba.org.uk
0870 770 3305   Mon-Fri 9.30am-5pm
Twinline 0800 138 0509
Mon-Fri 10am-1pm & 7-11pm, Sat-Sun 10am-10pm

Confidential support and information service for all parents and carers of twins (and more), and the professionals involved in their care.

Regional Co-ordinator for Bristol and surrounding area:
Jennifer Popham: 01275 859292
jennifer@mymadhouse.freeserve.co.uk.

Details of local clubs including non-TAMBA, tailored ante-natal sessions etc.

ADOPTIVE, FOSTER, STEP & ONE-PARENT FAMILIES

Adoption UK

Lower Boddington, Daventry NN11 6YB
sglos-auk@iname.com, www.adoptionuk.org.uk
01327 260295

Regional Contacts
Alyson & Nigel Hurst
182 Badminton Road, Bristol BS16 6NG
www.sglos-auk.freeserve.co.uk
0117 956 3680

Supporting families before, during and after adoption or long-term fostering.

Bristol Family Placement Team (Recruitment)

Social Services, Avonvale Road, Bristol BS5 9RH
www.bristol-city.gov.uk/fostering
0117 954 8545

Offers information, training and support to anyone interested in fostering children or young people. Welcomes applicants from all sections of the community.

Child Support Agency (CSA)

www.dss.gov.uk/csa
National Enquiries 08457 133 133
Textphone 08457 138 9924

Aims to support families with the cost of raising children, while recognising that the primary responsibility rests with parents.

Gingerbread - Association for One-Parent Families

7 Sovereign Close, Sovereign Court,
London E1W 3HW
office@gingerbread.org.uk, www.gingerbread.org.uk
0800 018 4318

Self-help association for lone-parent families. Provides advice, local contacts and activities.

One-Parent Families' Services

255 Kentish Town Rd, London NW5 2LX
info@oneparentfamilies.org.uk
www.oneparentfamilies.org.uk
Helpline 0800 018 5026   Mon-Fri 9am-5pm

Information on benefits, work, education, relationship breakdown and child maintenance, children and holidays.

Our Place

139 Fishponds Road, Eastville, Bristol BS5 6PR
ourplace1@btconnect.com
0117 951 2433

Offering foster and adoptive families opportunities to mix with others and share experiences. Fun activities, seminars & workshops run by professionals - no charges.

Single Parent Action Network UK (SPAN)

Millpond, Baptist St, Easton, Bristol BS5 0YW
annie.spanuk.org.uk, www.spanuk.org.uk
www.singleparents.org.uk (interactive site)
Annie Oliver: 0117 951 4231

Campaigns to improve the lives of one-parent families giving advice and support. Developing single-parent self-help groups around the UK.

SPAN Study Centre
0117 952 0626   Mon-Fri 9am-5pm

Focuses on training and support for single parents, further education and employment.

South West Adoption Network

Leinster House, Leinster Avenue, Bristol BS4 1NL
www.swan-adoption.freeserve.co.uk
Helpline 0845 601 2459   Tue-Thu 10am-2pm
                              & Tue 7pm-9pm.

SWAN is a post-adoption centre offering advice, counselling, support groups and workshops.

YOUNG PARENTS

Brook Young People's Services

1 Unity Street, College Green, Bristol BS1 5HH
www.brook.org.uk
0117 929 0090
Walk-in Mon-Tue 1pm-3pm, 4pm-6pm
Appt only Wed & Fri 12am-2pm
Walk-in Thu 4pm-6pm, Sat 10am-12am

Expert counselling and advice on sexual problems for under 25's. Provides all methods of contraception and emergency contraception; screening and testing. Connexions advice, and ACCSEX - a project aimed at young disabled people.

Off The Record

2 Horfield Road, St Michael's Hill, Bristol BS2 8EA
confidential@otrbristol.org.uk
www.otrbristol.org.uk
0808 808 9120
Mon 9.30am-8pm, Tue-Wed 11.30am-8pm

Counselling, information, advice and support to young people, 11-25yrs.

Young Mothers Group and Information Project
c/o The Mill Youth Centre, Lower Ashley Road,
Easton, Bristol BS5 0YJ
group@ymgt.fsnet.co.uk
0117 935 5639
Offers advice, support and out-reach visits to mothers under 25yrs. The Information Project is peer-led: trained volunteers talk in schools, colleges & youth clubs about the realities of young parenthood.

Young Mothers Group Trust
Unit 34, Easton Business Centre, Felix Rd, BS5 0HE
0117 941 5838
Provides housing for single homeless mothers (16-24yrs) or those facing homelessness.

RELATIONSHIPS

The Bridge Foundation
12 Sydenham Rd, Bristol BS6 5SH
bridgefoundation@tinyonline.co.uk
0117 942 4510
Consultation and therapy for couples, young children and families. Fees are charged, but discretionary for some.

Bristol Family Mediation
25 Hobbs Lane, Bristol BS1 5ED
mediation@bfmbristol.co.uk
www.bristolfamilymediation.org.uk
0117 929 2002   Mon-Fri 9am-5pm
Help pre or post separating/divorcing couples make mutual decisions and resolve issues.

Marriage Care
58 Alma Rd, Clifton, Bristol BS8 2DQ
Mrs Anne Reece 0117 973 3777
Free counselling service for adults - whether single, or in relationships. Fees by donation.

Relate Avon
133 Cheltenham Rd, Bristol BS6 5RR
relateavon@compuserve.com
0117 942 8444   Mon-Fri 9.30am-9pm
Counselling for those in relationship difficulties and psycho-sexual therapy for people in committed relationships. Fees on a sliding scale.

DRUGS AND ALCOHOL

ACAD - Advice and Counselling on Alcohol and Drugs
15/16 Lower Park Row, Bristol BS1 5BN
info@acad.org.uk, www.acad.org.uk
0117 929 3028
Group drop-in Mon/Tue/Thu 11.30am-1pm
1:1 drop-in Fri 10am-11.30am.
Free advice and counselling by appointment (or drop-ins) for people directly or indirectly affected by alcohol-related problems.

Al-Anon Family Group
Al-Anon Family Group, 61 Great Dover St, London SE1 4YF
alanonuk@aol.com, www.al-anonuk.org.uk
Helpline 0207 403 0888   Mon-Sun 10am-10pm
Confidential understanding and support for family and friends of problem drinkers. Details of local support groups.
Alateen, a service for young people (12-20yrs) who have been affected by someone else's drinking.

Alcoholics Anonymous
Alcoholics Anonymous, PO Box 42, Bristol BS99 7RJ
0117 926 5520/5926 24 hr
Frequent meetings held in various parts of Bristol. Free to join, the only requirement for membership is a desire to stop drinking.

Bristol & District Tranquilliser Project
88 Henleaze Road, Bristol BS9 4JY
Helpline 0117 962 8874   Mon-Thu 10am-4pm
Advice and support to people taking prescribed psychotropic medication. Runs withdrawal groups and offers individual counselling.

Bristol Drugs Project
11 Brunswick Square, Bristol BS2 8PE
info@bdp.org.uk, www.bdp.org.uk
0117 987 1500 (answer phone out of hours)
Drop-in Mon-Fri 9.30am-1pm, 2pm-5pm,
Drop-in with needle exchange Mon-Fri 2pm-5pm
Free, advice and counselling for anyone concerned about drug use. Crèche facilities on Wednesday mornings.

Narcotics Anonymous
0117 924 0084 or 07949 429 567
National Helpline 0207 730 0009
Information on Fellowship meetings
throughout the West Country and Wales, as
well as nationally.

BEREAVEMENT

ARC (Antenatal Results and Choices)
73 Charlotte St, London W1T 4PN
info@arc-uk.org, www.arc-uk.org
Helpline 0207 631 0285   Mon-Fri 10am-5pm
Support through the ante-natal testing
process and when an abnormality is
diagnosed; impartial help when making a
decision about the future of the pregnancy.

Bristol Miscarriage Support Group
Alma Church, Alma Rd, Clifton, Bristol BS8 2ES
www.bristolmsg.8m.com
Meet on 1st Tuesday of every month, 7-9pm.

Cruse Bereavement Care
9A St James Barton, Bristol BS1 3LT
0117 926 4045   Mon-Fri 10am-2pm
(answer phone out of hours)
Provides free 1:1 or family counselling.

FSID (Foundation for the Study of Infant Death)
Artillery House, 11-19 Artillery Row,
London SW1P 1RT
fsid@sids.org.uk, www.sids.org.uk/fsid
0870 787 0885
Helpline 0870 787 0554   Mon-Fri 9am-11pm
                                Sat-Sun 6pm-11pm
Working to prevent sudden infant deaths and
promote baby health. Funds research and
supports grieving families.

Miscarriage Association
C/o Clayton Hospital, Northgate,
W Yorkshire WF1 3JS
info@miscarriageassociation.org.uk,
www.miscarriageassociation.org.uk
Admin 01924 200 795
Helpline 01924 200 799 (answer phone out of hours)
Mon-Fri 9am-4pm

Support for those who have suffered a
miscarriage or are worried that they might.
Newsletters,information and local contacts.

Stillbirth and Neonatal Death Society (SANDS)
28 Portland Place, London W1B 1LY
support@uk-sands.org, www.uk-sands.org
Helpline 0207 436 5881
Enquiries 0207 436 7940   Mon-Fri 9.30am-5.30pm
                            Mon-Fri 10am-4pm
Supports parents who have suffered the loss
of a baby before, during or after birth.

The Compassionate Friends
53 North St, Bristol BS3 1EN
info@tcf.org.uk, www.tcf.org.uk
Helpline 0845 1232304   24/7
Admin 0117 966 5202   10am-4pm & 6.30-10.30pm
Self-help befriending organisation of parents
whose child (any age) has died from any
cause.

Twins and Multiple Births Association (TAMBA)
Runs a support group led by parents who
have themselves experienced a loss within a
multiple birth. See Babies & Children above
for contact details.

Winstons Wish
Clara Burgess Centre, Bayshill Rd,
Cheltenham GL50 3AW
info@winstonswish.org.uk, www.winstonswish.org.uk
01242 515157
Helpline 0845 2030405   Mon-Fri 9am-5pm
(answer phone out of hours)   Sat 9.30am-1.30pm
Helping bereaved children and their families
rebuild their lives. Also assists schools and
carers with the needs of bereaved children.

FOR WOMEN

Wellwomen Information
6 West Street, Old Market, Bristol BS2 0BH
services@wellwomen.freeserve.co.uk,
www.digitalbristol.org/members/welwomen
0117 941 3311
Women's Health drop-in and Helpline:

Tue/Wed 9.30am-12pm
Asian Women's Health drop-in and Helpline:
Mon 10am-12.30pm.

Available for women in distress or with other health problems. Counselling for those on low incomes.

Asian counselling service
0117 952 5023.

PRE-CONCEPTION & ANTENATAL

Pre-Conception Care

GPs give advice on pre-conception and sub-fertility problems, and will refer you to specialists if necessary. There are also organisations that help with pre-conception healthcare outside the NHS.

Foresight

The Paddock, Godalming, Surrey GU7 1XD
www.foresight-preconception.org.uk
01483 427 839

Offers dietary & life-style advice and general support to help couples conceive. Send an A5, SAE with a 33p stamp for more information.

Local contact
Elizabeth Season, Clinic of Natural Medicine,
126 Whiteladies Road, Bristol
elizabeth.season@netgates.co.uk
0117 946 6035

Life

81 Whiteladies Rd, Bristol BS8 2NT
life@bristol-life.org.uk, www.bristol-life.org.uk
Local Helpline 0800 068 5028
National Hotline 0800 849 4545

Free counselling service for women experiencing unplanned pregnancy, termination, miscarriage, still birth and infertility. Donations welcome.

NCT - National Childbirth Trust

www.nctpregnancyandbabycare.com
Enquiry Line 0870 444 8707
Membership line 08709 908040
Breastfeeding Line 0870 444 8708

Offers information and support in pregnancy, childbirth and early parenthood including ante-natal classes and breastfeeding

counsellors (available to non-members). See Antenatal Healthcare.

The National Endometriosis Society

Artillery Row, London SW1P 1RR
nes@endo.org.uk, www.endo.org.uk
0207 222 2781
Helpline 0808 808 2227   7pm-10pm

Provides support, information, local branch phone numbers.

Well-Being Eating for Pregnancy Helpline

Univ. of Sheffield, Dept of Reproductive Medicine,
The Jessop Wing, Tree Root Walk, Sheffield S10 2SF
pregnancy.nutrition@sheffield.ac.uk,
www.shef.ac.uk/pregnancy_nutrition
0845 1303646

Helpline offers scientifically valid information on nutrition for women who are pregnant, planning to be or are breast-feeding.

POSTNATAL

Association for Postnatal Illness

145 Dawes Rd, London SW6 7EB
info@apni.org, www.apni.org
0207 386 0868   Mon-Fri 10am-2pm

Telephone 1:1 support for mothers with post-natal illness. Callers are matched with a local volunteer, who has experienced the illness. Line is very busy, keep trying, answerphone messages responded to within 24 hrs.

Meet-A-Mum Association

www.mama.co.uk
National Helpline 0845 1203746
Mon-Fri 7pm-10pm, Mon & Wed 10am-1pm

Local Contact
77 Westbury View, Bath BA2 8TZ
01525 217064

Offers moral support and practical help (local groups) to women suffering from postnatal illness, or who feel lonely after the birth of a child.

Mothers for Mothers

PO Box 1292, Bristol BS99 2FP
Admin 0117 904 0065   Mon-Thu 9.30am-12.30pm
Helpline & Crisis Line 0117 975 6006   up to 9pm

245

Befriending and support for women suffering postnatal illness. Holds coffee mornings for mothers to meet.

IN CRISIS

Avon Sexual Abuse Centre
PO Box 665, Bristol BS99 1XY
Tue-Thu Office open
0117 935 1707 (answer phone out of hours)
Mon 9.30am-12.30pm, Wed/Fri 9.30am-5pm

A free and confidential counselling service available to adults, children and their families.

Bristol Crisis Service for Women
PO Box 654, Bristol BS99 1XH
www.user.zetnet.co.uk/bcsw
Office 0117 927 9600
Crisis Line 0117 925 1119   Fri/Sat 9pm-12.30am
(answer phone out of hours)   Sun 6pm-9pm

Helpline for women in any emotional distress; specialises in those who have suffered childhood abuse, and those who self-injure.

Gloucester Rape Crisis Centre
Confidential helpline 01452 526770

Next Link Domestic Abuse Services
5 Queens Square, Bristol BS1 4JQ
nextlink@mlha.freeserve.co.uk
0117 925 0680   Mon-Fri 9am-5pm
(answer phone out of hours)

Safe temporary accommodation for women and children experiencing domestic abuse. Offers other support services for women.

FOR MINORITY GROUPS

Bangladesh Association
Bangladesh House, 539 Stapleton Rd, Eastville, Bristol BS5 6PE
0117 951 1491

Advice, information and library service for the Bangladeshi community.

Bangladesh Association Women's Group
Bangladesh Centre, 35 Mivart Street, Easton,

Bristol BS5 6JF
0117 951 9777

Advice, information and support for Bangladeshi women in Bristol.

Bristol & Avon Chinese Women's Group
St Agnes Church, Thomas St, Bristol BS2 9LL
bacwg2@onetel.net.uk, www.bacwg.org.uk
0117 935 1462   Mon-Fri 9.30am-4.30pm (Fri 4pm)

Provides support to Chinese women.

Bristol Pakistani Community Welfare Organisation
454 Stapleton Rd, Easton, Bristol BS5 6PA
info@bpcwo.org, www.bpcwo.org
0117 952 3031   Mon-Fri 11am-4pm

Organises social, cultural, educational, religious and recreational activities, especially for women and children.

Bristol Racial Equality Council
Colston House, Colston St, Bristol BS1 5AQ
bristolrec@aol.com
0117 929 7899

Advice on racial discrimination. A directory of organisations and contacts for black and other ethnic minority groups, a monthly newsletter and weekly news bulletin.

Gay & Lesbian Switchboard (Bristol)
PO Box 49, 82 Colston St, Bristol
0117 942 0842   Mon-Sun 8pm-10pm

Provides information and support.

Home-Tuition Scheme
c/o Bristol Community Education, Alexandra Pk, Fishponds, Bristol BS16 2BG
0117 903 8815

Provides a volunteer home-tuition service for women wishing to learn basic English.

KHAAS
St Werburghs Community Centre, Horley Rd, St Werburghs, Bristol BS2 9TJ
khaas_bristol@yahoo.co.uk
0117 955 4070

Aim is to establish education, welfare and benefits for Asian children with disabilities/ special needs, and their families.

Overseas Chinese Association
9-15 Lower Ashley Road, St Agnes, Bristol BS2 9QA
overseaschineseassociation@southwest.fslife.co.uk
0117 955 5225
Advice for the local Chinese community. Also a club for the elderly, Chinese language group, courses and workshops.

Support Against Racist Incidents (SARI)
sari@sari.freeserve.co.uk
PO Box 642, Bristol BS99 1UT
0117 952 5652
Advice for people under racial attack or harassment.

Unity Group
Fulford Family Centre, 237-239 Gatehouse Ave, Withywood, Bristol BS13 9AQ
www.unitysupportgroup@angelcity.com
0117 978 2441
Informal support group meets on Thu at 1-3pm, with crèche, for black multi-racial families living in Hartcliffe, Withywood, Highridge and Bishopsworth.

MEDICAL CONDITIONS & SPECIAL NEEDS

General Support
Educational special needs are listed in Schools and Educational Support chapter.

Break
Mrs Davidson: 01263 822161
Subsidised or free holidays for children and adults who have special needs.

Contact a Family
209-211 City Rd, London EC1V 1JN
info@cafamily.org.uk, www.cafamily.org.uk
Helpline 0808 808 3555
Admin 020 7608 8700
Textphone 0808 808 3556
Supports families with disabled children, including those with health conditions and

rare disorders. Supplies information on special educational needs, benefits and local support.

Disability Information and Advice Service
Leinster Avenue, Knowle, Bristol BS4 1AR
reception@wecil-ltd.demon.co.uk
Admin 0117 983 2828   Tue/Wed/Thu 10am-1pm
Phone advice service provided by disabled people, covering all aspects of disability, also welfare rights, DLA and AA form filling service.

Disabled Living Centre
The Vassall Centre, Gill Avenue, Bristol BS16 2QQ
info@dlcbristol.org, www.dlcbristol.org
0117 965 3651 & Minicom
Appointments: Mon-Fri 10am-4pm (some Sats)
Professional, impartial information and advice on products and equipment to aid independent living. Also has a Multimedia Resource Area, coffee shop and garden.

Disabled Parents Network
Unit F9, 89-93 Fonthill Rd, London N4 3JH
information@disabledparentsnetwork.org.uk,
www.disabledparentsnetwork.org.uk
Helpline 0870 2410 450
A national network of disabled people who are parents or hope to become parents. Contact register, quarterly newsletter (available on tape), helpline, local and national events.

Family Link Scheme
The Heath Resource Centre, 2a Newton Rd, Cadbury Heath, Bristol BS30 8EZ
01454 866 251
Family-based short breaks for disabled children.

Hop Skip & Jump
Grimsbury Road, Kingswood, Bristol BS15 9SE
0117 967 7282   Mon-Fri 9am-5.30pm
Play centre for children with special needs 0-16yrs, children are looked after by qualified care workers, siblings welcome.

KHASS
Supporting Asian children with disabilities, see Minority Groups section, above.

Mind
PO Box 1174, Bristol BS99 2PQ
0808 8080 330   Wed-Sun 8pm-12am
Freephone helpline for those in emotional distress. Has a database of local organisations.

Parkway Parent and Child Project
Parkway Methodist Church, Conduit Pl,
St Werburghs, Bristol
0117 935 0205   Mon-Thu 9.30am-12pm
£3 (£2 with concession)
Disability/equality worker available for 1:1 support. Parent participation welcomed.

The Care Forum
The Vassall Centre, Gill Avenue, Bristol BS16 2QQ
admin@thecareforum.org.uk,
www.thecareforum.org.uk
0117 965 4444
Provides support, co-ordination and information services for voluntary groups, enabling them to deliver local health and social care services. Direct services include: The Complaints Procedure Advocacy Service (CPA), complaints about Social Services: The Disability Information Service (DIS).

Purple Pages Helpline
info@purplepage.org.uk
0808 808 5252   Mon-Fri 9.30am-4.30pm
A friendly and up-to-date helpline for disabled people, older people, carers and their friends, family and professionals in Bristol and surrounding areas.

The Yellow Book
Consumer Services Officer at South Glos
www.southglos.gov.uk
01454 865 924
A definitive guide book giving information and services relevant to caring for children with special needs in South Gloucestershire.

Time 2 Share
Unit 55, Easton Business Centre,
Felix Rd, Bristol BS5 OHE
info@time2share.org.uk, www.time2share.org.uk
0117 941 5868   Mon-Fri 9.30am-2.00pm
(answer phone out of hours)
For children with learning difficulties. Provides sitters and caters for individual needs. Families are matched on a one to one basis

with a volunteer; support and training is available.

SUPPORT FOR SPECIFIC MEDICAL CONDITIONS & SPECIAL NEEDS (A-Z)

Allergy UK
Deepdene House, 30 Bellegrove Road, Welling,
Kent DA16 3PY
info@allergyuk.org, www.allergyuk.org
Admin 0208 303 8525
Helpline 0208 303 8583
Mon-Fri 9am-5pm
Aims to increase understanding and awareness of allergy and to help people manage their allergies. Information, advice and support are available on most types of allergy. Membership £10.

Arthritis Care
Arthritis Care South West England, Constable Court, Fore Street, Heavitree, Exeter EX1 2QJ
swregoffice@arthritiscare.org.uk
www.arthritiscare-sw.org.uk
01392 437954
Helpline 0808 800 4050   Mon-Fri 12pm-4pm
The Source 0808 808 2000   Mon-Fri 12pm-2pm
for sufferers under 26yrs
Aims to empower people with arthritis to take control of their arthritis and their lives.

Asthma - National Asthma Campaign
Providence House, Providence Pl, London N1 0NT
www.asthma.org.uk
General enquiries 0207 226 2260
Helpline 0845 010203   Mon-Fri 9am-5pm
Publishes fact sheets and lists of support groups. Helpline staffed by asthma nurses.

Autism - National Autistic Society
393 City Rd, London EC1V 1NG
www.nas.org.uk
Admin 0207 833 2299
Helpline 0870 600 8585   Mon-Fri 10am-4pm
Local contact 0117 974 8400
The local group meets regularly and there are family social events throughout the year.

Birth Defects Foundation

BDF Centre, Hemlock Way, Cannock WS11 2GF
help@birthdefects.co.uk, www.birthdefects.co.uk
Helpline 08700 70 70 20   Mon-Fri 9.30am-6pm
                            Sat 9.30-12.30am
Dedicated to improving child health by
combating birth defects and supporting those
affected or at risk.

Blindness - RNIB Bristol

10 Stillhouse Lane, Bedminster, Bristol BS3 4EB
rnibbristol@rnib.org.uk, www.rnib.org.uk
National Helpline 0845 766 9999
Minicom 0117 953 7750
Mon-Fri 9am-4.30pm
Support and facilities for those with any level
of hearing impairment, including combined
sight and hearing loss. Sells a range of
equipment; offers information (education
and employment issues - New Deal & Access
to Work) on tapes and leaflets. Many other
services.

Blindness - Look West

C/o RNIB Bristol, Stillhouse Lane, Bristol BS3 4EB
www.lookswest.org.uk
0117 958 5323/967 0008
Parent self-help group of visually impaired
children and their families. Has its own
holiday caravan equipped to meet the needs
of a visually impaired child. Children's groups
include The Explorers and The Discoverers.

BLISS (The National Charity for the New Born)

68 South Lambeth Rd, London SW8 1RL
information@bliss.org.uk, www.bliss.org.uk
0500 618 140   Mon-Fri 9am-5pm
(answer phone out of hours)
Support and information for parents and
families with babies on, or recently returned
home from, special care baby units.

Brain Injuries - Cerebra

Kingsgate House, Church Road, Kingswood,
Bristol BS15 4NN
cerebra@org.com, www.cerebra.org.uk
0117 940 1111
Help for families and carers of brain-injured
children. Also funds research.

Cerebral Palsy - Scope Bristol

Unit 13 The Greenway Centre, Doncaster Rd,
Southmead, Bristol BS10 5YP
scopebristol@supanet.com, www.scopebristol.co.uk
0117 950 5099   Mon-Thu 9am-3pm, Fri 9-12am
(answer phone out of hours)
Services include: information, grants scheme,
evening club, Connexions Young People's
Information Point (YPIP), Lifestyles Project,
newsletter, physiotherapy.

Cleft Lip and Palate Association - CLAPA

235-237 Finchley Rd, London NW3 6LS
info@clapa.com, www.clapa.com
0207 431 0033
Information and support to all those affected
by cleft lip or palate. Specialist feeding
bottles, information leaflets, local contacts etc.

Cot Death - The Foundation for the Study of Infant Deaths

www.sids.org.uk
020 72332090
24 hour helpline and informative website.

Cystic Fibrosis Trust

11 London Road, Bromley, Kent BR1 1BY
enquiries@cftrust.org.uk, www.cftrust.org.uk
Admin 0208 464 7211
Helpline 0845 8591000
Information and list of local contacts.

Deafblind - Sense

The Woodside Family Centre, Woodside Rd,
Bristol BS15 8DG
0117 967 0008
The National Deafblind and Rubella
Association provides support to the families
of multi-sensory impaired children. Running
groups for babies, toddlers and children.
Facilities include: toy library, crèche and
sensory stimulation room.

Deafness - Acorns Resource for Families of Deaf Children

Elmfield House, Greystoke Ave, Bristol BS10 6AY
sue_horne@bristol-city.gov.uk
Sue Horne 0117 903 8442 (Voice/minicom)
For families with pre-school deaf children.
Drop-in centre for parents, access to advice

on sign language and communication. There is a crèche (Wed term time).

Deafness - The BUDS Group
Sensory Support Service 0117 903 8442
BUDS (Beginning to Understand Deafness) is a local group for Acorns. For families with newly diagnosed hearing impaired children.

Deafness - Avon Deaf Child Society & Bristol Centre for Deaf People
16-18 King Square, Bristol BS2 8JL
philipshielasaun@aol.com, www.ndcs.org.uk
Textphone 0117 924 9868
Minicom 0117 944 1344
Voice & Textphone 01275 843577
Mon-Fri 8.30am-5pm
Sign language and lip-reading taught to hearing impaired parents or those with hearing impaired children

Deafness - Family Centre (Deaf Children)
Family Centre (Deaf Children), Frome House, Cranleigh Court Rd, Yate, Bristol BS37 5DE
office@fcdc.org.uk, www.fcdc.org.uk
01454 315404
Minicom 01454 315405   Mon/Wed-Fri 9am-5.30pm
(answer phone out of hours)
Support, information, educational and social activities for hearing families with deaf children across the old 'Avon' area.

Deafness - Social Services Sensory Services Team
Centre for Deaf People, 16-18 King Sq, Bristol BS2 8JL
brssna@bristol-city.gov.uk
0117 924 0484
Minicom 0117 944 2168
Advice and social work services for deaf and hearing impaired people.

Diabetes UK
10 Parkway, London NW1 7AA
info@diabetes.org.uk, www.diabetes.org.uk
0207 424 1000   Mon-Fri 9am-5pm
Care line 0845 1202960
Specially trained staff offering diabetic advice.

Local Contact
Mrs S Gatehouse

7 Salisbury Gardens, Downend, Bristol, BS16 5RF
0117 956 4390

Downs Syndrome Association
155 Mitcham Rd, London SW17 9PG
www.downs-syndrome.org.uk
0208 682 4001

South West Development Officer
vr_dsasouthwest@hotmail.com
01275 858230

Local contact
Mrs Annabel Tall
annabel@dsa-bristol.org.uk
0117 935 1382
Information library, parents support network and mother & toddler group. Outings, events.

Dyslexia
Dyslexia and other learning conditions see Schools & Educational Support chapter.

Eczema - National Eczema Society
Hill House, Highgate Hill, London N19 5NA
helpline@eczema.org, www.eczema.org
Info line 0207 281 3553   Mon-Fri 9am-5pm
Help and support for those people affected by eczema. Local support groups.

Endometriosis
See Pre-Conceptual & Antenatal section, above.

Enuresis Resource and Information Centre (ERIC)
34 Old School House, Brittania Rd, Bristol BS15 8DB
info@eric.org.uk, www.eric.org.uk
0117 960 3060
Website provides advice and information on bedwetting, day-time wetting, constipation and soiling. Also provides forum to ask questions and read about others experiences.

Epilepsy - British Epilepsy Association
New Antsey House, Gateway Drive, Yeadon, Leeds
epilepsy@epilepsy.org.uk, www.epilepsy.org.uk
Admin 0113 210 8800
Helpline 0808 800 5050   Mon-Thu 9am-4.30pm
Fri 9am-4pm
Information, support groups and a newsletter.

Haemophilia Society
Chesterfield Hse, 385 Euston Rd, London NW1 3AU
info@haemophilia.org.uk, www.haemophilia.org.uk
Admin 0207 380 0600
Helpline 0800 018 6068
Patient group for those with haemophilia, von Willebrand's and related bleeding disorders. Information and advice, runs special projects for families, young people and women. 17 local groups across the UK.

Hyperactive Children's Support Group
71 Whyke Lane, Chichester, Sussex PO19 7PD
web@hacsg.org.uk, www.hacsg.org.uk
01243 551313   Mon-Fri 10am-1pm
Including allergic/ADD children. Advice and support with a non-medication bias for parents, carers and professionals.

Limb Disabilities - Reach
PO Box 54, Helston, Cornwall TR13 8WD
reach@reach.org.uk, www.reach.org.uk
0845 1306225
Association for children with hand or arm deficiency. Parent support group offering information and lists of local contacts. Membership £20 p.a.

Limb Disabilities - STEPS
Lymm Court, 11 Eagle Brow, Lymm WA13 0LP
info@steps-charity.org.uk, www.steps-charity.org.uk
0871 7170044
Association for people with lower limb abnormalities which offers information and support with local contacts.

Mencap, Bristol
127a Pembroke Rd, Clifton, Bristol BS8 3ES
www.bristomencap.freeserve.co.uk
Helpline/Info 0117 974 5165   Tue-Fri 9.30-12.30am (answerphone out of hours)
Information on disability problems; family advisors support families with newborn babies. 'Opportunity groups' held in Clifton and Withywood for 0-2yrs with learning disabilities.

Meningitis Research Foundation
Midland Way, Thornbury, Bristol BS35 2BS
info@meningitis.org.uk, www.meningitis.org
01454 281811

Helpline 0808 800 3344 24 hrs
Funds vital scientific research into the prevention, detection and treatment of meningitis and septicaemia. Offers support through in-depth information and befriending.

The Meningitis Trust
Fern House, Bath Rd, Stroud GL5 3TJ
support@meningitis-trust.org
www.meningitis-trust.org
Admin and Info 01453 768 000   Mon-Fri 9am-5pm
Nurse Helpline 0845 6000 800   24hrs
Financial and emotional support to sufferers and their families. Information and local contacts available on admin line.

Metabolic diseases - CLIMB
CLIMB Building, 176 Nantwich Rd, Crewe CW2 6BG
info@climb.org.uk, www.climb.org.uk
0870 7700325
Helpline 0800 6523181
Children Living with Inherited Metabolic Diseases (CLIMB) provides information to parents, carers and professionals. Local contacts, magazine.

Psoriasis Association
7 Milton St, Northampton NN2 7JG
mail@psoriasis.demon.co.uk
www.psoriasis-association.org.uk
01604 711129
Offers support and advice to children and adults suffering from psoriasis.

Sickle Cell and Thalassaemia Centre (Bristol) - OSCAR
256 Stapleton Road, Easton, Bristol BS5 0NP
oscarbristol@sicklecell.fsnet.co.uk,
www.bristoloscar.org
0117 951 2200
Providing information support and counselling.

Spina Bifida and Hydrocephalus - ASBAH
Asbah House, 42 Park Road, Peterborough PE1 2UQ
postmaster@asbah.org, www.asbah.org
01733 555988
Information and local group contacts.

SERIOUS & TERMINAL ILLNESSES

ACT - Association for Children with Life Threatening or Terminal Conditions and their Families

Orchard House, Orchard Lane, Bristol BS1 5DT
info@act.org.uk, www.act.org.uk
0117 922 1556   Mon-Fri 8.30am-5pm
(answer phone out of hours)
Information on support services available for families. ACT campaigns for the development of children's palliative care services.

CLIC (Cancer and Leukaemia in Childhood)

Abbeywood, Bristol BS34 7JU
info@clic-charity.demon.co.uk, www.clic.uk.com
Helpline 0117 311 2600   Mon-Fri 9am-5pm
(answer phone out of hours)
CLIC has 7 home-from-homes around the country (including Bristol) for parents and children, who live out of town, to use for the duration of treatment. It also funds 40 Home Care Nurses, play specialists and research.

Leukaemia Care Society

2 Shrubbery Ave, Worcester WR1 1QH
info@leukaemiacare.org.uk,
www.leukaemiacare.org.uk
01905 330 003   Mon-Fri 9am-5pm
Helpline 0800 169 66680   24hrs
Support through a national befriending scheme. Provides information, limited financial assistance and organises caravan holidays. Lists local contacts. Helpline staffed by those with direct experience of leukaemia.

The Jessie May Trust

35 Old School House, Kingswood Foundation Estate, Britannia Rd, Kingswood, Bristol BS15 8DB
info@jessiemaytrust.org.uk
www.jessiemaytrust.org.uk
Admin 0117 961 6840
Care Team 0117 960 7783
Providing palliative care service for children and young people who are not expected to live beyond the age of 19. Respite care, support, advice, terminal nursing care and bereavement support.

The Rainbow Centre

27 Lilymead Avenue, Bristol BS4 2BY
contact@rainbowcentre.fsnet.co.uk
0117 985 3343
Aims to provide the highest quality support and help to children with life-threatening illness, and their families. Bereavement support; art, play and complementary therapies.

LEGAL & FINANCIAL ADVICE

ADVICE ON ALL ISSUES

Citizens Advice Bureaux

Provide free, confidential, impartial and independent advice on almost any subject. Debt, benefits, employment, housing problems, relationship breakdown and immigration. Operates on a first in-line basis.

Bristol CAB
12 Broad Street, Bristol BS1 2HL
0870 121 2134
Drop-in, telephone and appointments:
Mon/Thu/Fri 10am-3.30pm Wed/Sat 10am-12am
Telephone Service only: Tue 10am-1.30pm
Outreach:
The Meeting Rooms, Greystoke Av, Southmead
Wed 10am-1pm (drop-in only)

Kingswood CAB
117 High St, Staple Hill, Bristol BS16 5HF
0117 956 9174

South Gloucester CAB
Yate Leisure Centre, Kennedy Way, Bristol BS17 4DQ
01454 318860
Outreaches:
35 High St, Thornbury
01454 318860
Patchway Library, Rodway Rd, Patchway
01454 865674

North Bristol Advice Centre

2 Gainsborough Square, Lockleaze, Bristol BS7 9XA
team@nbac.freeserve.co.uk
www.northbristoladvice.org.uk
0117 951 5751

Free, independent and confidential legal advice and assistance in social welfare law. General advice on debt, housing and employment issues. Drop-in and appointment sessions available in Lockleaze, Southmead, Patchway, Little Stoke and Lawrence Weston.

South Bristol Advice Service

Leinster House, Leinster Av, Knowle, Bristol BS4 1NL
admin@southbristoladvice.org.uk
www.southbristoladvice.org.uk
0117 985 1122 (answer phone out of hours)
Minicom 0117 909 9705

Confidential advice, representation, specialist debt and benefit services. Advice-points across south Bristol. Home visits for house-bound clients.

St Pauls Advice Centre

146 Grosvenor Rd, St Paul's, Bristol BS2 8YA
stpaulsadvice@btconnect.com
0117 955 2981   by appointment or drop-in
                              Mon/Tue/Thu/Fri 10am-12pm

Advice on benefits, housing, debt, and other rights issues. Tribunal representation may be possible.

DEBT

Bristol Debt Advice Centre

2nd Floor,48-54 West St, St Philips, Bristol BS2 0BL
mail@bdac.org.uk, www.bdac.org.uk
Helpline 0117 954 3990
Minicom 0117 954 399
Mon-Fri 9.30am-12.30pm

Free professional advice over the phone to people in debt. Sessions in Lawrence Weston, Knowle West, St Pauls & Lockleaze.

HOUSING

Bristol City Council Housing Services

Housing Advice Shop, 38 College Green,
Bristol BS1 5SU
tenancy_relations@bristol-city.gov.uk
0117 922 3847   Mon/Tue/Thu 8.45am-4pm
          Wed 10.30am-4pm, Fri 8.45am-3.45pm
See Telephone Directory (Bristol City Council display)

Advice to council tenants on all housing problems including homelessness and money advice.

Shelter Housing Aid Centre

31 Denmark Street, Bristol BS1 5DQ
0808 8004444   Mon/Tue/Thu/Fri 10am-1pm

A drop-in and telephone service providing advice and help on housing issues.

The SPACE Trust

St Nicholas House, Lawfords Gate, Bristol BS5 0RE
spacetrust@route56.co.uk, www.spacetrust.org.uk
Enquiries 0117 907 5355
Outreach Work 0117 907 3012

Christian charity working with families (from all cultures) housed in temporary accommodation. Organises and runs outreach clubs in hostels. Provides families with free furniture/household goods when rehoused.

Young Mothers Group Trust

See Young Parents section, above.

LEGAL

Avon and Bristol Law Centre

2 Moon St, Stokes Croft, Bristol BS2 8QE
mail@ablc.demon.co.uk
0117 924 8662   Mon-Fri 9am-5pm
Drop-ins for immigration   Thu 10am-12pm

Callers given telephone advice-line numbers on: immigration, employment (including discrimination), housing and debt, welfare benefits and community groups.

Solicitors Family Law Association

info@sfla.org.uk, www.sfla.co.uk
01689 850 227

Can supply a list of solicitors local to you, who are members of the Association.

The Law Shop

48 Gloucester Rd, Bishopston, Bristol BS7 8BH
rebecca@lawshopbristol.co.uk
www.lawshopbristol.co.uk
0117 944 1966   Mon-Fri 9am-5pm
                              Sat 9.30am-12.30am

Duty solicitor, £10 per 10 minutes

Self-help legal service. Selling legal forms, kits, books and CDs. Providing free access to the legal library, workstations for people who want to do the work themselves (work can then be checked by the duty solicitor) and low cost internet access.

SOCIAL SECURITY & TAX

Citizens Advice Bureaux
Provides free, confidential, impartial and independent advice on social security and tax issues. See Advice on All Issues section, above.

Inland Revenue
www.inlandrevenue.gov.uk
See telephone book for full range of helplines

Child Benefit
0845 302 1444   Mon-Fri 8am-7pm
Textphone 0845 302 1474

Working Tax Credits (including Child Tax Credit)
0845 300 3900   Mon-Fri 8am-7pm
Textphone 0845 300 3909

Self Assessment
0845 900 0444   Mon-Sun 8am-8pm

Bristol & North Somerset Area
Norfolk House, Temple Street BS1 6HS
01202 585 001   Mon-Fri 8.30am-5pm,
                         Thu 'til 8pm & Sat 9am-1pm
Local office providing help and advice.

Social Security
www.jobcentreplus.gov.uk or www.dwp.gov.uk
Bristol Office 0117 991 3000
Jobseeker Direct 0845 60 60 234
Textphone 0845 605 5255
Mon-Fri 9am-6pm, Sat 9am-1pm

Jobcentres and social security offices are now called Jobcentre Plus. They offer help for those seeking work, also with Jobseeker's Allowance, social security benefit, National Insurance Number applications.

Child Benefits	0870 155 5540
Tax Credits	0800 500 222
Benefit Enquiry	0800 882200
Textphone	0800 24 33 55
Disability Living Allowance	0845 712 3456
Attendance Allowance	0845 712 3456
Nat. Insurance Enquiry Line	0845 302 1487
Invalid Care Allowance	01253 856123

ACKNOWLEDGEMENTS

There are numerous contributors behind a publication like this, I hope I have remembered you all. Titch Hikers' exists because of you.

Special thanks from the Editor to the following:
All 12 researchers for their enthusiasm, dedication and patience, particularly when our IT capabilities floundered!

Other contributers
Marina Allan, Louise Bawdon, Katriel Costello, Kathrin Davis, Sophie Denham, Mick Dickinson, Bertie Ellis, Mark Ellis, Penny Hopkins, Rory MccGwire, Fiona MccGwire, Michaela Norris, Keith Potter, Peter Stonham, Julia Swan and Nikki Trott

Database design
Nick Adjerian, www.hatjoys.co.uk, & Jill Woodley, www.austinbusinessconsultants.co.uk

Website design
Simon Marchant, www.helmsedge.com

Book layout & design
Tim Potter

Marketing & brainstorming
Diana Beavon, Paula Brown, Carolyn Jenkins, Elspeth Pontin & Kath Sidaway

Personal thanks
To Tim for his inspirational IT contributions, endless encouragement and humour. To Fiona MccGwire, Angela Potter and Julia Swan for their loving childcare support. To my father, Bertie Ellis, for his enthusiasm, ideas and prose. Emily Shepherd who entrusted the editorship to me. Finally, to Kath Sidaway and Jo Smart for help with the last frantic edits.

Individual researchers' thanks:

Kath Sidaway - Out & About in the West Country
Thanks to Chloe and Mollie for patiently putting up with my wholesale hogging of the computer, and to Charlie for all the long distance IT support and encouragement.

Diana Beavon - Childcare 0-4 Years, Playgroups & Early Education 0-4
Thank you to the team at Bristol Council, especially Rachael Williams, for all their help and advice. Thank you to my family for helping out with childcare so I could research this project, especially Ian, my husband, who often needed to remind me that I was not the chief bread winner! Thanks to the Editor, who took me on at five months pregnant. It has kept me sane, made the pregnancy fly past and kept the brain working – so where have I left my son now?

Elspeth Pontin - Healthcare, Family Holidays & Weekends Away
As a freelance writer, I was delighted to be given a chance to research topics which not only interested me but related to my studies.
Thanks to Ben, William and Dominic. Ben for being so helpful and supportive, and the boys for being so patient.

Acknowledgements

Joanna Thirwall - Teen Guide

Thanks to the staff and students at St Bede's School for their help and ideas respectively, and special thanks to Mark, Ellie and Tom for their input and IT support throughout!

Thanks to those who completed the teenage questionnaire

Kate Allen, Katie Amato, Adam Baker, Danielle Banfield, Hayleigh Barrett, Kayleigh Bellamy, Rob Borthwick, Ben Bowen, Lindsay Bowen, Arron Browne, Emily-May Burke, Hollie Burns, Chris Butt, Chris Callaghan, Adam Clark, Lydia Clarke, Abi Clevely, Molly Collins, Georgia Comley, Siobhan Cordy, Francesca Costa, Charlie Crittel-Gilholm, Tom Cullimore, Lizzie Doherty, Hollie Davies, Cadi Davis, Jonathon Deeney, Aimee Donkin, Emma, William English, Barney Fairburn, Phoebe Farrell, Dan Forder, Michaela Fox, Andre Fry, Charlotte Goodman, Katie Green, Rose Harding, Harry, Verity Hope, John Howell, Rob Howells, James, Charlotte King, Alex Kite, John Lennox, Charlotte Lauda, Rachel Manning, Harry Marshall, Tom Marshall, Petronella Malata, Fiona Mason, Matt McCall, Danny Mcmahon, Siobhan Mitchell, Josh Morgan, Daniel Murphy, Becki Nelson, Helen Nelson, Sean O'Neill, Jessica Palmer, Josyane Palmer, Tommaso Parrinello, Shaun Phillips, Hannah Poulter, Natasha Reygate, Tom Richmond, Memory Rumuma, Daniela Sforza, Matthew Sheard, Molly Sherman, Emma Simmonds, Felicity Simons, Nick Smith, Paul Smith, Stephen, Jennifer Stephens, Laura Thayer, Alex Thomas, Emily Thomas, Gabriella Thomas, Laura Thomas, Kayleigh Voke, Catherine Wade, Joe Weare, Jason White, Shenagh Woodland, Ellie Woodward, Cameron Wysocki

Sharon Wagg - General Research

I thoroughly enjoyed researching for the Titch Hikers' guide and hope to use what I have learnt over the months to broaden my freelance magazine writing career.

I would like to thank all the many friends, mothers and children for all their help and encouragement during this project, especially Sabine Müeller, Diane Dickerson, Kelly Allen and Ioana Ibraim. I would also like to say a special thank you to my husband David for being so patient and understanding during this busy time, and my daughter Jessica (aged 21 months) who, without realising, made all the research great fun.

Titch Hikers' 8th Edition donated profits to: CLIC, the Jessie May Trust and NCT Bristol

INDEX

HOW TO NAVIGATE

Central Reference section holds
• Symbol keys for entry facilities
• Maps of Bristol & the West
• Tables listing sport & leisure centres

Index lists subjects as well as entry names
The book & chapter contents pages

Index

Index

Index

HOW TO NAVIGATE

Central Reference section holds
• Symbol keys for entry facilities
• Maps of Bristol & the West
• Tables listing sport & leisure
   centres

Index lists subjects as well as
   entry names
The book & chapter contents
   pages